Blue Star Love

From an Amazing Heart of Grace

Maia Chrystine Nartoomid

ISBN: 978-1-4525-6286-5 (sc)
ISBN: 978-1-4525-6287-2 (e)

Author can be contacted at: ElvisLightedCandle.org

Major editing, reorganization, rewrites, and proofing by Simeon Nartoomid
Minor editing, proofing and reorganization by Lina Daquinto
Cover Art "A New Day" and entry page "Elvis Horus Eye" from original paintings by Isabelle Tanner a.k.a. Elisabelle
Art Delight - P.O. Box 383, Elmsford, NY 10523
IsabelleTanner.com - ArtDelight@aol.com - TannerLandmark@aol.com

Balboa Press books may be ordered through booksellers or by contacting:
Balboa Press
A Division of Hay House
1663 Liberty Drive
Bloomington, IN 47403
www.balboapress.com
1-(877) 407-4847

Printed in the United States of America
Balboa Press rev. date: 1/28/2013

~ Unique Elvis memorabilia never seen before ~

~ A revelation, a teaching, an experience ~

~ A revealing tribute to a truly great soul ~

~ A one of a kind collector's item ~

For the children of the world, for Elvis dearly loved them and prayed as we all do, that through them, our lives will become more enlightened and universal.

"If we could all see through the eyes of a child,
the world would be a better place."

~ Elvis Presley

Contents

Opening Notes

As you read this book you will see many words marked by an asterisk*, denoting that this word can be found listed alphabetically in 'Appendix D: GLOSSARY OF TERMS' compiled at the end of the book.

In instances where the words are reappearing throughout the text the word will only be marked the first time it appears in each chapter.

This glossary is like a spiritual and metaphysical teaching unto its own. It might even be beneficial to read it before you read this book!

Additionally, there are endnotes indicated with superscript numbers in most chapters. You can go to 'Appendix F: Chapter Endnotes' and locate the chapter's section and find additional information on that particular topic provided there.

I hope that my efforts to provide these extra resources prove to be helpful to you!

Foreword

by Simeon Nartoomid

I was the husband of the author, Maia Chrystine Nartoomid, for 14 years and lived together with her for 16 years. Maia is still a very dear friend and kindred soul to me.

I did all of the major editing and provided publishing consultation on this book. This work extended over the entire period of time I was living with the author and for a couple of years thereafter thus spanning nearly 18 years.

I offered to write the Forward to this book because I am NOT an Elvis fan. I have never been a fan of Elvis' and I do not feel that I ever will qualify for that distinction. Yet, despite my lack of interest in Elvis' music I have come to love this man as a brother and a human being through being exposed to what appears in the pages of this book.

At first, even though I was in a significant-other relationship with the author, I was skeptical. I am a mystic myself, so I was not skeptical about her *mystical inner sources* as many others might tend to be. I was instead skeptical about the information regarding Elvis being so spiritually aware. Yet, every step of the way, Maia presented more and more information to me to back-up her positions in this book and about Elvis. She eventually dispelled my skepticism and gained my full support.

I have heard the tape with Elvis speaking to Wanda about his home on the Blue Star and some of the other taped conversation where he is speaking of other rather advanced metaphysical concepts and beliefs. These are some of the tapes that were submitted for authentication as being Elvis speaking on the tapes—this authentication is well-documented in "Appendix E: AUTHENTICITY."

The more I read and edited, the more in touch I also got with the amazingly generous and loving nature of this man we knew as Elvis Presley the rock super-star. He was so much more than most people realize. After hundreds of passes through this book editing, re-writing and organizing materials, I still weep when I come across some of the passages relating what Elvis had said or done, or what others whose lives he touched have had to say about him.

This man was one exceptionally incredible human being. If we had a world full of people like him it would be a different world indeed. I therefore feel this book has enormous value to us all, Elvis fans or not, in setting forth an example for what our potential as a human being might really be.

The author, Maia Chrystine Nartoomid, is also an exceptional human being. She also exemplifies many of the higher qualities that Elvis personified. In knowing her so closely for so many years I came to see what a very high degree of integrity she has. She is different, she is not like most of the people we meet today. She has a heart of deep goodness and love. Despite a life of much physical pain and suffering her loving, kind and caring nature has not been hardened nor eroded.

I therefore cannot say enough good things about the author of this book. I know that many people will be challenged to accept what is revealed in this book as being true. Yet, I can assure you that if Maia Chrystine Nartoomid did not believe it to be true with her whole heart and soul, and have reasonable reasons and even some proof to believe it is true, it simply would not be in this book.

I also know from communicating with Wanda June Hill that Elvis did not share the same things with all his different friends. Wanda felt hurt at first when she found out that he had shared some things with another of his phone friends that Elvis had not shared with her.

This happened fairly frequently, and Wanda came to realize it was nothing personal, it was just the way Elvis was. He only shared what he felt was right to share with each person. He was not being exclusive or trying to keep secrets either, he just wanted to have the harmonious relations with everyone and something deep inside of him was guiding that process. Personally, I am not sure Elvis even gave it much conscious thought. I believe that it was just so natural for him to say what seemed appropriate for and with each person that he just did it quite automatically.

Being a student of human nature I can say with a fair degree of certainty that Elvis had a somewhat child-like nature. He did not think like most people do. He just went with what was happening in the moment. The accounting of him telling the Bible story where he got carried away saying "they got his ass (Jesus')" in 'Chapter 10: THE TRICKSTER,' points to this part of his nature. He was so into the moment he did not even realize how he was relating that story. Yet, that is exactly how those people he was telling it to tended to speak, so it was natural for him to relate the story just that way.

There are also folks who knew Elvis quite well and who also knew of his spiritual nature. Some of these good people who helped Elvis with his spiritual life may feel somewhat hurt just like Wanda did when they read some of what Elvis shared with her if he did not share the same things with them. This is understandable and for anyone who is in this position I would simply ask you to hold an open mind as to the complexity and spontaneity of this amazing being we knew as Elvis.

Nobody knows everything about anyone no matter how much time they may spend with them. Always holding an open mind about such matters was something Elvis himself exemplified. He was an open book who always invited others to contribute some of their own unique pages to his story. He had his own persona, yet how he expressed it was always a work in progress. Except for one thing… he was very consistently generous, kind and caring. That was the true foundation of his being, and those are also qualities that I have found in the author and her friend Wanda June Hill.

I know that if you read this book with an open mind you will gain something valuable from it regardless if you are an Elvis fan or interested in spiritual matters or not. It is an exceptional and unusual story about an exception and unusual human being and icon in our history.

Preface

My intention in writing this book is to bring you an expanded understanding of Elvis Aaron Presley from my perspective—a mystic who is also an Elvis fan. The basis for religion and spirituality, in my view, is to broaden one's concept and experience of God. Since God is love, then the focus of religion or spirituality should be to broaden one's concept and experience of love.

Elvis exemplified love in action on this Earth and the love he inspired can be a springboard to higher levels of awareness. Elvis, in my opinion, started a 'church' of his own, one of the universal heart. Of course, he doesn't have a patent on that, only God could claim such a thing, but he certainly has strengthened that vibration on Earth through his heartfelt connection with his audience. Love in its higher expression is both a human and a supernatural phenomenon.

Therefore, this book poses some interesting alternatives which, to some, may seem foreign or even far-fetched. I ask you to reach into your hearts and allow the love that Elvis so exemplified to act as a bridge of acceptance. This will continue Elvis's good work and perhaps enable more people to become aware of a greater reality. Elvis touched people from all walks of life. Individually, their stories may have faded. However, I am bringing their voices together and they make an impressive collection.

I have been communicating with people from this and other realms since I was a child so it now seems quite natural. Combined with my astral communications with Elvis, you will see that he was one of the brightest lights humanity has known in recent times. It was only after I had these amazing experiences that I found Wanda June Hill and her conversations with Elvis.

My greatest hope is that the information contained herein will reach beyond the existing Elvis community so that his light does not diminish. Elvis' truly goodhearted nature and outstanding qualities became tainted by the media. It is scary but true that we are indoctrinated to believe certain things because it is presented as mass opinion. Those who know Elvis through his songs, understand his truth in their hearts. For those of you who have not known Elvis in this way, I hope this book will enlighten you to the true nature of this magnificent being.

Acknowledgments

Cover artist's poem for her artwork entitled, "A New Day"

A brighter Star is guiding us

on the path to a Higher Plain.

Its beckoning Rays of Glorious Blue

lights the Night into the Newest Day.

A heartfelt thank you to...

Wanda June Hill for her many contributions not only to this book, but to my life and experiences, awareness and knowledge of Elvis over the years.

JoAnna McKenzie for allowing me to share her beautiful story of friendship with Elvis herein.

Stephanie James, for coming forth with courage to publicly share her unusual and profound mystical story of how she learned that Elvis was her Guardian Angel and of a larger incarnative circle of reciprocity in this regard.

Simeon Nartoomid, my former husband and still dearly beloved friend, for all the countless hours of love and labor he has spent throughout the last seventeen years making this book what it is today.

Everyone who made various contributions through many, many years via the things they have spoken and shared about Elvis, and their genuine expressions of love for him as a truly exceptional soul.

The awesome power of the love that has made it possible for this book to be brought forth to reveal more of the true nature of the one we all love, Elvis Aaron Presley. This love truly is a representation of him in and of itself!

Elvis Aaron Presley, for I am deeply grateful for all the sacrifices he made in his short life so that he could extend his love to us through his music, biography and the kinship created by our love for him.

Maia Chrystine Nartoomid ~ the Author

About the Author

Maia Chrystine Nartoomid

I am a mystic, writer and digital artist. All my life I felt a close connection to Elvis Presley. Between 1969 and 1975 I was privileged to see thirty-six of his concert performances in Las Vegas, Tahoe and on tour. As 'Christine Hayes' (my birth name) I wrote articles and concert reviews for Rex Martin's Elvis publication in Great Britain as well as 'Strictly Elvis' here in the United States.

After Elvis died, I established a friendship with Wanda June Hill. She and her family had been a friend of Elvis' for the last fifteen years of his life. Both before and after Elvis' passing, I became acquainted with other persons who knew Elvis personally. All the information

I acquired confirmed Elvis was an exceptionally spiritual person. In 2004, I moved to Hawai'i. I now live on Kaua'i. Elvis is still very much loved in these islands, especially by native Hawaiians.

My Unusual Personal Story & Work

I was born in Caripito, Venezuela in 1949, where my father was working for an oil company. My mother was forty-five years old and I was her only child. Each night, from the age of four months, I would make persistent sounds which my mother seemed to instinctively know how to fulfill. Instead of popping a bottle in my mouth, she took me outside underneath a canopy of tropical stars. I pointed to the heavens, and said "star."

Of course, no one but my father believed her. She simply smiled to herself and began to chronicle my life. We left Venezuela when I was two. I remember looking out of the prop airplane as my mother told me we were flying over Angels Falls, deep in the jungles of the Amazon. As I stared into its frothing tumble, it appeared to be the gleaming wings of an angel. Something stirred deep inside me; perhaps a memory of those who guided and nurtured me.

In 1952 we settled on a dairy farm in the Ozarks of Arkansas. We had no television and seldom went to the movies. It was during this period I began to have very vivid 'dream' experiences, which I now believe to have been out-of-body travel. I would soar over a desert terrain (nothing like Venezuela or Arkansas) into a large mountain.

Once inside, I was greeted by nice-looking men who were tall and mostly blonde, and who dressed in skin-like white, seamless suits. They treated me as an equal and took me through their underground complex, explaining to me how their 'machines' (computers) operated in the most scientific of terms, which I completely understood. These computers did not look like any fact or science fiction of the 1950's. They more closely resembled what we now see in the Star Trek movies and TV shows. Yet bear in mind that these experiences were taking place in 1953 on a dairy farm deep in the Ozark Mountains of Arkansas.

When I 'returned' from my journeys, I would describe them to my mother. Once I drew pictures of different things I had seen which included what I called, "a clock controlled by the mind." My mother saved these drawings, typing at the bottom of each picture what I had said about it. I began to commune with the fairy elements of the beautiful Ozarks mountains and may have been referring to them when my mother heard me say at age three to no one in particular, "Their thoughts shared a lovely, dreaming time with the high hills."

At six I began philosophizing. One comment my mother recorded was, "I think that we could see a great deal more if we believed more. For instance, we look at something and see only a small part of it because we don't believe there is any more." I also plaintively asked, "Does it bore you to share my confidences?" She assured me it didn't! As I discovered the reality of others around me, through being exposed to the educational system, I felt very much alone. It was as if they were in one world and I in another. The whole process of education and the lack of sensitivity, for the most part, which I experienced there, was devastating to me.

Whereas my mother and father were receptive to my thoughts and feelings, the 'system' treated me as an underling who was expected to believe without question all they put before me. I sensed that much of it was either grossly incomplete or distorted. By the age of four, my mother had read to me, from cover to cover, 'The Greatest Story Ever Told' on the life of Jesus Christ. When she finished, I asked her to read it to me again, which she did without hesitation. 'See Spot Run' seemed like comparative dribble. I never reconciled to the prison of standard education. While I made fairly good grades in all but math, I struggled just about every day I spent in the educational institutions because of the limitations in thinking present there.

One day in my junior year of high school, my mother let me out in front of the cafeteria which served as a study hall. It was raining, so I decided to go inside the building. As I put my hand on the door, a 'voice' said inside my head, "Christine (my birth name), if you go one more day (to school) it will be dangerous." I was stunned, as I hadn't had any significant mystical experiences since the age of ten, after my father died. My mother was still there, waiting to see me go inside, as she knew how difficult it always was for me. I slowly turned around, came back to the car and got inside. When she queried me, I told her what I had 'heard.' She looked at me for a long few moments and said, "Let's go home." I never returned to school classes again.

Right after I left school, I began once more to receive from the Otherworld. I wrote my first book at age eighteen entitled, 'Under the Grey Moon,' a story of an ancient people in Canada. By the time I had finished the book, both my mother and I knew it was a true story which I had naturally gleaned from *my inner mystical sources.* One of the manuscripts I wrote next was 'Universe One,' a manual of high science and universal principal. My mother sent a letter and some samples of this material to Captain Edgar Mitchell, who had just returned from a voyage to the moon. She had read he was planning to retire from NASA to create a parapsychological research center which is now the Institute of Noetic Sciences.

After he was released from quarantine, he responded to her letter and sent for us both to be his guests while his parapsychological team evaluated me. On several occasions thereafter, he had us come to Houston where he would discuss at length with me these 'sciences' which I claimed existed in the universe. It was Captain Mitchell who told me that what I was receiving was valid, yet far beyond the known realm of scientific study. Eventually, he also confided that in order for him to make full use of this information, he would have to give up everything else to work with it, which he was not prepared to do.

I understood. Yet he had given me the gift of his professional evaluation. At that time, Captain Mitchell had more scientific credentials than any other astronaut in the NASA Space program. I continued with my work, and although my health began to fail, my mother was unfailing in her support and encouragement. She took care of all the physical aspects of life, freeing me to receive information and write. Beings of Light began to appear to both of us, sometimes when we were in the room together. We began to understand that we were communing with spiritual intelligences of exquisite love and wisdom. My mother made her transition in 1993. In 1994, I met the man who was to become my husband of fourteen years.

In 1980, I began my quarterly publication on ancient knowledge, inner Earth cultures, spiritual science*, nature magic* and planetary transformation* The material I receive is via a process I define as source translation*, the ability of the human mind, body and emotional system to align itself with the universal centers of knowledge that are connected to all knowledge. This knowledge can be transferred into the cerebral centers of the mind, where it is translated into English.

All universal knowledge which is a part of this wonderful planet is contained in recorded energy patterns along its energy centers. It's like a magnetic recording tape, the Earth herself is the tape and the universal knowledge is the source. This type of information can open the door to the evolution of humans by delving into the interrelatedness of Light, Form and Spirit as they create the dance of life in the human experience.

The application of this knowledge in a truly heart-centered way creates a movement of harmonies within ourselves and is a major endeavor within my work. This is the process of anchoring one's mind, body and soul to the rainbow of nature's true Spirit.

I have now written twelve books, three of which were self-published and one published by Naylor Company in San Antonio, Texas—'Red Tree' by Christine Hayes, still available as a used book through outlets such as Amazon.com. The rest, as yet, remain unpublished manuscripts on subjects including ancient pre-history, meta-science and spiritual philosophy. I have founded and co-founded spiritual orders and currently distribute the previously mentioned quarterly publications through my nonprofit ministry. I also worked as a spiritual counselor, healer and advisor.

What inspired me about Elvis was the commonality of our purpose in assisting humanity toward a greater harmony and transcendence of earthly limitations through heartfelt love.

My Personal Story With Elvis

I first went to see Elvis perform in 1969 at the Las Vegas International Hotel—now the Hilton. This was a very exciting opportunity, for a twenty year old girl, who had been an avid fan for seven years. In addition, I had been involved in mystical work for two years and when he appeared I knew why I had always felt such love towards him. Although I appreciated his immense talent, the spiritual grace he commanded was almost supernatural.

His unique persona could be compared to a fragrance—illusive, yet moving to the senses and the soul, creating a mood for further anticipation and joy. I am not always able to see auras*, but I never had any difficulty seeing Elvis' aura. In fact, his was the strongest, most brilliant aura I had ever experienced. It was mostly shades of blue, with some violet and deep purple. Very often a shimmering white light encircled these colors.

As he began to sing, his aura would expand, leaping up from the top of his head. Sometimes I would see Elvis' aura merge with one or more of his singers and musicians on stage. Often their aura would brighten if he spoke to them. I heard stories of others who came to see him from all over the world. There were revelations of miracles among these encounters, which were miracles of Spirit more than flesh. Yet I was told of some physical healing which took place as well, which I explore in more depth in Chapter 9.

In 1972, I began to give Elvis my mystical works from the edge of the stage. I first gave him my then recently published book, 'Red Tree'—published by Naylor Company, Texas. I had written a chapter on an ancient Lemurian★ healer named Kartum. Although I did not declare it in the book, I knew Kartum to be a past life of Elvis'. Inside I wrote, "To Kartum, in Remembrance." I brought the book with me to Las Vegas, intent on handing it to him, but not knowing at the time if he was at all open to anything of this nature.

Then I met a young woman working in the showroom as a photo girl who knew Elvis personally. Upon seeing my book and hearing a little about my work, she informed me that Elvis was a student of metaphysics and spiritual matters, and would be quite receptive. That night I was able to hand him the book from the edge of the stage, although considering my competition for his attention, it was most certainly ordained from the ranks of Spirit that I reached him.

When he took the book in his hand and looked at the ancient symbols on the cover, it was as if a shock wave passed through him. It seemed to affect him profoundly. Sometime later, the same young woman asked him if he had read 'Red Tree.' He exclaimed excitedly, "Oh, let me explain it to you." At this exact moment he was promptly interrupted by some men who worked for him—they were instructed not to let Elvis talk about such things.

In future stage-side encounters, I continued to give him select esoteric material from my writings based on the source translation process. Elvis never in all those years spoke one verbal word to me, as he usually did to those who gifted him on stage with roses and teddy bears. We communicated on an entirely different level, through a means that would be normally considered 'telepathy★.' At first I thought it might be my imagination, but it was soon proven to me that Elvis and I could, and did, commune through this means. It was a very deliberate thing on his part. He would mentally tell me that he had to be cautious in receiving my gifts—for my sake. At the time, I had no idea what he meant.

I learned later about the darker element clustering about him, which he constantly had to contend with and outwit in order to have some experience of his own inner life. These were forces sought but failed to blot out the light in his circle of brilliance. Elvis would mentally communicate to me at what point in the show he would be coming to receive my material. Then, at the prescribed moment, he would walk over to me. I had even 'asked' him in my mind to give me some signal if our communion of thoughts was truly a reality. He looked directly into my eyes, smiled and nodded before reaching over to kiss me.

I must say that while my experiences with Elvis might have been unique, I acknowledge there are many men, women and children who have also shared unique moments with him.

Let us all share a few more moments with his beautiful Spirit, as you read this tribute to a truly great soul!

Introduction

by Wanda June Hill

Author of: 'We Remember, Elvis' and 'Elvis Face to Face'

Wanda June Hill in 2012.

Wanda June Hill when Elvis knew her.

In 1980 I became acquainted with Maia, the author and mentor of this book. I met Elvis in 1963, he often spoke to me about many things, some that he didn't talk about often except in special settings with people he felt were friends and also receptive to his thoughts.

He was a very religious man, one who prayed daily, sometimes several times a day. Regarding this prayer practice he related that he did it, 'When I need help.' He meant when he needed help to do the things he had to do in order to 'please the crowds.' He also spoke of his childhood, relating stories which in his own words were about 'light men who came to talk to me.' He also spoke of how these light men had shown him images and scenes that he came to realize were, "scenes from my future."

I didn't understand much of what he spoke about, but he would read passages from his Bible and explain them in a way that made perfect sense to me. I had been raised Pentecostal as was he, but he was able to make what I had learned in church come to life and be real and useful for everyday living. After his death I and several other people who had a similar experience knowing Elvis, tried to bring the real guy to life in our 1978 book. Maia read our book and contacted me. Very quickly I realized she was like Elvis, gifted spiritually, someone who would understand his deep need to communicate.

Maia has taken Elvis' words and thoughts combining them with great understanding and realness. She has intertwined his beliefs with ancient knowledge and put a perspective to it all. She has also done so in such a way that most everyone will be able to gain a view of life and the past. The perspectives she brings forth help us to look past our questions and find the answers we need for today. That is what Elvis tried to do when he got a chance to "just talk with people." Elvis, I know is smiling and giving her that little nod of approval with those blue eyes shining like stars! I highly recommend everyone, Elvis fan or not, read this book. It might take a little while to read and comprehend, but it will be well worth the effort. One more thing, I would find a comfortable chair with good light because the information and images you will find are fascinating!

Wanda—Why Me?

Why did Elvis Aaron Presley, Superstar, who could have picked from any number of people in the world, choose to be my friend? I have asked that question thousands of times over the years. Elvis was as close as our telephone, as near as Los Angeles, Palm Springs or Las Vegas, and after he died, I continued to ask—why me?

In 1980, Maia Chrystine Nartoomid (then Christine Hayes) wrote to me after reading the book compiled by myself, several members of my family and some friends, all of whom had a personal relationship with Elvis Presley. I answered her letter, she wrote again and we began corresponding off and on over a couple of years. She sent me several booklets which she published that contained various information given to her through a type of channeling, most of which was out of my realm of understanding. However, as I continued to read these materials, I realized that many of the things she wrote about, Elvis mentioned to me, and some of what he said, closely followed what she was relating in her works.

It was as if a light suddenly turned on in my memory, almost as if he were speaking to me again. At first, knowing of his sincerity and of the ridicule and disdain he had received concerning his metaphysical interests from those closest to him during his last years of life, I was hesitant to reveal anything he had mentioned to me about it. I didn't want to bring further disrespect to his memory. But as Maia's and my own trust and friendship grew, I felt compelled to tell her what he had related to me. Once I began, it poured out as if that were the intent all along.

Maia immediately began putting together a book based on her knowledge and Elvis' impressions and wisdom gleaned from this spiritual quest and that of his own experiences, both during his life as Elvis and the many past lives which he felt he had lived and which Maia's channeling source could recount as well.

Amazingly, what he had told me and what her sources revealed matched in many ways, explaining why Elvis was Elvis and why so many people of all ages and circumstances, felt and still feel, such a rapport with him. Somehow, Elvis knew that, in time, I would pass on the things that meant so much to him, and so he 'seeded' my mind knowing that time would bring fertile ground in which to plant those seeds. Maia did just that, collecting and compiling information that she put into her book, 'Magii From the Blue Star' (the original title of this book—author).

In doing this work, Maia has given Elvis what he truly desired—a chance to share his thoughts, his knowledge and beliefs with everyone who would like to know the 'real Elvis,' the man behind the myth. Now, I understand and I am at rest with my own question—why me? Thank you, Maia.

Wanda—How I Met Elvis

I was in my twenties in 1963. Me and my husband and small daughter had just moved to Southern California and I was feeling very depressed and lost. Not only was I far from 'home' but painful childhood traumas were surfacing for me. In 1962 I felt as if there was no reason to go on living, except for my responsibilities to my husband and daughter. Then I went to the Laundry Mat and my life forever changed for the better.

On that day in the laundromat I met another young woman with a small child. While our children played amidst the washers and dryers, we talked. The other woman, Diane, mentioned to me that she worked as an extra in motion pictures and was currently in the Elvis Presley film, 'Kissin' Cousins' then in production. I was mildly interested since my husband, Jimmy, was an Elvis fan. I myself was not.

As a child raised in a Fundamentalist environment I had been told that Elvis Presley and Rock 'n' Roll were manifestations of the devil and to be avoided at all costs. I wasn't one to believe such things, but it had caused me to look elsewhere for my role models as a teen and young adult.

Honestly, I really didn't believe Diane when this new acquaintance declared that Elvis would be calling her at home that very night. Seeing my skepticism, Diane invited me to witness the event and maybe even to get talk to him for a minute myself. I almost said 'no,' but then I remembered how thrilled my husband would be if I could tell him I had spoken with Elvis… and well, I was also a bit intrigued by the possibility that Diane was telling the truth.

I went that night to Diane's house. Elvis DID call and I was able to talk with him. However, the 'minute' went on for some time, as when Elvis found out that I had only seen one of his movies and walked out in the middle of it—'Flaming Star', he seemed delighted to talk with someone who wasn't interested in 'Elvis Presley' and was responding to him in a normal, conversational manner. Elvis asked me a lot of personal questions. When he asked me what I wanted to be doing with my life, I said that I would like to work behind the scenes in the motion picture business. It was then that Elvis invited me to come with Diane to visit him on the set of 'Kissin' Cousins.'

My visit with Elvis is covered in my book, 'We Remember, Elvis.' At that time, he gave me his personal phone number and told me to call him "in the morning." Coming home with the phone number in hand, I did not expect to ever see or hear from Elvis again. I couldn't imagine that the number he gave me would actually ring him in his bedroom as he had stated. However, the next morning I called the number and Elvis answered. The rest as they say 'is history.'

Wanda—My Motivations

I wrote the following in the ELC Forums in response to questions about my motives with taping some of my conversations with Elvis:

"Elvis knew he was being taped. About the third year of knowing him, I asked him about taping a few conversations so I could share them with Jimmie and Starla and our relatives—some of whom he talked to (Jim's sister). He said 'okay,' and that was the beginning. They were quite awful tapes—quality wise, but we enjoyed them. I didn't tape many early ones—and I told him most of the time—a few were not but he didn't talk any different on any of them. Then when I worked at the law office all incoming calls were taped and some outgoing ones—the phone system was set up that way. Elvis would call there—talk to me sometimes and also to the lawyer his friend, if he wasn't busy. He kept him cackling in his office behind the closed door sometimes.

"They tried to top each other's dirty jokes. So that I didn't get in on. Elvis knew then he was taped when he first called—but his private conversations were not ever taped by the lawyer or me—I didn't control that anyway at the office—his secretary had that responsibility. I asked for and got copies of the conversations I had with Elvis during those office calls and Elvis knew it, I told him and he was fine with that. And he also knew he never heard a word about them anywhere and I didn't pass them around or sell them.

"So when the interview thing came up—actually started in late '75 but didn't get into it really until early '76 when he agreed to help his friend out at college—then we taped a lot of conversations and that was where most of the things came from. I have maybe twenty-three or so parts of conversations over fifteen years—that was NOT part of the interview stuff and most of that has been posted on ELC—Maia's Website ElvisLightedCandle.org—there is nothing to be 'motive' about—anyone who wanted to know can read them—I never sold anything, never used it for any purpose and turned down a hunka-hunka money several times for small portions of them.

"So that pretty much says what my 'motives' were I'd think—if I were going to be that type of person—sure would not have waited for nearly thirty years and then practically give them away in a book! As for the actual recorded tapes—I don't have much of that at all—it all went to him, minus as much of me as I could delete without cutting him out anywhere. It's like his writings—poems etc; I would not sell them but there they are, in the book for a small price—they get the whole thing—his handwritten poetic efforts. Wayne Newton paid a fortune for a few scribbled sentences thrown in the trash. And we give copies of ours away. Some motive huh? I can sleep peacefully—and that's good enough for me."

Wanda—Sharing A Couple of My Elvis Mementos

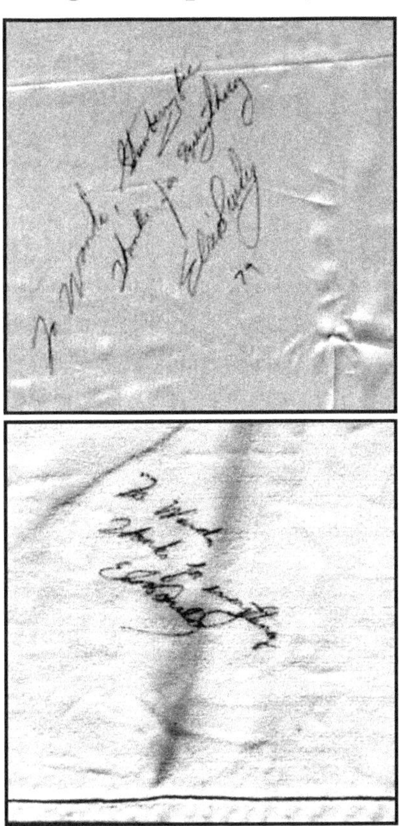

A Personally Autographed Green Scarf and Cloth Napkin

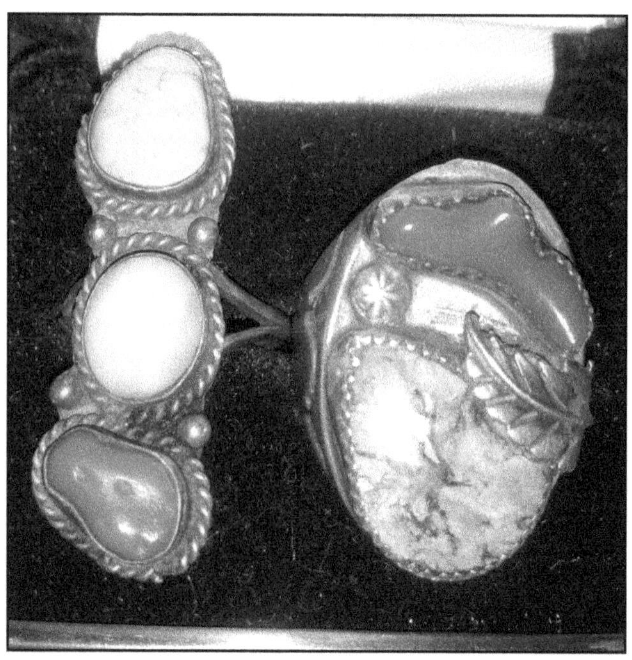

Rings Elvis gifted Wanda and Starla.

Above are shown two rings that belonged to Elvis. The large one on the right has coral in it which he found on the beach. Elvis had this ring made with that coral. There was an Indian silversmith that he had met while on location doing "Stay Away Joe" who is the person who made the silver bracelet Elvis gave to me. I believe it was probably the same person who made this ring because he did a lot of jewelry work for Elvis at that time. The other three stone ring on the left he wore in Vegas. He gave it to my daughter Starla simply because she mentioned liking it. Elvis was like that, always very generous.

Purpose

The purpose of this book is to reach a wide spectrum of people with the truth of who Elvis Presley was from my perspective as a mystic. In order to accomplish this feat, it has been necessary to include some esoteric and metaphysical-spiritual information alongside factual documentation and information that might appeal more to Elvis' devoted fans.

Some people will gravitate toward the book for its esoteric—metaphysical—spiritual content, others for its Elvis stories, memorabilia and collector's value, and others because it exposes a greater truth about an icon who has been buried in a media image. Elvis is the focal point for many paths of understanding within this book. I realize that in order for the reader to accept some of the spiritual information imparted in this book, they would first need to entertain the possibility that reincarnation is possible. While this may be contrary to some religious beliefs, it is not my intention. Rather my desire is to encourage an objective look at what might be beyond those beliefs in the hearts and minds of others in our world—one of whom was Elvis.

The concept of reincarnation, which Elvis devoutly believed in, represents our eternality in the eyes of a loving Creator. A Creator who would surely not create something as magnificent as a human being to only enjoy one lifetime in the vastness of the cosmos. Would it not also make sense that if God is eternal, and He created us in His image, that we too would be eternal? Some might construe this to be blasphemous, but it does not mean we are God, only that we share in His eternal Kingdom. Is not Elvis eternal in our hearts? How could that energy known to us as Elvis simply be no more? It seems downright preposterous if one thinks hard enough about it. We MUST believe Elvis is eternal or we would die inside, and if Elvis is eternal then might not we be?

Elvis was full of humanity—a combination of the ordinary and the unique. It is not so important to me that you believe he was from the Blue Star as it is that you understand his faith—here was a man who could accept his inner callings without self-reproach. He abided with what he knew inside himself rather than conform to what he was told. Because of this, and despite his many burdens, he was a happy and fulfilled individual within his spiritual center of being. His pain and sorrows were, as he put it, "but tiny thorns on the rose."

This book contains revelations about the whole personality of Elvis. They are in my opinion most revealing of a man who bled, laughed and cried yet who was somehow a miracle to others and set apart from the crowd. A human being is more than one strain or quality. He or she contains elements of the mundane that when strung together reveal the unique. Because of his immense fame, we find in Elvis those very human qualities we take for granted in ourselves and our next door neighbors, became especially appealing in him. Perhaps it is because we are all too aware of how money and fame can distort a person's grasp on the day-to-day humanities.

It will be obvious when you read this book, Elvis always and steadfastly remained the boy of the Tupelo misty morn from a Southland of novels and poignant reflections of days that are no more. And yet a man and a spiritual master are revealed as well; one who responded uniquely to wisdom in a reflex action of his empathy with all of life. Elvis has been portrayed as an immature child who never grew up. What is it about human nature that makes people uncomfortable with the thought that a man can have his ear pressed to the Earth and his eye on the Heavens at the same time? Why do we equate naturalness and an ability to remain innocent at heart in a world gone mad, with foolishness and immaturity?

If more people were like the man you read about in this book, would there be a child starving while the rich indulge? Would doors be closed to some and not to others? Would men and women still drain each other dry for sexual gratification and money, or would we turn to loving and sharing? What could the world become if every man, woman and child held one another? And yet we throw stones and deface memories of those whose example would show us the way. God bless Elvis. Wanda June Hill was Elvis Presley's friend for fifteen years. In 1979, I read her book, 'We Remember, Elvis,' which included her memories and those of thirteen others, all of whom had known Elvis personally over many years. Their main channel for this friendship was via the telephone.

In his loneliness and, from an innate quality of friendliness, Elvis reached out to 'ordinary' people he would never have been allowed to meet any other way through this medium. Few even in his inner circle, knew of his 'phone friends.' The men, women and children from all walks of life with whom Elvis communicated in this manner helped him to create a 'fantasy' wherein he was just one of them, and not one of the most famous human beings who ever lived. I was so impressed with Wanda June Hill's book that I wrote to her, thanking her and the other contributors for sharing their personal experiences of Elvis with the world.

Wanda responded warmly but briefly to my letter. Through the years, we would send each other a Christmas card or change of address, but no real friendship or in-depth communication developed between us until 1985, when I sent Wanda the 'Blue Star' material on Elvis which I had received via *my inner mystical sources.* As a mystical 'source translator*,' I had perceived Elvis' cosmic heritage. I then published it in my quarterly 'Doctrine of Sacred Inner Mysteries.' I wrote this original information in 1981, long before Ms. Hill alerted me to Elvis' startlingly similar story—a story that he first related to her in 1966 in a taped phone conversation. The transcription of the relevant portion of this conversation appears in Chapter 1.

In 1985, when Wanda wrote to me about Elvis' belief that he came from the Blue Star, we realized we had a purpose in knowing one another and in establishing an abiding friendship. Wanda and I felt Elvis would have wanted his message and mystical beliefs to be known because they were such an integral part of his life. As Wanda and I became closer, she gave me the transcribed tape conversations regarding what Elvis had said about spiritual-metaphysical subjects. She felt I was better suited to write on this topic than she and that the world deserved to share in the knowledge of the 'Inner Elvis.' This was accomplished in the first version of my self-published book, 'Magii From The Blue Star,' now re-titled as this book, 'Blue Star Love: from an Amazing Heart of Grace,' re-written with much less esotericism in order to share this special aspect of Elvis with many more people who love him.

A portion of this book is from transcribed telephone conversations between Elvis and Wanda June Hill, taped lectures given by Elvis at his home and from letters and cards sent by him to Wanda, her family and friends. This material has been validated as authentic. Some of that documentation is included in back of this book under 'Appendix E: Authenticity Documentation.' As these conversations reveal, Elvis believed sincerely that his soul had come to Earth from what he called the "Blue Star." He identified the Blue Star as Rigel in the constellation of Orion.

Elvis related to Wanda about the Light Beings who instructed him as a child in his birthplace of Tupelo, Mississippi. He spoke of wondering if the dreams he had were memories resurfacing from a past life and was it possible that he had lived in Egypt and served as a high priest to the Pharaoh Akhenaton and how these memories seemed to correlate with the frustrations he endured from being Elvis

Presley in this life (Chapter 4). In addition to Elvis' own thoughts, this book contains quotations from people of quite diverse backgrounds wherein they express profound feelings about a person who was much more to them than just an entertainer. Their statements form a testimony supporting the concept of Elvis' special heritage and mission in life. Some of these individuals knew him on a personal basis, many did not, yet all saw him as a special person endowed with the ability to help people from all walks of life, transcend the barriers of their travail and reach for the stars of a brighter heaven.

I felt it important to bring together into one place, all of the positive writings I have encountered that support the incredible spiritual goodness that emanated from this being we knew as Elvis. My apologies if any have been omitted, and I invite readers to share their experiences and writings for possible inclusion in a revised edition. Elvis' basic numerology* and his natal birth astrological* information are also revealed, based on the birth time given to Wanda by Elvis.

Most published natal astrological charts done on Elvis have given his birth time as that of his stillborn twin; also discussed are other mystical symbology's and his past-life incarnations. Tying this package together is the 'source translated*' material I received concerning the Blue Star and Elvis' cosmic heritage, and references that help substantiate what I am attempting to convey about this aspect of Elvis. While much in this book is in Elvis' own words, and will require reading with an open mind, it should not be too difficult considering the impact he had for twenty-two years of his life and continues to have upon millions. One must acknowledge there was something unusual about Elvis!

Bernard Benson, author of 'The Minstrel,' wrote, "It cannot be explained by his music alone." In 'Blue Star Love,' you will read Elvis' own explanation!

Art by Isabelle Tanner a.k.a. Elisabelle

Chapter 1: THE BLUE STAR

Wanda June Hill sat in the room, her attention focused on a dark-haired man. As his indigo eyes blazed in effort, his hand trembled above an ash tray on the polished top of the coffee table. His face began to pale and perspiration silvered his perfect features into a magic mirror of the mind. While Wanda and several others in the room held their breaths in anticipation, the large, heavy ashtray upon which this riveting young man had been concentrating, scooted across the table, just stopping before it would have crashed to the floor.

Wanda remembered in earlier encounters, having seen electrical sparks flash from his fingers in a darkened room. Not at all surprising she thought, for someone who had confided to her that his soul had come from another world, another star. He had once pointed his 'home' out to her as it laughed down upon them in the myriad twinkling of an evening sky. Even then it had seemed to call to his spirit. Surely, this world as well had singled him from the crowd, for few other human beings would be loved and admired by so many during their lives and long after their death, as Elvis Aaron Presley.

Such scenes as the above have repeated with variations throughout history. This is true of many aspects of the life of Elvis. To profile one such example would be the 18th century mystic and alchemist★, Count St. Germaine—a man of great charm, physical attractiveness and bearing. He 'Sang beautifully and often demonstrated feats which defied the known laws of science before small groups of privately gathered people.' St. Germain's death was mysterious as was Elvis's death. From Manly P. Hall's[1] introduction to 'The Most Holy Trinosophia':

> "Although nearly two hundred years have passed since his death or disappearance, research into the character and career of St. Germaine continues. He was called 'the man who does not die.' The true purpose for which St. Germaine labored must remain obscure until the dawn of a new era."

Like Elvis Presley, St. Germaine was ridiculed and wrongly judged by many. This is often the burden of the true spiritual teacher. Manly P. Hall asked Elvis to visit with him years ago, recognizing him as one who was among the few.

In 1979, I read a book written by Wanda June Hill, with contributions by thirteen of her family friends entitled, 'We Remember, Elvis.' Wanda and the thirteen other contributors had known Elvis from the mid-1960's until his death in 1977. Wanda, her husband and young daughter had an especially close friendship with him throughout these years and her book reflected the warmth and spiritual tenderness of Elvis the man.

I wrote to her in 1979 expressing my feelings about her book, and we continued to correspond through the years. In July of 1985, Wanda informed me that she was writing another book on her experience with Elvis. It was at this time, that she began to relate a great deal to me concerning his mystic nature, most of which she was hesitant to put into her book as those outside the world of spiritual metaphysics★ might find it too strange. It verified what I had written about him in 1981, having come from the Blue Star in my source translations★.

Wanda writes, "I remember Elvis saying so seriously (in 1966) and, with a look in his eyes like I have never seen before, that he was from the Blue Planet. He called it a Blue Star; that he was sent from there to Earth and he thought he was instilled into his mother's womb along with her natural son (Elvis' twin, Jesse) and that Jesse chose to die giving Elvis a path to an Earth life; that he always had visions even as a child, and, felt that he was somehow magical and not of this Earth, and was held to Earth to bring some new understanding and love to its people, to guide them to a higher realm of spiritual awareness through music or energy transmitted by music, and that he was doomed because he could not adjust to Earth's gravity and pressure—it was burning him up (Elvis' normal temperature was over 100 degrees).

"He was transformed—became different as he talked. It was dark, no moon at all and late, and he was lit as if from within. His eyes shone out of his head like miniature neon lights. He touched me and it was like getting an electrical shock from the tips of his fingers. I was almost spooked by him but there was a feeling of comforting warmth, of a good nature, that overtook the anxiousness I experienced. He talked fast, he sounded more southern and he gestured, shaping his hands differently than he did when just talking, almost as if using some kind of sign language.

"He began talking about all the things of his planet the Blue Star. He talked about the distance, time travel, astral projection*, and how his people astral projected to Earth and have for millions of years but they can't do too much as they are nebulous forms without substance and can't be felt. Some people can see them—only those who have come to Earth as (and have taken) human forms can see those who have not."

> *Author: I believe Elvis means that, those who are of kindred spirit to the star beings he is referring to, are the only ones that can see them.*

> "Those who are on Earth (from the Blue Star) are here to bring good and train mankind in any way they can without causing world conflicts. He then began talking about his home on the Blue Star; it had eight sides and eight rooms. The floors were of golden stones, the walls were crystal and many colors. The ceiling was a pyramid. He explained the principles of the power in the center that provided energy for all who lived therein. The beauty of his Blue Star was fantastic, he related, with birds that sang night and day. There were birds like peacocks, only more beautiful."

From my inner mystical sources, I was told about birds of paradise that were in Lemuria★ and Atlantis★, like peacocks, which I was told were also on the Blue Star worlds (planets of that sun). I was given information concerning the feline species and its place as a telepathic★ communicator on the Blue Star of Rigel. Wanda relates what Elvis told her about the domestic animals on his star home:

> "They had pets that were small, furry and like little dogs, only they didn't bark. Cats were important, he said. They were from his Blue Star planet—they originated there. Elvis then talked to her about his friends in that other world and about his constant physical discomfort on this planet. He began talking about several people, and their names kind of sounded like names in your pamphlet (the author's quarterly), but I can't begin to pronounce or spell them. He said that 'they were his family on the Blue Star—he had come to Earth, but was here too soon.' He should have waited; it was too soon. He said it softly, but so saddened and painful as if it hurt. (This was when he said), 'he was burning up; that the Earth was too heavy for him—he was going to have to leave early as a result.'"

From the 1996 'I Am America Prophecy' Newsletter and Catalogue No. 4, 'Following the Star,' by Lori Adaile Toye:

> "One of the most intriguing prophecies (of the Hopi Indians) is the appearance of the blue star—when the blue star appears, spiritual beings will destroy the conflict between material and spiritual concerns and create a new world."

My inner mystical sources indicate that the 'Blue Star' predicted by the Hopi is the Blue Star of Rigel in the constellation of Orion. From a transcript of a taped telephone conversation between Elvis and Wanda Hill in the early 1970's.

> Elvis: "See the air around us is filled with living spirits. We don't see them—sometimes they can be felt, but most of the time we are unaware until they want us to know about them. And if they can, they make us aware. The trouble is that we on Earth are too involved in living and we don't heed the ether* world. So there is little they can do for us, to help us or to make a contact. And it's a shame, but that's how it is. One day, in the future, not too far out of our reasoning either, it will be different. The time is coming when the portals will open, our Earth will be back on beam and those living on the other plane will be able to reach us, and us them. You see, when the Bible speaks of heaven, it is talking of the other plane—the existence of souls (who have) departed Earth bodies, and those who have not come to Earth in awhile, but plan to later.
>
> "Soon, in that time, it won't be necessary to take Earth bodies to help mankind, but people will pay attention to the spirit world… There are bad spirits, just as there are bad people—death doesn't change that, it only stops the Earthly process of growth and

development, but it doesn't always change the way the spirit is. Evil begets evil nine times out of ten, and there are those spirits who are evil. Satan after all, is alive and well and gathering forces, too."

Wanda: "You are really into all of that—spiritualism type of things, huh?"

Elvis: "What-no! Not spiritualism... spiritual development, soul growth and learning to develop the powers we all have lying innate. I'm not a conjurer of spirits. I don't have to, but I am not of this world, either. I know that, I know who I am. I am a man, a human being now, but what is 'me' is not from here. I am from out there. Did you ever hear of Rigel?"

Wanda: "No, is it a country or a person?"

Elvis: "A place, my home is near there—my other home—where I am from, and I have the Blue Star for my sun. I have eight moons and a mansion beneath the outer shell of my planet. You think I'm making this up, but it's true—you'll know that one day. You'll remember what I told you—before you die—you'll see some of it happen, and you'll be involved because you and I are tied together and you don't know it but I do. I can't tell you how—I don't remember it, but I feel it in my heart, in my inner self, and so do you.

"Why else are we talking about this? Why are you here? Why am I? I care about you because you are a part of my past as I am yours, and together it makes that tie in this life. Because of you and me things will happen—people will do things and have opinions and change minds and perhaps be more content, happier because of you and me knowing each other—that is life (perhaps Elvis was aware that

Wanda would contribute this information someday to be disseminated through this or another book)."

In the book 'The Star People,' by Brad & Francie Steiger, they relate their information, both channeled* and researched, on those among us who have memories, feelings and beliefs that, like Elvis, they came from up there—from some other world or dimension. Given in their book and also sent to the individual upon request, is a 'Starbirth Questionnaire,' a test one may take which will indicate whether or not one may be a 'star person.'

There are thirty-three questions involved. According to information from Wanda Hill, Elvis would have tested positive on all but two or three of these star people characteristics—determined by the Steigers in studying the personal histories sent to them by possible "star people". Two qualities that Elvis did not possess were low blood pressure and low temperature. Instead he had very high blood pressure and temperature relative to the norm. We do not know if he had an "extra or transitional vertebrae," but he did have one large spleen and several smaller ones, and a very much enlarged prostate gland and a smaller one.

While I have been told that it is not uncommon for twins to have multiple organs like this, the book 'The Star People' says this is also quite common to star people. Some of the other characteristics akin to star people listed in 'The Star People' book that Elvis possessed included:

- Compelling or heavy lidded 'bedroom' eyes,
- Good or outstanding personal charisma,
- Additional or unusual rib cage bones,
- Hypersensitivity to electricity and various forms of electromagnetic fields,
- Chronic sinusitis and general sinus issues,

- Can thrive on little sleep and often times work better at night,
- Star people are often times unexpected children,
- Love their parents but often feel they are not their real parents,
- May feel their ancestors and/or real family are from another world, another dimension, or some other level of consciousness,
- May long for their real home somewhere out in the stars,
- Often feel an urgency because they only have a short time on Earth to complete important goals, a special mission so to speak,
- As children, often believe they have unseen companions.

There are many more in this book and Elvis exhibited most of them. Another characteristic Elvis shared with his 'star' comrades was a memory of his true home planet as having two or more moons. He also shared with them the burden of being misunderstood by the more Earth-bound souls, but because of Elvis' high-visibility and fame, the intensity of such misunderstandings was increased a hundred-fold.

My inner mystical sources tell me that the cross-to-bear of the true spiritual initiate is evidenced by one who is blessed with spiritual insight and purpose, who does not conform to mainstream thought constructs and is seen as strange, perhaps stupid and foolish. In my opinion, never in modern times has there been such an intense, concerted effort to make a specific individual appear eccentric, foolish and un-intelligent as was levied upon Elvis Presley during his life and after his death.

The many sincere quotes and books written on this man have yet to receive their deserved coverage. Elvis once told Wanda Hill that you could tell how truly great a man was by how much he was slandered after his death (he was then referring to John F. Kennedy). By this standard, Elvis himself must have been one of the greatest. Perhaps I appear to border on what Elvis fans are accused of (most of them unjustly), which is glorifying King Elvis.

However, I am writing here not of any such 'King' but a man who was fallible yet capable of great insight and self-scrutiny. He was a man who, from the day he came into this world until the day he left it, dedicated himself to unconditional love and service to the people of the world. He did this for the masses, but covertly he gave of himself to individuals repeatedly in a way that was utterly unique, and I am not referring to the gifts of expensive cars and jewelry that he so willingly gave also.

> Wanda Hill: "Elvis would often speak to people visiting him about metaphysical subjects. He kept about thirteen or so of us captive one evening for over an hour while he talked about the Bible and the Hindu connection. He was spellbinding because he truly believed his words and it showed. He gleamed—that's the only word for it. His entire being actually seemed to shine—he was lit up like a polished piece of gold or silver, and his eyes were so alive, so brilliant that they held ours when he looked at us. When he was interrupted for trivia it vanished back into him and he didn't take it up again (that night). I often saw him look at his men—whoever it was that interfered (in these spiritual discussions) with a look of pity mixed with disgust and resignation, as though he thought they were to be endured."

In my previous writings from 1981, *my inner mystical sources* had indicated the man Ptah of ancient Egypt whose image was later deified as the God of Memphis, was an incarnation of Elvis Presley's. Wanda wrote to me about Elvis' knowledge and display of his powers:

> "He was writing down the relationship of colors to life just before he died. He was experimenting with pyramids,

> psychic energy and the ability to send thoughts to others. In 1966 he made an ashtray scoot across the table by holding his hands over it and thinking. I saw him do it. He said he could, people doubted and so he did it. The tray was heavy glass and it fairly flew down the coffee table, stopping just before it went over the edge. Elvis' hands trembled above it. He concentrated so intently that he broke into a light sweat and turned pale, but he did it (the story this chapter opened with). He could also make fire shoot from his fingers. It could be seen at night or in a dark room. It took a few minutes. He kept asking for silence and we all saw sparks fly off his index finger and seem to dance in the air before fading. He'd only do that for people he thought would be really motivated by it, and it was not something he ever bragged about or offered to do—he was kind of shy about it."

Elvis had spoken to Wanda in 1966 about the Blue Star, and that the ninth moon of Jupiter was somehow an energetic entrance or portal to his planet. *My inner mystical sources* tell me that Jupiter's ninth moon is an energy doorway to Orion and the Blue Star Rigel. After I had received Wanda Hill's letters on the subject of Elvis and the Blue Star, I was thinking about this connection as I went to bed. When I closed my eyes I saw clearly in vision form, a white elephant walking in the desert near a long, flat river.

A few days later, I received Joseph Jochman's 'Merrie Magi's Crystal Planetworks' newsletter for July of 1985. Reading it, I found information on the seven major chakras* of the body in their relationships to the initiatory temples of ancient Egypt. It was this passage from Mr. Jochman's newsletter that held my attention:

> "The animal symbol for the fifth chakra is a white elephant, which is directly related to Airvata, the elephant symbol of the first chakra. In the Egyptian system of initiation, there are two major deities of creation; Khnum, who shaped *man* on the potter's

> wheel, and Ptah, who shaped the *world* on the potter's wheel. Significantly, they are the gods and Masters of Initiation at Elephantine* and Saqquara* respectively, the first and fifth levels.[2] Saqquara, too, was designed as a healing temple, where the priests and Initiates of the God Ptah, called the Tongue of Ra, learned to produce sound at absolute pitch and direct that sound for healing of the physical, mental and spiritual bodies. The fifth chakra is of course the throat chakra, the source of producing sound. Devotees of the fifth chakra were said to be able to overcome disease and attain long life."

According to *my inner mystical sources*, Elvis' mission here on Earth was oriented quite heavily towards assuming world karma*, which to a great degree negated his ability to 'master' the afflictions within his body. In essence, Elvis soul made a decision prior to his birth to forgo his own physical health and bodily wellbeing in order give the gift of redemption to whatever degree he could facilitate that, to the world. As a result of this soul decision, Elvis' body did indeed "burn up" as he had predicted it would eleven years before. The autopsy concluded that he had the arteries of an eighty year old man.

He had many health problems throughout his life including acute insomnia caused by a genetic disorder, blinding headaches and recurrent pneumonia. In the last years of Elvis' life he suffered from glaucoma, detached retina, inherited liver disease, pernicious anemia, bleeding ulcers and cancer. He was thus impelled to take prescribed medication that included strong pain killers towards the end of his life. His medication and his misunderstood metaphysical pursuits have been grossly distorted by the media with help from several persons whom he had trusted as friends. Quoting Elvis' true friend, Dr. Harry Rosenberg, from Wanda Hill's, 'We Remember Elvis':

> "When Elvis died they said he had drugs in him. He should have had more, the way he suffered in his last few

months. With his condition, he was courageous beyond all reason if that's all he had in him."

As souls who come from the Blue Star are oriented heavily towards world service, usually at the expense of their own experience in the physical world, we can see that Elvis' life did indeed follow the typical pattern these souls incarnate under.

These souls truly understand sacrifice for others, generally without recognition in the physical world. From a writing of mine in 1981, I profiled Elvis Aaron Presley:

> "Among his incarnations in the outer world of Earth were those of both Lemurian* and an Atlantean Melchizedek Priesthood;* the Roman statesman Pericles; the Greek mystic, poet and scholar of celestial and nature music, Orpheus; the Egyptian, Ptah who was a physician, author and intellectual and the brother-in-law of Hermes Trismesgistus."

Elvis' soul was also a follower of Jesus Christ when he walked the Earth (see Chapter 4 for further information on these and other past lives).

Thoth Hermes, my main inner mystical source, said:

> "Elvis Aaron, a soul who brought the flame of love into this life experience, was destined to relive the pain of Calvary, of the Master (Jesus) whom he so loved. Elvis' presence for good still abides with the Earth—in his life as Elvis Aaron, this entity longed to reveal his inner knowledge, which was abundant. Yet it was his plight to remain a Hidden Priest."

I have presented evidence that Elvis comes from another star and planet system other than our own both from his perspective and our own. Of course, the reader must be able to accept that there is life in other places in the universe, and that reincarnation is possible before this can be an acceptable hypothesis. If you are not sure about your beliefs concerning such matters, I simply ask that you hold an open mind as you read the remainder of this book. In the very least, Elvis so exemplified such an extraordinary love, that one must consider if this in and of itself might be the only indication needed that he hailed from another world more evolved than our own.

Love comes unasked and unsolicited.

It doesn't confine, condemn or criticize.

It frees, protects and uplifts the beloved.

It is a gift from God, to be nurtured and cared for.

So many people think it is their right to own another person, that isn't love.

It is possession and will not survive in times of crisis.

If it were not for God, His hand in my life, I would have nothing.

I believe I am doing the thing I was put here for and
hope that by my conduct and my example, somehow
I can be worthy of the opportunity to be here.

It's silly to think we're the only life with billions of planets in the universe.

This planet is obviously being monitored by superior beings,

to prepare us for the transition into the New Age.

~ Elvis Aaron Presley

Chapter 2: SACRED BIRTH & MARK

"That cold January morning the woman's first son came into the world lifeless, but as the man wept their loss the mid-wife cried out, 'There's another baby to come out here!' Some minutes later the man went outside, raised his eyes to Heaven and thanked God for giving them one live child. As he turned back to the house, he saw streaming down from the sky a glowing blue light bathing the humble home where lay his wife and new born son. And the man said twenty-five years later, 'I knew Elvis had to be a special baby, he had the light of Heaven on him from birth,' so said Vernon Presley of his famous son's entrance into the world.

> "That 'special' baby grew to be a unique and special man whose talent ranged far from mere entertainer to that of one who was gifted, beloved of millions and one never to be forgotten. I knew Elvis for fifteen years. He had a quality one could only call magical and of a special nature. I believed him when he said, I'm not from here; I came from up there, from the Blue Star. One day you'll know that's true." ~ From Wanda June Hill.

Several sources have told about the blue light which shone down upon the humble Tupelo shack the night of Elvis' birth, lighting his father's way to the well. It has further been stated that all the medicine bottles inside the house rattled violently on the shelves, several of them actually shattering. While the outside of the building was bathed in blue, the inner rooms were lit with a violet light. One can only imagine what must have gone through the minds and hearts of those who witnessed this event, keeping it largely a secret for the duration of Elvis' lifetime.

Such phenomena certainly fit the pattern of 'sacred births' throughout the ages. Those who are born to serve the masses in a unique way, beyond the normal role of leadership, have had situations of conception and birth that were far from normal in their circumstances. I do not imply here that Elvis was a 'god,' but I do see his birth, life and death as paralleling other human beings who were destined as spiritual leaders in various degrees of brilliance. It would seem that select human souls are chosen in major cycles of planetary development to enter into roles beyond their personal humanity. These souls are bestowed with a special grace. They are knighted to do battle with the dragons of our corruption, and emerge as symbols of the greatest good, which we can and must strive to release from within ourselves.

One sign of a 'sacred birth' is often a special birthmark. Elvis had this as did others of his generation before and after him. Generally, such a birthmark is not present solely on the one of 'Divine birth' but appears in a somewhat similar form among members of the same family throughout the many generations as a sign of the 'royal lineage' which produces select individuals with a particular destiny.

Due to differing personal and soul conditions, many times people of these royal lineages are not consciously aware of their genetic heritage. Elvis Aaron was born during what the Native Americans call a 'crying moon' which is a condition where the lower half of the moon is darkened, light appearing to stream from the upper half down to Earth. This occurrence takes place only once a year.

The birthmark Elvis said he had was a diamond-shaped

discoloration, bearing a cut-out upside down bowl or crescent of normal pigmentation within the upper left hand corner of the dark diamond, eclipsing the left edge of the birthmark. The birthmark was on the upper thigh or groin area.

Quoting an abstract for an article in the 'Society for Scientific Exploration's Journal,' Volume 7, Number 4: Article 4, Page 403 entitled: 'Birthmarks and Birth Defects Corresponding to Wounds on Deceased Persons' by Ian Stevenson of the Department of Psychiatric Medicine, University of Virginia, School of Medicine, Charlottesville, Virginia:

> "About 35% of children who claim to remember previous lives have birthmarks and/or birth defects that they (or adult informants) attribute to wounds on a person whose life the child remembers. The cases of 210 such children have been investigated. The birthmarks were usually areas of hairless, puckered skin; some were areas of little or no pigmentation (hypo-pigmented macules); others were areas of increased pigmentation (hyper-pigmented nevi). The birth defects were nearly always of rare types.
>
> "In cases in which a deceased person was identified the details of whose life unmistakably matched the child's statements, a close correspondence was nearly always found between the birthmarks and/or birth defects on the child and the wounds on the deceased person. In forty-three of forty-nine cases in which a medical document (usually a postmortem report) was obtained, it confirmed the correspondence between wounds and birthmarks (or birth defects).
>
> "There is little evidence that parents and other informants imposed a false identity on the child in order to explain the child's birthmark or birth defect. Some paranormal process seems required to account

> for at least some of the details of these cases, including the birthmarks and birth defects."

Elvis' birthmark correlates to the above circumstances, in terms of a wound, from the perspective of the 'Wounded King' archetype[3]*. It can also be extrapolated that, if the scientific community has seen rather conclusive evidence that birthmarks can be an indication of past life occurrences, then Elvis' birthmark may also be as result of the past service his soul has seen in service to God and humanity—God's sign to us. We can draw a corollary here to some ancient myths and legends regarding this birthmark with its peculiar placement to further support the idea that Elvis was a unique soul with a specific purpose for being here on Earth. If the birthmark is seen as a 'wound' (the greater expression of a blemish) then the 'Wounded Thigh' analogy can be used.

The 'Wounded Thigh' or 'Wounded King' is an archetypal symbol[4] of several ancient myths and legends, given various interpretations. One meaning is that of someone appointed for spiritual service, whose body is wounded or maimed (also correlates with Elvis' illnesses) in order to release illumination to the people. The concept here is that in order for the world's wrong doings to be resolved, there must be someone who is willing to 'pay the price' for humanities debt, which many times is in the form of suffering, to balance the energy deeds that have been tallied in imbalance within the world over time. This is a similar function to Christ's except his was a much higher level of experience.

I feel that the birthmark on Elvis' thigh is quite symbolic of the 'Wounded Thigh/King' representation within the myths and legends, especially when one considers what his life was truly like, and about. I feel this will become self-evident as the reader progresses through this book. The diamond in Elvis' birthmark is a representation of the hermetic* axiom, 'As Above, So Below,' for it contains two triangles merging—one pointing to Heaven and the other to Earth, indicating a reflection of the macrocosm in the microcosm, or the Greater Mystery of Spirit reflected in the Lesser Mystery of Life.[5]

The crescent is an image of the Goddess, the Magical Realm of Gaia, the Living Earth. These energies are expressed in love of the Earth, animals, humans, and all natural being. Certainly as you will see, Elvis lived and breathed love for all things. The Merovingian Dynasty* of France is said to have originated from the genetic lineage of Jesus Christ. The kings of this dynasty reportedly all had mysterious birthmarks. Elvis' heritage was French, as well as American Indian, Scotch, Greek, and Jewish.

In the book, 'The Glastonbury Zodiac,' by Mary Caine, she tells of a Jewish legend from the Middle Ages which is representative of the 'Wounded Thigh' myths and legends. In her book Caine speaks of how the Hidden Name* was secretly inscribed in the innermost recesses of the Temple and had a lion in the form of a statue as its guardian. If an intruder saw the Hidden Name the lion would issue forth a supernatural roar so intense that all memory of the name would be driven from the intruder's mind. She goes on to say that Jesus knew this and he successfully evaded the lion. He then wrote the Hidden Name, cut his thigh open, and hid it within the wound and closed it by magic. Once Jesus was out of the Temple he then re-opened the incision and took out the Hidden Name.

Lions, usually in pairs, were seen by the ancients as guardians of sacred knowledge. One only need to stand before Graceland, and see the two white lions poised in motionless command at the threshold, to envision the Temple Elvis had created—whether consciously or unconsciously)[6]—upon this site. What sacred knowledge does it possibly contain within it, still waiting for its revelation to us? In Chapter 5, this subject of the 'Wounded King' archetype is explored more in depth. It is only mentioned here as it connects symbolically to the sacred birthmark.

In mystical ways of thinking, everything that is known to us as part of our physical reality is as the result of energy patterns in the unseen realms. In other words, one could use the analogy of the electricity flowing through the wires to light the light bulbs, or run the motor in your fan. One cannot see the electricity, but it is there, and it has a definite result when it is directed to the physical device that makes use of its power. One does not have to know how the electricity works within the devices to be able to throw the switch and turn them on.

In much the same way, this birthmark could be seen as a result of the power of the energy in Elvis' bloodline and soul respectively. As the body of Elvis formed in his mother's womb, the energy present from these previous experiences perhaps left its signature upon the babe about to be birthed, that he might remember who he was. A mark of remembrance of times past, of the greatness he was here to express, of the Divine link his soul communion with God so exemplified.

Chapter 3: GRACELAND

> "Few people who have ever lived are less dead than Elvis Aaron Presley. A little of all our hearts will be forever Graceland" ~ Donald Lyons

Graceland was Elvis' home from 1957 until his death in 1977. It was built in 1939 by Dr. and Mrs. Moore on a thirteen and three-quarter acre site that at the time, was heavily wooded countryside. Previous to the Moore's ownership of the land, this site had been a part of a 500 acre Hereford cattle farm established in 1861 by S.E. Toof. The whole spread had been named 'Graceland' after Mr. Toof's daughter, Grace. Certainly there could have been no more appropriate name for the home and final resting place of Elvis Presley.

In the book 'Graceland—The Living Legacy of Elvis Presley,' published by Collins Publishers San Francisco, it revealed that people who go to Graceland are like pilgrims, some of them being spiritual and some not. It is also stated that these people are totally open and unashamed about their love for Elvis and their pilgrimage to Graceland in honor of him. During the short span of his life as Elvis, he opened his soul and let the starlight shine onto those who may never have known just how beautiful the stars could be. As one writer said, "He made it all his, then revealed it as ours." Now his followers have only the garden, wherein the laughter of a man and his child still echoes.

He left them his Graceland, his sanctuary, to read from as prose sweetly filled with the life of a man of grace, who knew how to live greatly, gently, and with love for every living thing, No flower was kept from growing by his shadow. He reached like a soaring redwood far above us, but he brought down to our realm the benefits of his blessings. Beyond Elvis the man is the Elvis mystery. In this context the word mystery is used to denote a hidden and not commonly understood spiritual entrainment to a heart-mind consciousness, rather than something that can simply be learned through the study of books or such.

A mystery of this genre is a labyrinth journey to reach the center of a particular knowing that is essentially catalytic in nature. It connects to other mysteries and paths of consciousness, once the individual has penetrated the central chamber of enlightenment sustained at the labyrinth's core. All mysteries have a secret that guards and empowers their purpose. According to *my inner mystical sources* Nostradamus predicted the Elvis mystery and its secret when he wrote:

> "The divine voice shall be struck by heaven so that he cannot proceed any further. The secret of the close-mouthed one shall be closed, that people shall tread upon and before it."

When a mystery reveals its secret, it is no longer empowered. It must contain drive, that impelling force which is hidden in order to draw upon the subconscious mystical instinct of the masses choosing from among them those destined to follow that path. Without the secret, the seeker is not challenged. To move into some mythological metaphor, as the masses come to Graceland, so they enter the realm of the Quest, into which each seeker must journey. It is akin to the passage of King Arthur* in Avalon* and the search for the Holy

Grail*. No matter the mystery, this scenario is duplicated in some form. In this instance 'The Crystal Isle*' of Avalon has become Graceland.

Elvis is the 'dead king,' that Arthurian representation of a Knight who has finished his Earthly quest and has ascended into the dimension of an archetype, where through the masses who loved him, he has received grace. The king is never seen as being without stain in these myths. He is that being who emulates the Christ, but who is also very human and thus makes at least one crucial error resulting in his death. But this error is never of an evil or debauched nature. Instead, it is a result of placing trust upon those who betray him.

The lesson is, even the very good can err through their relentless belief in the essential purity of all things. In pursuing this virtue they are robbed of Earthly breath but are claimed by God's Light and glorified in the hearts of those who followed after them. The 'king' is one who is able to touch the heart of his realm—not just the individuals within it but the very center of the collective heart, transferring this love throughout the kingdom. When touched by the love of the king the people are aroused to press upon the door of illumination; to enter unto their own questing. Without 'hero-kings' humanity would not be able to rise above the turmoil within and without.

Mankind must have its representatives, heroes, and martyrs. Through their mysteries, so do the masses conquer the profane—seeing in the image of the dead king the living entity within—Jesus Christ was the perfected mystery, from which the dead king gave life through the ritual of communion. Elvis, as an archetype, has become a beacon to those still questing. This mystery is prefaced by the questions: WHO was he? WHY was he? WHERE is he now? This ultimately personalized in the seeker: WHO am I? WHY am I? WHERE am I going?

Elvis as a man was a reverberation of every man/woman at a soul-level, for he was as a little child—without guile, possessing a great sense of compassion, adventure, loving, and humor. He was HUMAN, he erred. Yet he was noble, and through it all his integrity remained chiseled in the foundation stone of his heart. In the body of the dead king, we do not see decaying flesh, but hallowed ground, for wherever a Knight of Christ is buried, so there a garden grows. It is that bit of Earth transformed by the heart, to which the flowers of his followers gather to root, to remember that once there was a Camelot.

Toward the end of his life, Elvis told Wanda Hill that from backstage, after a performance, he could hear fans calling his name—chanting for him. Often he continued to hear these voices in his head, calling to him even in his sleep. He said that his astrology chart predicted he would be even more famous after his death. Elvis expressed disbelief to Wanda about this, saying, "What are they going to do, come and chant around my grave?"

Indeed, this is what has happened, they come and chant, sing, cry, meditate and pray. Author, Ted Harrison, in his book, 'Elvis People—The Cult of the King,' writes about people praying to or through Elvis to God: He says that many of his fans feel he had a mission here that was imbued with divine purpose. That he has touched so many people with his music that he can no longer be considered an ordinary human being. Harrison states, "they feel they are justified in praying to or through Elvis."

Others have said similar things. In the book 'Elvis People—the Cult of the King' there is a fan named Marie being quoted saying that she believes God chose Elvis for a purpose on our planet and that this purpose is related to bringing people closer to God. She indicates that she believes this happens through the love that is exchanged between Elvis and his fans via the medium of his music. The Candlelight Service around Elvis' grave in Meditation Garden on the Graceland estate has become an annual prayer ceremony beginning on the night of August 15th, and continuing into the early morning hours of the

16th, the date of his death. A first hand personal accounting of the 1982 service…

> "The most moving moment for me was the occasion of the fifth anniversary of his death. A candlelight procession around the grounds is held every anniversary. This time there was a torrential downpour all day but at ten minutes to midnight it suddenly stopped. Some 17,000 people, each carrying a lighted candle, moved along the driveway, lined both sides with flowers, up the hill, round the mansion then down to the grave. It was almost like a religious ceremony.
>
> "We moved in single file. In front of me was a Mexican couple with a young baby. They had saved for years to make the trip to Memphis. The ceremony took nearly three hours (Elvis sacred music was played in the background). The moment it was over the rain lashed down again. It was uncanny.
>
> "Elvis was known by those around him to on occasion, control the weather in shamanic fashion. On the last day of Elvis' life, his cousin Billy Smith complained to him about the drizzle that had been coming down for hours. Elvis went outside, lifted up his hand to the sky, closed his eyes for a moment and the rain had stopped! As the sun shone down upon him, Elvis turned to his stunned cousin and said with a crooked grin, 'You never know, Billy, you never know.'"

Elvis was noted for his unconditional giving under an infinite array of circumstances. This is something that Graceland and his fans have carried forth in his memory; another testimony to the power of God's Light that was unleashed through the heart of Elvis. Elvis' father, Vernon Presley, recalled that as a child, despite the poverty in which they lived, Elvis was always giving his meager toys away to those who had even less. On one occasion, his father and mother had eaten corn flakes for several weeks in order to save enough money to buy their son a tricycle.

Finally, the day arrived. When they presented little Elvis with his trike, the child was ecstatic. However, several hours later, the tricycle was missing. When Vernon inquired of his son where the shiny new toy had gone, Elvis informed him that he had given it to another child who didn't have one. Vernon recovered the trike, only to have Elvis give it away again. This time, his father gave up. He realized that as long as Elvis encountered those who had less than he, the child could not be content to enjoy his own possessions.

Kathy Westmoreland quotes B.J. Baker, background singer and vocal choir conductor for Elvis' TV Specials, as saying that he was totally awed by the generosity, innocence and desire to do good that Elvis exhibited. He goes on to say that Elvis just never stopped giving and never allowed the darkness of others to taint his open trusting nature. Marty Lacker, a friend and employee of Elvis' for many years went on record to say, "Elvis was the epitome of the Biblical joy of giving. He gave without wanting anything in return. He loved to make people happy."

Jeweler Lowell Hays remembers Elvis buying a ring from him which was to be a gift for Sammy Davis Jr: His recounting of this story goes on to say: "Then Elvis asked how much he owed me. I told him fifty-five thousand dollars. He said, 'You gotta be kidding.' No Elvis, it's got an eleven and one-half carat diamond in it. 'Well, all right,' Elvis smiled, then looked at me with that lopsided grin and said, 'Now I want to do something for you Lowell. What do you want?'"

J.D. Sumner of the Stamps Quartet, Elvis' backup group in the 1970's said, "The man made $4 billion; I didn't say million, in his life, and gave over half of it away."

In the book 'The Best of Elvis' by Cindy Hazen and Mike Freeman it is related how Elvis gave all the credit to his fans for his success. He was so grateful and appreciative of them that he felt whatever he had was theirs and allowed them to sleep on his lawn at Graceland in full understanding of how far they had traveled to visit him. Graceland and Elvis' fans have carried this spirit of giving forward in tribute to Elvis, and in God's name.

The 'Elvis International Forum' states the following regarding the 'Elvis Presley Memorial Foundation':

> "A $25,000 scholarship endowment fund for acting and music students has been established at the University of Memphis by the Elvis Presley Memorial Foundation Inc. The foundation presented a $25,000 check establishing the endowment to Richard Ranta, Dean of the University's College of Communication and Fine Arts. The scholarship is set up to help those students in areas where Elvis made his mark, which was in acting, music, television and film. Jack Soden, chief executive officer of Elvis Presley Enterprises Inc., said the donation is the beginning of what he hopes will be a growing endowment fund for art students.
>
> "Soden, whose company established the memorial foundation in 1985, said he plans to encourage Elvis fans to make other contributions to the fund. 'There are many, many entertainers who give great thanks to the early influence of Elvis Presley and his music.' Soden said the purpose of the endowment is to help talented students, who may be struggling financially, to get started. Ranta said the University has for years worked closely with Graceland on special projects for Elvis Week, as well as on the presentation or

> an annual distinguished achievement award given to outstanding artists in the name of Elvis Presley."

International Elvis Week is an all-out tribute week to Elvis sponsored by Graceland each year on the anniversary of Elvis' death (August 16th, 1977). While Graceland is the hub of this activity, much of the city of Memphis participates, with many thousands of people from all over the world coming to Graceland during this time.

The highlight of the International Elvis Week is the candlelight vigil at the grave site in Meditation Garden at Graceland on the night of the 15th into the early morning hours of the 16th, when as many as an estimated 125,000 people have passed by the grave of Elvis Presley. From Graceland Express, January-March 1989 issue, excerpted from an article by Patsy Andersen entitled, 'For the Love of Elvis—His Generosity Continues through His Fans':

> "Everyone knows how Elvis loved to give, whether it was a lavish present, financial aid to an individual or a charity, or his even more important gift of himself. Now, his fan clubs carry on this tradition of giving in his memory."

An Elvis Fact from 'Elvis International Forum':

> "It is estimated that Elvis Presley has sold over one billion record units since 1982 (meaning from the beginning of his career until 1982), more than any individual or group in the history of recorded voice. To give the figure perspective—that's enough for every person in America to have four Elvis albums or singles in their collection—or enough for one out of every five people on Earth to have one. These one billion albums and singles could encircle the Earth at the equator twice and then some."

Graceland attracts more visitors than any place in the USA except the White House in Washington, D.C. Since Elvis' passing in 1977, an estimated 700,000 make their pilgrimage there each year. As the throngs of fans, followers and those drawn for reasons they do not even understand, file through Graceland each year, some are moved to leave a piece of their hearts behind to share with others. Sentiments etched by 'pilgrims' on the stone-walls around Graceland…

> "Pray for us and always remember us."
>
> "Elvis, a man before his time who will live forever."
>
> "We traveled from Germany to be near you."
>
> "Elvis, we believe, always and forever."
>
> "Elvis, the world needs you."
>
> "He touched me and now I am no longer the same."
>
> "Elvis, thank you for being our guiding light."
>
> "Every mountain I have had to climb, Elvis carried me over on his back."
>
> "I heard the call, I made the pilgrimage, I came to Graceland."
>
> "Wanted to be here before I died. I made it."
>
> "Elvis, eternal spirit, blessed by God."
>
> "Elvis, from one of your newest fans, take care of us all."
>
> "Elvis, your spirit lit my way, I hope to see you again."
>
> "How Great Thou Art."
>
> "Beam Me Up, Elvis."

"Dear Elvis, I missed you at the Dome but I'll see you at the rapture, Love from Texas."

"When he shall die, take and cut him out in little stars, and he will make the face of Heaven so fine that all the world will be in love with night and pay no worship to the garish sun—Shakespeare."

"In ancient times the prophet spoke and told of visions he had seen. This modern world need not despair, there's wisdom from your songs to gleam. If only I could sit all day and grovel at your very knee, I'd be the wisest one of all and die to love you tenderly."

From Elvis International Forum, author unknown:

"Thank you God for giving us Elvis and showing us the way to love our fellow man; Thank you for the family of Elvis; We will try to be worthy and will spread his love; Every single day, as much as we can."

By Donna Rose Zaeko about the mystique of Graceland:

"All alone in a confusing and somewhat congested world, it stands high among the trees—surrounded by a winding road of precious memories. Its gentleness streams across each blade of grass and the trees quietly nod, as if to almost welcome you. Tall and proud it awaits, calling me to come into the glory of peace and rest. He lies there, sleeping in a garden, seeing it all and smiling ever so gently. He knows that I come to see him, he can feel me as much as I can feel him. How long have I waited to enter upon these gates, how long have I waited to be with my friend?

"I am here now and all is still, except for the

> pounding in my chest and the rushing of feelings running inside my heart. I am free now, to remember and feel. This is our time together, no one can take away this beauty or lessen the tender moment, between me and my friend."

This chapter was intended to be a tribute to not only Elvis, but to Graceland and the fans who continue to perpetuate the pure essence of Elvis' love for humanity. It is this divine essence of giving unconditionally, of helping others in any way one can with no thought of self that was the most outward sign of the Light of God that shone through Elvis' heart.

Truly, this kind of light IS Graceland, for while there is a unique and wonderful physical place called Graceland, it is only a representation of the state of mind/heart that all of it represents and that can be found anywhere that love expresses itself unconditionally. Graceland is a state of the mind/heart that resides within everyone, and Elvis reminded us that it was there, just waiting to be revealed in all its shining splendor and glory, the beauty of God manifest on Earth.

> "In Graceland, in Graceland, I'm going for reasons I cannot explain, there's a part of me that wants to see Graceland. And I may be obliged to defend every love, every ending, or maybe there's no obligation now. Maybe I've a reason to believe we'll all be received in Graceland." ~ From the song 'Graceland,' by Paul Simon

Chapter 4: THE GOLDEN THREAD

> "And finally he died, and his voice lived on and his music lived on—and he was overwhelmed with joy!"
> ~ From 'The Minstrel,' by Bernard Benson

Sean Shaver, wrote a highly mystically inspired statement in his book 'Elvis—Photographing the King' when he said, "According to Einstein's theory of relativity and time, all the past and all the future are still out there in the ether*. If so—out in the mists somewhere—comes the golden voice we have all grown to love—He now belongs to the ages."

Each human being is a rich tapestry of experiences, woven not only of the many variances of a single life, but from the different fabrics, color and forms of life after life, through which a soul makes passage in order to redeem its lost sight. This is the 'Golden Thread' of continuity that each human soul follows throughout all of its experience. In each life we enter a magical moment in which we are given the key to this sight and return again, in different habit and circumstance, to peep through the keyhole and dream of opening doors, as we lie sleeping with the key in our hand.

Among us are those who are living keyholes—souls who offer windows for us to see through into the Light of the Infinite. Every baby is surely a window of light, a keyhole to God's Light. However, as we mature that window is often sealed through fear, frustration and disillusionment. Only a few humans are able to resist the strong urges to shut the window because of non-acceptance by the world around them of anything but the 'norm.' Perhaps these few who do pull free, it is their great sense of loving and their ability to appreciate being loved, that sustains the unmasked light shining through them, overcoming the fear of being 'different.'

This acute 'loving sense' beyond what we consider the normal, is a product of many lifetimes in spiritual service. It is a service through which that soul both succeeds and fails in varying degrees but understands the reasons for failure, accepts it and rises above it to move on. It is the 'loving sense' that secures each one of us to the bow of the Divine ship and in some it becomes a mission unto itself.

What exactly is reincarnation* and what are the spiritual-scientific laws under which it operates? There are many different opinions concerning this belief. I choose to focus more on the essence of reincarnation rather than its linear fact. I see the connectedness of all experiences, and therefore our souls are connected to all points and experiences everywhere at once. I view our 'past' and 'future' lives as points within our subconscious and sometimes conscious minds, that are receptive to Spirit recreating a flow of perception or self-aware knowledge through the physical, emotional and psychological experience.

It is this self-aware perception that individual souls accept as part of their beingness. Many times we have feelings and behaviors, both good and bad, that are not explainable through normal deductive analysis based on the current conditions. These are generally emanating from a past-life experience that Spirit is bringing to our current awareness through the feelings to be recreated in a more proper or spiritually aligned context. Exactly which points of experience will merge with our current self-awareness are determined by our individual roles as co-creators with God. Both 'karma*'—the balance of cause and effect—and 'dharma*'—soul destiny or Divine order for the soul—form the pattern for this expression.

Through the years before and after Elvis' death, I was able to translate information on many of his past-lives, or 'receptive points.' The following is a listing of what I believe to be some of Elvis Presley's past-lives. I have accessed these from what many call 'The Hall of Records' or the 'Akashic Records.' This is a continuous stream of thought into which all memory is impressed. Mystical and metaphysical thought has it that every thought and feeling ever experienced by anyone at any time is recorded energetically in the ethers much as a magnetic tape records your voice in a tape recorder.

A sensitive can 'read' or source-translate these thought-feeling records as though they are reading a book. As a mystic this is one of my unique gifts.

The following information is not meant to represent a complete review of Elvis' past life sojourns, but is instead a selection of major archetypal roles that his soul's essence has embraced in its evolution. This cataloging is not in precise chronological order, although I attempted to arrange it in more or less an advancing sequence through time. First appears the name he had in these previous lifetimes, then a brief description of who he had been and in some cases a bit about what went on in that lifetime for his soul.

Elvis' Previous Incarnations

Aarnon

A member of the Sun Bow Clan*. This Clan was composed of the first beings of human origin who were part of the original human race, and who inhabited the Earth in the 'Time of the Light.'1

Poniciah

An ancient Lemurian* Emperor, much loved by the people, and also the son of the Great Lemurian Emperor, Ramu I.

Kartum

A healer, prophet and governor of Urasia, a nation under the supremacy of the Lemurian Empire. Kartum healed thousands, and once again, was greatly loved. He was also a fine singer. The life of Kartum is profiled in my now out of print book 'Red Tree,' which appears on the book list Elvis gave to Wanda June Hill.

Ebonaron

An Atlantean priest in the Order of Melchizedek* and guardian of the Holy Tone*.

Amuil

A Master within the Temple of the Lion, also known as the Great Pyramid at Giza in Egypt. He was involved in the energetic charging of the pyramids through the use of star-energy*. In 1974 I had a medallion made, resembling the one Amuil wore during that lifetime. I gave this medallion and its information to Elvis from the edge of the stage at Lake Tahoe.

Mayah-Metahraptah

One of the identical twin male Pharaohs of Egypt, in its most ancient and distant past. Elvis' twin Jesse, who was born dead in this last incarnation, was the soul of Mayah's twin. The following is my seer's view of a past life memory as experienced by the soul of Elvis Presley while incarnated as Mayah-Metahraptah. This scenario is based solely on my own paranormal perceptions, and not on any experience he verbalized to another person to my knowledge.

"He lay sleeping, finally. The pain had gripped him

tightly in its fist for so many hours he was reduced to a dulled pantomime of feeling, no longer connected to the present world. And so he slept. Or was it sleeping? It was as if he had become a mirror held up to the sky. He felt empty, yet full of hidden spaces. A gentle and steady wind swept into the sails of his mind. He shivered a moment then relaxed. His soul became a ship, its bow cutting through the darkness, breaking into a silver sea, spilling stars in its wake.

"It was not an uncharted course the wind had embarked him upon for surely as he soared on wings of light, he was homeward bound. Within each soul there are many ports where the lanterns are lit for our returning memory. As lost sailors we may someday re-appear for a moment out of time to recount our struggles, pleasures, and rewards in a life now far removed from our shore. He knew this, and he knew also that he was now upon such a journey. Suddenly, all about him a swirl of blue light twisted and turned in a dance of mists, invoking him in a surge of happiness, of belonging. From the center of the blue depth a vaporous form took shape. As a shade from the past, the form grew more visible, until he could see it fully under the brilliant sun.

"He realized he was now standing upon a vastness of sand, the sky swirled as a tender rose in the first blaze of dawn. But for the imposing figure before him, he felt alone. He was a speck of light upon an amber marble in a sea of glass. The form that had taken shape in his sight appeared to be a great golden falcon its pinions raised towards the sun. The protruding beak of the creature glinted in silence, yet the large rounded eye, turned toward him and spoke into his heart.

"A door opened inside him and he saw himself in the ancient land—the Egyptos before the Deluge when the masters had walked the Earth. He was tall and straight, with pale blue eyes the color of Siberian quartz. He wore a shirt of white with golden threaded braid. A similar braid encircled his head. In repose at his feet lay a white tiger, his yellow eyes synchronized with some distant motion.[5]

"He saw that he was in the open air standing before the steps of a massive temple. Before him a small gathering of men and women stood, waiting expectantly. He knew they awaited his response to their need. A great and tedious drought had laid siege to their land. As a descendant of the Blue Star he was seen as a god among mortals, and it was therefore within his power to control the elements. He instinctively beckoned an aid to come forward from behind him.

"The man carried a cage containing seven white doves. As he took the cage from his aid, he knew he was committing this act upon the scroll of time once again, as he had done in that age long ago. It was as if he must repeat the act for the benefit of relieving the drought within his own soul. He lifted the cage toward the cloudless sky. Like the eye of the falcon it shone down upon him, unblinking. He heard himself speak, 'I, born of Horus★, given breath by Ra★, who descended from the One Star[6] in the Day before Creation; I set free the living waters that reside in the abode of the Ascended, wherein all abundance is manifest.'

"In that minute, a small vapour appeared to rise from the long slash of brown water beyond the Temple.

The vapour became a small cloud, lingering near the horizon. He who was Mayah-Metahraptah, Solar Monarch, Living Throne to the One Star, placed his slender fingers upon the golden clasp of the cage and released into the morning breath of Egyptos, a chariot of doves. Feathered emissaries to the gods, they were set in a slow motion of soft white, chorused by the psalm of tiny silver bells encircling their legs. As a melody of wings swept the bell notes higher upon the scales of the wind, Mayah-Metahraptah opened his throat to the voice of Heaven, and the gods gave pause to listen to his song.

"The doves gathered and circled about the cloud, their bells faintly tracing a harmony over the land, dipping and rising, weaving with the lifted voice of the Pharaoh. From the east there came a low incantation, like a beast struggling from a pit. It echoed across the face of the day, devouring the delicate tinkling of the dove bells, usurping the spaces above the desert with its profound message. Dark clouds impressed patterns of shattered bronze upon the Earth, brandishing spears of lightning before them. Then, as if no barrier were left to hold back the storm, rain streaked a gray sky in its flight to refuge. He could go now. He had sung his song to the heavens once again. His soul was quenched."

Baleck

A master rejuvenator in the Temple Beautiful of ancient Egypt. He employed the use of color and sound vibration for the healing and rejuvenation of the human body.

Ptah

A physician, author and architect of Egypt, he was also the peer and brother-in-law of Thoth Hermes—whose true name was 'Raismes,' and is my main inner mystical source. Ptah was deified long after his death, and called the 'God of Memphis.'

Sitirus

The Pharaoh Akhenaton's supreme personal astrologer in the Egyptian city of Akhenaton.

White Magician's Son

One of the identical twin brothers (Jesse was the twin again in that life) who guarded Pharaoh Tutankhamen and sealed sacred vaults, temples and King Tut's tomb with protective energies.[7]

Aaron

The brother of Moses in the Bible.

Chetilezan

The Leader and Master of Sciences for a Central Earth Incan Clan*.

Quiasmuvaldi

The Incan son of a Royal Divinator*. He was visited by a cosmic emissary* in his twelfth year of life. As a man he made a perilous journey from Peru to Mexico, installing an energy wheel in the Pyramid of the Sun.[8]

Zapotec Amazul Amakuklal

The Aztec prophet who organized what was then known as the Brotherhood of Hooded Light. He was murdered by Aztec priests, along with most of his followers, for attempting to put an end to human sacrifice and trying to preserve ancient records attesting to the principles of one omnipotent God.

Om-Siris

An Egyptian spiritual leader who met a similar fate as Amakuklal.[9]

Kyndakori

An American Indian shaman in central California. Collected pre-deluge[10] records and artifacts, sealing them away in a chava or shaman's★ cave.

Malalinque

A Mayan girl who was a gifted mystic, and who communed with Angels. She died at the age of ten.

Kameah

A Hawaiian leader from whom King Kamehameha I was a later descendant. Kameah also founded a colony in New Zealand.

Emeriah

An architect, alchemist★ and artisan. A Master craftsman under King Solomon's★ Master architect, Hiram Abiff★. Emeriah was also a fluent linguist and talented singer.

Uaerus

A follower of Pythagorus who was a master of the Sacred Sciences and geometry in Greece.

Pericles

A Greek statesman whose name was given to the greatest period of Athenian history. He was a leader of the Athenian government for thirty years.

Harmahark

An architect to Ramses II. An interesting correlation to this incarnation is found in an announcement for Cottonland Tours in Memphis—Memphis means 'Abode of the Good'—Tennessee:

> "Cottonland Tours is incorporating the King, Elvis Presley, with the ancient king, Ramses the Great (II). In honor of the Ramses Exhibition visiting Memphis from April 15-August 30, 1987 we have put together several tour packages including one highlighting Ramses and Elvis. Both kings have strong ties to Memphis. Ramses the Great ruled ancient Egypt's capitol, while Elvis Presley started his career and lived in the present day Memphis. We will be offering this special one day tour including admissions to the Ramses Exhibition, Graceland and lunch throughout the length of the exhibition (including 'International [Elvis] Week')."

Myyrith

The grandson of Merlin. In this incarnation, Elvis became his own father, in that at Myyrith's death, he re-entered immediately into the womb of his love, and was born from his own seed inseminated previously. He then was born to become Bran, baptized as Galahad*.

Galahad

My inner mystical sources state that Elvis' soul was incarnated as this legendary figure as outlined above for 'Myyrith.'

Corinne Heline in her 'New Age Bible Interpretations' writes:

"Galahad, in the Vulgate★, is the name of the great-grandson of Joseph, and is the same as Gilead, Numbers 26:29; Judges 10:18. His lineage is obscure on his father's side; but through his mother he descends from 'the first Bishop of Christendom,' Joseph of Arimathea★."

My inner mystical sources claim that Galahad's birth name was Bran, and that his father was the grandson of Merlin. They further state that the soul that was Merlin's grandson and great-grandson were the same soul, meaning that the father incarnated as the son via the process described under the previous lifetime as Myyrith. Thus, Elvis' soul was incarnated as both the grandson and great-grandson of Merlin. Since Merlin, according to these same sources, descended from the Arimathea lineage, so Bran or Galahad was then also related to Joseph of Arimathea on both sides of his family tree, rather than only his mother's as Corinne Heline suggests.

When reviewing the birth of Elvis Aaron under the canopy of blue light emanating from the heavens, and his communion with Angels in early childhood, the following quotes from 'Mysteries of the Holy Grail' by Corinne Heline concerning Galahad's beginnings are correlative.

> "Those who are appointed 'Ambassadors of Spirit' appear to have, even from infancy, some recognition of their destiny. The Abbey mural shows the infant Galahad. The nuns who have him in charge gaze upon him in awe—he sees what they cannot see and hears what they cannot hear—from angelic worlds."

In addition, both Galahad and Elvis as archetypes★ demonstrate the journey of the Divine through the labors of the material existence, which is the path to redeem Spirit within matter.

Temojen

A Persian prince, who was also a student of poetry and architecture, and a friend of Omar Khayyam.

Oaluhamen

A Burmese prince.[11]

Damjinisk

An Irish bard (poet minstrel). The unusual name for an Irishman was due to the fact that he had been orphaned as a very small child, fending for himself in the streets. He had no real name, but when he began his profession as a minstrel he took an exotic name that came to him one night in a dream. It was actually an ancient Celtic name, meaning 'music is freedom.' He had been bestowed this name by his Spirit guardian who was incarnated with him in a former Celtic life, in which this bard's name had once before been 'Damjinisk.'

Uwick alias Squire Brenton

A Master Tomer★, collaborator and communicator for the perpetual choirs★ of England in the 12th century. He was also a Template★ in the secret Order of the Sacred Three within the Druids★ of the White Grail★.

Jonathan Anders

A Quaker carpenter, lumber mill owner and import/export merchant. He was involved in a mystical order in Massachusetts in the 1600's.

Marcos Costa

A Mexican of semi-affluence who desired to become a priest, but because of feelings of unworthiness, turned to fortune hunting. Marcos returned to the ancient Aztec city where he had lived as Amakuklal. He saw in a dream the location of golden records he himself had buried as the Aztec prophet. Marcos recovered the records, only to later bury them at another site, revealed in yet another dream.

These records eventually found their way in a relay process to where Joseph Smith was led by the angel Moroni. It was upon these elusive golden plates that Smith founded the Church of Latter Day Saints. Elvis was told about these records by his 'Mormon' friend, Ed Parker.

Sequoah

A Cherokee Indian who created the alphabet of the Cherokee nation.

Henry Cross

A privateer who sailed the seas in the era of Jean Lafitte. The illustrious Lafitte and Cross often collaborated in their efforts to stop the Spanish from funding an overthrow of the U.S. government. This soul who was incarnating as Henry Cross, was at the same time, Sequoah. It occasionally happens that souls inhabit more than one body in the same time frame. This occurrence has been researched by Dick Sutphen, well known past life regressionist.

My inner mystical sources tell me that, with the exception of certain feelings, impressions and dreams, the two, or on rare occasion three physical forms of a single 'soul,' are not aware of the other's existence and will never meet in that time frame which they share. It is of even greater irony that both Sequoah and Cross knew Lafitte, but were never in his company at the same time! Sequoah had only several brief encounters with Lafitte, while Cross was a good friend and peer of the famous patriot and privateer.

Giovanni Giocondo

In 1992 Elvis came to me in Spirit twice, giving me the name of one of his past life identities whom he wished me to look up in the encyclopedia each time. The first, he told me was a "Giovanni," who was a Renaissance architect. I noted to him that "Giovanni" was not a sir name, but he said "Look it up anyway." As it turned out, the last name was Giocondo.

It was thus, 'Giovanni Giocondo.' I am certain it is the right Giovanni because he is the only one who was a Renaissance architect just as Elvis had said. I wondered why he gave me this information, but in reading about Giocondo, I found that he worked on Chateâus in France. Rennes-le-Chateau*, in Southern France, has been renovated several times in the past. It is from the Rennes area that the Christic Merovingian* blood line can be traced, and it is from that bloodline, that Elvis descended.

Dagobert II

The second time he sent me to the encyclopedia, was to look up his past life as "Dagobert" in the Merovingian Dynasty. I did find Dagobert, several of them, all of the Merovingian Dynasty. The one Elvis then told me was his incarnation was Dagobert II, also called Saint Dagobert:

> "(b. c. 650, d. December 23, 1679), Merovingian Frankish king of Austrasia. He was the son of Sigebert III. Dagobert was packed off to an Irish monastery after the death of his father in 656, and the Austrian throne was taken by Childebert the Adopted, son of Grimoald, the Austrasian mayor of the palace."

To make a long story short, after a lot of heads rolled, Dagobert was finally found and restored to the throne, only to be murdered three years later. Recently, I read in the book, 'The Cult of the Black Virgin,' by Ean Begg: "...one of the most important acts of Dagobert II... was to continue the ancient tradition of Gaul, the worship of the Black Virgin[12]... is Isis, and her name is Notre-Dame de Lumiére."

It was in 1977 that I source translated Elvis' past life as Akhenaton's personal astrologer. In 1986, while reading through the transcripts of conversations in 1975 between Wanda and Elvis, I found Elvis speaking about his belief that he had a lifetime with Akhenaton. He does not give the correct name for this ruler, but by his description of historical places, events and other names, it was obvious to me that he is discussing Pharaoh Akhenaton and his City of the Sun—Akhenaton means the 'Horizon of Aton.' Here is a portion of the conversation Elvis had with Wanda June Hill that supports this lifetime I brought through.

Wanda: "When you were king."

> Elvis: "No—I wasn't exactly a king—just a high court priest—it had something to do with religion—I'm certain of that! Where he (Akhenaton) took his people when he left Egypt's court to start his own lifestyle with his followers. He was a peacemaker—a ruler who formed a new religion of Sun worshipers[13]—and they built temples and courtyards to do that. They didn't make war and they farmed—but he wasn't much of a ruler—in fact, he was one of the first hippies you might say—and he-he-he stole Nefertiti from her family and took her for his wife—I'll bet that I have a burial temple with artifacts somewhere—I can see it sometimes.
>
> "I see a chamber below the ground, square-walled tunnels and a room full of baskets and urns—grains and such for my journey to the Home of the Ram. We worshiped the ram, you know. And on my casket is the head of a-a ram—it's gold-gold-and-and-dark-God! I hate the dark! I'd rather worship the Sun—darkness scares me—makes me cold. (shivers, sucks in his breath). Ohhh-lord! Talk about somethin' else…"
>
> From Secret Places of the Lion, by George Hunt Williamson: "Akhenaton—Pharaoh was addressed as 'the King, the Ra, the Sun.' This signified his position

> as leader of the 'Goodly Company' of starborn beings dedicated to the salvation of the planet!"

Orpheus

I would like to share with you one more lifetime of Elvis Aaron's. The name Orpheus is poetic and legendary, but was a true personage of Greece. He was a musician—a teacher of geometry and the cosmic frequency of music—and as a mystic, he was founder of a sacred order based on this knowledge. Following are some correlative quotes for those unfamiliar with the legends and myths surrounding Orpheus. In 'Mystic Masonry and the Tarot,' by Corinne Heline, she states, "The occult science of the ancient Magi★ was concealed. This sublime alchemy was the science of… Orpheus."

Ms. Heline also states in her 'New Age Bible Interpretation, Vol. V', "As we grow in Christ power, there comes… the full corn in the ear, or the wondrous fulfillment of the Christed mind producing a man whose light shineth."

By the fruits of his labor, Orpheus established his purpose and lifted minds of an age long ago into the Light to whatever degree possible, he returned as Elvis to do the same. Ms. Heline fleshes in the spiritual portrait of the historically illusive Orpheus by saying, "(He) was an incarnation of Apollo★ and his music was the music of the spheres★."

The legendary story of the god Orpheus continues through many trials, typical of the Greek Mysteries. Eventually, the gods changed him into a swan and placed him in the heavens as Cygnus the Swan, near Lyra the constellation of the Harp. Ms. Heline goes on to relate, "This glorious Harp floats across the heavens on summer evenings with the great star Vega blazing like a blue jewel in its heart."

Interestingly, according to my inner mystical sources, Vega is one of the major connective energy centers linking the Living Lights or celestial hierarchies to the 'Crown' stars, the supreme of which is Rigel in Orion, the Blue Star of Elvis Presley's spiritual heritage.

Antiochus I Of Commagene

There are quite a few 'Antiochus' in history and even at least one other 'Antiochus I.'

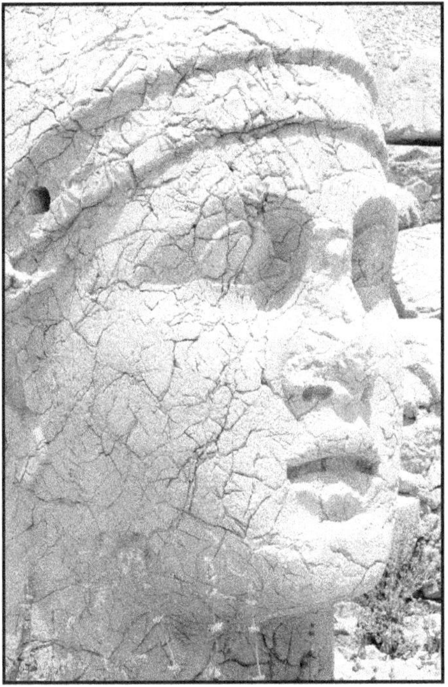

A statue of 'Antiochus of Commagene' a startling resemblance to Elvis Presley

It is difficult to find any tangible history on him except but a few dry facts. However, doing a web search, I did find an article entitled 'Magi—The Quest for a Secret Brotherhood' by Adrian Gilbert from his book by the same name. In this article Antiochus I of Commagene is mentioned as follows:

> "I believe that this man, Antiochus I of Commagene, was closely linked with the Sarmoung brotherhood of his day. His funerary monument indicates he knew a great deal both about astrology and the Hermetic tradition… gives two astronomical

> dates which I believe relate to his birthday and his initiation... there is a mysterious shaft, angled at 35°, 155 meters long and leading nowhere. Archaeologists have long been puzzled... was intended to give two significant dates, including the 'Royal Birthday' of the Kings of Commagene. This was when the sun is conjunct the star Regulus in Leo, which in that epoch would happen on 29th July."

I find this especially interesting, since with the original version of the manuscript for this book I had felt compelled to entitle it 'Magi From the Blue Star.' I also received a message through Elvis on his incarnation as Antiochus I of Commangene. It was obvious to me as I received this message I share below that Elvis was delivering it to me in the personality and memory of Antiochus I and not as Elvis or Rhama Azul.

> "When I was born as Aladudadius (birth name), son of Mithridates I Callinicus and Laodice VII Thea Philadelphus, I was born on an auspicious day of the stars, known now as July 7th, 62 B.C."
>
> "This date was called the 'Day of the Lion Eating the Star.' It is commemorated in the stone carving at Nemrud Dagi (Antiochus' religious sanctuary and tomb site in Turkey) of the lion with 19 stars, 2 planets and a crescent moon. This became my royal seal. (Author: July 7th, 62 B.C. was given by archeologists as the date represented on the stone carving of the lion, stars and crescent, and said to either commemorate Antiochus's birth or his ascendancy to the throne.)
>
> "I was an only child, greatly loved by my parents. I had been a twin, but my brother died at birth. Later, my mother miscarried a girl-child. I was groomed all my life to become the next king of the empire. I was also seen as a religious figure. Not a 'god,' but

one blessed by the gods. As all Kings of my lineage it was my responsibility to 'know the gods,' to embrace them within myself, so that the people would have an entrance to their power through their ruler (the king) on Earth.

"Due to my auspicious birth on the 'Day of the Lion Eating the Star,' (Author: some kind of massive supernova event) I was seen as even more 'in touch' with the cosmic forces and thus the gods or powers of the universe. I thus felt a strong responsibility and duty to become the vessel or mouthpiece of the gods for my people, whom I dearly loved.

"In my undefiled tomb within Mount Nemrud, the sacred things through which I was initiated into the sacred mysteries are present. They still radiate the LIGHT of the power I nourished and performed for the people. Both before and after my lifting into the stars (death) many made pilgrimage to my Place of Mysteries (Nemrud Dagi), wherein lies the entombed remains of my mortal body."

All but one of the reincarnations of Elvis which I present in this chapter are male. However, I feel that Elvis had more female lives than one. Perhaps his male lifetimes were more relevant to his Blue Star mission and thus were revealed to me because of that. Undoubtedly, he also had lives that were less glamorous, but probably not too many, as it is the pattern of 'missionaries' from the Light Races★ which come to our Earth and incarnate from other more advanced worlds, to lead very active lifetimes in the performance of the spiritual duties which they were sent here to accomplish.

Thus, we have an insight into the Golden Thread that is woven through the experiences of the Earth sojourn of Elvis' soul. If you do not necessarily believe in reincarnation, I suggest you try to feel the essence of what each of these lifetimes represents in relation to the human being the world knew as Elvis.

I do not refer here to the Elvis the 'media world' knew, but the one millions knew within their hearts. Through this exercise, a determined individual will be able to see that it matters not whether this lifetime information I have shared on Elvis is a figment of my imagination or not, so long as the essence of what it represents can be felt. The more creative readers can live the reality of what is presented here to their own delight. For which is more real: the dream or the dreamer?

Chapter 5: ARCHETYPALLY FOREVER

Elvis' features were strikingly similar to the ancient statues of gods, patriots and kings of many different cultures. Some of the most prominent resemblances are Alexander the Great, Pericles[1], King Mausolus of Asia Minor[2], Charioteer from the Sanctuary of Apollo at Delphi, and the statues of Hermes among others. Elvis' photographs were used as studies to re-build Old World statues damaged during the bombings of WWII. Here are a few photos of these ancient Greek statues that demonstrate this remarkable resemblance to Elvis facial features.

Statues Resembling Elvis

Pericles

Known as the 'first citizen of Athens,' Pericles was an aristocrat, soldier and statesman behind the building of the Acropolis.

Pericles

Alexander The Great

Alexander is depicted as a charismatic, brutal warrior and eccentric. However, there are some documents written by those who knew him personally who tell a much different story. A conqueror, yes. This was the mode of life in those days. Boys were raised to not only defend in battle, but to conquer territory.

Some were strategically better at it than others. Yet he was also shown to have been fair, and even compassionate to his enemies. It was also written that there had been some kind of conspiracy against his reputation after his death by those who scorned him. SOUND FAMILIAR?

Alexander the Great

Hermes

The Greek version of the Egyptian Thoth, God of healing, architecture and writing. As Hermes he was known as the 'Messenger' and thus was often depicted with wings on his helmet and heels.

Hermes

It is revealing to note that these various statues sculpted in different eras and in many separate empires of the world only slightly resemble one another, further signifying the complexity of Elvis' features which in the various stages of his life went through transformations wherein several archetypal 'world images' were represented. His face, expressions and growth of self were as mutable as were his artistic talents, which grew with the advancements of the times in which he lived. Yet despite his parity with the world, he remained singular, unique, and quite apart from the symbolic archetypes he represented in our culture.

Before we go any further, an explanation of archetypes would be in order. An archetype is any prototypal pattern which can be repeatedly duplicated in thought or form. This could be as simple as the prototype model for an object to be manufactured, or as complex as consciousness patterns. There are many different variations on archetypes. The noted psychologist Carl Jung identified many different archetypal patterns of human thought. These represented ways of thinking and behaving that humans would adopt, many times without being fully conscious of the pattern they emulated. These patterns influence an individual's perception of the world around them greatly.

Carl Jung's archetypes are those born partly of God essence, and partly of humanity's own lesser variations of that essence. There are also sacred archetypes of consciousness that were created by divine beings that are much more pure. These are the archetypes that we as humans would do best to emulate. To emulate them we must first be able to identify what they are, and who in our current experience might be exemplifying these archetypal qualities whereby we might contemplate that individual, and what makes them different.

It is in that light I attempt to give the reader an understanding of the divine archetypes that Elvis exemplified in his life, and in his past lives, as they all are connected. In addition, there are archetypal types of faces and bodies. Elvis' face was definitely purely archetypal, as you can see by the accompanying photos of ancient statues. Metaphysical principle states: 'As above, so below.' One perspective on this statement would be that anything that exists in the unseen spiritual realms (such as consciousness), will have its counterpart in our physical world.

An archetypal face that is associated with a certain divine archetype of consciousness is an example of this principle. In other words, there have been, and will continue to be, individuals who are working archetypally with certain consciousness components. These individuals will have this reflected in their physical features, and there are others in the past who worked with the same archetype that would have had similar physical features as well. This is what I attempt to point out with some of the statue photographs in this chapter.

In the assessment of those who loved Elvis, the one face which captured our hearts and impressed itself upon our minds will never be duplicated regardless of whether it is through an act of God or the hand of a plastic surgeon. To look into Elvis' eyes in the flesh was to behold a sense of balance within the delicate and often over complicated ligaments of humanity. He seemed to see beyond the horizon, and for a moment his eyes burned into yours, and you shared the vision with him. Such is the power of truly great souls. Like the Gods of Olympus, there was a sense of prophetic furtiveness in his gaze, a taste of hemlock upon his tongue. Yet there was no morbid rush in him to encounter his seat in Valhalla★.[3]

It was instead a simple knowing and a faith in things yet unborn. It was his to conquer grief, to expose the tenacious rays of hope and lift sorrow from deeply embedded roots, transplanting love in the gaping hole of the unknown. In his face were engraved the fine lines of eternal youth which echoed with trust unquestioned. He accepted his future as he did his past, without regret, and led by an innate understanding of his own birth and death.

From beneath the eclipsing burden of this knowing, a brilliant Sun burst forth. Elvis' joy and humor shone because like the Sun, the soul's natural reflex is to be radiant. Elvis' happiness did not perform entirely as a puppet to his life experiences. His joy responded instead to the call of Spirit, of one soul touching another. For this reason, no sorrow could fully penetrate him. His smile was exquisite. The crook of his lip revealed in the shyest way a suppressed delight.

The flash of teeth molded to his grin like a roller-coaster to its trellis in a perfect match. Elvis possessed a noble bone structure, the envy of Shakespearean advocates, with an immaculate hairline accenting the broad intelligent forehead. The explosion of well-groomed sideburns, ending in a sweeping flourish at the peak of high cheekbones gleaned from his Cherokee blood and the boldness of his jaw, set the visual stage for a scenario of impending revelation.

The wide set eyes, which did on occasion betray their fascination for blue to become tinted with smokey grays and greens, were the supreme reward one sought when gazing upon Elvis. Like a shimmering pool, the beholder tumbled into the depth of them and into the secrets of the ages they contained. Photographer Sean Shaver in his book, 'Elvis In Focus' comments on Elvis' face, "His skin glowed, and his eyes had a shine. Here was perfection out of a dream. When Elvis entered the room everybody turned—you felt his presence—some invisible power he had."

Even at a distance, Elvis was unique in form with his squarely broad shoulders, impressive six-foot frame and gleaming hair of black satin. He possessed a special 'looseness' permeating his movements. He seemed in perpetual readiness to spring upon some target unseen by less wary eyes, yet this tension was suspended in the weightlessness of rhythm that exuded from his presence, whether dancing, walking or at apparent rest. Indeed, Elvis was never truly 'at rest' until he departed his wearied cancer ridden body on that August day.

His eyes cut from side to side, alighting briefly on faces, seeming to recognize them in mystic communion. His hands could vibrate in almost violent drama, deftly piercing the air in talon-like precision. However, within their power they preserved a gentleness in an always open gesture as if expectantly awaiting the clasp of a child's hand. The legs, especially the famous left one which he shook on stage, were never completely still. There was forever sufficient motion in the left knee to cause the spray of feathered locks on his forehead to undulate in the wake of a barely perceptible tremble.

The piecing together of this collage in the mind creates a picture of a man of intelligent instinct, able to discern the false and superfluous. We see a human with great humor and a tolerance for the weakness in others. Yet the stern set of the jaw revealed that he had little patience for his own weaknesses, and a quicksilver temper, the fury of which was more often turned upon himself than hurled at others.

An inner loving which ran very deep in his nature pervaded the tender actions of his mouth in speech or song, unveiling his gentle heart and total commitment to all things of Spirit. He lent mystical insight to those who would see with him beyond the horizon. With his eyes he could make you believe he was a savant from another planet, and indeed he was in Spirit! Marble statues—of mortals imbued with the divine—are gathered in the ancient sepulchers; mute testimony of days when magical signs and wonders wove dreams into their own reality for races of a Golden Age*. Similarly, Elvis Presley's image is with us now, raised as an epistle of our own story in time to an age of new miracles.

It memorializes a time when we began to understand the burnishing of our own flame, and how glorious it could be to dance to the music of a sweet soul who would lead us through an all too brief passage in history. He gave us knowledge of ourselves, not through divine appointment but with a stroke of human grace, knowledge of a love that escapes the encounters of lesser men. We learned in a joyous awakening, what fun it is to be alive.

To those who shake their heads in bemusement at such inspiration, I can only say that those of us who lived the experience saw the marble of the ancient statues come to life, the eyes quickening the cold blind stare into a living sapphire light, and the stone mouth quiver into a tempting smile. For us, the revelation was complete. We will never forget. The photographs of ancient Greek statues I have included in this chapter bear an uncanny resemblance to Elvis. The statue of Pericles shown earlier in this chapter represents an actual prior lifetime that Elvis had (see Chapter 4). Here are a few other unnamed Greek Deity statues with very archetypal-type faces that bear quite striking resemblance to Elvis as well.

See also the 'Antiochus' image in the previous chapter. There are actually two main archetypal facial forms present in all of these statues and in their relationship to Elvis. One of these forms personifies eternal youth and vigor, just as Elvis did in the early stages of his career, with his joyful exuberance in front of an audience. This chiseled face is tranquil on the surface, almost disinterested; and yet smoldering beneath the smooth muscles and full lips. There is anticipation resting in the deep spaces of the sinews, that even in marble or bronze seems to be ready to pounce upon the observer. Yet such tension beneath the relaxed exterior is not malevolent. It only serves to entice the spectator to becoming more involved with the statue. This was true also of the young Elvis, who reached beyond the petulant expression into the fiery core of his being and brought the interactive individual into close proximity with the register of his flame.

The second archetypal form is exemplified as controlled grace and measured performance encompassed within the stroke of a visionary's world offering. These faces reveal men with a sense of their own power and an awareness of their personal fate. Held in the balance, is the strong resolve cast in the far-reaching gaze, and the tender mercies evident in the set of a sensitive mouth. Certainly, this also is a description of Elvis in the early 1970's when his face held all the complexities of the world and all the beauty of heaven in one single lightning struck moment.

> "Elvis believed that our 'Light' (soul) came from the Light of God—this may explain why Elvis seemed to 'glow.'" ~ Gail Brewer-Giorgio

What follows is my examination of Elvis' spiritual purpose, during his lifetime and beyond, using pure archetypes. These archetypes or patterns, in their purest form, move beyond identification with personality archetypes and into the realm of ancient paths of association and integration with spiritual principle.

It is here that archetypes can also be seen to be represented in symbols, colors, images and/or combinations of these. I have created the first three of the seven categories with the intention that they represent the inner structure of spiritual purpose for which Elvis Presley was born to demonstrate how this works.

1—The Moonstone Path/Divine Synergy

This pure archetype of consciousness, expressed in our current world, represents harmony within the social arena; recognition that you are not separate from others and therefore may see yourself within them; the balancing of the physical, more practical portions of one's life with the spiritual aspects. Working together with others for the good that can be manifest for a common cause, and bringing out the best in others.

Elvis brought together different realms of reality by attracting a wide spectrum of people. He created social harmony through music by encouraging the audience to see him as the singer and the song. His versatility and expressiveness unified people despite their cultural and musical differences allowing them to feel in control of their lives once again.

Elvis saw the audience as an extension of himself, embracing them with more compassion and forgiveness than he was able to extend to himself. By extending love, he received love. He strove for a balance between the physical and spiritual attributes of his innate expression. Elvis' highly developed spirituality made him very different to most people, particularly in the era in which he lived. It was difficult for him to be objective about the gifts he had in comparison to others. In such cases, the physical and emotional desire to aspire to greater heights of spiritual expression, and the longing to have a deep spiritual communion with other humans, often overshadows acceptance of their abilities.

As Elvis was always in pursuit of helping others, he also saw that spark of God within each and every human being he ever had contact with. By almost naively recognizing only that divine flame within them, he assisted these souls to see that aspect of themselves more clearly at whatever level they were able to. He never let their own self-judgments cloud his vision of their potential, and humanity being what it is, we tend to live up to others expectations of us. Elvis had great expectations of others divine potential, and helped them to step into that role within themselves.

2—The Ruby Path/Divine Motivation

This pure archetype of consciousness represents a prime movement of energy, an unconditional and absolutely trusting love of all beings, development of the sacred heart, humility and an absolute faith in God, dedication to giving one's life to spiritual purpose and living that life strictly from one's inner sources. Elvis most certainly moved a considerable amount of energy, not only through his music and dancing, but within the heart. Audiences felt uplifted and excited by the sensation of being alive. Thus, they tended to modify their existence to accommodate their emerging faith in life. There are many stories of hope rendered to the hopeless, simply by exposure to Elvis' voice or image.

Elvis was able to uplift the soul through his presence alone because he always lived from his inner strength. He was fed by deep wells of Light that gushed up from the greatest part of him, that portion of his self that was still harbored in the star of his spiritual birthing. It was a point of Light he focused upon so intently that he made us see it with him, and we suddenly viewed the ordinary as magical and special. WE became magical and special. Listen to Elvis burst forth in the live performance of 'The Wonder of You' from his 'On Stage' LP. He was expressing this very sentiment to us. Elvis knew what his purpose was in this lifetime from a young age.

He might not have known all the details, but he felt the essence of it, and was even shown some of the components by his 'angel guardians.' As such, he humbled himself to his peers, and thus to God. As Christ washed the feet of the disciples, Elvis expressed his humility in many ways. The most visible way was by not becoming ego-centered about his phenomenal looks, voice, wealth or fame. He trusted implicitly in the process of his purpose here, and used his God given attributes to serve others in the only way he knew how.

3—The Sapphire Path/Divine Feminine

This pure archetype of consciousness represents evolution of matter, the nurturing of all beings and life, moving past limiting fears of mortality, becoming comfortable with one's own body and deciding how to best present that to the world for the greater purpose, becoming aware of the balance of divine male and female aspects needed within oneself. Elvis' evolution throughout his life was evident to those who watched his music change.

He expressed his nurturing self through the male form extraordinarily well as discussed elsewhere in this book. Therefore, I will only say here that the most obvious expression of this quality was seen in his ability to console others in times of distress. His body image was archetypically representative of the mythic spiritual warriors and real heroes of the ancient past. His face was an obvious reflection of the gaze from Mount Olympus*.

There, a godly race beyond the mortal pale, reached into the wake of man in order to experience the kiss of life and death. With wings bruised and broken by this attempt at mortality, they returned to their mountain home beneath the Sun that knew no night—Elvis Aaron's physical beauty was exceeded by a greater beauty within his soul. This combination of inner and outer connectivity was borne in a seal of features struck in similar casting throughout history. It is the mark of mastery.

In our sub-consciousness we knew this, and so his physical form was instantly recognizable to us as an image of 'the gods.' With this knowledge, we were awakened to the balance of the divine male/female archetypes within each of us. Elvis never feared death. In fact, toward the end of his life he welcomed it. But never did he view death as a morose inevitability. He saw it as a doorway to the true home of the soul.

It is our challenge now to release his image from any sad thought and to see him joyous in sunlit rapture, embraced by the kindred company he knew was there waiting for him in his 'other Home.' It is a vision that we too may make our own reality; to find release from the clutch of the Raven's death and be at peace in the thought of the door opening for each of us one day, as we are received into the eternality of Spirit to begin a new phase of our soul's journey in God's Kingdom.

Elvis' physical trials were a lesson in understanding that the purpose of suffering is not always for he who suffers but to create an empathic link with the Earth and her children. *My inner mystical sources* refer to 'World Karma*,' and say that most of Elvis' unhappiness in this life was not a result of his own unfortunate karmic circumstances, but rather because he was assuming the role of transforming 'the sins of the world.' This was what the Master Jesus accomplished through his crucifixion, but on a much larger scale than Elvis. You might see this as a form of purifying the world's life blood through the parts of the body (beings like Elvis) that have the greatest ability to withstand pain through love. Elvis' body was a sacrificial component in the body of the world that needed to be purified.

In the next part of my examination, I have chosen four additional categories of archetypes representing the Four Pillars or balances within Elvis, which sustained his inner structure of spiritual life purpose outlined in the first three categories.

4—The Emerald Path/Divine Knowing

Completion of one's cosmic purpose, merger with the reality of the soul, clarity of purpose, absolute knowing of the purpose for incarnating in the current lifetime, the understanding of the totality of one's experience through all of their lifetimes as though there were no time barriers at all. Elvis possessed an innate comprehension of his place in time and the cycles of manifestation that brought him here.

This gave him clarity to the degree of a visionary and philosopher. It enabled him to keep his focus on the stars, and not allow worldly influences to blow him off course. Yet he had the ability to be in this world fully so that others could relate to him. Without the ability to connect with others on the grand scale he did, his spiritual purpose here would have failed. He saw that all of his current experience was a part of the grand completion for his soul, in preparation for the next journey, whatever that may hold for him.

5—The Lapis Path/Divine Physicality

The bringing together of all experience into the present, protection of all aspects of the vulnerable self, utilization of the sexual/creative energies for their true purpose so that one may become enlightened and enlighten others, realization of the divine truth manifest in this real world. From his many past experiences and willingness to serve humanity, Elvis was empowered by the 'Tantric forces*,' which are a creative energy of the Spirit. It is the Kundalini* fully received into the higher consciousness centers of the spiritual body.

Kundalini relates to the sexual/creative activity in humans, but there are many expressions of that energy possible, from the lowest sexual act to the Immaculate Conception of Jesus. In between these two extremes are many differing levels of expression. I do not feel Elvis' sexuality was ever vulgar, as the old press clippings of the 1950's would have you believe—you will readily see this demonstrated as the remainder of this book unfolds.

He became more spiritually aware by the 1970's. He wanted to enlighten others about the sacredness of the act; that the true power of sex was in the heart. This knowledge brings the individual into 'Gnosis,' or truth. God reached down to him in those moments when he was not able to reach up to God, and will do the same for each of us, if we ask. In addition, his talents as a musician were an aspect of this archetype as well as the creativity and professionalism required to sustain his career.

6—The Amethyst Path/Divine Fulfillment

The realization of the fruits of following the path of intuition, increased ability to use all the physical senses at a new level of awareness, the merging of one's cosmic being with their sensual self, fulfillment of all physical and material needs beyond one's expectations, unlimited flow of creative energy for the greater purpose. These are all expressions of Elvis' life. He implicitly followed the path of his inner guidance and was able to tailor his performance to each audience.

It was evident to those of us who closely watched Elvis' that he became more aware of his cosmic expression on Earth. He certainly experienced material abundance, which was a result of his creative energies. As he expressed in his speech to the Jaycees in 1970, his childhood dreams had come true beyond his greatest expectations. In addition to his spiritualized sexuality, he exuded a mystical sensuality and was creative in weaving the divergent aspects of his life together. This flexibility and easy grace in the midst of decadence was one of his most valuable empowerments and his greatest test.

7—The Diamond Path/Divine Victory

Spiritual victory, through action that may seem foolish to others; the completion of the ultimate chess game, where you trade your most powerful and prized piece to gain the victory. In the final analysis, Elvis was victorious as he inspired others to overcome challenges and he continues to inspire many who were born after his death, invoking invoked dramatic action and change throughout the world.

He was aware of the greater good and his memory will not be diminished. He traded his most prized physical possession, his body and life, for the greater goal at hand. He readily accepted his early death and knew it was coming long before the medical community. He welcomed death with an open mind and heart trusting implicitly in the process. To me, of all the divine attributes Elvis exemplified, this stands as his greatest. His early transition preserved his memory for posterity.

The information in this next portion of the chapter is more esoteric and metaphysical and perhaps optional for some who may wish to simply scan through the material and then read the last paragraph. For those interested in metaphysics, spiritual matters, the Inner Mysteries or simply a new adventure, this information should prove to be nectar for your hearts.

The following esoteric study came together for me as a result of several years of inner understanding finally coming to blossom, and pulls together the other seven pure archetypal consciousness patterns previously addressed into a greater vision yet. Some of this material will relate to aspects of metaphysical interpretation with which you may not be familiar. I suggest that you not try too intently to understand every word, but rather take the greater message of this work directly into your heart.

This relates directly to my comments on Elvis' greatest gift of all in the closing of the 'Diamond Path/Divine Victory' archetype.

The 'Wounded King' Archetype

Elvis' greater overall archetype is that of the Wounded or Lame King. This is found within the Grail Legends★[4] and is also known as the 'Fisher King.' There are various interpretations to understanding the role of the Wounded King. I am choosing to follow the illumination given to me from *my inner mystical sources.* It is important to keep in mind that the 'Grail Mystery★' is an outer representation of an inner search for our own complete God Self, or nature in God.

The Wounded King is generally the guardian of the Holy Grail consciousness although not adequately empowered to carry out the job. The Wounded King must be healed, but this is not possible until the rightful recipient of the Grail consciousness comes along and claims the Grail. The Wounded King's plight is reflected in the barren wasteland that his kingdom has become (i.e. the consciousness of the world he lives within). The Grail consciousness cannot be reactivated until the individual worthy of it appears and asks the right question proving they are worthy of such a treasure. The questions would be; "What is the true sacred purpose of this Grail? In whose name does it serve?"

In the asking of these questions, the seeker proves he is aware of the king's plight and the state of his kingdom, and that they have a true compassion for the king's experience. The only purpose for the activation of the Grail consciousness must be for the benefit of others, and not glorification of the self. Who will achieve the Grail consciousness?

In this role we may find any and every one who in their seeking asks this question within. In seeking the truth of this knowledge, so we are quickened to release our own spiritual wounds and receive the Grace of God. For in the asking comes acceptance of our own separation from our true God Self in its balanced wholeness, and in the acceptance we open to the necessary healing. Elvis in the role of Wounded King (he was/is not the only Wounded King but one of those who assumes a major aspect of this role on a world scale) allows us to understand his physical suffering from a spiritual perspective and indeed his entire life as well as his current link to humanity.

In his Wounded King role, Elvis Aaron was assuming world karma in order to facilitate healing for the masses. Certainly he had/has his own karma, and it was reflected to a degree in his life, but the broader spectrum of his 'Elvis experience' was as a result of a World service, according to *my inner mystical sources.* The Wounded King's suffering serves the purpose to bring greater wisdom, knowledge and insight to the people of his kingdom. He offers his life force to the greater cause to release those he loves and cares for from their suffering if possible. Certainly we can see this in the way Elvis gave all for his fans, so that they might experience a moment of happiness they might not have had otherwise. He lifted them from the doldrums of everyday life into the heights he inhabited at great expense to his own physical being.

Another format where the Wounded King may be referenced from a different perspective is the pattern of the 'Gaia Matrix Oracle' divination deck and book by Ms. Rowena Patty Kryder. I have compiled a dynamic of the Life Mystery of Elvis Aaron Presley. *My inner mystical sources* chose the particular archetypes (cards) through me that held peak correlations to Elvis' life within the correspondent 'Four Phases of Creation and Regeneration of Gaia*.'

Elvis' childhood up to the age of nineteen and his army years, were preparatory phases and not the actual full manifestation of the archetypes themselves. The final phase began at his death on August 16, 1977, and continues through to an unrevealed (to me) future time. The portions in quotations and the terms, Involution, Evolution, Sacrifice and Eschaton, as they relate to this application, are from Kryder's Gaia Matrix Oracle book. The rest was given me by *my inner mystical sources*:

INVOLUTION: The inward flow of consciousness, where self-discovery and greater self-knowledge is forthcoming. This phase played out for Elvis from 1954 (age 19) through 1957 (age 22). Archetype/card selected: Immortals—"Inherent joy of Spirit." The sheer joy a young and innocent Elvis experienced and gave through his singing. Here was the 'Mystery' in its first stages of being. The mystery was not yet aware of its own devices, and so it is active through the autonomous power of life itself. In other words, the mystery begins by mirroring the sheer joy of the universe instead of acknowledging one's own singular persona, character or direction.

EVOLUTION: The movement outward to greater knowledge and realization of truth as a result in the inward focus becoming an inherent autonomous process. This phase was active for Elvis from 1960 (age 25) through 1967 (age 32). Archetype/card selected: Hero—"Helping others by being true to yourself." In the 1960's Elvis lived the second phase of Creation and Regeneration by working inwardly on his wholeness, which was expressed outwardly by the great feeling of love focused toward his fans.

In the 1950's his followers had primarily been swept along by unthinking joy, Elvis Aaron was now, however, refining his definition of Self, and thus was generating a deeper more consciously aware love from his inner being toward his followers. While it was largely an inactive period for Elvis on the screen, most of the music he generated at that time was soothing and reassuring. Even the fast pieces contained the emphasis on essential beingness; 'I know who I am, thus I am better able to serve you.'

SACRIFICE: Places into motion the greater healing of self and humanity. The giving of all for the greater purpose at hand. This phase was prevalent from 1968 (age 33) through 1977 (age 42) in Elvis' experience. For this third phase *my inner mystical sources* have chosen three archetypes instead of one, because in this last earthly phase of Elvis' life, he was encompassing a greater degree of the 'Mystery.' 1st archetype/card selected: Heart of the Sun—"Seeing everything as a sign of divine glory in the light." 2nd archetype/card selected: Blue Pharaoh—"Allowing the breakdown of the physical vehicle while heightened cellular (consciousness)[5] changes occur." 3rd archetype/card selected: Black Buffalo—"Experiencing oneself as a fulfillment of the divine image in the human, empathy for all life."

As Elvis entered phase three, he experienced a surge of return to his own divinity. All the love he had poured out toward the World in Phase One and, Phase Two especially, were now streaming back into him. As he increased his love outwardly in response to this melting pot of Love, he created a bridge of light continuously in motion, moving from him to his followers and back again. This movement was also escalating thus a spiral was manifesting. The point of the spiral touched the Elvis Mystery in mankind and the wider end reached into the divine continuum, the heart of God. It was at this juncture defined by the development of the Golden Spiral* of Love, that the Heart of the Sun archetype was expressed.

The immense energy sustained within the physical body of Elvis Aaron at this point was tremendous. There were millions of human beings FOCUSING LOVE ON THIS ONE MAN with an intensity that perhaps has never been known before. During their lifetimes, not even Buddha or Jesus Christ had that much concentration of human energy infusing their bodies, since there was no media of communication to accommodate it, and not as many people on the planet even if there had been mass communication ability.

Elvis experienced love and admiration more than many other entertainers and, not only love, but karma. Unfortunately, human love is not yet pure. It is projected through the persona, and that persona is a vehicle for the karma of the individual. While there were great spiritual benefits to Elvis in receiving the world's love, he was unable as a single human being to fully strain out the lumps of karma. Taking upon himself the karma of the world, his physical body began to break down.

Matter is the 'Corpus*' of the karmic embodiment. Yet because of the Golden Spiral of Love, his spiritual body incorporated more and more Light into its higher state of being. This enabled him to continue to sing with such power and glory, even to the end. All of his music during this third phase reflected the magnificence of angelic choirs, sounding to the reverie of the soul. Elvis Aaron's body shifting from matter to light is paralleled by the Blue Pharaoh archetype. It was awe-inspiring to compare the changes in his physical body. During his last years, the suffering wrought by disease took its toll. However, long after death it attained a sublime hue, an indication of his important role during this lifetime.[6]

Throughout the third phase, Elvis radiated the message of the Black Buffalo, but we can also see this archetype as a consummation of his entire life up to that point: "Experiencing Oneself as a Fulfillment of the Divine Image in the Human, Empathy for all of Life."

ESCHATON: "This is the phase completing spiritual consummation of the Earth, received through a fiery burst of experience, much like Joan of Arc on the burning pyre. It can be painful or glorious, but it is always illuminative to the point of total surrender. One can no longer claim anything tangible. It must all be given up to the divine flame in perfect knowing that the greatest possession is to BE possessed by God." This fourth phase began for Elvis and his Mystery at his death. There are two archetypes chosen for the Elvis' Eschaton phase: 1st archetype/card selected: Mother of the World—"All embracing compassion for all beings." 2nd archetype/card selected: Fool—"Whole-hearted presence."

With the Mother of the World archetype active in your life, "You can now free yourself totally from giving your power away to another." Elvis did give a great deal of his emotional power away to others, by trying too hard to fulfill the demands made upon him by his fans, friends, and family. This was a contributing factor on a personal level to his grosser physical depletion. He no longer does this, for now he is able to give without being pulled upon.

The Fool archetype represents innocence and instinctual response. It is the essence of purity that has not been tainted by limited thoughts of the world; the part of self that has no ego or personality to obstruct its vision. In some schools of thought, the Fool is represented by the wounded swan, which in turn represents the fall of humanity from grace. The swan frequently symbolizes purity, love and grace.

There is a story involving the wounded swan in relation to the legend of the Holy Grail. In this story there is a character who represents the innocent hero by the name of Parcifal who shoots a swan wounding it, and in the process wounds himself. Through this experience he becomes conscious of the nature of suffering which leads him to the discovery of greater expressions of love.

There is a connection between the wound that has been inflicted upon the swan, and evolving consciousness, all represented in the swan's body as it appears in the picture on the Haindl Tarot card for the Fool. Though the neck twists in pain it forms a spiral curling into the sky. Consciousness does not move upwards in a straight line, but spirals toward the heavens. But the golden beak does point almost straight upward, like an arrow directing us to the heavens. The swan's wing arches upward, creating a vision that makes us feel we could climb to heaven through the experiences of love and pain[6].

Take a moment, and form the following picture in your mind: It is the end of an Elvis concert. The lights create a mesmerizing, spiraling radiance about his body. The jewels on his suit flash in a twinkling maze of fire, and his face seems to glow from an inner source. With humble expression, he raises his head and stretches out his arms, holding the ends of his cape. A horizon of crimson fans upward—he forms a cross of color and light upon the stage. Is this not the swan of the Fool, the wings lifting upward, his gaze like an arrow shooting into the heavens? The red wound pours into the Cup of Darkness and he is received into the folds of time as a dazzling diadem of light…

"LADIES AND GENTLEMEN, ELVIS HAS LEFT THE BUILDING"

For those of us who have experienced this revelatory transmission with Elvis in person, nothing more need be said.

> "That Elvis, man he's all there is. There ain't no more. Everything starts and ends with him… it was like he came along and whispered some dream in everybody's ear, and somehow we all dreamed it." ~ Bruce Springsteen

Chapter 6: PILLARS OF FIRE

From the Bible, Revelations 10:1, 7, 11 & 11:1, 3, 4, 7, 8, 9:

"And I saw another mighty angel come down from heaven, clothed with a cloud: and a rainbow was upon his head, and his face was as if it were the Sun, and his feet as pillars of fire."[1]

"But in the days of the voice of the seventh angel, when he shall begin to sound, the mystery of God should be finished, as he hath declared to his servants the prophets."

"And he said unto me, Thou must prophecy again before many people, and nations and tongues, and kings."

"And there was given me a reed-like unto a rod: and the angels stood, saying, rise, and measure the temple of God, and the altar, and them that worship therein."

"And I will give power unto my two witnesses, and they shall prophecy a thousand two hundred and three score days, clothed in sackcloth."

> "These are the two olive trees and the two candlesticks standing before the God of the Earth."
>
> "And when they have finished their testimony, the beast that ascended out of the bottomless pit shall make war against them, and shall overcome them, and kill them."
>
> "And their dead bodies shall lie in the street of the great city, which spiritually is called Sodom and Egypt, where also our Lord was crucified."
>
> "And they of the people and kindreds and tongues and nations shall see their dead bodies three days and an half, and shall not suffer their dead bodies to be put in graves."

It is my conviction that Elvis' soul prompted me specifically to write this chapter, and wanted me to name it 'Pillars of Fire.' I feel he also guided me to the above verses in 'Revelations.' What was he trying to convey? I honestly do not know if I understand it completely. However, let us explore what Elvis may have wished me to reveal. Perhaps we will find clues to the deeper, hidden purpose behind these words.

The Harmonic Convergence 1987

On August 9, 1987 I was in contemplation, reflecting upon the date of the Harmonic Convergence*, which was soon approaching. This was the two day period when Jose Arguelles, author of 'The Mayan Factor,' said that according to the advanced galactic science of the 'ancient' Maya, the dates August 16-17, 1987, are precise points when the process of global civilization can phase out of a myth of progress into a myth of synchronization and global cooperation.

The dates of August 16-17, 1987 are also recognized by various Native American and South American medicine people as a significant moment, particularly in terms of the prophecies of the ancient Mexican god-hero, Quetzalcoatl*, also referred to as the Feathered Serpent. All over the world on these two days in August there were planned gatherings of meditation and prayer for a better world.

Jose Arguelles stated that there was an underlying assumption or belief among many of the people involved in planning and implementation of these events that embraced the concept of 'The Hundredth Monkey effect.' Simply put, this belief has it that when a certain number of human beings arrive at a common vision and resolve, that the 'idea' or vision of global peace will spontaneously leap through the imagination of a significant majority of the members of the human race, and a manifestation of that vision of peace would then occur.

There is a saying used in Germany amongst the artistic communities there, that whenever there seems to be a popular theme arising in what everyone is committing to art, that the idea is 'in the air.' This then is the same concept. After the Harmonic Convergence Jose Arguelles has stated that by 1992 it will become evident that a new era is dawning, one as distinct from the industrial era as the industrial era was from the long agricultural era that preceded it. The shift will not be easy. He felt that under a five-year mobilization plan for peace, much could be accomplished. If we were able to so quickly mobilize for 'World War II' and change the face of the world, then without the prospect of bloodshed even more could be expected from a total mobilization for peace.

August 16, 1987 was by destiny or coincidence, the 10th anniversary of the death of Elvis Presley. Over 70,000 people were expected to arrive at Graceland in Memphis, Tennessee for the Decade Memorial. I could not but believe that it was destiny which brought together these two events, and as thousands proceeded to walk upon the grounds of the Graceland estate, and filed before the grave as Nostradamus had predicted.[2]

I also feel there was a commonality between these folk and those consciously attuned in prayer and meditation with the Harmonic Convergence gatherings. Surely Elvis' soul would be a part of this, for he so wished for peace in the world and wanted to contribute to the goal in whatever way he could. That is what his followers truly gather together to honor—his desire for God, good, helping others and peace which was so infectious during his lifetime, and still continues on through his memory via the efforts of his fan clubs, Graceland and close friends he deeply influenced with goodwill for all.

As I contemplated this, I drifted back to events of several days before. I had received a very strong telepathic signal from Elvis' soul to write a particular gentleman whom I admire as a dedicated metaphysician, and give him a message from Elvis Presley. I did not know this man well at the time. This message was that Elvis and he had known one another in a past life in Egypt, Elvis had been Ptah★, brother-in-law to Thoth Hermes★.

Elvis and the Sphinx

Elvis told me a small underground pyramid near the Sphinx had an elaborate capstone which had more recently been buried under the sands of time. I was informed the capstone was designed by Elvis (as Ptah), John (the man I was to write), and his colleague Joe. It had originated from ancient blueprints revived by Thoth. The actual craftsmanship of the capstone was accomplished by a being then known as Ra Ta, known to our present world as the mystic channel Edgar Cayce.

Elvis revealed to me that the Sphinx contained a series or arrangement of acu-points★ and meridian lines★ much as a human body does. Each acu-point, which is a result of certain meridian lines intersecting, was connected energetically in a process similar to telepathy, to the pyramid complex at Giza, Egypt. The small underground pyramid, called the Zenaph, also contained an acu-point upon the Sphinx, which when activated by a light beam of a specific color in ages to come, would reactivate the Zenaph, which would in turn act as a 'supercharger' (Elvis' definition) to the Great Pyramid.

Elvis wanted John to know this and that the two of them had worked on this project together. Some days after I sent this message, having no idea what John might think of a 'message from Elvis Presley,' I received a call. He had just finished reading the message and informed me that he too, had been given a communication from Elvis—on January 8th, 1987, the date of what would have been Elvis' 52nd birthday. It was a message concerning Elvis' role as, to quote John, "a messianic figure."

I interpret this as one who is a planetary healer and redeemer through the Christ Ray of Love. To my knowledge, John is not an 'Elvis fan,' making this experience all the more profound. Sometime later I was told by Wanda June Hill that Elvis had mentioned to her that something important was buried near the Sphinx. Wanda also related that recently Japanese scientists using electronic sensors had located a metallic object in that area. No one has attempted to uncover it at this writing. To quote Wanda's letter to me concerning Elvis' visions of the Great Pyramid and the Sphinx:

> "Elvis said the pyramid (at Giza) was a landing base (UFO's) and had rooms etc., laid out so as to effect a non-gravity base[3] for space ships and people to 'transform.'[4] He said someday they'll learn this. The Sphinx was a part of a chain of 'transformers' for this purpose and had several chambers no one's seen (in known history).
>
> "The foot of it contains a large 'plate' of precious metal and stones and is a 'conductor' for this special magnetic force field. He said in my (Wanda's) lifetime (he did not say in his!) they'd locate this. The Japanese have done so but don't yet know what it is. He also spoke of the Mexican and South American pyramids being part of a 'grid'[5] for this force field."

The following is from a letter sent by Elvis in 1970 to a friend whom I shall call Alice, and her husband whom I shall call Roy:

> "So, Alice, I'm going to Vegas, if you and your family would like to come and see us there it'd be nice. Let Joe know and after the show we could get together. I'd like to talk to you about transference of thoughts. I've tried it and had some success - it would appear to me that I am a sender as well as a receiver. I've had better luck sending, however. Stanley's book helped me, I think you'd like it and I have a copy for you. Roy won't mind if we talk; I'll ask him, not you. It would be nice if I could have some time away from everything but not now, not here. Besides that, I have some personal problems with it too, Priscilla doesn't enjoy anything of that type.
>
> "You have a good man in Roy, he does understand us. Alice, I've been thinking about the Egyptian trip and I really want to go. If I can work it out with my schedule count me in! God, to see the temples and walk again on the same steps! It sends me! I want to see the lions again, go inside them. I guess that's impossible now though, but maybe I could remember. I remember so much, have lost so much, but with you there I could, I know it. I want to go so much it hurts, but you understand that, don't you? I have dreams, dark places and hidden steps down and tunnels with oil lamps on the walls and boxes, long boxes with grain and many golden figures around them.
>
> "I dream of blood, spilling out, flowing over my feet and staining the hem of my robe and of screams and cries and black hoods and flashing knives. Swords they be with cutting edges and points and oh, the blood is everywhere. God, it chills me. I feel I did it.

I wake up wet, cold and shaking and so sick at heart and I am filled with sorrow for the lost souls and the agony I caused.

"Could it be so? Am I he? Is this why I feel such a debt to the people I play to? Do I owe them this joy, this pleasure because I took so much? Is this my way of atonement? I do not know, God, I do not know! Alice, help me find out if you can. I have done all you said to do and I'll be ready to let you take me back. (*Author: to the knowledge of his past lives*).

"My life, Alice, is yours, guide me through and please make me see the reasons. I'll look forward to seeing you soon and Roy also. I have something he'll like from the game! Don't mention this to any of the guys or all is lost for us. I won't say a word here... Always, Elvis."

From *my inner mystical sources*, I received the truth about Elvis' frightening and troubling vision with the knives, black hoods and blood. It was a lifetime in Egypt when he had been a spiritual leader (see his past life as Om-Siris, Chapter 4). He had placed faith in those who were actually his enemies. Because of this, a band of his followers had been murdered before his eyes. Elvis felt responsible for the murder of these trusting souls through his misplaced trust.[6] When reading the verses in 'Revelations' mentioning the 'Pillars of Fire,' I suddenly realized I had read a portion of them before, in Wanda's first book 'We Remember, Elvis.' I hadn't read this book in several years, but went to it immediately, and found the following.

"Elvis always wanted to go to the Holy Land and see where Jesus lived and walked, and he longed for Jesus to return to Earth. From reading and studying the Bible—Daniel, The Book of Revelations, and Matthew, and other parts as well—Elvis developed ideas about the return of Jesus, which he discussed with preachers and people who should

> know. When all the prophecy is fulfilled, after the famines, floods, earthquakes, wars and rumors of wars; the time would come for Jesus to return and claim His people—all those believing in Him and following His teachings. They will be spared the time of great torment and tribulations to follow.
>
> "He also spoke of the Bible's mention of two prophets returning to Earth and being killed for their influence upon mankind, and for three days all nations would 'see them lying' in the streets. Until there were television satellites, he believed this could not have been fulfilled, but now we are able to send pictures around the world in minutes. Someone like Martin Luther King or John Kennedy could be one of those prophets."

Because, he said a 'prophet' does not necessarily mean a person who speaks of visions or predicts the future, but one who tells of what a thing could be—as Martin Luther King told of his 'dream.' I am now wondering as I recall all of his words, could Elvis Presley have been one of those prophets? He too, influenced the world and spoke to the masses. Should he have chosen to lead, he very easily could have commanded great forces in whatever capacity he selected, and for three days we saw him 'lying' in the streets as we witnessed the masses mourning his death via television. "And their dead bodies shall lie in the street of the great city, which spiritually is called Sodom and Egypt…"

It is noteworthy that Elvis died, 'lay in state,' and was buried in Memphis, a city in Tennessee named after an ancient city in Egypt—the city which claimed Ptah as their 'God of Memphis.' Martin Luther King was also slain in Memphis. Elvis and JFK share important numerological* similarities and both King and Kennedy were revered by Elvis. Of course, that makes three 'prophets' instead of two, but could it be that the number 'two' in the Biblical context is a number code and does not necessarily refer to only two individuals? Perhaps there are several people who compose the 'two witnesses,' the two perhaps representing some type of principle rather than an exact count.

When Elvis was a child, he went to a Pentecostal revival where the minister practiced 'speaking in tongues,' a mysterious ability of some to speak in an unknown language—this was accomplished by several of Christ's Apostles and mentioned in the Bible. After the Pentecostal minister finished his speaking in tongues he was supposed to stand and translate what he had just said. This time young Elvis stood instead, rendering a meaning of these words to the satisfaction of the assembly.

In the 1950's, when Elvis first became popular, he was not accustomed to the intensity of energy focused on him by his following. It would often make his nose bleed. When he came offstage, he sometimes fainted from sensitivity to the energy blasting he received from an enthusiastic audience. Unconscious, he would begin to speak in an unknown language. Regaining consciousness, he had no memory of the occurrence. Consequently, on one occasion a friend tape recorded his trance-like jargon. Upon listening to the tape, Elvis did not recognize the language, but took the recording to a language expert, who identified it as 'ancient Hebrew.' This, Elvis told Wanda Hill, was what began his deep study of the Bible.[7]

Elvis believed his cosmic heritage was linked with the Sun. In 'The Mayan Factor' Jose Arguelles writes of the Ahau Kines, the Mayan name for 'Priests of the Sun' and 'Diviners of Harmony.' He states that the Ahau Kines or Lords of the Sun have remained ever vigilant and attuned to the principles of God. It is due to their influence, which comes to Earth at times in the form of energy patterns called archetypes★, that the consciousness of humans has been elevated, directed, or received through the religion of the Sun, which is mystically representative of the higher mind of God.

Ra was a deity assigned to represent the Solar mind of God. He was commemorated and consecrated in the secret thirteenth chamber of the Great Pyramid★. This was intended to pierce humanity like a ray of pure light evoking a lasting memory of the higher evolutionary purpose for being on Earth at the initiation of the cycle represented by the Harmonic Convergence. Elvis, in his past life as Ptah and similarity to the Horus* archetype, was a focus for the Ahau Kines re-patterning of mainstream human consciousness. His music carried the vibrations of higher consciousness in its ability to open one's heart. In this way he is intricately linked to the 'Solar Lords' or Ahau Kines consciousness and purpose.

On the day of Harmonic Convergence, the 10th year of Elvis' passing, a black male newscaster stood in the Trophy Room of Graceland, next to what he thought was Elvis' Mayan Sundial suit, but was in fact his Aztec Sundial suit (no matter—the Aztecs adopted their 'sundial' calendar from the Mayans). Elvis wore the Aztec suit for his last performance. To his television audience, the newscaster said (paraphrased):

> "August 16 (1987) is a unique day—it represents not only the great tribute being presented all this week for an American entertainer, but it is also the day of the Harmonic Convergence of the planet Earth. It so happens that the Ancient Mayans ended their long range projected calendar with the date August 16th, 1987.
>
> "Elvis was interested in Egyptian, Mayan and Indonesian cultures and had designed a suit resplendent with the Mayan Sundial upon it for his final nationwide appearance before his death. Elvis was a spiritual, sensitive man, deeply moved by the plight of his fellow humans. His message to the Earth was one of love, peace and brotherhood toward all races. His memory is one of a great man, a leader for the good of all."

After a failed attempt to steal his body at Forest Lawn Cemetery in Memphis, he was moved to Graceland's Meditation Garden. Elvis' father requested the valuable rings buried with him be removed before re-interment. Opening the casket, all present were astonished to find Elvis' body in an uncorrupted state. Despite embalming, the corpse had an other-worldly look of transparent beauty. Elvis was fascinated by the ability of Yogis and Saints to achieve transition of the physical realm and studied the teachings of Parahamsaji Yogananda whose body remained in an un-deteriorated state for quite some time after his death.

I feel Elvis wanted this chapter written, highlighting unsolved mysteries about this 'Prophet of Power.' The Pillars of Fire - the ancient pyramids, are a legacy from the race of Blue Star Rigel which Elvis mentioned to Wanda June Hill as being his true home. These temples are also true 'witnesses' of God, as are those souls like Elvis' who served within them in ancient times. Elvis' undying love for humanity stands as a 'Pillar of Fire' for all to see.

Chapter 7: THE STUDENT

In 1971, Stan Brossette of RCA Records, said that Elvis was fascinated by words and would ask about their meaning and how they could be used. Elvis began to read metaphysical literature through his friend Larry Geller, author of 'Elvis, His Spiritual Journey,' and 'If I Can Dream.' Wanda Hill recounts:

> "Larry said that he started him out on lesser, simple books, and Elvis went through them so fast, devoured them, that he could not keep him supplied. The more difficult, advanced books went just as quickly. Elvis would know what they said from one reading—would explain them to Larry in details often above the actual book, going into more serious, complicated study without having anyone or anything to guide him.
>
> "So Larry got more and more advanced metaphysical books and Elvis whizzed right through them, to the point Larry thought he was not reading them. He then questioned Elvis, and Elvis would again relate it in detail, enlarging on the matter until Larry was out of his depth and couldn't go on with it any further. Larry said that he didn't know where to take him, what to do with him or his desire to learn more.

Larry had nowhere to go with it. He was lost, couldn't please Elvis and felt bad but began looking for more and that's when he got him the last books. He had just begun to read them when he died. Elvis told Larry, when Larry gave the books to him, 'I don't think I'll finish these, but you did fine son, thanks.'"

Ed Parker, a good friend of Elvis' for many years wrote in his book, 'Inside Elvis,' that Elvis used to carry a lot of books with him when he traveled. He would use the books to research and learn. Ed also relates how Elvis had a photographic memory and could retain and recall what he read years earlier with uncanny accuracy.

Wanda June Hill gave me a book which Elvis had given to her entitled, 'The Search For a Soul—Taylor Caldwell's Psychic Lives' by Jess Stearn. It is a copy especially autographed for Elvis by the author.

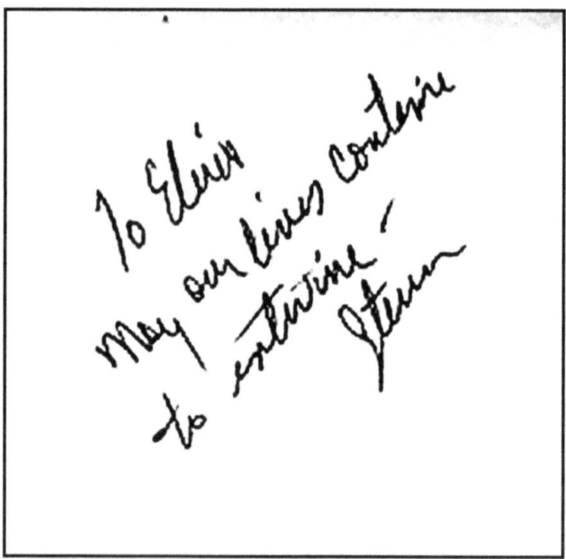

Typical of the way Elvis devoured books he had many passages of the text underscored. The following photograph is typical of how Elvis marked up the books he read.

The session got off to a good start. Not even having been told of Marcus' death or his deathbed vow to his wife, the Reverend Gilbert still tuned in on both incidents.

"Will there be the return of the husband in any way to let her know that there is life after death?" she asked her guides.

Before there could be an answer, she also had a practical question for her masters.

"What will be the outcome of the project, with Janet Taylor Caldwell, and the new book to come forth?"

Without waiting for an answer, she took a deep breath, filling her lungs with oxygen, and then proceeded to address the subject, Taylor Caldwell:

"You have known for a long time that the main thing that was necessary for you to do was to control the emotional problem within yourself. And it is then, when you then go within, go alone, that you have been able to attune to the higher self [Janet Reback versus Taylor Caldwell], and receive a direct answer of cause and effect that would enlighten you and give you the key to face your problems.

"Very often this occurred in a dream state, at night. You would awaken with strange dreams, and strange memories. At other times, the experience of the past would run through your consciousness, revealing scenes to you, not for the principle of curiosity, nor for the satisfying of the ego, but to tell you exactly what was operating at your life at that time, the mistakes that you had made in the past, and how you must correct them."

After correctly picking up on the author's dreams, the life reader tuned into the practical changes in her life since Marcus' death.

"For the past two years there have been many changes in your life. You have been under emotional stresses in being

I found it especially revealing that 'Jupiter'[1] was underlined, as was the name 'Pericles' whenever they appeared in the text. Many years previous *my inner mystical sources* had told me that this Roman statesman (Pericles) was one of Elvis' incarnations.[2]

220 THE SEARCH FOR A SOUL

gone, I'm hearing better, and I've got all this energy, with nothing to do with it." Her eyes twinkled mischievously.

"You're getting rid of things that have bothered you for many lifetimes," the hypnotist said. "You're getting liberated."

"Liberated?" she said with an expression of mock dismay. "You mean like Women's Lib? Never, I couldn't stand it."

"You're in a category by yourself," he said.

Affecting relief, she shifted comfortably under the blanket. "It's the only way I can keep warm," she said.

"That feeling of being cold will pass," said he gently, already beginning his suggestion. "It will pass and you will feel warm and strong and healthy in every way."

Her head started to nod, and he stroked her lightly. "I want to go back in time now," he said, "back to the days of Hippocrates, Helena, Aspasia. Back . . . back . . . way back to Helena and her friend Aspasia."

Her eyes closed, her breathing even, already in trance, she hesitated only a moment.

"Oh, Aspasia has the school of mathematics." She, too, seemed to be making a transition from her original occupation. "It is such a joke. Heracleus says that Aspasia will be the first to 'square the circle.' I confess I do not know what it means. Do you know what it means to square the circle? We must ask Aspasia."

"Who does Aspasia live with? Spell it."

She spelled out Pericles.

"Is Pericles prince or king?"

"The king of all of Greece and Attica," she replied extravagantly, with the pride of knowing him.

Since Pericles was not king, though he controlled Greece with his alliances, it was obvious we were not getting her conscious mind, which was of course aware that the democracy of Athens had no kings at this time.

Also, the word 'cancer' (the disease) is underlined throughout the book. And then there is the following passages from 'The Search For A Soul' which Elvis underlined, expressing an innate sense of his own destiny:

as being caused by overindulgence, when we know today that it is essentially a glandular imbalance, affected but not caused by a partiality for sugars and sweets.

Perhaps because it was so specific, the medical material out of the past had appeared properly evidential to me. One could not help but be impressed by the authoritative manner with which she discussed homeopathy (the particles from the spider webs), the body as a connected whole in sickness or health, psychosomatic medicine, the abortive drugs such as ergot, with that quaint story of its discovery through observing miscarrying cows in rye fields, and the Hippocratic concept of the function of the heart, brain, and the four humors of the body.

I could compare Helena's eloquence as a lecturer only with the knowledge and wisdom of Keptah the master physician in *Dear and Glorious Physician*, or with the well-articulated skill of Dr. Jonathan Ferrier in *Testimony of Two Men*. When she spoke of cancer as being contagious, I knew of course she was wrong, but then a few days later, after she had departed for the Orient on the *Rotterdam*, I read with some surprise the new medical theory that some cancers might indeed be caused by a virus which could infect others.

And it was some twenty-five hundred years ago, subconsciously at least, that the fair Helena, formerly of the house of Aspasia, was saying all this in the Hippocratic school of medicine in old Athens.

All through her regressions she marshaled one fact after another—correct names, dates, terms, and places. But no matter how plausible her narration, what clearly impressed me most was the emotion with which she relived those dramatic events, the subtle changes in voice, the gestures, the complete detail with which she described the surgery of Hippocrates' day, the medical practices, and in a different area, the envy

On page 269 Jess Stearn wrote a very beautiful and poetic paragraph, the essence of which was: "Somewhere in the secret heart of you… you have been a preparer of the way… to prepare many to be ready and able to receive Him." In the margin next to this passage, Elvis wrote, "I am."

see what you had been preparing for and attempting to help make the way ready."

Hannah had told many people of her dream, recollecting one day that he would be five years of age at that time, if her dream were truly prophetic.

Violet Gilbert, again paralleling the life of Hannah, a Hebrew variant of Anna or Ann, saw that she had lived into the beginning of Christ's three-year ministry, but not through it.

"You were still in body when he began his ministry. But by this time age had come upon you, and in even that great knowledge that was within, you had only asked to live to see his mission placed into motion. You had not asked to remain to see it completed. And so it was that at this time [in Jerusalem during the stoning] your spirit left your body."

Even the great dark secret of the mysterious Presence was hinted at, with the suggestion that Janet Caldwell was an instrument of enlightenment to an earth in desperate need of a new revelation.

"Somewhere in the secret heart of you, you have known many things that you have not spoken to man. In this lifetime you have been a preparer of the way, because in time to come, very near in the future, there will be that attempt from the most high to bring the world of light unto man again. And you have been used to put forth the word that would help to prepare many to be ready and able to receive him."

After this exciting experience, there was another lifetime for Taylor Caldwell, whether she liked it or not, in which she would become a proponent of the fourth dimension—psychic communication—in the new Golden Age of Aquarius.

"In this age, you will become a direct teacher to aid man in this new dimension of time. To do this, there is one phase

On page 14 of this book Elvis underlined the following sentences: "(She) felt at times an over whelming link with a universe full of shadowy personalities… This hovering Presence had the eeriness of another life, and another planet, and in its largeness seemed to fill the room… The Presence came and went unexpectedly."

The following sections in this same book were also underscored by Elvis: On page 40, the paragraph beginning with, "Look on your wife with love…"

40 THE SEARCH FOR A SOUL

other manifestations of this disease, especially in children, who invariably die of it. It would be interesting to talk with these children, who, even in their tender years, are possibly of a greedy disposition, caring only for self. We can do nothing but prescribe the leanest of meat, the starchless vegetables and fruits, and restrict or omit the sweets or starches. Little, however, will be accomplished except painful deprivation and prolonging of a restricted life, unless the patient has an awakening of the spirit and thus is enabled to love beyond himself."

Dr. Griffiths thought Keptah's analysis—and advice—essentially sound.

"Look on your wife with love," Keptah admonished. "Say not, 'She belongs to me, and she will serve me!' Say in your heart, rather, 'This is my beloved wife, and what can I do to make her the happiest of women, so that she will say she is married to the kindest and noblest of men?'"

Griffiths was of the opinion that few could have better instructed a pupil in the value of psychosomatic medicine and patient attitude as factors in understanding the origin and progress of disease.

Lucanus had asked, "Then this is not an organic disease?"

Keptah stopped and pondered. He finally said, "There is no separating the flesh from the spirit, for it is through the flesh that the spirit manifests itself. You are wondering how it is that some people contract illnesses in epidemics and others do not. Hippocrates talked of natural immunity for those who escape. One of his pupils believed that those who escape manufacture some essence in themselves which repels the disease. But why? Could it be that certain temperaments resist infection whereas others do not? Immunity? If so, then it is the immunity of the spirit, though other physicians do not believe this."

On pages 52 and 53 the paragraph with: "There will clearly have come from another planet at the time appointed… If a soul is weary after its sojourn on any of the worlds, it may rest… Then it must engage in the work of God…"

On page 182, where the Mormon founder Joseph Smith's accounting of the angel Moroni's appearance to him is given: "(I discovered) a light appearing in my room… a personage appeared… he had on a loose robe of most exquisite whiteness… glorious beyond description and his countenance truly like lightning."

182 THE SEARCH FOR A SOUL

"While I was thus in the action of calling upon God," said the prophet, "I discovered a light appearing in my room, which continued to increase until the room was lighter than noonday, when immediately a personage appeared at my bedside, standing in the air, for his feet did not touch the floor. He had on a loose robe of most exquisite whiteness. It was a whiteness beyond anything earthly I had ever seen; nor do I believe that any earthly thing could be made to appear so exceedingly white and brilliant. . . . Not only was his robe exceedingly white, but his whole person was glorious beyond description, and his countenance truly like lightning."

This was the angel Moroni appearing to Joseph Smith by divine revelation. But an apparition by itself, seen only by one person, was hardly validating. Yet, as I read on, a slight chill ran up my spine. For there was much, much more on the gold plates and where they came from; and it rhymed with what Taylor Caldwell had said in trance:

"He said there was a book deposited, written upon gold plates, giving an account of the *former inhabitants of this continent*, and the source from whence they sprang. He also said that the fulness of the everlasting Gospel was contained in it, as delivered by the Savior to the ancient inhabitants."

Somehow now, the whole thing seemed possible. The legendary White God who had appeared to the Aztecs long ago, and whom they mistook for Cortez—was it he who had brought the golden plates, promising one day to return?

How little we know of the affairs of man beyond a few thousand years, and then only skimming the surface history of Western Europe, the Middle East and the Orient. All else is the subject of idle speculation, with the obvious usually dismissed as fable because it doesn't conform with our notions of what the past should be like.

There are many other passages which Elvis also underscored in this book, but I feel those presented here are the most significant in regard to his personal life journey, and comprehension of his spiritual purpose.

In the inside of the back cover of Elvis' copy of 'A Search For A Soul' Wanda found a paper napkin tucked inside. On it, in Elvis' familiar handwriting, is written the following (spelled exactly as it was written by him):

Elvis' Abilities and Aspirations

1. Psychic abilities

a) able to 'see' events

b) hearing acute

c) impelling force

d) filling of dangerous surroundings

e) certainly pray

f) constant search for peace

g) need for quiet

h) necessary to mediate

i) control emotions

(Author: he skips item 'j')

k) control stress

l) control physical urges

m) patience

n) fairightedness

o) teach others

p) love all

2. Things to Perfect

a) control of self

b) meditation

c) control temper

d) patience

e) more time of quiet

f) love of all races

g) relaxation

h) concern

i) love Priscilla

j) understand Daddy

k) wheight (*Author: weight*)

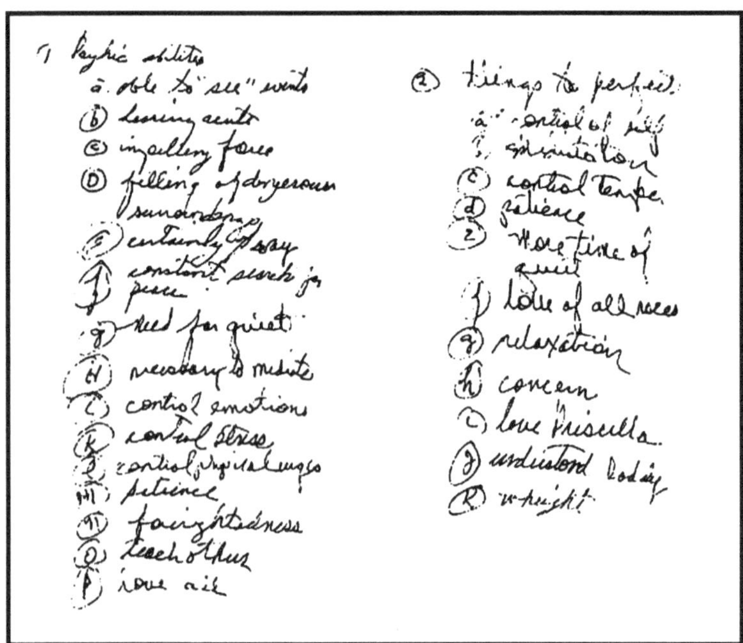

In one of the books Elvis gave Wanda June Hill, she had found a bookmark at a later date, upon which Elvis had written the words 'Melchisedec Priests.' I was astounded when I learned of this as I had been given mystical inner information years ago on the Melchisedec or Melchizedek priesthood as having originated on the planet Venus, which is an energy access point for the Blue Star Rigel.

I have written about this priesthood in some detail through the years, and Uwick, alias Squire Brenton, whom I perceived to be the name of one of Elvis' past-life identities, was indeed a Melchizedek priest in the 'Order of the Sacred Three.'

Wanda told me that Elvis had been studying for years to become one of the few 'Elder' priests of the modern day Melchizedek Order, but as his marriage began to fail he withdrew from the order, telling Wanda that he felt 'unworthy' of the station. It is my perception that Elvis already was a Melchizedek Priest, his soul having been ordained eons ago. Once this type of initiation becomes part of a soul, there it remains eternally.

From my previous writings in 1984, "There was a fear of persecution as the 'Sacred Three' was all that remained of the true Melchizedek Order, finding its way into the Druid experience via the Phoenicians, who were latter day Atlanteans."

Uwick was a Template* of the Sacred Three, meaning that he was one of six Council priests. To them was entrusted the most sacred knowledge of the remnant Order—Great Britain in the 12th century. Because of my previous mystical information on the Melchizedek Priesthood and Elvis' past life as a Melchizedek Priest in England—he was also within this Order in several other lifetimes—I find the 'revelation' of the bookmark to be some of the most profound 'outer' evidence to verify Elvis' mystical heritage that I have yet to encounter, surpassed only by his speaking to Wanda of a 'Blue Star Rigel' heritage. You can see Elvis' dedication also represented in this note pictured below that he wrote entitled 'My Vow.'

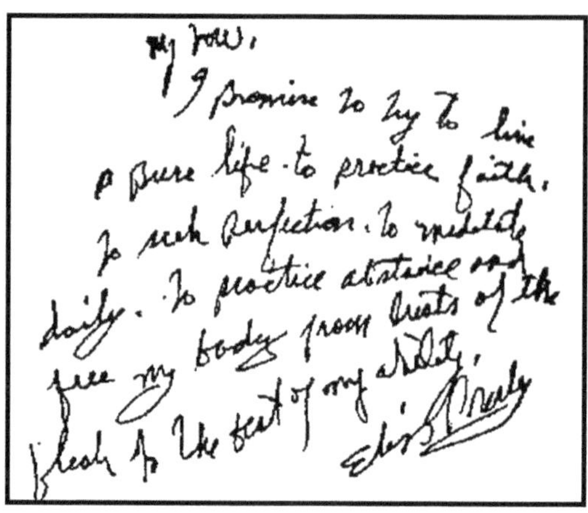

My vow,
I promise to try to live
a pure life. to practice faith.
to seek perfection. to meditate
daily. to practice abstinence and
free my body from lusts of the
flesh to the best of my ability.
Elvis Presley

Below also appear some photos taken of Elvis Presley's copy of 'The Teachings of Buddha' by B.D.K This copy was given to Wanda June Hill and contains Elvis' handwritten comments and underscoring of text so typical of many of the books he read and studied.

6 SAKYAMUNI BUDDHA

deeply affected by the tragedy of these two little creatures. He sat down in the shade of a tree and thought about it, whispering to himself:

"Alas! Do all living creatures kill each other?"

This spiritual wound was deepened day after day as he grew up; like a little scar on a young tree, the sufferings of human life were more and more deeply carved into his mind.

The King was increasingly worried as he recalled the hermit's prophecy and tried in every possible way to cheer the Prince and to turn his thoughts in other directions. At the age of nineteen, the King arranged the marriage of the Prince to the Princess Yasodhara who was the daughter of Suprabuddha, Lord of Koliya castle and a brother of the late Queen Maya.

So true

3. For ten years the Prince was immersed in a round of music, dancing and pleasure, in the different pavilions of Spring, Autumn and Winter, but ever his thoughts reverted to the problem of suffering as he pensively tried to understand the true meaning of human life.

"Luxuries of the palace, healthy bodies, rejoicing youth! what do they mean to me?" he meditated. "Some day we may be sick, we shall become aged, from death we can not eventually escape. Pride of youth, pride of health, pride of existence,—all thoughtful people must cast them aside."

"A man struggling for existence will naturally look for help. There are two ways of looking for help,—

42 CAUSATION

controlled by his will; third, some say that everything happens by chance.

If all has been decided by destiny, both good deeds and evil deeds are destiny, weal and woe are destiny, and nothing exists outside destiny, then all human plans and effort for improvement and progress would be in vain and humanity would be without hope. The same is true of the other conceptions, for, if everything in the last resort is in the hands of God or of blind chance, what hope has humanity except in submission? It is no wonder that people holding these conceptions lose hope and relax their effort to act wisely and avoid evil. No, these three conceptions and viewpoints are all wrong:—everything is a succession of appearances whose source is the concurrence of causes and conditions, and these causes and conditions can, in a measure, be modified and controlled

control thy self and rule the body. gain eternal peace.

120 THE WAY OF PURIFICATION

more danger in the reaction to pleasant things than to evil things, because one is tempted to please the others regardless of the wisdom of the act. For instance, there is pleasure in music and entertainments and dancing; in themselves they seem harmless, but in their reaction there are evils against which one should be on guard. Music after all is only an exciting of the emotions, and the dance is but the act of a crazy mind to cover the desire for something quite different. Those who seek enlightenment can well afford to avoid the allurements of music and dancing; and those who are seeking to realise a quiet mind should avoid entertainments and only smile when they face something pleasant.

oh?

9. Better than a selfish mind that desires and seeks after pleasant things for oneself, is a mind intent on following the Noble Path. One should get rid of a selfish mind and replace it with a mind that is earnest to help others. An act to make another happy, inspires the other to make still another happy, and so happiness is aroused and ... bounds. Thousands of candles can be lighted from a single candle, and the life of the single candle will not be shortened. Happiness never decreases by being shared.

Those who seek enlightenment must be careful of their first steps. No matter how high one's aspiration may be, it must be attained step by step, and first steps must be taken first. The first steps on the path to enlightenment must be taken in our every-day life, today and tomorrow and the next day.

178 DUTIES OF THE BROTHERHOOD

and teach what words he will use; third, he must be concerned about his motive for teaching and the end he wishes to accomplish; fourth, he must be concerned about the great compassion of Buddha.

To be a good teacher of the Dharma, first of all, a homeless brother must have his feet well set on the ground of endurance, he must be modest, he must not be eccentric or desire publicity, he must constantly think of the emptiness aspect of things, he must avoid thinking of things as this good and that bad, as this easy and that hard, he must not become attached to anything. If he is thus concerned, he will be able to behave well.

Secondly, he must exercise caution in approaching people and situations. He must avoid people who are living evil lives or people of authority; he must avoid women. Then he must approach people in a friendly way; he must always remember that things rise from a combination of causes and conditions, and standing at that point, he must not blame people, or abuse them, or speak of their mistakes, or hold them in light esteem.

Thirdly, he must keep his mind peaceful, considering Buddha as his spiritual father, considering other homeless brothers who are training for enlightenment as his teachers, look upon everybody with great compassion and then teach anybody with friendly patience.

Fourthly, he must let his spirit of compassion have free course, even as Buddha did, unto the uttermost. Especially he should let his spirit of compassion flow out to those who do not know enough to want to be enlight-

244 THE APPENDIX

possible will obtain this book and as many as possible of our fellow-men will enjoy and bathe in the Light of the Great Teacher.

THE TEACHING OF BUDDHA

昭和46年9月10日 第15版発行

© 1966

財団法人仏教伝道協会

電話 (453) 0749

108 19249

¥450

Shortly before his death, Elvis gave Wanda a list of his favorite twenty-two (twenty-two is a master number in numerology) books, saying to her that if she didn't do anything else in her lifetime, that she should read these books.

Elvis' List of Books

- The Impersonal Life, Joseph Benner.
- The Initiation of the World, Vera Stanley Alder.
- The Prophet, Kahlil Gibran.
- The Mystical Christ, Murdo Medowald Bayne.
- The Secret Doctrine, Helena Petrovna Blavatsky.
- Life and Teachings of the Masters of the Far East, Vol. I-V, Baird Spaulding.
- The Leaves of Morya's Garden, Vol. I and II, Morya.
- Red Tree, Christine Hayes (this author by her former name).
- The Philosophy of Shopenhauer.
- Life of Christ.
- The Autobiography of a Yogi, Paramahansa Yogananda.
- Cosmic Consciousness, Richard Maurice Bucke, M.D.
- The Intimate Way, Joel Goldsmith.
- Sacred Science of Numbers, Corinne Heline.
- The Inner Reality.
- The New Age Voice, Larry Geller.
- Just One Voice.
- The World Around Us, Hillstrom-Svercik.

- The Bible (old, new and revised versions and lost books thereof).
- The Agony of Christianity, De Unamuno.
- Joyful Wisdom, Reinhardt.
- The Scientific Search for the Face of Jesus, Frank Adams.

See also 'Appendix B—SPIRITUAL BOOKS ELVIS READ' for a more comprehensive list.

Elvis also really loved the Bible and had given a Bible to Jim Hill (Wanda's husband) for his birthday. Found tucked inside it was this poem written by Elvis in 1977. It read as follows, and a photo appears after the transcribed version.

Poem by Elvis 1977

I sit here alone, thinking, watching how the moon's light glows.

Meditating upon the garden water there below,

I've only just begun to spend my life, to have some fun-

But as I think of all I've lost, the hurt hangs on; so slow to go.

I'm now full grown and called a man—but really,

is that what I am?

My heart's so young, it feels like new-

To think I'm getting old makes me very blue.

Lord, Just let me laugh and be the clown I am.

Please give me dignity and grace-

So I can have the strength to face

These final days that seems to race

Let me have some time to do all I can

So facing death won't be such a task.

Please Lord, thy will be done, that's all I ask.

~ Elvis Presley 1977

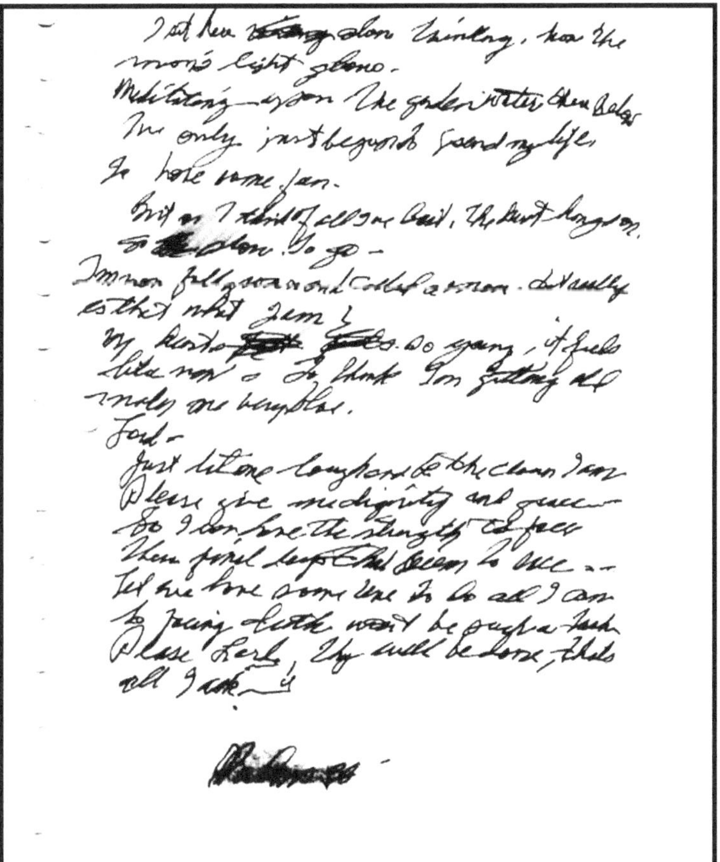

Elvis was also a student of Yogananda's Self Realization Fellowship* and became a friend of its then worldwide head, Sri Daya Mata, whom he affectionately referred to as 'Mother.' Elvis' friend and employee Charlie Hodge wrote that when Elvis asked Daya Mata, "Why did God make me Elvis Presley," her response was to hand him some ancient manuscripts, saying that he might find the answer to his question within them. Larry Geller devotes a whole chapter in his book to Elvis' experiences with the Self Realization Fellowship and Sri Daya Mata.

In this book entitled 'Elvis—His Spiritual Journey,' Larry Geller writes, "He (Elvis) would have liked to have emulated Yogananda, but was bound by a different destiny." Larry revealed that Daya Mata told Elvis, "You must take care of your body. Your mind and Spirit do not worry me. They will be fine, as you meditate and grow calmer inside. You have done splendidly in these areas." In 1977 Wanda felt inspired to ask Elvis, "What is something you did to build discipline?

Elvis on Building Discipline

> Elvis: "I forced myself to conform to things that I might not want or like - in order to learn concentration and patience. In order to control and build the will one must control the self—the willfulness of self, the desire of self, the irrational self—and to do that one must use strict measures at times. At the same time one has to learn who one is, what one is, and why one is that person.
>
> "In my own case, I had too much praise, too much flattery and fawning over and I needed to remember me—who I was, where I came from. I especially needed a reminder so I chose to do it with something I needed daily and also looked forward to having—my meals—food, if you will. I would find a meal I especially enjoyed and force myself to eat it until it was distasteful then I kept on eating it. At times, for weeks—in order to teach myself discipline, steady control of one of our strong appetites—also a necessity to life. When I learned to overcome my own cravings, I'd change, but not until I felt I needed a reward for my control. Maybe that sounds silly or a bit crazy to you, but it worked for me."

I believe what Elvis was attempting to relay here is that his method of overcoming his cravings was to give the lower nature what it desired to such a degree that its reward became its demise.

Wanda: "What's something you ate in that way?"

> Elvis: "Oh—I loved pork chops, gravy and such—I still do, but only as a treat now. I ate them until they almost ran out my ears—but it taught me control. And meatloaf—one time I called a relative in Tupelo. It was Christmas and they were havin' dinner.
>
> "I asked what, and she was kind of quiet, then said 'meatloaf.' I was kind of shocked as we'd had the best, you know—turkey, ham, steak—everything. She just said it was near to the first and they'd run out of money so they just had meatloaf. It hurt me. And so I ate it for about eight months—every night, so I'd remember where I came from and remind me of how many people were unable to have what I did. It was kind of—penance, but also a strong lesson in discipline. You understand me? Perhaps it was drastic, but I'm a strong will and need a heavy hand to control—and I have to do it—no one else will."

Wanda Hill spoke with Elvis in 1973, just after his worldwide performance via satellite in Hawaii, which was seen by more people than the first landing on the moon. Following are excerpts from this conversation, in which Wanda asked Elvis if he has any hopes and dreams which he has yet to fulfill.

Elvis' Goal

> Elvis: "Yes, there are things I would like to do. It may sound silly to some people, but there are things I would like to do that I haven't done yet. I would like to somehow, by my life, by my personal example, not just my career, outside my career; I would like

to be able to do something. I don't feel that I have contributed to anything of major importance.

"Music-wise I'm a singer, that's okay (but) that's not what I'm talking about, you know? That isn't what I'm talking about at all. I'm talking about personal experiences, a meaningful, worthwhile endeavor that I could do to help people. I mean, I can give money, I can be charitable, I can do all those things, but that's not enough somehow, it doesn't satisfy the need that I have to—I guess what I'm trying to say is I would like to be important in more than the music field, I would like to do something outstanding."

Wanda: "Well, before you put yourself down too far, you have done some very outstanding things. You've influenced a lot of people. You may not realize it, but your life has been a major influence on thousands of people, and still is."

Elvis: "Ah, that's real nice of you to say, but that-that's true I-I know that's true, but you don't understand. There's more than that, there's the inner being, the spiritual self. My spiritual self, my inner being is hungry for personal contact with other people's spiritual selves and inner beings on more than the physical label, er, level. I was about to have a new record here, physical label."

Wanda: "I know what you're talking about, I really do, I do know what you're talking about, and I try to understand."

Elvis: "I know, some of the things that I think are kind of far out—and I don't meet a lot of people that I can relate to, and those that I do meet that need to know more about their spiritual selves, I do the best that I can, but I would like to be in a position to reach these people that are out there, I know that, and I-I can't get in that position. My career won't allow it, my management won't allow it, my friends won't allow it, and I—I don't want this on—on—I-I don't want you to use this, because what I think is above and beyond what the majority of my fans think, and they're not ready for this, they're not ready to hear me say these things, so let's just keep this to ourselves, alright?"

Wanda: "Sure, absolutely. I wouldn't—no, don't worry about it, don't worry about it."

The decision was made to include this information in the book, as at that time Elvis didn't feel his fans were ready for the truth of who he was, but we felt that this is a different world over 20 years after his death, and Elvis would want the world to know this information now.

Elvis: "I-I can talk to you about it because I've brought you along."

Wanda: "That's true, you have. I don't always understand, but I'm willing to listen, and I do learn."

Elvis: "I know you do. But you understand what I mean woman, things are not just black and white. Now, there was a time when things were black and white. I could see this side and that side and there was no middle. And now, with my age and experience, and the things that I have learned from reading and from people that I have met—I've been fortunate in that I can, if I read something that somebody has written, and I'm intrigued by it, or I need to know more, I can contact them.

"And chances are, they'll respond because of who I am, and that's good because it's helped me, and in helping me, they've helped other people, but I have this need for more, and its driving me crazy, it's driving me crazy. I'm going to be a blundering fool

> if I don't solve this somehow. I-I don't know, maybe time will straighten it out. Time has a way of doing that, you know."

Wanda: "Why not the classes that you belong to? Don't you belong to some religious order or something? Aren't you involved in something like that?"

> Elvis: "Uh, I really—I really don't want to talk about it. It's very dear to my heart, very personal. But the answer to your question is yes, I do, and I do the best I can, my time is so limited I can't really be a part of it, I have so little time, which is unfortunate. But I—time is worth more than silver or gold to me. My time is very valuable. My time to myself, that's what I'm referring to, my time to myself."

Wanda: "Well, I'm taking up a lot of your time right now doing this, you don't mind, do you?"

> Elvis: "No, no, no, I-I read, no I-I don't mind, because I like to talk to you. You don't, uh, you don't look at me like I have two heads."

Wanda: "Three, maybe."

> Elvis: (chuckles softly) "Yeah, but you know what I mean, you-you know what I mean."

Wanda: "I know what you mean—You told me one time that you had some real unusual experiences when you were growing up. Would you like to talk about any of that?"

> Elvis: "No, no I wouldn't. I don't want them to think I'm completely off my rocker. They already think I'm a squirrel come right out of the trees, but I don't need to prove it at this point in my life."[5]

Elvis was a student of all life; he saw an opportunity in the most mundane situations to glean a bit more wisdom, to understand the intricate nature of God in humanity and himself. I feel the following insights from Elvis demonstrate the unique and inherent ability Elvis possessed to be that student of life and Spirit, which is evident through his observation of the situation at hand within these quotes.

In a sense we are all students, so I would like to conclude this chapter with a final delineation on the nature of Elvis' 'student-ness.' The information presented in this chapter clearly demonstrates that Elvis had a craving for spiritual knowledge, and he recognized that this knowledge must be put to use for the benefit of all.

However, his role as a student goes much deeper, diving into the unexplored recesses of the human heart. The extreme difficulties he had to overcome during this lifetime highlighted the depth of his true learning and his mission to expand his love to even greater levels of expression. What better way to do that than to have been given the extraordinary challenges he faced. Could any of us have been so forgiving and loving under similar circumstances?

Let us join our hearts together through our common love for Elvis and further what he came to learn! Nothing would make Elvis happier!

Chapter 8:
THE TEACHER

"Christ's Spirit taketh breath again within the lives of Holy Men." ~ W.C. Braithwaite

Elvis told Wanda June Hill that he was awakened from a sound sleep by someone in a dream telling him the words to the following poem. He said he had been searching his heart for his 'reason' for being and he felt that he had been given an answer by this poem. "Praise God," he said, "He never lets me down!" Quoted here in part:

Elvis' Reason For Being

For you are the chosen from these generations

To lead, to display, to guide, teach, to obey,

This is your purpose, and this is your existence.

Praise God for your life, and turn away from all strife.

For all must suffer if they learn lessons from life,

You are one chosen from the moment of birth.

Another verse written in 1976 by Elvis quoted from 'We Remember, Elvis,' by Wanda June Hill:

He tries to describe the loves he cannot become,

Failing the wildest dreams of the mind,

And settling for visions of God.

But remember Him, do not forget, because in forgetting,

He will lose even memory of life.

In the early 1970's book 'Elvis' by Jerry Hopkin, a twenty-three year old student from Polson, Montana, speaks of how she had so many dreams and experiences and even memories with and of Elvis that they would fill a book all by themselves. She states emphatically she had no control over these experiences and that they were the result of unseen powers and forces that were pulling her towards Elvis.

During my trips to see Elvis perform, I was told by several young ladies about their experiences as part of the esoteric circle Elvis brought together in secret. They were all young, attractive women, because they were the only ones Elvis' employees allowed up to his suite. This was something over which Elvis had no control. He would select some of the women, take them into his bedroom and close the door, as this was the only place he could find any privacy from the scrutiny of his men. There he would arrange them in a seated circle on the floor. He then sat in the center of this circle and would read and discuss spiritual, metaphysical concepts with them. It was this type of thing that reached the sensational press via several of the men in his employment as Elvis' sex orgies. The following are transcriptions from tapes made of Elvis speaking on spiritual subjects to a small group of people, mostly young women, in 1966:

Elvis Sharing Wisdom

Elvis: "There is a light brighter than anything we have ever seen on Earth and it is visible to those who are on the verge of dying. As they begin to leave their human flesh body they are given sight of this Heavenly Light. It is the Light of God and is a Light filled with a sense of warmth and belonging as no other, as not experienced on this planet Earth. It is greater than family belonging, or loved or lover belonging, but is a oneness with God our creator. We are like the light, only our light is so little in comparison and all the time spent on this Earth, our Light Being, our Spirit Self, longs for return to that one great brightness, that oneness with God.

"The light is representative of the sum total of all knowledge. From eons ago, it is held in some vast storage center and is given out to us in small lots, each lot equal to our understanding as we progress mentally and spiritually. Some of us never do progress and so we share little of that knowledge—others strive for education and growth and get more.

"Some—few, are born ready to receive the knowledge, yearn for it and wish wholeheartedly to obtain it. Then they become the educators for those who have not accepted or are not ready to receive without help. There are few here—not many, who are placed in positions of power—the ability to reach others—not power for obtaining possessions, etc.—who are meant to educate but who at times get side-tracked. They must come again and try over.

"Those few who do find their place and do try to achieve their aim here on Earth, do not have to try again, unless they wish to. Sometimes they come too soon, and have to make adjustments or perish. Sometimes they are unable to adjust and so cannot fulfill their aims for that reason, and then are not held responsible for that karma*.

"Then there are a few who educate, do all they can to achieve progression of their souls by accomplishing a purpose for the good of all; they are the ones who enter a different plane when they return to Heaven's Light. They achieve soul growth and are blessed of God. Sometimes we meet people who shine—who seem to have a glow and whom we wish to be around because they brighten our own lives—not by material gains or such trivia but by their mere presence. We are attracted to them. They are the further progressed souls, and we know that so our soul's Spirit wants to be near them as they are nearer to heaven or God than we are.

"Those who have that nearness are the ones that can reach people; people automatically love them, desire them, want their company, strive to be like them in some fashion and those are the beloved of people. It is of utmost importance that those nearer ones are of good quality and good morals and good hearts or they lead many to their doom. Like evil is black, swallowing up all Light, they swallow up all good and take people with them into blackness. Blackness is hell—what we think hell would be; something we do not want physically, but imagine our delicate spiritual Light Beings thoughts about that—fear incarnate!

"It would be foolish to say that it is not true that we are a creature like the light—the Bible says of Jesus, I am the Light and the Way. All ye who enter must enter this way. He tells us He is light—as we are part of Him, His children, therefore we too, are light—a being of fine particles of light—many colors—each of us have a light of color, of varied colors as is our personalities. We respond to those colors and thus we like this color or that, are comfortable in this or that and look better, etc. in that color or this one.

"Myself, I prefer blue and white. I like green and blue and I like them mixed with gold or yellow-gold because those are the colors of my light. I know this because I was told. I won't tell you now, how I was told, it's not important. To say more would confuse you today. But I am also to soon have lavender among my light—I know this and want it.

"To change colors you have to be spiritually ready to study, to expand your heart and soul and obey the laws of God. I hope to have reached that point, but if not, I'll try harder. God does not like lazy, shiftless and wicked people—he admires effort and determination and desire for good. Be good, do no evil thing to anyone or any living animal on this plane because if you do, you implant evil into your karma and sooner or later will have to atone, have to face it again in some form or other and it won't be any easier the next time. It's much easier to be good in the first place—atonement is a hell of its own.

"The light I wanted to tell you of is God's love, His understanding love for each of us and the knowledge he wishes to give us. Don't fear the brightness that comes to you in dreams, the colors you might see while asleep. And don't fear the feeling of being weightless in sleep or just before sleep—unless you are on drugs, then you can get in trouble and be filled with evil incarnate which is what happens to many of the poor souls in mental institutes—no one was there to help them.

"And if you have a dream which seems real, which you cannot explain but you feel strongly about, try to find someone to explain it. Examine it for answers to your problems. So many of us are filled with self and self's wants that we don't hear or see the answers being given to us. Take the time to meditate, to ponder and think—your heart will tell you. It is the radio of God, our transmitter and receiver, so to speak. So turn it on and listen now and then."

Young girl: "Elvis, what about astral tripping? Don't drugs help with that? Or is it dangerous?"

Elvis: "Honey, drugs don't ever help with spiritual matters. They only open all your doors and let anything in that wants in. Sometimes it might be good spirits, but most often it is not. Evil spirits come to confuse people; they lie, take forms that appear good but in reality are not. The way to tell good from evil is to look at the light—is it pure? Is it comfortable? Do you like and want the feeling it gives you, or is it something sensual and not something that you would like forever?

"If you say 'yes' to that, then maybe you can trust it. Test the feeling. Don't be foolish and jump in feet first. Drugs are wrong. They confuse and distort the heart and mind while making the body responsive to earthly things. Don't think it is right to use them."

Young girl: "Elvis, want to get high on some good pot and test your theory?"

Elvis: "No, honey. I don't use pot or any mind

altering drugs for the reason I just told you and you should not either. Pot will destroy your DNA and make you have problems with future plans for children. You are playing Russian Roulette with your life, dear."

Young girl: "You don't use anything—not even with all this mumbo jumbo?"

Elvis: "No, I said not. Aren't you listening? Do you want to leave?"

Young girl: "Don't get testy—I want to take you into another room."

Elvis: "We won't do anything there that we can't do in here."

Young girl: "In front of all these people?" (several giggles)

Elvis: "Honey, if that's what you came here for I'm not going to oblige you now or later, so you might as well go and let someone who wants to learn about this come in. You're wasting my time and yours." (voice soft, patient, slightly disgusted)

Young girl: "I don't want to go—just go on, I'll listen."

Elvis: "Honey, what do you want out of life? Your most heartfelt desire? Other than makin' it with me, that is." (patient tone, more giggles from girls present)

Young girl: "I don't know... maybe get married and have a home—if I don't make it in the (show) business soon. Something important."

Elvis: "Dear, a family, children raised to God's

plan for their lives is the most important thing a woman can do—if she finds her true mate. Are you one of these girls who—sleeps around—don't answer me—just listen! If so, then you are weakening the light vibrations for you. That is wrong. Sex, the ability to feel love and devotion for another, is a God-given thing. Sex is not just a haphazard thing given to the human animal to keep the species going—it is a power, a key to Divine Love.

"It relates to God, is likened unto God's love for us. To waste it is wrong. To give yourself, to any guy that comes along that you're attracted to, or for any other reason, is asking for trouble both in the body and spiritually. It will not make you happy, it will not satisfy the deep inner need you have for love; and to let yourself in for all that misery, loneliness and disharmony is to be foolish.

"We have to learn to restrain feelings and place them in the proper perspective for life. Love, true love, is not to be played with, it is to be treasured. The lower emotions of lust, desire and need—physical need—can be controlled, channeled, into more lasting and worthwhile endeavors. It can be used accordingly to benefit the one you care for, the one you love. (It is) something more lasting than a few hours, minutes, or whatever, of pleasure or excitement that is going to be forgotten, not used to further the love for that person—the commitment, the benefit and good for that person.

"That's wrong; I learned that—you're wrong if you think that it means nothing to me. You are young; you can learn it from me now, from my personal experience. If you listen, pay attention, you won't have to find it out later on, maybe after it's too late. Don't be one of these who throw themselves to the winds, then find out too late that it could have been so beautiful if you had waited, been more selective and held out for the real thing. This Earth, its inhabitants and creatures are not by chance. Everything has a purpose, a meaning, and you as a female are invaluable—every aspect of your body, mind, heart, spirit and soul. You are a temple. Don't dirty that temple. Do you see what I'm telling you?"

Young girl: "I'd like you to teach me whatever you know—bet it's plenty!"

Elvis: "Yeah—I can see that you would. Like I said, I'm not going to waste my time on your fantasy. So make up your mind—either leave or shut up and listen." (very stern tone).

At this point, the girl begins to insult him in crude language, and Elvis tells her to leave, which she does.

Elvis (to remaining people): "Okay—it makes me wonder how such girls can go through life like chaff on the wind. One of these days that one will meet someone she cares for and perhaps because of her past attitude will find that he is unattainable and she will spend her days in the hell of regret's arms—if she doesn't come down with some illness caught during one of her lapses, that is." (end of tape)

Elvis responding to a question from Wanda:

Elvis: "I guess the most important thing—the very most important thing would be—is—is that I try to teach my daughter to respect other people, to see their needs, not just listen to their wants, and to understand and know that there is a God, an all loving and caring God—the Father, in whom she can always look to for spiritual guidance—eh—any comfort in times of trouble. All parents have that duty, to give children a foundation of faith, hope and charity."

Elvis on the Spiritual Impact of Colors

Elvis geared this presentation to beginners on the subject:

Elvis: "Color plays an important role in the life spectrum."

"**RED**—We associate red with the Devil. Why? Because it is a color of heat, of strife, of emotional turmoil, of energy—good and bad. It is related to sexual tension and sexual activity. It is the color of erotic passion and dreams. It is the color for blood, the life force, the energy transmitter of animal life and human life. It is the ultimate force color—RED! Its name even emotes energy when spoken or when thought. It warms in a room it provides warmth and passion giving radiance to the setting.

"**YELLOW** is control. It is the warmth of the sun. It is comforting, yielding and encompassing. It is compassion, truth and trust and it is relaxing to the human psyche. It is also the color of integrity and spiritual strength. It has a calming effect and is a family color.

"**GREEN** is life, touching everything. It is comfort, security in the ever-growing life force. It is relaxing and soothing to the spirit and provides an atmosphere of sleep. It should be used in bedrooms and in places where serenity is desired.

"**PINK** is compassion, it soothes. It relaxes the mind and tends to put one in a happy, youthful mood.

It is related to females and makes the male more aware of the comfort women can provide. It is also the color of truthfulness and is often used in pictures related to Christ.

"**WHITE** is pure. Related to the Christ it is capable of pure energy. It is a 'cool' color and yields to all others. It is spiritual and is the color of love.

"**BROWN** is warmth, the Earth and mothering. It is compassionate, soothing, nurturing and enveloping as the Mother Earth. It works best in cold atmospheres and lends it's self readily. It is a female color.

"**BLACK** is associated with death. It swallows every color up and is depressing to life. It can also be a strength color as it is the strongest color of the spectrum. When used with red or yellow it provides contrast and creates gray energy. Its depth bounces off light colors and can draw magnetic force from them and channel it back. It is ageless and projects male strength and power and considered a dangerous color.[1]

"**VIOLET** is a spiritual color. It is a blended color and is The Christ love color. It should be used in the house of God and where ever one desires the peace and tranquility of spiritual love. It is a meditation color and gives the spirit strength.

The following is on the 'Golden Key to Happiness,' by Elvis, 1970, from taped conversations with young girls during one of his many tours.

Elvis on Auras

"There is around all of us a kind of curtain made up of our own personal vibrations. Each of us is entirely different in this respect. We have a vibration like no other. It is called an aura—this vibration can tell us many things. As when someone walks up quietly behind us, we sense it. It can tell us when someone is talking or thinking about us too. It can be very sensitive and again if we have not become aware of it—can be very un-sensitive. Most people will admit to knowing that they, for some reason, are aware at times of things they cannot explain.[2]

"To some people this is scary. A person with a narrow unseeing understanding is to be pitied for they go through life missing most of life's joys and blessings. God provided us with a brain, with a soul and a Spirit-Being and the ability to tie them all together and tune into His manifest power in Light and Wisdom. And that ability is in our aura which is us, the Light-Being within which is our Spirit body, made in God's image. God is ethereal, God is Light, and so as such is part of us. We are one with Him, encased in a body of human flesh to live out the karma of our souls, many souls, for we are many bodies with one Spirit and one soul. Our soul has come in many human flesh bodies, usually connected in some way with each coming to Earth.

"But that's off the subject—now I'm talking about our auras, our Light Body which surrounds us, comes from within us and is our protection system if used wisely. We ought to be careful when we meet someone that sets wrong with us, that we feel uneasy with, as they do not correspond with our vibrations—(they) in some way distort it, and if two magnets with opposite ends—(are) trying to force together, they do not vibrate evenly and will cause strife, discord and probably get us in trouble if we don't leave them alone. This is the warning system built into us, in our aura. Use it, listen to it, and be wise.

"Our human will is also a gift tied into our aura and can be used for a direct source of strength. God intended us to have a will or He would not have given it to us. We ought to be strong, but tender—powerful—(yet) able to sense a need for gentleness, and unbending except in love. If you allow your will to weaken then you open the door for evil and evil waits like a hungry jackal to leap upon the weak. Positive thought is strength to the will; use it. Never be negative unless it is not wise to be positive.

"The need for the will goes further than being able to say 'no' and mean it. It goes further than refusing to do a wrong thing to another. It means that you are able to judge when to be strong and when to be tender—that you are wise in your character, steadfast in your heart and determined to be true to your principles. Don't give in just because someone wants you to and you feel you have to in order to keep their friendship when they ask you to do something you feel is not quite right. For if you do that, it weakens your will and the next time wrong is so much easier, until at last you have no will but that of (a) physical sense. Your spiritual will, your Light-Being, will weaken and be of no use to you, or to anyone you care for.

"To strengthen the aura light around you do this: Pray fervently and honestly by asking for strength, understanding of fellow man, and for courage to live on the Earth's plane among the confusion and discord of so many Spirits all trying to fit into this unbalanced vibration. For only those with open chakras*, with

Ki* (pronounced chee), and with balanced channa* can truly know the Key of Wisdom and help others find it too. Meditate, practice peace and quiet several hours a day. Take the time daily to be quiet, to look deep inside and listen to the being within you, the most holy being living inside who guides you if you will listen to Him.

"Let that light glow, let it fill you and hide it not. The Key to having confidence is first to know yourself. Have high ideals, store them on your mental shelf and hold fast to faith and principles. Listen to your heart, it knows. It is the key to your aura, your light being, your ageless self that lives forever from ether to ether and plane to plane in human and spiritual forms, eon after eon, forever."

Elvis on the Bible

"Read Roman Mythology and Greek Mythology and compare this history to that of the Bible, you will find it corresponds. Read all religions, compare— for only then can you have true knowledge and understanding. It is wrong to go through life being empty, believing that only one way is the way—or each book is history—our history, God's history of Earth, written in different styles, by different races of mankind, but all telling the same story based on that race's life style, yet saying virtually the same thing. Don't be so foolish as to say 'no, that can't be right,' when you don't know, do not have knowledge but accept what someone else believes without question.

"That is to let in a foolishness that can damn you to the fires of regret, the hell of knowing you had a chance and blew it. Hell is of the mind—the mind

> brings physical hell. Nothing is so painful as the seed of regret growing into a vine of remorse and heartfelt sorrow. The thought of knowing I could have and did not. Oh, that I had more time! That I was more wise, more able to say what I feel, but I am only me, a man with a humble soul, a heart full of need and only silence upon which to lament my inability to put into your minds and hearts the wisdom you need—must have, in order to survive."

Wanda June Hill, in her book 'Elvis, Face to Face,' writes about another of Elvis' spiritual discussion sessions with young girls, at which she was present:

> "He began talking about God and how He is everywhere, just as the air we breathe and as radio waves are sent around the Earth, His Word is also. 'He transmits on special frequencies,' Elvis related, 'one that we can tune into if we have faith and believe.' He told us, '….God sends, we receive, and we can even receive pictures as a television set, if we are willing. Great visionaries such as Martin Luther King, who saw a better tomorrow but was killed before he reached enough people with his message; were able to receive God's transmission in vision form.'
>
> "Elvis asked us to pray with him, bowed his head and recited several passages from the Proverbs and Psalms before saying one of his own. He asked for world peace, understanding and companionship among all races and that we who were with him, would be blessed as we opened our hearts and minds to God's will. When he said 'amen,' he reached out to touch each face as if imparting his own blessing. He stood, accepted several kisses as he said goodbye, asked one girl to wait as he had a book for her and told me he would see me later. As the group went out and down the hall I listened as the girls talked.

"They commented on how 'great, sexy, and sweet' Elvis was and I asked what they thought of his 'talk.' One rolled her eyes saying she'd listen to anything he had to say as long as he was the one saying it! Another was more thoughtful. She enjoyed his lecture she said, and related it was one of many talks she had taken part in. I asked how long she had known him. 'Since I was thirteen,' she replied, and added that her sister had brought her up to the house as a birthday present. Elvis had sung 'Happy Birthday' to her, then taken her to his bedroom, gave her a book of Bible verses and then proceeded to explain salvation to her. She said that he told her not to be promiscuous, not to smoke and to always listen carefully when spoken to, as what was said was not always what was meant. 'I love that man,' she grinned, 'he's the best there is!'"

Elvis' mind was apparently also a dynamo of other-worldly and innovative information. Wanda June Hill relates more…

Elvis on Turning Trash into Energy

"Elvis once had an elaborate scheme to make normal, everyday trash into an energy source which would leave nothing harmful as residue in the end. It was over my head, but he was going to meet with the Tennessee officials who were involved in such things through the government and tell them of his idea. He did meet with them, and they listened. Later, he said the idea was going to be used on a trial basis. Not everything he said was understandable, so it was too early for them (to fully employ).

"Now in the State of Tennessee they are developing and using his idea and it is working. There was a write-up in a trade paper about it. I knew at once when I read it that it was the plan Elvis devised, only had been turned into an everyday kind of idea (his proposal had been more advanced).

Consequentially, there are no vast waste dumps in Tennessee. It is all converted into power—electrical and gas, and the man doing it was a friend of Elvis'—the one Elvis had initially approached with his idea. But Elvis was not mentioned. After all he was just a singer."

Elvis said: "An image is one thing, and a human being is another."

It might also be stated that the 'image' is only a surface reflection of the hopes and dreams of individuals gazing into the mirror of the teacher's face. Elvis polished the dark coals of ancient fires within us until a brilliant diamond emerged. It is our deepest desire to fulfill the quest of love; a quest that must always begin and end in the ability to love ourselves.

Elvis opened this door to many people. By so freely loving them through the inner message of his music and his personal friendliness and giving of himself, he enabled people to see their worthiness through his act—they were worth the love of a special person. It is very simple, yet quite profound. Human beings seek to love themselves through the love others give them. The difference with Elvis was that he gave this love unconditionally to a unique degree. When we looked into his face, we saw a familiar friend. When he looked into ours, he saw for the most part strangers.

Yet, like a boy searching for his favorite pocket knife in the recesses of his trousers, Elvis dug deeply into the treasures of his soul, and always managed to pull some memento from his heart to bestow upon the individual. He possessed an ability to form an instantaneous and bonding recognition between himself and the individuals within the masses.

This, in my opinion, was his greatest spiritual talent, for in doing so he taught many to do the same. In support of this I offer the following quotes. Ed Enoch, one of Elvis' backup singers in the 1970's gave an interview for the 'Elvis International Forum,' which appeared in their First Quarter 1992 issue. He told of a touching experience he had with Elvis, exemplifying the unique sensitivity of this man. He relates how he and Elvis were at the Las Vegas Hilton talking about Jesus Christ of all things rather than women, music or ordinary things. Ed said to Elvis, "Isn't it funny, a nothing, a poor old nobody like myself being able to sit here with you who has everything." Elvis grabbed his face and said, 'You are not a nobody! You are my friend!'"

> 'Nell Lee,' one of Elvis' phone friends[3] wrote, "He was full and overflowing with love for all people and creatures, with a tremendous capacity to forgive those who inflicted hurt and shame upon him. His was the pure, tender heart of a child, and he was like a child in so many ways. Yet if the occasion called for it, he had a very business oriented, steel trap mind. He lived far ahead of the times, in mind as well as dress, and lived more in his short forty two years than most people could in two lifetimes. Through knowing Elvis, I have come to know a new closeness with God, to live my life with a little more kindness, a little more patience and a lot more love."
>
> Author unknown: "Thank you God, for giving us Elvis and showing us the way to love our fellow man. Thank you for the family of Elvis. We will try to be worthy and will spread his love every single day, as much as we can."

Chapter 9: THE HEALER

> "He (Elvis) firmly believed he had the powers of psychic healing by the laying on of hands. He believed he would be reincarnated. He believed he had the strength of will to move clouds in the air, and he was also convinced that there are beings on other planets. He firmly believed he was a prophet who was destined to lead, designated by God for a special role in Life." ~ A news clipping

Through Elvis' unconditional love of everyone, he opened his heart to the emotionally troubled and physically afflicted and they flocked to his performances and waited for him patiently outside his home. Even today, over twenty years after his passing, many people in wheelchairs attend the annual candlelight service at Graceland. He did not respond to them with pity or condescension. I have seen him enfold people in his arms who were in obvious emotional need; some physically marred, others only broken inside. Many were women who were quite homely. His communion with them was natural. He did not reach down to them, but across to them, "Like a bridge over troubled water, I will lay me down." When I looked into Elvis' eyes, as he extended his hands to those in need of him, I saw a reflection of their pain and knowledge of their sorrow.

Deep within was a living wound, not solely from this life experience. Those more aware and caring humans such as Elvis, do not hold themselves as separate from the misery of the world. This was what I saw in the pools of blue light coming from Elvis' eyes—it was the suffering of the world, but also, ever so much as brightly, the hope of the world. Like the Unicorn*, Elvis was a rare creature of air and light, drawn to the lap of grace, only to find his captors not far behind. We see this symbol in the tapestries and paintings of old, where the Unicorn lays its head in the lap of the maiden, and in a later scene, is struggling in vain against the cruel ropes and snares of his attackers. These are men who would kill him and take his precious horn as their own, for the horn is a symbol of strength and beauty.

Despite the implicit threat of his own demise, Elvis continued to perform. Shimmering in white, like the flank of a Unicorn, he would kneel before his audience. Grasping hands often tore his flesh in their ardent desire to touch the 'sacred creature' hoping to ignite the same within themselves. What I saw and experienced was not illusion, nor did it dissipate when the curtains closed and he disappeared. The magic remained upon the air lingering in every corner and cloaking people as they left. It was tangible, it was real. It was a touch of grace that left an indelible mark on us all.

There were stories of both physical and emotional healing. Some of these healings resulted from the actual touch of Elvis' hands and lips upon them, but many occurred by simply having been in his presence; and it did not end there. Souls around the world were, and still are being healed by Elvis in various ways, without ever having been near him.

Elvis Helps Girl with Cerebral Palsy

After Elvis' death, Lena Canada wrote a book entitled, 'To Elvis, With Love,' in which she related her experiences with a young girl named Karen and her love for Elvis Presley. It was in Stockholm, Sweden in the 1960's when Lena, a 19 year old aide in an institution for handicapped children met Karen, a nine year old with cerebral palsy. Karen was unable to walk, her body deformed. Her mother had left her in an institution from birth. Karen lived a lonely and isolated life except for Elvis.

Lena relates how Karen would collect Elvis records and memorabilia. Karen knew all about his personal nature and life right down to his habits. Young Karen believed in Elvis so deeply she talked of him as if he were an old friend. Lena shares how she finally suggested that Karen write Elvis a letter, almost regretting it because she thought it unlikely Elvis would respond.

Karen of course was thrilled about this possibility! Lena relates how Karen had an unwavering faith that Elvis would indeed respond. When months passed, and no response from Elvis was delivered into Karen's waiting hands, Lena became desperate as she saw the child's despair. Then one day she came across a movie magazine with an article on Elvis by a reporter who claimed a special friendship with him. Lena wrote the reporter, pouring her heart out to her about Karen. The outcome of Lena's compassionate action alerted Elvis about Karen and her letter to him. In his first letter to Karen he told her that he was sorry that he had not received her letter. He said that he very much wanted to become her friend, and gave her a special address where her letters would always reach him. As a result of the letter, Lena shared that Karen took on a new glow and started healing. Many of her problems started improving from that day forward and she became much more relaxed and manageable.

Elvis continued to write to Karen, each time encouraging her to write to him in return. He also began sending her presents. Samples of the correspondences between Karen and her 'friend' Elvis appear in Lena's book and are a must read for anyone seeking to delve into the real character of Elvis as a healer and compassionate person. They are very touching. Lena noticed that as more letters and presents from Elvis came, Karen 'blossomed' more and more. In the end, Lena relates that longevity was not to be for Karen. The young girl died while writing to her friend Elvis. Lena concludes by sharing her story of how sometime after Karen's death she heard Elvis had also died. This is what inspired her to tell Karen's story in her book. Lena wished to return the good Elvis had done for Karen by sharing what an exceptional person Elvis truly was.

Elvis Helps Girl with Downs' Syndrome

In Dr. Raymond Moody's book, 'Elvis After Life,' he tells the story of another little girl's devotion to Elvis and how he came to her in the moment of transition from this life to the next. The story begins with her parents, Sherry and Jimmy. They were both Elvis fans and played his music for their daughter, who was afflicted with Down Syndrome. When the child Jennifer was born, her parents were also informed that she had a hole in her heart. They were cautioned she would not live to be very old. Jennifer loved Elvis. She would sit and listen to his music for hours. When she saw his television special from Hawaii in 1973, she was ecstatic.

When she was five years old, her parents took Jennifer to see Elvis at one of his concerts in their city. According to her mother, the little girl squealed and laughed, loving every minute of it, later telling anyone who would listen to her, "I saw Elvis!" Jennifer did not seem to understand death and when Elvis died it seemed as if he were still alive, and so he was deep within her heart.

In 1980 Jennifer approached the moment of her own death. Sherry said the child suddenly lit up stating, "Here Comes Elvis," and tried sitting up in bed. She began holding her arms out as if trying to reach out and hug them. The child said "Here comes Elvis" twice, then collapsed and died. Sherry related, "She had the most beautiful smile on her face as she died, like an angel."

"She saw Elvis when she died." Jimmy recalled his daughter's death. Even though he'd never been religious and barely believed in

God, Jennifer's radiant smile while reaching out for Elvis changed him. He knew in his heart his daughter would live on with God forever.

Elvis' Healing Music

An Elvis fan in 1974 related that, "I've had my problems and recently I tried to kill myself. While I was in a trance I heard a neighbor playing an Elvis record, and like the coming of the dawn, my will to live came back." The song this woman heard playing was 'How Great Thou Art,' a gospel piece.

> Another testimony read, "I have a little sister who has had nine operations. She is retarded. The doctors gave up on her four times. She can be crying—but when we put on any one of Elvis' records she quits crying and laughs and plays as long as the record turns."
>
> Elvis' friend Larry Geller related, "From the moment we first met, I knew Elvis had a spiritual quality. I had never seen so much power in one person. The effect he had on people was tremendous. He could silence an entire room full of people just by walking in. It wasn't just his fame that caused that—it was his aura of power."

Larry Geller Witnesses Elvis The Healer

> Larry witnessed Elvis' healing power in action. "We were on a bus when he saw a man fall into the gutter with a heart attack. Elvis stopped the bus and he put his hand on the man's chest. The man said, 'It's you, it's you,' and got up."

One article stated, "Leading religion experts say he's (Elvis) actually answering his followers' prayers—in some cases, miraculously saving their lives."

> "It's as if Elvis were a saint," says Raymond Moody, a psychologist and author of the book, 'Elvis After Life.' "People are praying to him, begging them to heal them out of their troubles. People are having visions of Elvis just like they have visions of Jesus or Joan of Arc or Saint Christopher. They travel to Graceland like pilgrims to Lourdes."
>
> USA Today newspaper, March 30, 1984—from Toronto, Canada: "The 14th annual convention of the Popular Culture Association is being held in Toronto. Among the topics being studied by university scholars: a slide show of Elvis Presley publicity photos in which the singer is shown as a spiritual, introspective folk hero and finally as a 'spiritual being who almost had healing powers.'"

Deaf Girl Hears Elvis' Music

Elvis described to Wanda June Hill the most touching thing that happened to him in 1975:

> "I-I-guess, when this little girl who is deaf, totally deaf, wrote to me a note and handed it to me at a concert and said she could hear me sing—my voice—and would I please speak to her. I leaned down—had to lay on the stage to reach her—and I said, 'I love you, you're beautiful,' into her ear. She shook all over and grabbed me. There was such a power surge, I mean, between us—like-like voltages of electricity, and there was like a bright light around us.
>
> "Charlie saw it, James and the rest too, and my whole body was jolted. And she looked into my eyes

> and said, 'I heard you!' Then she kinda fell and the guards took her to her seat. Later at the hotel, her folks sent a letter up to me sayin' that she told them what I said. She couldn't have read my lips, she didn't see them. And they said in the letter she knew all the words to my records and claimed from childhood to be able to hear me! But she was totally deaf! I have to say that touched me in a unique way, more than anything that's happened since. But I understand it."

Elvis Heals Singer with Cancer

Joe Esposito, a friend and employee of Elvis' through the '60's and '70's, reveals in his book, 'Good Rockin' Tonight,' an incident in which it would appear that Elvis' healing touch was nothing short of miraculous. Sylvia, one of the Sweet Inspirations back-up singers, had been diagnosed with cancer. Elvis came to her dressing room, put his hands on her stomach and began to pray. The next day, when Sylvia went to the hospital further tests concluded there was no sign of cancer in her body.

Elvis was and is a healer. He touches the wound, whether of mind, body, heart or soul and the afflicted responds by loving him/herself into wholeness. Perhaps this is an over-simplification, but it needs to be understood that although Elvis was certainly a "unique and enlightening man" as his daughter described him, he was also one of us. His ability to heal us from loneliness, depression or illness of the flesh, is really our own God-given ability to heal ourselves. He gives us the recognition of being able to see our own wholeness through his eyes, and we supply the spiritual energy from within our own God center.

Others could do the same, but Elvis manages to make this revelation a great deal more joyful somehow. Not all of us have people who are there when we need them. Elvis is always there in our memories, records, videos and in Spirit. In prayer and contemplation, so are Jesus Christ, Buddha and other enlightened Masters. Granted, Elvis was/is not Christ or Buddha. He was a very human man, with exceptional godly intentions and gifts. To me, he represents a link between understanding ourselves and believing that God abides in us despite our imperfections.

Elvis' Spirit Visits The Sick

V. Anderson of California: "Elvis has been around me for about a year. I have learned that I can call on him when I need help. He is very tender and compassionate with sick people because he suffered so when he was in his body. I'd like to share an incident I had with him on the morning of December 12, 1991. I had gone to bed the previous night feeling ill. One of my eyes was pink-rimmed and swollen. My head ached, and I felt weak and dizzy. I knew I was running a temperature.

"I slept deeply for several hours then awakened. I still felt terrible. I said, 'Elvis?' Instantly he was there. He said quietly, 'Yes, baby.' I said, 'I feel really sick and I have so many things to do. Can you help me?' Then I saw his entire body for the first time. He was pure white shimmering Light and he knelt and placed his hands on the sides of my head. I fell asleep again and when I awakened two hours later I felt so much better that I was able to get up and start to work."

From a friend of mine, Flora Haas, San Antonio, Texas: "To my deepest regret, I was never lucky enough to ever see Elvis in person. All my knowledge of him comes from watching him, listening to him for umpteen hours, reading every scrap of information, whether positive or negative. In 1980 I had my first serious illness, which was the beginning of the end for me. In 1981, I totally collapsed and had to retire from my job, quit driving, quit going out in public and couldn't do my housework anymore.

"The doctors found I had a progressive, deteriorating heart disease as well as a lung disease that had apparently been there for years. With the new diagnostic machines, they found two heart defects that I had at birth and that explained all the health problems I had coped with all my life. All through the years of raising children, I ended up in the hospital at least once a year and sometimes twice. So now I felt the axe had fallen, and my life was over.

"For about two years I was completely depressed and couldn't function mentally or physically very well. I was on all kinds of medication for depression, anxiety, etc. Having been a pianist all my life I couldn't even play the piano anymore. Then one day I put on an Elvis gospel album. (In 1983) I began to listen to Elvis more every day and found that I began to feel less tense and anxious. The more I listened, the more I wanted to hear that beautiful voice.

"He reached me when no one else could, it seemed, and I was even able to pray again, something I had not been able to do for some time as I was angry with God, too. Elvis made me see how foolish I was and I turned back to God in my daily prayers as I had always done before. Elvis's love of God came through to me. Then something very eerie happened and I hesitate to tell it, because it seems so strange, and yet it happened and maybe the telling of it will help someone else.

"You see, my sons had always played guitars and harmonized when they got together. (I have five sons). I had taught them music when they were small and they went from the piano to the guitars—one night my sons were all in my living room, playing and harmonizing as always, but you see this was a dream. I was standing there watching them when I noticed that Elvis was with them. I thought to myself, 'What in the world is Elvis doing here and how did he get here?'

"I was so excited at seeing him in person and as I was standing there staring, in shock, Elvis turned around, saw me and came over to me. He was dressed all in black and looked exactly as he does in the '60's movies where he wears black and has that one curl over his eye. He came up to me, took both of my hands in his and smiled that gorgeous smile. I could see his beautiful blue eyes and that smile just made me freeze. All he said was, 'I'm so glad you like my music.'

"At that point I woke up, and my body was trembling and I was in a cold sweat. I was so shocked that I actually got up from bed and went into the living room to look and see if he was still there! His presence was so real I could still feel it after I awoke and it stayed with me for days. That experience affected me so deeply I was in a daze. I just knew that I had been in Elvis' presence and no one will convince me that he did not come to me with his beautiful Spirit, because from that day on, I never took another pill for depression. Elvis brought me out of my well of despair and kept me from falling back into that state ever since."

Elvis' Spiritual Brother

Elvis occasionally comes to me in Spirit, and sometimes he asks me to give others messages for him. Recently, a man awakened me from sleep with a call late one night needing counseling, as he was very depressed—spiritual counseling is part of my work. I had only talked to this gentleman briefly once before, on the phone, and really knew nothing about him personally because our conversation consisted mostly of my answering his questions on spiritual and metaphysical subjects.

After this last conversation with him as I was drifting back to sleep, Elvis suddenly came through, asking me to wake up and listen to him, which of course I did instantly. He told me that the man I had just spoken with—let's call him Bob, was his (Elvis') "spiritual brother." He wanted me to tell Bob this and to also tell him that he (Elvis) would be helping him to overcome his sorrows at this time. That was all.

Bob had not mentioned Elvis to me nor I to him. I had no hint as to whether or not he might be receptive to such a message from 'Elvis Presley.' When I gave Bob Elvis' message to him in person, tears came to his eyes. He was visibly shaken. He had to sit down and compose himself for a moment and then told me that he had always had a special feeling for Elvis. Bob's brother died around the same time as Elvis, and as he traveled through driving rain in Kentucky during that period, Elvis' song 'Kentucky Rain' was playing on the radio. His music helped Bob make his journey home to his brother's funeral, as Elvis' music was playing much of the time on the radio during those days in August of 1977, near the time of his death.

When Bob drove through a rainstorm in Kentucky years later, 'Kentucky Rain' again guided him. Several years later, Bob had a relationship with a woman who gradually became more and more obsessed with Elvis. She was emotionally unstable and created a dark fantasy around Elvis. She would constantly compare Bob to Elvis, telling him how he failed to measure up to Elvis in every way. For a while Bob endured, but finally he ended the relationship. He told me, "I feel I owe Elvis an apology." Bob had allowed his experience with the disturbed young woman to embitter him toward the man he once loved as a "spiritual brother." He became almost ill when he would even hear his music.

Now, as I revealed Elvis' message to him, it was as if a dam burst for Bob. Later he would confide in me that because of Elvis' message and his help, he was now able to think about and release much of the sadness in his life. He has not entirely rid himself of the many sorrows he experienced, but is able to open the wounds and work with emotions that were too painful for him to confront before. He no longer feels resentment toward Elvis and has begun to play his music again. Bob told me he is a singer and songwriter himself and also a serious student of the same karate that Elvis practiced - in fact, the 'lineage'[1] of his teacher is through Ed Parker, Elvis' first karate teacher!

Many of the letters Wanda June Hill has received in response to her two books on Elvis have been from those who knew him, most of them briefly, and yet he seemed to enter their lives when he was most needed. Several of the women who wrote to Wanda stated that Elvis had "saved their lives." He touched them in a way that reversed their destructive life-pattern. Such is the power of true spiritual, cosmic love. One of these letters to Wanda was so moving and relative to the message of this book, permission was given for it to be quoted in part here.

Elvis' Compassion for all People

In 1974, this woman whom we shall call Sarah was invited by one of the men working for Elvis to a party after one of Elvis' performances. Elvis was not present at the gathering, but asleep in one of the adjacent rooms. Sarah, as she explains in her letter, was extremely overweight and unattractive. She was eager to please those whom she considered to be Elvis' friends, and to be as popular as her slim-figured girlfriends. The only way she was allowed to come with her attractive friends to the party was as a joke. She was to dress in a hippopotamus suit with a pig face mask.[2] It was degrading to her of course but she so wanted to be accepted and to possibly get to meet Elvis, so she agreed.

> As Sarah tells it… "Elvis wasn't at the party but was asleep in the next rooms. The party was wild and there was sex and drugs and I was drinking and doing things to get laughs and wearing the pig mask. Things were loud and Elvis woke. He opened the door and saw me on the table half-naked and dancing in a hippo suit and the men cheering at me—everyone doing wild things. He was standing there staring, disgust on his face."

At this moment, Sarah relates, several of the men present did something especially insulting to her—nothing I wish to print in this book.

> When Elvis saw this he, "Stormed up, jerked them away and pulled me off the table, cussed his men and took me to his rooms. He wiped my face—it was smeared and I was so ugly and fat, and he was so kind and he talked to me for so long. He put me in the shower and I was so miserable and sick too from drinking and pills and Elvis had to hold me up and got wet too. He bathed me and then he was helping me to bed and he got in and held me in his arms and talked and I finally stopped crying and he was so sweet and he told me how important I was and that I was worthy of life and love. I'd get it all together if I changed my lifestyle. He kissed me when I cried again.
>
> "Elvis was so sweet and good and he made me feel like a really pretty woman. I mean I was 187 pounds

> and five feet tall and ugly, stringy hair. He said I was beautiful and that I made him feel very male, very sexy. He had a lady do my hair and make me up and he whistled when he saw the change. He held me on his lap which was a feat as I was so fat, and he talked and talked."

He began to tell Sarah about Biblical figures, and how much adversity they faced, yet they overcame all obstacles with God's help, and that all God's children were beautiful.

> Sarah continued, "Elvis wouldn't let the guys take me home. He wouldn't let me leave for two days until I was over the drugs. He was afraid I'd be depressed and that I'd kill myself as I said I was going to do. Elvis made sure I was okay and then he said he wanted to hear from me now and then and made me promise to diet and keep in touch. I was so in debt to him. I did diet for Elvis. I got a job, I got an apartment and I kept in touch for a long time, then they'd not let me talk to him. And he was so sick. I knew it wasn't drugs. Elvis would not do that—he was too smart, too good.
>
> "Elvis told me I was God's child, beautiful, made in His image, and that's what I believe forever. I love Elvis Presley. I'll always love him and one day I'll see him again in Heaven. I'll always remember him, his smile and his kindness to me, a low-life girl, used and dirty as I was. Elvis gave me my life. He was wonderful in every way a man should be. God smiled on me when Elvis opened that door. And God used him to reach me. I know that and someday I will tell Elvis that also."

This is but one of many stories relating Elvis' personal service to individuals who so needed a saving grace in their lives at the moment

Elvis 'opened the door' for them. As to the reason why he endured the kind of men in his employment who taunted and degraded Sarah, I refer the reader to the upcoming Chapter 15—Shadows. Through no direct personal fault of his own, Elvis had become more than just a prisoner of his fame, but also a physical captive of those who desired the power Elvis had over people—a power the dark ones continually seek but can never control—the power of light and love.

Italian Woman's Vision Restored

A news article of March 1986, told the poignant story of Rosa D' Angelo, whose home in her native country Italy had burned down three years before. Rosa had rushed into her flaming home to save her Elvis records. She had been successful, but at great cost. Cinders fell into her eyes, blinding her with resultant scar tissue.

> The article states that, "After the fire, Rosa had her children play these records for her daily, claiming she always found comfort in the sound of the King's voice. 'He was like a god to me,' said Rosa. 'I believed he could do anything and when I heard his voice, it elevated me to such a high spiritual plane, I felt sure I was floating among the angels.' In her prayers, Rosa called upon Elvis as an intermediary for healing. 'I know he heard what I was saying,' she insists. 'Sometimes I even felt his Spirit beside me in the bed.' Rosa says a cool, misty breeze would gently blow over her as she lay in her bed. 'Then I would hear his voice call me by name. He would tell me not to worry, that I would soon be fine.'
>
> "Rosa adds even in her blindness, she could see Elvis' ghostly image floating over her bed. 'I would feel his hands on my face, and I saw tears falling from his eyes as he gently kissed my own eyes.' His spirit visited me almost every night for two years. Then, on

> one of his visits, he told me soon I would no longer need him. I opened my eyes to beg him to return, and saw a blur of colors.
>
> "It took a few seconds, but gradually the room came into focus. 'On my dresser I saw the photograph of Elvis I had kept since childhood. All my records were neatly stacked beside the phonograph, and there were the pictures of my husband and sons,' Rosa exclaims. 'I started screaming for my family to come quickly. I kept yelling that I could finally see again.' At first, my family thought I was having a breakdown of some sort. I grabbed a book and began reading it to them,' she declares. 'Then they believed me.' Rosa says she knows it was the Spirit of Elvis that restored her vision."

Whether it was the image of Elvis in Rosa's mind that made her faith strong enough to heal herself, or Elvis' Spirit did truly touch her need with the ability souls in Spirit have to awaken the human element to wholeness, Elvis would be pleased to know her sight was restored through his presence in Rosa's heart. Being able to heal by 'laying on of hands' as the Master Jesus did, was always a gift Elvis sought to give.

One last story which demonstrates the lengths to which Elvis was prepared to go to serve his fellow man. Certainly the saving of a human life in a time of dire emergency can be classified as an act of healing, for it matters not whether it is the Spirit, the body or the potential trauma that has been healed. The following is from an article concerning Elvis coming to the aid of a young pregnant woman and her child in a most dramatic way.

Elvis Rescues Family from Fire

In this article, a witness to the event recalled seeing an auto crash. The Pinto car burst into flames. The people nearby stood there in shock, no one making a move to rescue the woman and infant daughter in the vehicle. An eye witness remembers...

> "Suddenly, a man, who I later found out was Elvis, came speeding up to the fiery crash. He leaped out of the car and immediately ran towards the burning wreck. He yelled for someone to help him yank the door open but everyone just froze and started to run the other way because they knew the car was going to explode. I don't know how he did it, but he ripped the door right off the hinges by himself and dragged the woman out of the burning vehicle.
>
> "She was only semi-conscious and obviously in shock, yet she kept screaming, 'My baby, where's my baby?' Elvis instinctively knew what she was talking about and raced back to the car and leaped inside, emerging a few seconds later with the child in his arms. Just as he got several feet away from the car, there was a second, more violent explosion and the whole car was destroyed. The impact was so great that it knocked Elvis down. But he acted like nothing had happened. He just jumped up and started mouth to mouth resuscitation of the child who had stopped breathing. About 30 seconds later, the baby began coughing and a doctor in the neighborhood took over.
>
> "It turned out both the woman who was pregnant and the child, suffered bruises a few broken bones and burns, but were fine after hospital treatment. The unborn infant was unharmed. Elvis was bleeding and burned on a part of his hand and arm but he insisted he'd have it treated later. All he cared about was the condition of the mother and child. I heard from a nurse friend that Elvis visited the mother and child

> every day for a week and after he found out that the woman's husband was a liquor store employee who was killed in a holdup two months earlier and that she had no money, he insisted on paying the entire hospital bill and even bought her a brand new car. He didn't have any ulterior motive. In fact, after that week was over, neither the mother nor daughter ever saw him again."

When it comes to utilizing our God-given gifts to restore wholeness in mind, body and Spirit, we are but 'babes in arms.' We are only now beginning to move beyond self-imposed limitations to see our own power. Jesus knew this when he told an ailing world that the 'miracles' He performed were but a natural inheritance of our spiritual beingness. The way He had put it was, "All this ye can do, and more, if ye but believe." Elvis believed!

Elvis The Bridge

> "I like to think of myself as a bridge on which people can travel and leave their troubles behind" ~ Elvis Presley

Chapter 10: THE TRICKSTER

Elvis on Laughter

> Elvis' drummer in the 1970's, Ronnie Tutt:, exclaimed about Elvis, "He loved to laugh—had a great sense of humor—you could see his eyes sparkle when something funny was going on—was most of the time, if he had anything to do with it. It was great to play music together, but it was also great to laugh together."
>
> Elvis: "It's pure freedom, like being a kid again."

This chapter is named 'The Trickster' after the mythic being who brings individuals into greater knowledge of their inner self and the intricate workings of subtle worlds through humor, revealing that while one should always take Spirit seriously, the ego self can only evolve through seeing the 'lighter' side of the struggle. Native Americans present the Trickster in the form of a Coyote who leads people to find themselves through the unexpected. Only by remaining open to the humor of the moment, can they hope to receive the true message of Spirit the Coyote has to offer them.

The Trickster is also represented esoterically by 'The Magician' archetype. One of the paths that lead to spiritual enlightenment is humor. To relate to the Magician we must embrace humor both as a power that can liberate us from the shackles of limitation and despair, and its inverse or shadow side which is that of the malicious prankster. Through the Magician Archetype we can learn to laugh freely at ourselves, rather than maliciously at others in an attempt to make ourselves feel better about who we are at another person's expense.

Elvis loved to shake up people's illusions of him in a playful way. There was never any malice connected to his pranks, only an impish Spirit. He was a man of contrasting mood who could be very mature, intelligent and serious in his deep understanding of Spirit and Life. Yet, in order to remain sane in the atmosphere which had collected around his 'image,' he sought relief through humor. I believe unconsciously he wielded it as a means of teaching others the true joy in living.

Larry Strickland, former base singer with the 'Stamps' Quartet, who sang as backup with Elvis in the 1970's, commented in 'Elvis International Forum' on Elvis' marvelous sense of humor by telling a humorous story of how one night they were all jamming and telling each other about Roadrunner cartoons they had seen. Larry relates how Elvis was actually lying on the floor and laughing so hard he was holding his sides. He was on the floor right next to piano player Tony Brown whose mouth was literally hanging open in disbelief at what he was witnessing!

> John Lennon: "It was his sense of humor that stuck in my mind. He liked to laugh and make others laugh, too."

The 'Trickster' in Elvis was revealed on many occasions. When he performed in Las Vegas, he would often have a few people up to his suite after the show. Some were other entertainers, but often they were simple people, mostly women from the lobby that his employees chose to bring up for their own diversions. Nothing wild went on in Elvis' suite however, he would not have permitted it. In fact, he would not allow women to even lie down on the couch if tired or sleepy. He would tell them that if they were fatigued, they should go home[1]. When he would come into the suite, all eyes would be upon him and all conversation would instantly stop. If he smiled, they smiled. All present duplicated his every mood or inclination.

Elvis' Practical Jokes

One evening Elvis decided to shake them up a bit. He dressed in his finest and fanciest clothes. He looked great. He strolled into the suite of those waiting to gaze upon him, and began to make a little speech. According to a photographer named Sean Shaver,[2] Elvis told his guests, "I thank all of you for coming here." He went on to say that he loved performing and his fans. He gave them a very serious dissertation on how the Elvis on stage was not who he was behind the scenes, saying he just liked to be himself. He mentioned the fancy clothes he wore on stage and how he preferred casual attire when off-stage.

The people in the room were trying hard to conceal their puzzlement and uneasiness, as the Elvis standing before them was dazzling in black leather pants and a multi-colored soft leather jacket with two-foot fringe hanging down the seam and the back of the arms. His jewelry included a heavy gold cross containing seven or eight green emeralds, accompanied by two smaller necklaces.

> Elvis continued speaking to them, "When I'm on stage I'm a performer. When I'm off stage I am who I am. I hope that you all will not be disappointed when you see the real Elvis." At this point, Elvis gave the people in the room one of his brilliant smiles. This was the 'punch line' to his speech. Every other tooth appeared to be missing. He had blacked them out, so that his usually sexy smile more resembled

> Lucille Ball in her 'Hobo' routine. Amazingly, no one reacted, other than to all smile back. Elvis blinked in disbelief. When he left the suite that night, he shook his head in defeat, as his gag had most definitely backfired. But then, Elvis often laughed the hardest when the joke was on him."

Another tale told by Sean was the wild bus ride Elvis gave his base singer, J. D. Sumner. Not long before Elvis' death, J.D. and his quartet 'The Stamps,' had purchased a state of the art bus for their tours. It was large, comfortable, and full of all the amenities of home. While playing back-up for Elvis in Las Vegas, J.D. proudly gave him a tour of the bus. After he had walked through it, Elvis very politely asked the base singer if he would let him drive it for a short spin. J.D., anxious for Elvis to receive the 'full treatment' the bus could offer, agreed. So with Elvis at the wheel, the two of them set out on what the lead Stamps member expected to be a nice little drive around the block. But in just a few moments, J.D. realized it was to be far from a peaceful journey.

Once out of town, as Sean Shaver writes, "Elvis cranked the wheel... drove completely off the road. The bus was bouncing up and down... Elvis was flopping up and down... laughing like a kid." All the while J. D. was praying for a miracle to save his brand new $125,000 bus. Finally, J.D. could contain himself no longer and yelled, "God damn it Elvis you're tearing up the bus!" To which a still laughing Elvis' replied, 'Hell J.D., so what? If I do, I'll buy you another one—just hang on!'" As Sean describes the next series of events, "Elvis tried to cut a donut... he was unable to get the bus to slide sideways... hit the ditch at an angle, and the bus leapt onto the paved road in a cloud of dust. Elvis was yelling and screaming..." After they were once again on the highway, Elvis drove the bus back to the hotel parking lot like a little old lady on a Sunday drive. As he turned off the engine, he looked into the ashen face of his friend and broke into fits of laughter again.

I remember seeing Elvis in 1970 perform 'You've Lost That Loving Feeling.' He would begin the song with his back to the audience and a single spotlight on the back of his head and shoulders. When the music built to a certain point, he would swing around in a dramatic and graceful flourish. It was always a heart stopping moment in the performance. However, Elvis became bored with that routine and decided to add a bit of fun to it, so the next time he sang the song and swirled around amidst a timpani of drums and horns, he looked somewhat different. The audience gasped. Could it be that he had suddenly grown a beard—all over his face? It took people a few moments to realize that Elvis was wearing a gorilla mask!

Elvis loved to play with his audiences. One incident which exemplifies this was his water pistol skirmish with several members of the audience. The fans knew Elvis loved water pistols. As a result, some fans had brought fully loaded squirt guns to the show, and were shooting at each other occasionally in the front rows.

Then the moment came when they handed Elvis a water pistol of his own. He couldn't have been more delighted. His friend Ed Parker described the scene in his book, 'Inside Elvis,' by stating that when Elvis got his water pistol he started playing too by shooting water at J.D Sumner and Charlie Hodge and then the audience! This was when pandemonium pursued and a whole bunch of people began getting into the act with their own water pistols. They were all shooting at Elvis now! By time it was over Elvis was soaked, but he and everyone else were totally delighted! This endeared Elvis to his fans, made him like one of them.

Wanda June Hill also recalled a close encounter with an aquatically armed and dangerous Elvis when she worked in the MGM mail-room in the 1960's. Elvis came in with a water pistol and decided that Wanda made an easy target. As she later wrote about the incident in her book, 'We Remember, Elvis':

> "He took aim and fired a blast in my face. I stared at him, shocked and then, without thinking who he was, I picked up

a paper cup with melting ice from a Coke and tossed it in his direction. It got him, right in the chest, and splattered up his face. The look on that face would have been worth millions on film! He was stunned and speechless. For a few seconds I thought surely he would kill me, as his expression changed from shock to surprise, then anger.

"Then he slowly relaxed and his handsome face began to smile. He tossed back his head and laughed. Then, brushing off the ice and slowly raising his water pistol, feet spread apart, hip out, he turned slightly and with the meanest and most deadly look I've ever seen he drew aim at my heart and fired his water pistol. Well, it was nearly empty and the stream sort of dribbled at me. That was too much; we fell all over the office laughing. Elvis went off to refill and I went back to work, wet, but totally sure Elvis was something else—just what, I hadn't yet decided."

Wanda June Hill in 'We Remember, Elvis'; "One day while I was staying at the Hilton Hotel (in the 1970's), I was outside for some fresh air when I noticed a group of people staring up at the top of the hotel. Curious, I walked over and looked up. Sailing through the air were several little paper airplanes, and way up on the 30th floor was a tiny figure of a man, waving to us below. It was Elvis, curing his boredom flying paper airplanes and watching the people running after them—after all Elvis Presley had touched them! What I did not know was that he also put messages on the airplanes, written in baby talk, and he laughed as the people found them and read his messages while he was observing through his binoculars. It was just silly Elvis putting people on again!"

Wanda tells about the time a female Hollywood reporter[3] was determined to get into Elvis' suite in the Las Vegas Hilton to spy on the 'wild parties' she had heard (and hoped) he was having. She disguised herself, as that was the only way she would have been allowed in. However, Elvis knew she was coming…

> "Well, Elvis had a great sense of humor and when he learned of her plan he had an idea. He hired some Las Vegas girls to come over and had them dress or undress for various roles. He also warned friends who were at the party. When the reporter, in disguise, arrived at his suite, Elvis staggered from his bedroom with a naked woman hanging onto him. He pushed her away, staggered to the coffee table, and said, 'clear off the table; who's up next?' and he grabbed the reporter. She was horrified (or pretended to be) and told him off. Elvis couldn't keep a straight face. He cracked up. The whole room exploded in laughter."

I personally remember Elvis in 1975 on stage in Las Vegas, holding an enormous gold fish bowl filled with slips of paper. He informed us that the names to many of his songs were in the bowl. They had been collected from the audience before the show. He was going to sing a few of them, by drawing the song names out of the bowl at random. He went through a whole discourse about how he was going to sing whatever song was revealed on the slip of paper that he would draw from the bowl, as these were the songs his fans desired to hear.

The audience was in suspense as Elvis reached into the bowl and carefully swirled his hand around. He paused then moved his hand around some more. Finally, he drew out a piece of paper. Everyone was quiet, as Elvis stood there with the big glass bowl encircled in one arm, and holding the tiny bit of paper in the other hand. He stared down at the paper as he read to himself in deep concentration. The fans bent slightly forward in their seats. Then Elvis frowned. Without even looking up at the audience, he threw the slip of paper over his shoulder and thrust his hand back into the bowl. He came up with another slip, only to shake his head and toss it away, too. After several attempts, Elvis finally found a song he wanted to sing.

The audience chuckled as if they were one large entity, at this display of 'pure Elvis.'

Once in the 1970's, Elvis became self-absorbed with his own rendering of the story of Jesus in the Garden of Gethsemane. It was in the early 1970's in Elvis' Palm Springs home. Elvis stood in front of a large picture window with the mountains and valley in the distance, perfectly complimenting his own natural beauty. As usual, he was regally dressed, but holding an 18th century walking stick which he would use to punctuate his talk.

His friend Charlie Hodge documented Elvis' telling of the sacred story in his book, 'Me 'n' Elvis.' Charlie tells this great story of how Elvis told the story of the events in the Garden of Gethsemane where Jesus was betrayed by Judas. Elvis got very animated while telling this story in an almost comical way. He was waving a large jeweled cane about like some kind of biblical prophet or something. He ordered some men out when they began laughing uncontrollably. At the very end of Elvis' rendering of this Bible story Charlie relates that Elvis says:

> "'And Jesus was dead right,' he said. 'It wasn't another fifteen minutes before a bunch of Roman soldiers with torches marched in with Judas and they got his ass.'"

All was perfectly quiet in the room. No one dared to laugh. That night, Elvis noticed Charlie and some of the others acting funny, so he pressed them about it. Finally they told him the words that he had used in his rendition of the Bible story. Charlie wrote about what happened next:

> "...he (Elvis) slapped his forehead with an open palm and gasped, 'Oh, my sweet Lord!' Then he went outside and fell in the grass and lay there laughing, looking up at the desert stars."

The Phantom of Hill House

During Elvis' lifetime, Wanda June Hill was awakened one morning by a loud pounding on the wall right next to her side of the bed—it was three distinct thumps, as if a man were banging his fist against the wall with all his strength. She bolted up in the bed and heard Elvis' voice say, "Wanda, Wanda!" Her little poodle screeched and ran under the bed. Wanda got out of bed, wrote down the time, which was 3:15 A.M., and then retired again.

Later that morning at 7 A.M. she woke to the ringing of the telephone. Upon answering it, she heard Elvis' voice on the other end say simply "3:15 A.M.," and laugh wickedly. He had told her previously that someday he would transfer his energy to her at a distance, and so he did. He planned it at a precise time, proving to her that it was indeed him. Apparently he had 'seen' her reaction and her poor little dog's fright. He found it amusing that he had scared the daylights out of them both!

Elvis and the Key Chain Gang

Wanda told me that most of the people who contributed to her book, 'We Remember, Elvis,' were her friends because of Elvis, as he personally brought them into her life. This was also true of several other friends who did not contribute to the book. As an example, she told me about two ladies, whom I shall call here Nancy and Jo. Elvis was looking through a free paper carrying advertisements of all kinds, when he came across their ad for 'Elvis Key Chains.'

He called them, saying his name was Walter Goolick, the name of his character in the motion picture Kid Galahad.[4] He asked about the key chains, also wanting to know a lot about them as individuals, which frightened Nancy and Jo, as they suspected him to be working for Colonel Parker, who might put them in the slammer for infringing on Elvis' paraphernalia merchandising rights. 'Walter' told Nancy that he would send a woman by to pick up some samples for him and then he would call them back the next day.

Wanda's next door neighbor was on Elvis' phone list, as when Wanda first moved there she didn't have a telephone, so Elvis called her at her neighbor's house, then he paid to have a telephone installed at Wanda's, and paid all the phone bills on it for one year—including those calls he charged on her line himself. Since Wanda had been gone when Elvis called her to ask her to be his messenger for the key chains, he left this request of her with her neighbor. All the message said was for her to go to a certain address in her county and pick up sample key chains which she was to deliver to the home of one of Elvis' other friends.

So Wanda drove seventeen miles to get to Nancy's house, and found the two ladies poised to greet her, pale and wary. They handed her a big jar of key chains, which were really high-quality and attractive, etched in metal. Wanda told them that 'he'—she didn't know whether he had told them he was Elvis or what pseudonym he had used—only wanted a sample, but they insisted that she take the whole jarful! It was then that one of them mentioned his name was Walter.

Elvis did call Nancy back the next day and talked to her about his hometown Memphis, chatting about a lot of different things—still calling himself 'Walter.' Then he asked for some more key chains. She inquired of him as to what he did with all these key chains, and he replied, "Oh, I give them to friends." She said, "Well, they are $2.50 apiece." Elvis replied, "Oh, I thought you gave them to me—I would be happy to pay for them." At this point, it finally clicked in Nancy's head and she asked, "Are you Elvis Presley?" To which he responded, "Yes Ma'am." Elvis continued to call these two women, and so did Wanda. As a result, they all became friends. For Elvis Presley, this was one of the few ways he had to reach out to normal people for friendship, and he did it in a typical Elvis way.

Here is a great section entitled 'Elvis' Great Escape' as an excerpt from 'The Interview' portion of 'We Remember, Elvis,' the revised edition by Wanda June Hill:

"During the first two years Elvis played Vegas he was more accessible to his fans in various ways. He would go into the ladies powder room and flirt, kiss and talk with the women who were totally stunned. And he went door to door on a couple of hotel floors near the one he was staying on (the penthouse was unfinished at the time) going in and talking with surprised guests and inviting people up where he held court behind a roped off section near his bedroom door. He loved meeting the people—and it showed. I remember the time Elvis "escaped" in 1970 from that hotel "birdcage in the sky" as he called it then, bringing a friend he called "Bill" from his onstage group with him, knocked on our hotel door several floors down from his penthouse suite and practically carried one of my women friends in with him so quickly did he come through the door she had opened.

"We were totally surprised, in our night clothing and waiting for him to call the room, because he said he would after his last show. He told Bill to watch the door; this would just take a few minutes, and then winking at us said, "Thought there was going to be three women here?" I said, yes, one went downstairs. He looked at the two beds and said, "We better get to it—don't have much time!' And he quickly unfastened his belt (like the red one with the chains on it but this one was white and blue), and dropped it on the floor and then made as to undo his pants. Bill's face turned dark red; he stared at Elvis with bugged eyes and then turned away and sat down facing the door with an, 'Oh God, what am I doing here!' look on his face.

"Elvis struggled to keep a straight face and failed, breaking into giggles. He sat on the first bed, my friend nearly jumped over it to get pillows off the other bed for him to lean back against. He accepted her help graciously, murmuring, 'Thank you dear, that's nice.' Then with his long legs stretched out on the bed, he leaned back and asked questions—how'd we like the show, what else had we seen in town and so on. I remember how fire seemed to blaze from his eyes; he was still 'on' from doing the show, was still sweating and kept wiping his face on the towel he wore draped around his shoulders. one foot keeping a beat all its own and he laughed joyously as my friend, who was hugging his belt kept exclaiming she couldn't believe Elvis Presley was right here!

"Finally he said, 'I don't believe it either, an' we got to go, 'fore they call out the police to find me!' He kissed her bye, put on his belt and then turned to me. I had put some big rollers in the front of my hair earlier but removed them when he showed up. He put his fingers in my hair and gently pulled the curls loose and grinned that grin before kissing me on the forehead. He said 'Bye, bye ladies' and left in a rush, after 'Bill' who had recovered from Elvis' joke, checked the hall for any search party. They went down the fire stairs Elvis told me later, and then took the elevator up and when he came off the guys were forming search parties. He told them he had to take a leak and all the bathrooms were bein' used—what the hell is the fuss about? Not long after those days, his 'escape door' was locked to 'protect' him but really, so that he couldn't sneak out again."

In the 1970's, Elvis frequently performed at the Las Vegas Hilton. The showroom was gaudily decorated with plaster cherubs which Elvis called, "fat, funky angels," and statues of men and women in renaissance garb, dancing what appeared to be the minuet. Elvis thought the whole display to be quite tasteless. Having had his fill of it, one night he and a few of his employees snuck into the showroom with flashlights and a can of black paint.

Elvis stood on the shoulders of one of his men, painting furiously while he snickered, wobbled and laughed. In the morning, the hotel staff was aghast to see a white gentleman in powdered wig and lace, dancing with a striking black female bearing a powdered bouffant hairdo. That night during his show, Elvis watched the reaction of the audience, as he gave a sly look to his Afro-American back-up singers, the Sweet Inspirations, who were laughing heartily at Elvis' attempt to integrate history.

At his homes in both Memphis and Los Angeles, Elvis spent time with his fans who would gather near the gates. With the younger girls, he would often talk seriously with them in regard to continuing their schooling and other topics. But he would also have fun teasing and joking with them. Gate fan Sue Wiegert recalled in her book, 'Elvis—For the Good Times,' how Elvis would stop to talk to them and often displayed his crazy and humorous side.

She tells the story of how he talked about his miniature horse named Geesh that had green stripes in his rear end as he played with his fans! When he was on stage performing, especially in the 'cozier' setting of the Las Vegas Hilton, Elvis would frequently continue his 'stories.' Sue Wiegert also recounted in her book how Elvis told his audience a funny story about a harelip squirrel while pantomiming the behavior of the squirrel. This totally cracked his fans up and they loved him all the more for it!

Wanda: (late 1970's) "…just don't forget, I will listen to you when no one else will. And I'll try not to beat your wings down, okay?"

> Elvis: "Deal." (A thoughtful silence for a few seconds as we both had turned serious all at once.) "Honey?" (questioning, warm voice)

Wanda: "Yeah?"

> Elvis: "How 'bout comin' up 'n stayin' with me? Since we understand each other so well, we'd get it on good too, huh?" (dead serious, but I KNOW he's teasing)

Wanda: "WHAT? Elvis you had better be kidding!" (I know he is, but I play along)

> Elvis: (laughter) "Hey, had you goin' a minute, didn't I? Man, you sounded funny—it was worth it for that!"

Wanda: "Oh, you think you're such a hot number Elvis Presley! I thought maybe—(he's still laughing) Now, you listen to me! I thought you'd finally flipped your lid!"

> Elvis: "Sure you did! I bet you got chills 'n a flippy heart at the thought, huh?"

Wanda: "Bull! You must be kidding! I was worried about your mind, that's all! For heaven's sake, I know you'd never consider such a thing, so you had to be losing your paltry brain!"

> Elvis: "Paltry? That's a new one! Oh, you're funny, it was worth it—damn, it was!"

Wanda: "Boy, you must've had your Cheerios this morning. I'm glad you can laugh about something, even if it was dumb."

It is ironic that in much of the media coverage of Elvis, most especially the screenplays, and the derogatory books written on him, he is depicted as a brooding figure shut away from the world in his own deep misery. It's understandable that a man who was terminally ill for many years, who had a difficult marriage with a heartbreaking ending, and who was threatened and held captive against his will,[5] would have more than a few moments of depression. But for the most part, despite his extreme hardships, Elvis was a man of joy and laughter no matter how bleak the picture of his life seemed to be. He would not allow such dark presences to smother the candle that burned so brightly within him.

His defiance of such destructive powers was most exquisitely evidenced in the force of his laughter. It was a clarion call to arms against the tides of tyranny. True to his nature, even at the very end of Elvis' life the Trickster still prevailed, as he deprived death of its dark grip upon his soul. He was for the most part happy and cheerful that last day in full knowledge that it was indeed his last, not because of any thoughts to end his life with suicide as has been suggested because of his precognitive knowledge of impending death, but because he chose to accept that which he knew spiritually in his heart, as God's call to greater works to be accomplished.

He laughed in the face of death in order to move forward unflinchingly, much as he had laughed in the face of death to save the mother and child from the burning vehicle[6.] Elvis viewed all of life and death as part of one continuous cycle whose individual parts would dance in the shadows with each other, the part in the light always laughing at the part in the dark. Elvis' laughter still rings through the hearts of all those who heard it and, if Einstein is correct,[7] it rings throughout the universe and always will.

Chapter 11: MUSIC OF THE SPHERES

Songwriter Mae Axton, who wrote one of Elvis' biggest hit songs, 'Heartbreak Hotel,' once stated that Elvis "thought God had a purpose for him." She related further that, "He believed that purpose was to let music be completely universal. He combined the music of a little bit of everything and I think this exemplifies his caring about people of the world."

Elvis never limited his music. He was, without question, the most versatile singer who ever lived. Aside from exploring the many facets of American culture with his song, during his career he sang in German, Italian, Spanish, and even a bit in Chinese. He not only sang in these languages, but his accent and feel for the language and culture in which he sang was native to that nationality. Writer Nick Cohn spoke about Elvis' musical versatility in a 1975 article where he stated, "Somehow, he seemed to have the ability to assimilate everything, draw it deep down inside himself until it became his own... he sucked in sounds and became a sort of musical kaleidoscope."

Ironically, the man who was known as the King of Rock'n'Roll performed very few true 'rock' numbers. Rock, like its progenitor rhythm and blues, is generally not accepted in modern spiritual, metaphysical, or as they are so often called, 'New Age' circles. Rock, jazz, and most up-beat music is considered, at the very worst, detrimental to spiritual flow and, at best, not as conducive to enlightenment as classical music and the other slower, sequentially ordered and melodic musical styles. The assumption is often quite true. Yet some of this music which is outcast by the New Agers is very much a part of the Music of the Spheres* and the driving pulses of the universe and should not be omitted from the initiatory phases of spiritual development.

In order to fully understand how music affects our spiritual-cosmic journey, let us begin with the song of the atom. I am going to get somewhat technical for a bit here, but please bear with me as I believe you will glean something from this discussion, even if you don't completely understand it all. According to *my inner mystical sources*, each particle within an atom emits a sound whose harmonics are determined by the distribution of its mass. The larger the particle, the more internal sub-particles it contains, which in turn each contain sub-systems of particles and so on, down to the smallest unit.

Each of these particles within an atom, each proton, electron, neutron, and their subsequent subatomic particles emits a sound[1] that is one harmonic of the sound emitted by the entire mass of that atom. As particles join to form atoms, and atoms join to form molecules, the harmonic sounds join together and increase the complexity of the overall sound emitted by the atom or molecule. This can be compared to many voices coming together to form a choir, and then many choirs coming together to form a grand symphony of sound.

The ancient pre-Pythagorean* study of this Music of the Spheres was known as the science of atonic harmonies in the pre-historic[2] cultures of Lemuria*, and also later in Atlantis* and Egypt. The word aton (atonic) can be translated in its most basic frame of reference as the Holy Tone*.[3] Light and sound were interchangeable types of energy to the ancients, the term aton referred to light as well as sound, but qualified as light becoming sound.[4.] Stars are far more musical than planets due to the fact that the level of their atomic energy activity is greater.[5] However, planets in their various sound harmonics, give stability and direction to the musical dance of the stars.[6]

The ancient study of atonic harmonics is extremely complex. In order for me to explain its workings in relation to Elvis and his music, I must of necessity address only the basics in a simplified approach. There are two basic patterns within atonic harmonics; 1) 'singular escalation,' which is a more or less unbroken escalation of sound vibration producing fluidity, evident in semi-classical, classical, and most New Age music, and 2) 'synquaser rhythms' in which the driving pulse that can cause subatomic stimulation of matter is evidenced. The primal force of synquaser rhythms is orchestrated in R&B, rock, country and other up-beat music. Many tend to associate primal force with disorganization and chaos, and therefore assume that it's non enlightening and even degenerating to spiritual progression.

According to *my inner mystical sources* this is untrue. Pure primal drive is at the fountainhead of creation[7] and is essential to the journey of our spiritual Selves. Much of the great classical music, while it is predominantly singular escalation, also contains the driving pulse of synquaser rhythms. The only problem with primal force is that it is very easily violated. Its structure is not complex enough to maintain an ordered state if its energy field is tampered with and weakened. Weakened energy fields produced by singular escalation type harmonics will release their force through random activity. Yet this type of violation does not occur naturally. It takes sentient minds, such as human consciousness, to interfere with the volatile purity of primal energy. What we are really addressing here is karma* (also known as sin in the Christian traditions). Karma is the interfering factor in the universe and it affects the most sacred purities which are to be found in the beginnings of Creation, herein also referred to as the primal force.

Returning more directly now to music, many of the up-beat styles in varying degrees, are violating primal force harmonics, and therefore produce decay, decadence and chaos in varying stages, dependent upon the degree of weakening the energy fields have experienced at the hands of the humans making the music. These violations interrupt the cyclic exchanges of harmonious musical tone. The violated and incomplete musical cycles leak energy, eventually de-vitalizing and weakening the listener also cause psychic numbing of the body's energy centers, called chakras*, to occur. There is no denying that primal force, and consequentially its atonic harmonics in a pure undefiled state, are stimulating.

Elvis and Synquaser Rhythms

Were the universe devoid of stimulation there would be no existence, and certainly no cosmic consciousness either, since all higher thought and awareness of the divine, is revealed to humans via a stimulation of the higher senses. On Earth at this time, there is singular escalation type music imbued with synquaser rhythms that comes close to the actual universal type driving pulses of the sounds that stars emit. However, much of this depends upon the proper orchestrating of these up-beat melodies, and the delivery of them by the musical artist(s). This brings us back to Elvis and his masterful execution of a music that contains synqusar rhythms.

Elvis' mission in light was communicated through his music with not only his beautiful voice but also his empowerment of the mastery of balance. This combination enabled him to synergize the singular escalation and synquasar rhythms of the energy universe without violating the primal force. His music was free of negative karma[8] in its later development (1969-1977). It was also of the divine dimensions of reality relating to the spiritual hierarchy*. The divine beings such as Archangels and Angels exist within the stellar bodies in another dimension somewhat higher in energy vibration than ours. These beings are referred to by *my inner mystical sources* as the 'Living Lights.' Elvis' later performances were imbued with the atonic harmonic splendor of these Angelic Living Lights, ascending beyond the trivial pursuits of this earthly world into the dominion of the heavenly hosts.

An Elvis fan named Virginia Kelly once stated, "I've never heard such a spiritual sound coming from anyone; it was the sweetest most beautiful singing in the world."

In a message I received from *my inner mystical sources*, I wrote:

> "Elvis was essential in establishing upon this planet, a blending of the root synquaser sound with a tempered classical issue, producing a sound different from and of greater hierarchical (angelic) quality than either parent sound. He brought about, through this merging, an amalgam unique to Earth. This new pattern was taken from combinations of the quaking star symphonies—the Music of the Spheres produced by numerous star sounds combined—which had been unheard even by the ancients of Earth. As a fiery comet, Elvis presented the Earth with a musical birth which shall continue to manifest into the Golden Dawn[8]. It is a vital translation of power for the Earth's ultimate transition.
>
> "Elvis Aaron arrived as the musical priest—a master of the Holy Tone. As Elvis progressed his musical art (from the more basic energy incantations of the 1950's to the rhythmic classical anthems he produced in the 1970's) he brought a greater dimension to his musical consciousness, releasing through his talent a measure of this consciousness to mankind. Within the last eight years of his life he entered into the Golden Section (spiritual maturation) of his priesthood, gathering deeper into the wellspring of unheard musical scales and bringing balance to

> the synergistic potential of singular escalation and synquaser harmony combinations on Earth."

Elvis was not merely the singer of these symphonies. He created the combinations of music as well. To this, he added the cosmic dance. He was the Star Dancer.

Elvis' Music Stirs the Chakras

In his book 'Inside Elvis,' close friend Ed Parker shared that Elvis not only had a vivid imagination but "...was also endowed with a rare gift, the ability to hear sounds individually or collectively in harmony in his head..." Ed goes on to relate how Elvis could just lie there and hear all these musical arrangements in his head then go make improvements on them as he wished in order to make his next performance even better. Glenn D. Hardin, Elvis' pianist in the 1970's spoke of how Elvis always really made things happen for them. Glenn relates how Elvis could completely change an entire show with nothing more than a glance towards his musicians. "You kept your eyes on him or you fell off a fast moving train." Glenn said he had never felt more alive than when he was with Elvis.

Elvis had studied the revelations on music, color and light by Rudolph Steiner, Corinne Heline and other esoteric authors. He quoted Pythagoras, and one of his most treasured books was Manly P. Hall's 'The Secret Teachings Of All Ages.' Mr. Hall, a renowned metaphysician, requested to meet Elvis, as he considered him a unique spiritual teacher in his own right. When listening to Elvis' live recording of 'Polk Salad Annie,' one can imagine the primal stirrings of giant suns and mystical quasars sending sonic challenges of their dominion, like humpback whales, chorusing through the celestial sea. *My inner mystical sources* comment on Elvis' liberation of the human energy centers—also known as chakras in the Eastern spiritual traditions:

> "In coordination with his music, Elvis affected the cosmic dance. In the early stages of his performing

career Elvis elicited a loosening of energy fields normally held tightly about the solar plexus, which have become constricted through the centuries in the human body. Others followed his expression, some none too adeptly, but the ultimate result was a cultural, mystical release of the solar[10] force within the human energy body.

"As Elvis' abilities matured, he brought the cosmic vital energy movement upward into the chest cavity and the arms and head. Once freed from immobility, the solar plexus generated an expansion of new impulses to the seat of the soul—crown chakra at the top of the head—and to its attending energy centers or chakras of the upper torso. It was intended that Elvis open his soul for all to see.

"Consequently, his auric energy field was loosely bound like a child's, so that the Light of his soul could be seen more prominently than it is in most adults. While this was not uncommon to the highly developed first humans on Earth, it is a rarity in the present age. It is true that certain negative impressions arose from the karma others attached to the initial musical 'revolution' (more aptly evolution) Elvis began.

"In an imperfectly structured world, all positive outputs affecting the masses must displace the inertia of decay and chaos. This process of displacement includes the stirring of the karmic kettle, bringing the dregs up from the murky bottom. These karmic forces must act out their roles in the scheme of things. Eventually, the water clears so that the true form may emerge victorious."

Elvis' Thoughts on Music 1973

From a taped lecture with Elvis on music he played in 1973 at a jam session in Memphis, Tennessee:

> "Music is the universal language, appealing to all races, creeds and cultures. Even the deaf can respond to music in feeling vibrations of the notes. It can soothe, arouse, or just relax one to a state of getting things done. It brings harmony to the senses and this is why some of the more energetic forms of musical compositions can be harmful to the senses.
>
> "Those discordant notes and vibrations that are not harmonious together, now being put into 'music' can make one have ill feeling, headaches, and in general be confused emotionally. Some Rock'n'Roll is like that. It is too bad, because it will give Rock'n'Roll a bad name, bringing those people some worked so hard to convince, back into thinking of it as evil and harmful, which it can be when used wrongly.
>
> "What I do, the kind of music I like to perform, is not disharmonic, it is soothing or stimulating as I wish it to be. I try to give them what they came for, in a musical sense. Most of the time I can, but on occasions when I find it impossible to reach them, to respond because of some disharmony, perhaps in the building or the location, or even the people present, it drains me instead of giving me the necessary drive…
>
> "I can't overcome certain negative forces… then I feel so bad that I haven't been able to give them anything. I guess that I have to have those occasions or I might get so swell-headed I'd have a time wearing my hats."
>
> *He then laughs, winks and leaves the room.*

In her book 'Elvis & Gladys,' Elaine Dundy discusses Elvis' impact musically on the minds and hearts of the billions of people his sound absorbed into its rhythms. She speaks to the power Elvis' music had to literally embed itself within all of these people as if each one had another record being played inside them. Elaine relates how Elvis used his perfect voice in combination with Gospel music as a celebration of God that conveyed his own beliefs to all who listened. She further expounds that Elvis combined both an explosive power and a tenderness that resulted in sheer ecstasy which could lift the suffering of others.

> A Baptist Minister once stated that, "Like most black people in the South and in whose soul God has pressed down a harp of a thousand strings, it only needed tuning. Elvis' voice was that kind of voice that agreed with a thought of Calvary. He was a bundle of energy set to music, and that echo will never die."
>
> Elvis stated that "Gospel music is the purest thing there is on this Earth."

Elvis Records his Music in Other Languages

Elvis also felt a close bond with Latin-Americans and Jews. He loved Spanish music and recorded songs in that language, as well as in Italian, German and even Chinese! His accent and feel of these languages, especially Spanish and Italian, was near perfect. Elvis saw to it that both a cross and a Star of David[11] were placed on his mother's tombstone.

It was true that Elvis Presley incorporated all the people of the world not only into his music, but into the recesses of his heart as well. Gregory Sandows, a professor of music at Colombia University once said of Elvis' voice that it stood up well classically. He noted the vast range of his voice and suggested he might be considered a "lyric baritone with exceptionally high notes and unexpectedly rich low ones." Sandows then goes on to explain that what was important about Elvis Presley's voice was not just an impressive vocal range (2½ octaves), "But where its center of gravity is. By that measure, Elvis Presley was very nearly all at once a tenor, a baritone and a bass—the most unusual voice I've ever heard."

Elvis' Spiritual Music and Dance

As a student of the deeper esoteric mysteries, Elvis purposefully employed Corinne Helene's[12] understanding of music in his performances. In other words, in his 1968-1977 live performances, he consciously used his music to awaken the true spiritual heart in the listeners. If the spiritual heart can be stirred and awakened in individuals, then they will begin a greater questing for their true spiritual purpose for being alive. All the while he kept control of these audiences in that he never allowed the power of the dynamic he had created to unleash a 'beast.' His whole purpose of performing in this manner was to infuse the individuals in the audience with a spiritual impression of their own limitless being.

He worked selflessly—never for the greater glory of Elvis. True, in the early 1950's he had the power on a more instinctive level, and didn't yet know how to control it, but then he was only 19 years old. He learned quickly, and utilized what he learned for the benefit of humanity. His on stage dance movements in the 1970's were a combination of martial arts and obvious (to me) sacred dance of ancient cultures, most especially Lemurian. In 1972, I put together a book which I handed him from the stage, in which I identified many of these specific stances and motions for him (using photos of his performances). There are only two copies of this book—Elvis had one and I the other.

Employing a combination of his movements, his 2½-octave voice, and his marvelous choirs of gospel and opera voices—black and white, male and female—with a full orchestra, Elvis re-created the harmonies of the perpetual choirs of the past. Something he had accomplished in several previous lifetimes as well. In Spirit and in reality, he created with his music—most especially his on-stage 1970's music—a sacred geometry of sound, a living cathedral of spatial energies. Through this living cathedral induced by the vibrations of Elvis' sound, Spirit was able to move into matter, and matter thus actuated was able to release its inherent Spirit for all to experience.

From the song 'The Legend of a King,' by L.W. and D.W. Jacks.

> "And as tears give way to memorial, and memorials to life times, the scattered sons and daughters we've yet to spawn will sit still in the panoramic temples and speak with awe of the man, the legend, who changed it all.
>
> "And I'd like to think when I look up at the stars, in the times I have left to ponder, that all the music he ever made still moves, still echoes somewhere out yonder."

Chapter 12: THE ELYSIAN SONG

Corinne Heline writes in her, 'New Age Bible Interpretations, Vol. V,' about the role of teachers and angels and how they guide and test their aspirants. She indicates that the aspirant will "undergo many trials wherein his strength, will power and perseverance are tested." Heline goes on to state how if the aspirant passes the tests and trials then he will be rewarded, "as his Spirit is bathed in Elysian air… companioned by angelic beings of transcendent beauty and splendor." Surely, by Corinne Heline's definition, Elvis Presley's life was an initiation of the 'Elysian Song'.[1] He underwent "many trials wherein his strength, will power and perseverance" were "tested to the utmost."

The Child Elvis Talks to Jesus

As a child he was visited by Heavenly Beings who showed him his destiny, and told him that they would be with him until he no longer had need of them. Elvis' Aunt Lorene was once noted as having recalled a very young Elvis when she related that: "On one occasion when we missed him and finally he came down out of the pasture and said he had been talking to Jesus. He had tears running down his little cheeks."

Tupelo Neighbor Remembers Little Elvis

Mary L. Jones was seventy-four when Wanda June Hill visited her in 1979. Mrs. Jones held dear to her heart the memories of an Elvis no journalist could have invented. She is a simple woman, with simple memories of a young boy, bared by poverty not of his making, struck to the bone by the cruelty of a time and place far from his true spiritual home. Mary lived near Elvis and his parents in Tupelo, Mississippi—next to the same one room dwelling in which Elvis had been born and over which the strange blue light shown on the night of Elvis' birth, lighting his father's way to the well.

Later, she then moved into Memphis as did Elvis and his family when he was thirteen. Mary shared with Wanda her recollections of Elvis as he was then and also the tragedy in which he lived in that past time, when Elvis Presley the singer was still only a dream, a faint song in a lonely boy's heart. Mary Jones sat in her rocking chair, spitting tobacco into a nearby pint jar, as she unrolled the canvas of her memories, and painted a tender yet graphic story for Wanda on that rainy day in 1979. The following is Wanda June Hill's condensation of Mary Jones' conversation with her:

> "Mary knew Elvis from his birth. Elvis adored his mother, cried after her and always obeyed her. He was very small, thin and sickly and he had fevers and colds often, and very bad coughs every winter. Mary would worry about it, give him medicine she had for her own kids and gave him hot drinks and food. Elvis was so polite often he wouldn't take it or anything until he had asked his mother.
>
> "When he was three he nearly died from fever, he was paralyzed and couldn't breathe and Gladys (Elvis' mother) was beside herself. There was no money for a doctor and Vernon (Elvis' father) was out of town looking for work. An old black woman took Elvis, wrapped him in hot towels and kept him alive. She breathed into his lungs for him (artificial mouth to mouth resuscitation) and then when his fever cooled she

began putting him in tubs of warm water, making him move his legs and arms and taught him to walk again.

"Gladys was working in the cotton field and left Elvis with the black ladies who watched the little kids. Elvis ran around all day naked, brown as the Negro babies he played with while his mother worked. The black woman would put him in the pot they had washed clothes in just before Gladys came in, then they dressed him and he was spiffy for his momma, come evening time. Elvis was the favorite of the black women, they held him, played with him and cuddled him all day and he got stronger and stronger and was happy that summer. Mary said (speaking about Elvis), 'He was such a sweet boy, so good-hearted and kind and was especially nice to old people and kids and needy people.' Mary's son was killed in Korea. Elvis had followed him about and worshiped him as he grew up in Tupelo.

"When her son died, Elvis was a singer and doing well. He heard about it and came to visit her. He brought her $500 in cash and gave her a $400 check to buy her son a tombstone. He brought her a bouquet of red roses, sat in her house and cried over her son, told her how much he had thought of him and how he loved her and felt close to them all these years. He said when he left that he thought she could use a new roof. The next day roofers came, put one on, then painted her house and put down new carpet.

"Elvis used to sneak off (as a small boy) from home to go to a creek that had a small cove with still water and he went there to pray and to talk to Jesus, he said. He also said he talked to the 'angels' on the water and they sang to him. He told his mother when she came and caught him, and she said he was evil, doing evil things and whipped him. She also spanked his hands with a board once because he was 'using devil sign language' (hand signals of some kind). Elvis was small, yet he didn't cry even though she hit his hands until they were bright red.

"He told her when she started crying, 'It's okay Momma, you don't understand, it's okay.' Then he cried too and hugged her. Elvis also liked to sit in the moonlight and stare at the sky, but when asked what he was doing he would say, 'getting moon beams in my heart' and said he could hear music in the heavens—beautiful singing, angels on high (*Author: the Elysian Song?*). His mother told him never to tell people because they would say he was evil, crazy, and lock him up. And his grandmother said Gladys often washed his mouth with soap when he did talk about hearing voices and seeing things. So Elvis learned to keep quiet and only told a few who understood about people with 'the gift' as Mary called it. Elvis, she said, had 'the gift' and had it in abundance. She told him to treasure it, that it was God talking to him.

"He hugged her and said, 'Thank you Mrs. Jones, I know.' He'd say to her, 'Someday, I'm going to tell people all about God and they'll listen to me! I'm going to make them listen to me all over the world!' And they did—he reached the world with his singing gospel. Mary said that when Elvis was about twelve he was crying and she asked him what was wrong. He said, 'Mrs. Jones, I got nobody to talk to and I need to so bad.' She said to him. 'Talk to your Momma,' and he said, 'Mrs. Jones, my momma don't understand—I can't explain—she just gets upset and I can't upset her with this. I got nobody and I'm scared that no one will ever understand. Do you know, Mrs. Jones, what it is to be all alone in a place that is not ever going to be your home? I am going to be there—and I got nobody to understand.' And he cried until he shook."

Gladys and Vernon Presley

> Elvis' mother, Gladys Love Presley was quoted as saying, "Elvis (as a child) would hear us worrying about our debts, being out of work and sickness and so on. He would say 'Don't you worry none. When I grow up, I'm going to buy you a house and pay everything you owe at the grocery store, and get two Cadillacs; one for you and Daddy and one for me.' Little as he was, the way he'd look up at me, holding onto my skirt... you know I'd believe him."

In a January 1978 interview with 'Good Housekeeping' magazine, Elvis' father Vernon Presley spoke of his son, and the insight he had concerning him by saying:

> "I believe Elvis' career and contribution to the world were fated from the first. For during his early life, certain things happened which convinced me that God had given my wife and me a very special child for whom he had very special plans. Gladys and I were so proud of Elvis and enjoyed him so much that we immediately wanted more children. But, for reasons no doctor could understand, we had none... When Elvis was about 10 years old, the reason was revealed very clearly to me in a way I can't explain. I can only say that God spoke to my heart and told me that Elvis was the only child we'd ever have and the only child we'd ever need.
>
> "Elvis was a special gift who would fill our lives completely. As soon as I realized that Elvis was meant to be an only child, I felt as though a burden was lifted. I never again wondered why we didn't have additional sons and daughters."

During his son's life, Vernon had difficulty accepting Elvis' spiritual beliefs, and yet after Elvis' death, he came to acknowledge what he had really known all along what had been whispered into his inner mind about this 'very special child.'

Ted Harrison, from 'Elvis People, the Cult of the King,' related that Elvis believed in UFOs and read a lot about esoteric matters including such topics as the lost continent of Atlantis and beings that have visited us from the planet Venus that were from a brotherhood of very advanced beings.

Elvis and the White Brotherhood

Larry Geller, in his book, 'If I Can Dream,' related that, "Elvis believed that he was working under the aegis of these masters—the White Brotherhood, meaning of white light, not the white race[2]—including Jesus." Larry goes on to explain how Elvis felt connected to these Masters and that they were in some way helping him. Larry goes on to explain that, "In Elvis' mind, his life was being directed divinely by the brotherhood… enlightened entities that have existed since time immemorial."

The following dialogue was transcribed from a telephone conversation between Wanda June Hill and Elvis in 1973:

Wanda: "You look like your father's side of the family—and your mother's also—they are all nice looking people."

> Elvis: "Yeah—you know, I look like my people. We all look pretty much the same, straight nose and all, and we are blonde. I don't like being blonde—I wanted to be different. It fits this incarnation—fits what I am here on Earth—to be dark (haired), I mean."

Wanda: "You mean your former life?"

> Elvis: "My former entity—my home out there—where I am from."

Wanda: "How did, I mean, when did you figure out that you are from out there, as you say?"

Elvis: "When I was about ten they told me."

Wanda: "Who?"

Elvis: "The two men who talked to me—have talked to me since I was five when they first presented themselves to me and said, 'I am that I am and you are you—we will be with you, as your Lord is with you until you have no need of us again.' And they showed themselves to me—as light forms, and one of them touched me and I felt light inside me—floating sort of. And the other one said when he put his hands on my head, "You are now and you will be for all time." I didn't understand then—I was scared, but they said not to be and told me to speak of it to no one. But I told my mother and (he laughs) she washed my mouth out with soap and spanked me for making up things and lying. So I never told her anymore about them."

Wanda: "How often did they talk to you? Just when you were alone?"

Elvis: "At night—when I was alone and sometimes when I was in the - the closet."

Wanda: "The closet?"

Elvis: "Yeah—hiding or-or being punished or something—you know."

Wanda: "So you heard voices—what did they tell you?"

Elvis: "Nothing—just to listen. They played music for me, showed me things—instruments like in sounds, and they told me about my home and who I used to be and still am—and that I would-

would-would be a great person in this life—and they showed me a guy dancing, kind of, on stage under lights dressed in-in white, with colors all around, and they said-said to learn. I didn't know what he was doing—the man, you know, but then I later saw karate and I knew immediately then—it was me—they had showed me the future."

Wanda: "What else—what did they tell you about?"

Elvis: "Oh, many, many things. Most of it too far over my head—I was just little—but it made a deep impression. I had dreams—dreams about being on stage and singing—but I didn't realize it was me—it was like I was seeing a silent movie. And..."

Wanda: "You mean no sound? No music?"

Elvis: "No-no at first none, then they talked to me, told me to listen hard—in a quiet place to listen. And so I got so I listened to everything—music especially. I loved the way-way it made me feel inside—so-so good. I don't know the words to-to ever tell anyone about it. It is like unto a great sense of-of soaring, of freedom and a-a rushing of my-my emotions through something that-that sort of (is) like being cleansed. I can't tell you—it's a feeling.

"But I can tell you it is the best feeling I have ever had that was mine alone, a personal feeling not shared with another—not like sex—I'm not talking about that kind of emotional feeling; though I would liken it to that in intensity. But it is better-better! It's divine, celestial, Godly, I don't know the words. Sometimes I feel so stupid—they are right there, and I don't know them! In fact, the English language is so-so lacking in expression, all of them (languages) are as a matter of fact. It's—this is silly, I know, but sometimes I feel like I could talk, speak, whatever, in some other tongue, but I am not sure what it is. You know? It's like, I know it, but I don't consciously know it or something. Like maybe, I used to, but have forgotten."[3]

Wanda: "Did the men who talked to you speak it?"

Elvis: "I-I-don't-know. Maybe they did and I heard it in English? Hell, I don't know."

Wanda: "When did you start hearing music? Were you on stage in dream then?"

Elvis: "Oh yeah—it was—it came slowly. Simple at first, then I began, as I listened to the radio and such, to hear more and to put my own ideas together, and I wanted so to have a piano or something—Momma taught me at church and I loved that. So they got me a guitar—it helped, but I heard more complicated things."

Wanda: "How old were you?"

Elvis: "Six or so—yeah, six. Funny, now it all makes sense. I wish they'd talk to me now…"

Wanda: "They don't?"

Elvis: "No—not much—it's not like it was—kinda hard to hear them now—so much is in my head—you know—the music, the noises of the crowd. I can't hardly hear them for it—I can't-can't shut off the noise."

Wanda: "Who else knows about your voices?"

Elvis: "Oh, Charlie—some of the guys—they think I'm crazy though—they—they don't understand—it's way over their heads. They think I'm talking to ghosts or something—they don't-don't have any grasp of it. But that's okay—I don't need them to understand anyway."

Wanda: "You know, you are pretty weird—but I want you to know that it does not seem strange to me, only curious. I've heard voices, seen some strange things and so you seem pretty normal to me."

Elvis: (laughs) "The weird talkin' to the strange, huh?"

Wanda June Hill described to me two photographs of a young Elvis that were shown to her by Mary Jones:

"He was so pathetic looking—so thin, sad-eyed and woeful in all but one. In it he had caught a big fish and he was grinning and his eyes were shining as he held it up so proudly. Vernon stood beside him, so young! He was really slouchy-poor looking. Elvis was standing with his fish, wearing shoes that looked so old—one foot turned on the side as if they hurt his feet and his pants were patched on the knees. His shirt was too big and his hair too short and he had on a hat that was too big, too. But he had the happiest smile and eyes—one of the few pictures of him young that looked happy. She had another of Elvis and her son. Elvis was little, looking up at him adoringly and the young man was giving Elvis a toy pistol which Elvis wore in a holster and belt that was about to fall off his little hips. He was barefoot but there were patches of snow on the ground. The bigger boy had a coat—Elvis had none and was bareheaded. Their old car, a Zephyr Lincoln, sat in the background with a flat tire on the front. It had snow on the window and hood."

Elvis to Wanda: "Sometimes when it's late and I can't get to sleep, or else I've woke up early 'n' everyone's quiet, I lie here thinkin' about before-

before now. It's kinda scary considering, I mean, I wasn't anyone special, just a poor white trash kid with nothin' goin' for him 'n' not much better ahead either. I mean, I wasn't smart! I'm still pretty stupid in many ways. I'm not a brain, hell, I damn near failed in school.

"It's a wonder I graduated—they took pity on me! I was already a year older and behind a grade so-so they passed me on. It sure as hell wasn't 'cause I was smart or anything. And then, what was I doin?' Goin' to 'lectricians school, studyin' to repair appliances and such, 'n deliverin' stuff for a hardware. Man, a real definitive goal in mind!

"But you know, I dreamed. I dreamed of doin' something big. I wasn't sure what—then too, I wanted to sing, get in a gospel group, or somethin,' I really did. I spent every minute in music. I went to every singing I heard about and could reach. I listened to the radio—Momma said, 'Son, you're gonna have to grow yourself some more ears the way you're listening so hard.' She was right. I tried to hear everything—not miss a show. And the-there was the-the feelings I had. I wanted so much to do something big, to have things for us and for the family. It hurt me so to see how some of 'em lived. We were so much better off, even though we didn't have much either.

"We were living like kings in comparison. Really hard to picture—huh? But it's so. Some of my relatives were farmers—most of 'em, really. Sharecroppers and such. You don't get rich farmin' somebody else's fields—not then, not in those times, I mean. My family didn't 'n I don't recall anyone else doin' so either. Back then, to me, doin' well consisted of havin' a roof over my head—that didn't leak! Food on the table three times a day, a car that would run 'n cash enough left over for gasoline 'n maybe a movie on Saturday night. To me, in those, days, wealth meant havin' money left after all that! It's funny, I've never forgotten those days, the feelings and wants from those times. I hope that I never will.

"It keeps my feet on the ground 'n my head out of the clouds. Because when people forget where they came from they also start thinkin' too much of themselves and that's when the trouble begins. You never get so high and mighty, full of self but what you can't get knocked down. It's better to keep a level head about it in the first place.

"I've been doing this (performing) since I was nineteen you know, 'n it's been a trip. Man, it's been something! I wouldn't trade this life for anybody's existence. No one I know man, equals my life. I'd do it all again—there are a few little things I'd do differently, but mostly, I'd do it just the same. (pause—takes a deep breath) Damn, I'm a fool—huh? (laughs, then becomes serious) It was worth it all, every tear, every heartbreak, every fear. It was worth it all."

Elvis and the National Jaycees 1970

In 1970 Elvis was chosen by the National Jaycees Association as one of the ten men in the U.S. whom it considered to be the most outstanding in their field of endeavor for that year. This function was held in Memphis, Tennessee in order for Elvis to be able to attend. He was awarded for his outstanding contributions to the humanities. A visibly shaken Elvis approached the podium with tears glistening from his eyes. He spoke to the assembly:

"I've always been a dreamer. (as a child) I read

> comic books, and I was the hero of the comic books. I saw movies, and I was the hero of the movies. So every dream that I ever dreamed has come true a hundred times. And these gentlemen over here (gesturing to the nine other men chosen by the Jaycees), most of these type people who care, who are dedicated—do you realize that it is not impossible that they might be building the Kingdom of Heaven? It is not too far-fetched from reality. I learned very early in life, that without a song, the day would never end. Without a song, then you don't have a friend. Without a song—so I just keep singing a song. Thank you very much."

Elvis' life in so many ways exemplified the path of a spiritual initiate, as witnessed by the many hardships he endured from a very young age without complaint and with total love in his heart and consequently was graced at key moments in his life with direct experience of the Angels and their Elysian song, which he in turn sang from the depths of his heart to the masses of humanity clamoring for a glimpse of something beyond their mundane existence.

From the song 'The Impossible Dream' sung by Elvis Presley.

> "I know if I'll only be true to this glorious quest, that my heart will lie peaceful and calm when I'm laid to my rest. And the world will be better for this, that one man, scorned and covered with scars, still strove with his last ounce of courage, to reach the unreachable star."

Chapter 13: SIGNS, SYMBOLS & WONDERS

This chapter is oriented towards the metaphysical, spiritual and esoteric meanings of both the obvious and obscure signs, symbols and wonders associated with Elvis, rather than the more traditional interpretations. With these signs, symbols and wonders I offer a further validation to the other-worldly and spiritual nature of Elvis, but leave the final decision as to the meaning of these symbols up to the reader.

> Wanda June Hill, in her letters to me, wrote that, "Elvis—believed for a fact with every bit of sincerity in him, that in past lives he had been different rulers and educators. He said he felt strongly tied to Egypt and always had. Later he was told by the Edgar Cayce[1] people in Virginia Beach, Virginia, that he had been an important personage of that period and was from a town in that life which was later named Memphis, and it was on the Nile River. He felt so tied to Memphis, Tennessee and loved the river.
>
> "Elvis also said that he heard voices from the time he was a baby, telling him things, but his family thought of it as 'evil nature' and so he did not tell them or talk much about it. His mother was the only one who knew and she wasn't too keen

on it either except for the 'pretty things' he told her. He said they told him about space, his 'other life' and gave him the power to go on stage when he was too scared to move on his own.

"When he was very ill a blonde 'Indian-looking' young woman came, stood at the foot of his bed, sprinkled something in the air and chanted over him... it was a vision... his mother thought he was delirious and dreaming. Later (as a man) when he had eye surgery she came again, did the same thing and never spoke to him except mentally... he was afraid I would think he was crazy as did some of his male pals, and was so relieved when I said I didn't doubt it. He thought she was his guardian angel. He had two men who 'talked' to him and who told him 'complicated things,' his words. They 'help me,' he said. They guided my music."

In 1985, I did a past life reading[2] for entertainer Starla Hill, Wanda's daughter, whom Elvis taught to play 'Twinkle, Twinkle, Little Star' on his guitar when she was three years old. In the reading, I came across a life Starla had in Burma. She had been one of several little princesses, whose older princely brother was Elvis' soul in another incarnation. Of his many younger sisters, she had been the closest to him. As a young child this little princess developed a severe ear infection and was close to death. Her brother (Elvis) was moved by Spirit to put his hand on her ailing ear and take the sickness from it. He indeed healed her in that life and she grew into womanhood because of him. After listening to the cassette tape which I sent Starla containing this information, Wanda wrote me the following:

"It blew me away, because it brought back a memory I hadn't thought about—for one thing, I met Elvis through the actress who played the Burmese dancer in 'Girls, Girls, Girls.' But also, the day that Elvis met me in the duck pond across from Knotts Berry Park (in the late 1960's), Starla had been having severe earaches—she had the problem from infancy, and often had tonsillitis with it. I had taken her to a doctor who wanted to remove her tonsils and I refused and took her to another doctor.

"I was telling Elvis of this while Starla was on the Merry-Go-Round because he asked why she was wearing the 'helmet,' he called it. It was a heavy stocking-type hat with ear flaps that covered her ears and tied beneath her chin—I didn't want the air to get into her just healing ears. I told him the reason for it and he said not to let them operate on her, that we needed every organ of our bodies and we should never let them remove them unless it was severe trauma, etc.

"When we took Starla off the Merry-Go-Round after having been on it for thirty or forty minutes, she was angry, refused to talk to him or me and was acting like a brat (she was not quite seven). She stood with her arms folded, her face sullen and her back to us. Elvis walked up behind her, reached down, sort of clapped his hands over her ears, and almost lifted her by the head, it appeared (though he didn't intend to do that—she sort of slumped like she was falling) and at the same time he called her 'little princess' and said some more things to her. As I recall it now, from that time on her ear problems improved and she quit having such severe pain. We often spent the night working with her—but from then on she got over it—could it be history repeating?"

Elvis' Unique Clothes

Wanda wrote me about Elvis' kinship and understanding of certain symbols, and how he employed them consciously in his personal as well as professional life:

"He had them on clothes, on jewelry, on personal things like pens, desk sets, belts; and doodled them off when talking—naturally, as if he had known it all his life. He did not mention it often, unless someone asked then he would explain in great detail, way over the questioner's head, I know. His use of belts, owl buckles—anything that the normal person wouldn't have found or wanted—Elvis wanted it."

Elvis presented all the basic designs for all his on stage costumes to his designer, Bill Belew. They were each a masterpiece of mystical art, reflecting both universal and ancient Earth symbology, sparkling like a tapestry of diamonds in the sky. Clothed in these suits of higher consciousness design, he appeared grand and illuminating, yet as naturally born to them as a Prince of Burma. Elvis' Cherokee Indian blood accentuated his striking features to promote the quality of ancient Light that enhanced his splendor before us. There was no narcissism—only reflections of a greater Light; and there was joy at the sheer pleasure he received from his audience's attunement to what they were seeing and experiencing.

In his book, 'Inside Elvis,' Ed Parker wrote about how Elvis had jumpsuits with pictures and designs of all sorts of things such as animals, birds, artifacts from history and symbols of tribes, cultures, myths and nations and the matching decorative belts Elvis used with these jumpsuits. Ed also mentions the capes Elvis used between 1971-1975, how he would use them with a highly dramatic flair to his spellbound audiences as if he wielded some sort of magical powers—as you have gathered by now, he actually did!

Some of Elvis' most impressive and intricately designed suits included his peacock suit. It had varying shades of blue, a jeweled-feathered design trailing down his pants legs; a fabulous tiger inspired by his martial arts philosophy and the fiery oriental dragon. This also came from the symbology attached to the ancient spiritual concepts embodied in martial arts. One of his suits displayed a modified rainbow in shades of blue, another the entire Aztec calendar in gold upon the front and back of the suit. There was also his American Indian jumpsuit, and one with the symbols of East India upon it.

Ed Parker related that Elvis had a preference for the white

jumpsuits over other colors, he felt the white suits seemed to bring out the magnetic qualities that Elvis had in such abundance. Despite the workmanship of these costumes, in Elvis' case, the suit did not make the man. As Wanda June Hill disclosed…

> "Sean Shaver and others have spoken of this too—Elvis' clothes were so drab and unglorified—when hanging on a hanger the material was even ugly! But when he put them on—WOW! And when he walked on stage, my gosh—his clothes even took on a radiance, 'glory,' as he called it—he shone head to toe and it was not just the lighting! It was from inside him."

The 'glory' Wanda referred to was what he called the radiance he meditated upon, concentrating it about him. His mother, Gladys, taught him the early stages of this when he was small, and he continued to practice it throughout his life. Wanda explained:

> "He told how she (his mother) would hold him up to the mirror, telling him how handsome, strong, talented and intelligent he was and would grow up to be; how he could do anything he wanted to do. He said, 'I sometimes—well, nearly every day, stand before the mirror and stare into my eyes and tell myself—I'm going to stay young, look good and be healthy. And I thank my Father in heaven for helping me do that. Then I pray and ask for things I need. I guess it's kind of silly, but it helps me. I believe it creates the power of faith in me and I can do the things I want.' He said karate gave him the stamina, the inner source of power and self-control and the determination to carry it off. It helped him form his mind and that the image he projected was his 'inner self—the me that wants and needs their love.'"

Charlie Hodge, Elvis' close friend and on-stage assistant once told me that originally Elvis began handing out scarves he wore during the show to fans because they continued to ask for them, but he discovered through an Eastern Master that this was a practice of the High Llamas* in Tibet. They would bless silken scarves and give them to those in need of the blessing. After this, Elvis became more devoted to this practice in his life, and saw to it that his silken scarves were handled by no one before him but Charlie.

Elvis' Special Ring

A long time ago Wanda June Hill was given a very special ring by Elvis which she re-discovered in August, 2006 in her vault. This ring shown below had special meaning and symbology for Elvis.

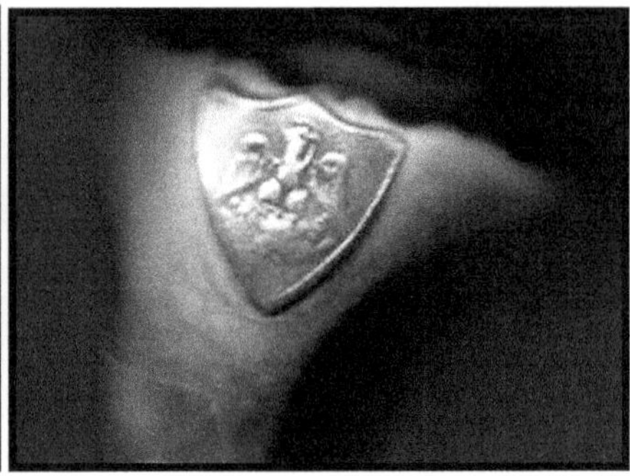

Wanda wrote to me about this ring saying that, "This ring is very heavy, made from metal, not silver, not all gold and seems to be brass and something? It is big. On the sides are shields with the three point top and oval/rounded sides and bottom. On the shields that can still be seen somewhat, it's very well-worn and old, are eagles with the wings spread and the head sideways—they are small and they are standing on big boughs it looks like, though hard to tell it's so worn.

"There is blue inlay of some kind below the bough and rounded areas that seem to be water maybe or perhaps clouds in the sky? Above the eagles head is a curved long vine or something with one arrow head looking leaf at the end? That's on the sides of the ring. The top has a large base that is beveled to look like to me, sun rays all around a center that has a raised bed of what looks like copper, and on top of that is another 'set' that is about ½ inch long and a tad less wide with a cut off top and bottom to the whole thing. I will try to draw a picture of this entire thing.

"In the center of the top setting is some kind of design that has gold set into it or onto it in the very center—when the light or sun hits it is sends a bright light out of it. The top is a rough cross as far as I can tell—it is worn down too and there is behind the cross red color inlay. Across the whole bed is some white inlay that looks like maybe a robe—or part of one—it's worn down too. At the bottom are about 4 curved narrow blue inlays. The entire set, with the color and markings, is edged in gold. Around the under bed is a wreath of leaves that go all around the top setting of metal and colored areas. I can't tell what it is exactly, but I think it has religious meanings in some way—spiritual meanings of some type. The entire thing is strange as it was very old and hand-made; roughly hand-made but extremely well detailed I imagine when new.

"This ring was given to him, he was supposed to give it back when he didn't complete the necessary steps etc., that it took to reach his goal—to be a priest so he could really help people in need of spiritual guidance. This was when he was wearing those big scarves over his shoulders—different colors—white for step one, gold for step two, and there was two more—with the last one to be lavender. I don't know the third now. He gave it up because Priscilla (even though they were separated and divorcing) and his father ridiculed his efforts and desires so much, and convinced him he wasn't able to handle his own problems—how could he even think he could handle anyone else's? Anyway, he felt he couldn't do it—plus he couldn't rid himself of the sleeping pills entirely at that time either. He thought they were wrong for what he wanted to be and do also.

"Anyway this ring was supposed to be more than 100

years old and I believe it—they would not take it back from him because they felt he should have it—he was very moved by that. He didn't tell me much, just that it was old and that it carried within it all the 'saints' who had gone before, given their life for their religious beliefs and to save mankind from evil and that it belonged to the master priest—which he was striving to become one of. They gave it to him at his second ceremony and he was to take full charge of all it meant at the 4th but he never completed the 3 or 4th—and they wouldn't take it back as it 'belonged with him' the head master told him. He ought to have it. But to wear it sparingly as he had not fulfilled his full training and it was 'powerful.'

"He said it was the only one, the original handmade and designed by those who formed the society of the brotherhood. He would not say who, what or where—didn't want to talk about it. I think I have seen pictures of him wearing it—on stage shots—but only a very few times—he gave it to me and said that I should keep it as it was valuable and the spiritual background of it was sacred. He wanted me to keep it, put it away safe and leave it there until I found the right place for it—that it would show me when the time was right. I should never wear it except when I needed to have spiritual strength and understanding as it would 'protect and guide me' and then he said those many spirits from its past—would be there for me.

"Well, as I said, I have been going through things and I had totally and completely forgotten that ring! It was kind of scary to have it, I put it up and forgot about it! Anyway, I have it out now and I thought maybe I can get some photographs of it. I don't have a clue as to what it is on it or what it represents at all. He said it had come from European background and he was looking forward to being 'worthy of it' and I think that is why he quit wearing it—he didn't want to keep it for fear it would 'disappear' or he'd 'lose' it somehow. I think he was afraid someone would take it or discard it because it's not actual gold or white gold—but it does have some on it. That center strip is almost like a lightning bolt but its worn and you can't tell really what it was—but it certainly reflects the light! As does the edging which is very tiny and delicate."

My inner mystical sources also say that Elvis' soul is one of those known as the 'Children of the Sun.' In correlation with this Elvis told Wanda June Hill that he began his career in August, the month of the Sun, recorded his first record at Sun Studios in Memphis, where his first hit was 'I Don't Care If the Sun Don't Shine,' and that he worshiped the Sun in a past life. He continued making comparisons to his life and the Sun. He died in the month of the Sun[3] and the last of his mystic costumes which he wore was the Sundial suit.

Robert Charroux, in his book, 'The Mysteries of the Andes,' writes about some mysterious gold tablets from the Gobi Desert. They were written in an unknown language, had a numerical quality and apparently there was a good translation of it available at one point. "The very thin tablets, bound together by rings, formed a kind of book called Thor Heliohim, or 'Book of the Children of the Sun.' It was confiscated by the Inquisition."

In 'Secret Places of the Lion,' George Hunt Williamson reveals a legacy of Ancient Days when Star People known as the 'Goodly Company' aided (and are still aiding) mankind by incarnating as humans on this planet and working with, inspiring and distributing knowledge to the people of the world. Mr. Williamson uses as references ancient records located in a monastery in the Peruvian Andes. Regarding the entombment of the Egyptian Pharaoh, Tutankhamen.

Mr. Williamson discusses two young men, twin brothers with extraordinary psychic abilities, who served as bodyguards for Tutankhamen. They were, "sons of a great White Magician"[4] who were there to protect the Pharoah as well as various tombs, temples and secret chambers. They used their special psychic abilities to protect these areas by placing a vibrational thought pattern about them which endured long after they left the mortal coil.

Elvis and Jesse Protect the Pharaoh

It was these brothers, so the ancient thought records tell me, that sealed King Tut's tomb with a special magical energy to protect it from wrongful entry[5]. *My inner mystical sources* relate that these two sons of the White Magician were later to incarnate as Elvis Aaron and the near incarnation of his stillborn twin, Jesse Garon. After Elvis' birth, his twin Jesse's soul hovered over him throughout his life, integrating Jesse's energy with Elvis' in order that he be empowered for his special service to a higher degree.

Elvis and I Re-tune the Pyramid of the Sun

Long before I had read 'Secret Places of the Lion' I was instructed by *my inner mystical sources* to go to the pyramid of Teotihuacan in Mexico in 1973, to act as a human energy connector for a re-alignment of Earth and cosmic energies on the planet[6]. I was told there was a small wheel like device implanted within a secret chamber of Teotihuacan's Pyramid of the Sun by a past incarnation of Elvis. This wheel had been inserted for the purpose of helping the Earth maintain a certain balance in energy over a period of time. But in 1973 the wheel needed re-tuning. I was to perform this function in unison with Elvis' live satellite concert in Hawaii, which was to be witnessed by 1.5 billion people throughout the world—it would be shown at a later date on tape to the U.S..

I was told by *my inner mystical sources* that Elvis would be harnessing the raw energies of the masses through his music and performance while being within the relatively neutral energy of Hawaii, while I would be helping to create an attracting type energy within the pyramid in Mexico, which would draw those energies from Hawaii into the Mexican pyramid like a large magnet. I was to arrive at the summit of the Pyramid of the Sun at sunrise on the day of his performance, in January of 1973. For the occasion I wore black, as I had been told by *my inner mystical sources* that I should wear black and that Elvis would be in white, and so it was, I came to find out later.

The use of these two colors was necessary for the proper male-female balance. Elvis represented the Sun or male energy within the Lunar or female energy of Hawaii, and I represented the Moon's feminine power coming through the Sun or male energy of the Pyramid of the Sun. Elvis' suit bore the emblem of the American Eagle in red and blue on the white background—the Eagle of the alchemist* is traditionally known to be the transmuting power of the astrological sign of Scorpio, which symbolizes regeneration and immortality. Elvis' birth sign was in Capricorn, and I am Pisces, the sign of humanity. Capricorn is Earth, Pisces is water, the combined energies of which were used to carry the effect of this whole process through the fire energy of the Pyramid of the Sun.

I do not know how consciously aware Elvis was of this event or how much he knew or felt about his part in it. I suspect now, he knew or at least felt, a great deal. At the time I did not know he was conscious of esoteric and mystical knowledge nor that he actually spoke of his home on the Blue Star to Wanda. At the end of that satellite performance, Elvis tossed his cape into the audience. He had never done this before. When asked why he did it, he only replied, "I had to."

A year later I read a report of an 'invasion' of UFOs occurring on that exact day in January of 1973, in which a fleet formation of UFOs flew over the U.S. coming from the direction of Hawaii, and were joined by a formation fleet of the same type, flying in from the direction of Mexico! I was not surprised considering that it was the 'space brothers' or 'ultra-terrestrials,' as they refer to themselves through telepathic communications with me, who had originally directed my journey to the Pyramid of the Sun.

A spacecraft had even escorted the commercial jets I traveled in to and from Mexico. I had been told in advance they would do this and shortly thereafter the captain of the returning flight called it to the attention of his passengers that an unexplained light was following the airplane—some kind of reflection, he reasoned. There is a pattern of light within all of us, bonding us to our true origin; each family grouping of souls bears the same energy 'signature' or pattern upon them, radiating like a beacon out into the universe. These patterns, varying only slightly among individuals of the same soul groups, are then integrated into our worldly symbols, designs and creations.

Like spiders we weave our webs in the likeness of our inner energy patterns, each silvery thread a collection of distant star memories residing within the subconscious, like a seed awaiting it's time to grow. Elvis passed to Wanda June Hill one such 'star memory,' as she related in her letters to:

> "He gave me a crystal paperweight that has a pyramid on top and is round on the bottom. He had one on his desk that was a pyramid and was more reflective than mine. He told me to keep mine in the (natural) light and it would bring me good luck."
>
> Wanda wrote that when he gave her the crystal, he spoke something to her that was, "like a prayer, he recited it and put his hand over mine as I held the crystal and then put his other hand on top of my head. I felt as if my brain flew out as he lifted his hand above my head."

It wasn't until 1986, when Wanda decided to take some photographs of the crystal Elvis had given her, that she realized the striking comparison between the paperweight and Elvis' description of his home on the "Blue Star Planet." As she peered through the magnifying lens of her camera, she saw the sunlight fill the crystal, as a soul infuses a body with life. It was then she could hear Elvis saying to her of his otherworld home…

> "It had eight sides and eight inner rooms. The floors were

of golden stones, the walls were crystal and many colors. The ceiling was a pyramid."

What she was witnessing through the mystical eye of her camera at that moment was exactly as Elvis had described his star home those years ago! Aside from the physical shape of the crystal being identical to the Blue Star home's geometrics as described by Elvis, viewed under magnification in the natural sunlight, it came alive with the qualities of light and color that completed Elvis' vision of his star palace. It could be pondered as to whether Elvis might have had these two crystal paperweights (hers and his larger version) custom made with that very purpose in mind.

Elvis, the Lightning Bolt and the Unicorn

"The Divine voice shall be struck by heaven."
~ Nostradamus, 15th century

The logo Elvis chose for himself in the early 1970's was the lightning bolt. He added the letters 'TCB'—taking care of business, for himself and his male friends, and 'TLC'—tender loving care, for the women. The lightning bolt and TCB was emblazoned on pendants, rings and the tail of his airplane, the Lisa Marie. It is now on his tombstone as well. From a mystical point of view, his choice of a lightning bolt for his symbol is evidenced as a stroke of destiny.

In the ancient Hebrew Kabbala*, the lightning bolt is seen symbolically as 'the sword of the Spirit.' In the book 'The Secret Tradition in Arthurian Legend' by Gareth Knight, the author relates, "There is a particular glyph related to the Tree of Life (*Author: the Kabbala*) which is known as the Lightning Flash. This concerns the descent of power in the creation of life and it is frequently depicted with a handle, like a sword."

Within the Kaballistic Tree of Life*, there are ten points of Light called the Ten Holy Sephiroth*, connected by twenty-two different lines. These lines are referred to as paths, and together with the ten spheres, they form the thirty-two Paths of Wisdom spoken of in the ancient spiritual traditions. As the individual experientially enters into each sphere with their consciousness, so they encounter a path leading them even further up the Tree of Life. This journey represents the ascent from matter to Spirit, from knowledge to wisdom, from human limitation to God's Grace.

In 'Simplified Magic,' Ted Andrews writes that the interconnecting paths are steps which we take to awakening to a greater realization of the mysteries of the universe and finding our rightful place within it. He relates the unfolding path of realization as, 'Awakening the God-Spark.' Ted Andrews goes on to say that there is a dualism in each of these 10 spheres or Sephira in that they represent both an aspect of the creative Divine Spirit or God, and human consciousness at the same time.

He explains how they represent an unfolding creative process, one flowing into the next that is esoterically known as the 'Path of the Flaming Sword.'[7] The 'Flaming Sword' is seen symbolically in this esoteric reference as a lightning bolt, like Elvis used in conjunction with TCB. Esoterically, the lightning flash is also a symbol for the Divine Word, manifesting into the elements of this world as a spiritual command from upon high.

Subconsciously perhaps humanity recognizes this as evidenced in mundane statements which have been made for time immemorial along the order of, "I came into the realization as if struck by a lightning bolt." In this comparison of the lightning bolt and the Divine Word, the lightning bolt can also be seen as any vocalization of a spiritual nature, which would be demonstrative of one level of the Divine Word being actualized through a human being. Certainly Elvis' singing was from the Spirit, and was a form of vocalization.

This is the strongest link between the lightning bolt and Elvis' true purpose—as an emissary of the Divine Word through his song—the 'lightning strike' of the Divine into our hearts. I believe Nostradamus was correct in calling it a "Divine voice"[8] for Elvis not only influenced an entire world but positively changed it forever, beyond visible cultural patterns and impressions—surely the work of God manifest through him. Long ago, there was a spiritual practice which honored three forms of fire as sacred.

The third type of fire correlates to the lightning bolt as a Divine symbol, it could only be approached in this ancient practice by the most holy of individuals and had been actually lit by lightning. On stormy days they would wait for lightning to strike a tree and they would then run to the site and bring the burning embers back to their sacred temple and kindle them into a flame, which was then maintained with additional fuel for as long as possible, night and day. For each altar they provided such a flame, and it was used to symbolize the link between the flame in the heart of man and the flame in the heart of God.

Another symbolic form of the lightning bolt or flash is seen in the spiraled horn of the Unicorn* as they are mystically known to emit a sacred sound from their horn—again the Divine Word comparison comes into play. If Elvis could be seen symbolized as an animal, I feel this mystical creature would be the most appropriate, for it represents beauty, love, loneliness and sorrow. The Unicorn's attraction to humanity is from the heart, rather than the head. The thought of its very existence, whether one chooses to believe in its physical reality or merely see it as a symbolic virtue, brings us pleasure.

The symbolic depiction of the Unicorn in medieval times was of a creature so loving and of Spirit that it was not able to withstand the harshness of the physical world and thus like Christ, was slain by the hunters who represented the realm of lower desire, lust and greed. As a Capricorn, Elvis is also linked astrologically to the Unicorn. The main purpose of Capricornian energy is to bring the individual born under its sign into illumination or enlightenment.

It must be understood that the there are many different levels to the potential this can represent to different individuals. The Capricornian has three symbolic representations, the first is the goat, the second is the crocodile and the third is the Unicorn. Each of these three representations is actually a phase of spiritual development containing certain tests within each. Skipping the first goat phase because I feel Elvis' soul was beyond that expression, the second two phases are as follows starting with the crocodile phase.

The tests within this phase which an individual must undergo and pass before the greater spiritual blessing of enlightenment may be bestowed upon them are as follows:

1. Conquer lower desires—money, sex and material possessions.
2. Expand their consciousness beyond the personality and learn to include the intuitional realm and live a creative life.
3. Overcome fear and the feeling of loneliness.
4. Conquer pride and worldly ambitions.
5. Develop the spiritual ability to maintain a steady level of contact with higher God based forces.

These five tests were obvious in the unique life of Elvis Presley, and I believe that he passed all of them with the possible exceptions of overcoming the "feeling of loneliness" and the constant maintenance of "spiritual ability to maintain a steady level of contact with higher God based forces." Although, in my perception, under the unusually volatile circumstances of his life he did very well in keeping spiritual channels open to him.

The third phase is represented by the Unicorn, which is the higher representation of the goat, and as previously mentioned these are the symbols for the astrological sign of Capricorn, Elvis' birth sign. The third phase of spiritual development is an initiation always taken symbolically in the 'high mountains.' The energy the Unicorn symbolizes has the ability to climb to the summit pinnacles of experience with determination, and with spiritually aligned willpower the Unicorn (higher representation of a Capricornian) masters the difficulties confronting them.

The horn in the middle of the Unicorn's forehead (remember the lightning bolt comparison) is the symbol of Divine determination, and is comparable to the lifted sword of the spiritual warrior. Once the individual has spiritually formed this sword upon their forehead, their direction is clear. They know their goal now, and no one can cause them to deviate from that goal. In this way the Capricornian—Unicorn phase—transcends and becomes a great spiritual warrior, or a great server of humanity.

The keynote of the Unicorn is incredibly beautiful. They stand on the top of the mountain of their being after the long journey upwards and say, 'Lost am I in light supernal, yet on that light I turn my back.' They do this to serve humanity. This means that instead of leaving this world behind to its misery, in favor of their own receipt of that light, they face toward the need of the world and radiate that supernal light back to help humanity. The mountain is also a symbol of the spiritual Trinity, and only those who have contact with such a source of purity, beauty, and integrity can serve a nation, and serve humanity in a selfless way.

In summary, during the goat phase an individual searches for himself. In the crocodile phase an individual learns to serve groups or nations. But the Unicorn phase brings synthesis, unity, cooperation, rhythm and harmony and stands for the service of humanity. In that service they must renounce all separate interests. This I believe was the phase in which Elvis operated within his Capricornian influence.[9]

One last comment on Elvis' selection of the Lightning Bolt and TCB symbol to lend further credence to the notion that it had a mystical value. 'TCB' in the meta-science of numerology* amounts to a number seven, which is commonly referred to as a 'sacred number,' and is esoterically considered the number of the spiritual temple.

Elvis and UFO's

Returning to the Blue Light which shone over the humble shack of Elvis' birth the night he was born. Elvis' father, Vernon Presley, discussed this phenomenal occurrence with Elvis which was later documented in 'Elvis, a Spiritual Journey' by Jess Stearn and Larry Geller. The authors relate that Vernon confided to Elvis that he had seen a blue light illumining the area around the house the night Elvis was born. Vernon indicated that at the moment he saw the blue light the incessant wind stopped blowing and that was the moment Elvis was born! Vernon and Elvis had together witnessed a UFO over Graceland at one time, and in addition Elvis' favorite color was blue, which he said he often saw in his meditations.

1974—Elvis talking to Wanda June Hill about seeing a UFO in the 1950's while camping:

> "We were off away from the fire (in the desert) and we saw this light in the sky—movin' weird you know—not like a plane or anything like it. And it was different looking than a plane—it got brighter and it was comin' in closer. Hell, it was way up-up there but we could see it on account of the moon and the way it was lit up. It was cigar-shaped, oblong and rounded and had some window portholes on one end and had lights along the bottom, but the damn thing had no wings, no means of bein' up there at all that we could see. Well, we were watchin' it and the guys at camp started hollarin' 'cause they saw it too.
>
> "And then we all ran to each other and got quiet and we heard the sounds it made—it was like electricity, buzzing and metallic sound, not like any engine we ever heard—and then it got kinda over us, still high, mind you, but up there over us. Our hair began to prickle—it stood up on my arms and on my head and I got his weird feeling like I was about to

float any minute. Like when you have two people put their hands over the top of your head and then lift you off the floor and you're real light, go up fast like an elevator—you ever do that?

"Well, I thought they were goin' to take me, man! But we all felt it and then Lamar started groanin' and he fell on his face—man! Flat in the sand on his face! And we all kinda got spooked 'cause he was like dead! He had no heart beat and I started to pound his chest and Jerry was givin' him mouth-to-mouth, you know, and he came around fast—he was yellin' about flyin' saucers takin' him off—but the thing was gone when he came around. We didn't see it leave, but then we stayed up all night lookin' for it.

"We called the base that is not far—Marine base, you know—Air Command post—and they said there was a UFO report but it was nothin'—you know how they are. But man, we saw it! And that's not the first time either—a bunch of us saw one, one night comin' out of the studio. It was right over us—right over LA and big as life—man it was weird. It was round! Like a saucer and that night there were blackouts around the area and across the country. You can't tell me they aren't doin' that—checkin' out how our things work, I mean, they are comin' and God damn I hope I'm here! Man, I want to see one! I want to see 'em up close! Hot damn! That would be a blast! I'm from out there, I told you that."

Wanda: "I know you did—and darn, if I don't believe you!"

These photos are of a page in Elvis' copy of the book 'Strange World' by Frank Edward wherein he made comments in the margins regarding UFOs. Also shown is Elvis' signature that was also written in the book.

STRANGE WORLD

veston hurricane, some fishermen on Prince Edward Island found a huge box, covered with moss and barnacles, floating in the shallows. It contained the coffin and body of Charles Coghlan, including the silver plate which identified him. He had come home at last to the little island three thousand miles from where he had been buried, just as the Gypsy fortune teller had predicted so many years before. Charles Coghlan—brought home by the sea—was finally buried in the cemetery beside the church where he had been baptized sixty-seven years before—one of the strangest true stories on record.

21 UFO OVER HAWAII

When the so-called "flying saucers" were first noted in sizable numbers, back in 1947, their appearances seemed to follow no given pattern. Later, however, studies showed that they were systematically visiting important military bases, industrial centers, and communications centers. The same studies showed that the strange objects, officially known as Unidentified Flying Objects or UFO's, appeared most frequently in the spring and summer in the Northern Hemisphere, and in the balance of the year went to the southern half of the globe when warm weather moved to that area.

In the years of 1960, 1961, and 1962, the strange objects appeared with predictable regularity at the time of satellite launchings. They were on hand when we conducted hydrogen bomb tests in the Pacific in 1962. A group of objects moving in formation followed Captain Joe Walker as he made a test flight in the rocket plane X-15, traveling at several thousand miles an hour high above the atmosphere. Walker's wing cameras photographed the formation and, although the public was told that the things which followed his plane were only gigantic "ice flakes," officials flatly refused to let the public see the films.

About 8 P.M. on the night of March 11, 1963, a glowing circular object was sighted high in the heavens over Hawaii. Hundreds, perhaps thousands, of persons saw the thing

55

Laura Mundo, in her book, 'The Mundo UFO Report,' relates how in 'People Magazine' of September 10th, 1978 the magazine reported thirteen UFO sightings over Elvis' grave at Graceland. Ms. Mundo says there were saucers with orange lights hovering as close as twenty feet over the tomb, shining laser type lights onto the stonework around the grave. This information was given to the magazine by a security guard who wished to remain anonymous for obvious reasons. This guard indicated these UFOs made frequent appearances, usually between 2:00-4:00am.

The security guard also indicated that, on one occasion, there were very strong electrical sounds and energies around as if he were near high tension power lines. He was very frightened and although he was there to make sure nothing happened to the tomb and the body it held, he was unable to even reach for his gun. Shortly after the UFO zoomed off into the clouds, he tried to use his walkie-talkie but it had so much interference on it he couldn't even talk to the guard at the front gate who was still clueless. Just about everyone who worked there had seen these UFOs at one time or another but they were under orders to remain silent.

Three suburban Memphis teenagers, who made constant vigils at Graceland, also claim they saw UFOs there one night. Sixteen year old Sandi Lee Smith related:

> "I like to sneak out in my Mama's car and drive there late at night. The night I saw the UFO I was with my friends Debbie Barnes and Rhonda Flowers. We saw the flying saucer dart down from the sky. There was a strange humming in the air. It was raining. A beam lit up the tomb. I jumped out of the car. The UFO started to go away but it came back and hung around for ten seconds or so before disappearing. We drove to the (front) gate and told the security guard, but he said to get the hell out of there and not tell

> anyone or they would call the police and say we were on pot."

According to Larry Geller, Elvis told his step-brother David that he would not see him again here but in "another time and space" the day of his death. Can we perhaps understand the frequent 'Elvis Sightings' as visitations by an exceptional being who is now in the Spirit world?

In President Bush's 1992 State of the Union Address, when speaking on the influence of America in the world, he commented that during WWII, G.I.s wrote on the walls, "Kilroy was here," but in the Persian Gulf War, they wrote "We've seen Elvis!"

A dramatic report in U.S. papers concerning 'Elvis Sightings' indicated soldiers in the Gulf were saying they had actually seen Elvis. One account was given to commanding officers in the field by several soldiers who together saw Elvis walking toward them in the desert while they were on patrol. They all reported that he was wearing a turban, came within a few feet of them and said, "Everything is going to be alright." Then he disappeared before their eyes.[10]

Chapter 14: NUMBERS, NAMES AND STARS

This chapter discusses etymology*[1] numerology* and astrology* as pertaining to Elvis. Elvis strongly believed in numerology, the science of numbers. He recognized the unity of the universe which is mapped in an interlacing pattern of light, form, space and dimension. The transformative power of this pattern is found in the essence of numbers which reveal the life force within Earth and our human potential.

In mystical circles of thought, there is a whole science devoted to numerology, as with astrology. In fact, the two are linked—in astrology numbers are paramount to figuring the chart, numerology looks at the significance of numbers in their relationship to a more abstract essence—spiritual. Each number has a 'feeling' or characteristic to it, a specific energy vibration or frequency.

Here we see the merging of the more clearly understood realm of numbers, as applied in mathematics, and the less clearly understood realm of emotions, feelings and the higher archetypal* significance of numbers. When I say more or less clearly understood, I am speaking relatively. The minds which are generally considered to be the most functional (i.e. normal) in this world, are those who are able to grasp the day to day functions of numbers and business etc., while those who are equally adept at issues of love, or feelings, are considered to be inadequate in our world if they do not also understand and operate well within the 'normal' modality.

I suggest both are equally important, and one without the other is only a partial picture. We must understand this principle and its implications to us as a race. We can no longer go forward with the perception each of us is a separate island—we must learn to incorporate the best, the shining glory within each of us, in an intricately woven tapestry which, when completed, allows each and every thread to be viewed for its contribution.

Yet all are seen together simultaneously as being infinitely more beautiful than singularly. Elvis came to show us love relates to higher principles. Unfortunately, many humans are too busy to give serious thought to this aspect. He represented the love and feeling side of numbers, the higher archetypes lost to our mechanized goal-oriented world.

With this in mind, let us take a look at Elvis' numerology in order to gain some further insight on the man. If the sciences of numerology or astrology are foreign to you, or you are not quite sure what to make of them, allow this to be an adventure whereby you can explore these realms through Elvis and see if you find any truth in them within your own heart.

Before going into the numerology let's have a brief etymological look at his name. The unusual name Elvis may be derived from the ancient Norse 'Alvis' which means 'all-wise.' In Norse mythology, Alvis was in love with the daughter of the god Thor. Another possible historical source is the Teutonic Elwin, Alwyn or Elvin meaning 'famous, noble or godly friend.'

From another mythological reference it is said to mean 'friend of the elves.' The Biblical Aaron was the older brother of Moses[2].

In Egypt, he was the head of the priesthood and spokesman for his people. Aron is the Hebraic form and may mean 'teaching' or 'mountain' based on various old Hebrew words. In Arabic, it would mean 'messenger.' Elvis' last name Presley is a modern form of the English last name Priestly, meaning a person who lives near the priest's land or woods.

In numerology, the full name of the individual at birth is considered the most accurate in containing the essence of personality and potential of that person.[3] It is because of this that I come to a difficult decision, as although it is purported that on Elvis' birth certificate his middle name is spelled Aaron, he wrote his name as Aron. It was not until shortly before his death that he requested 'Aaron' be written upon his tombstone, and it was. Thus, I feel that both versions of the spelling of his middle name should be regarded as numerologically significant for Elvis A. Presley.

The following is a condensation of the basic numerology of Elvis Aaron Presley, using the interpretations given in the book 'Numerology and the Divine Triangle' by Faith Javane and Dusty Bunker. In this book, the numerics of one's personal make-up are divided into four parts: the Life Lesson number, Soul and Outer Personality numbers, and the Path of Destiny number. Together, they form a picture of the individual's entire personality.

Elvis' life lesson number was nine: this is the number of universal love of humanity and patience, "Someone who is kind and understanding and at the peak of life's expression, who must turn and show others the way." They are well suited for marriage, being strong in passions and compassions. Acquiring money and wealth comes easily for a nine. They are not petty individuals and can deal in broader concepts, usually attaining success despite great difficulties. They very well may become an orator, writer, communicator or statesman, and leadership positions are quite suitable for a nine.

Among other likely careers listed for this number are explorer, magician, narcotics agent, scientist, preacher, doctor, and surgeon.

There are also career possibilities for nines as artists, musicians, lawyers and spiritual healers. It is interesting to note here that Elvis had very much wanted to be a doctor. He bought an entire medical library and studied it extensively. A friend of Elvis' who was a mortician allowed him to watch and study embalming procedures, because of Elvis' acute interest in the medical structure of the human body.

Elvis was also a 'narcotics agent' of sorts. President Nixon assigned a special narcotics agent badge to Elvis in 1970 when Elvis wanted to be of service in fighting drug abuse (see Chapter 15 for more of this story). He was also certainly a musician and a spiritual healer as well (see Chapter 9). A further delineation of Elvis' nine, as reduced from twenty-seven[4] reveals that it is a number of, "Great spiritual strength—just and wise—these persons have a fertile, creative mind and a love of beauty and art. Civilizations are built upon the stuff of which they are made. All business enterprises will succeed beyond expectation. Their influence over others, coupled with an ability to lead, bring them wealth and comfort."

As Aron (vs. Aaron), Elvis' soul number was eleven. Eleven is a 'master number' meaning that it places more demand on the individual, as it is more open to the expression of the soul. A person will fluctuate between the master number and its base digit[5] as it is difficult for an individual to maintain the intensity of a master number. I feel Elvis lived his eleven most of the time and chose Aron which gave him this number (whether consciously or unconsciously) to put himself into circumstances requiring greater mastery over himself and therefore oneness with his soul. Perhaps this is partly the reason he wished to become 'Aaron' again before his death, which would reinstate the soul number of 39 = 3 (i.e. 3 + 9 = 12, then 1 + 2 = 3) expressed as 39/3, allowing for more of a personal self, something he had not experienced much of in his life.

Eleven as a soul number indicates one who has been on a spiritual path for a long time, learning the mysteries of life and death. This is a person with, "Courage, talent and leadership abilities, understanding and often clairvoyant with extremely sensitive ESP abilities and strong spiritual leanings." Three as the soul number for 'Aron' indicates someone whose philosophy in life is the knowledge, "That inspiration and imagination will bring the best results when used to help others."

Love is important to a three. A further delineation of the soul number 39/3 indicates selection of a life of service to others. "They offer love and sympathy in order to help make the world a better place in which to live. They are crusaders who want to feel that the world has benefited because of their sojourn in it—surrounded by friends and loved ones. The love they give is returned abundantly, which fills their cup even fuller, until the love must overspill into the lives of those who are in need—they will communicate this love to all they contact." Since the essence of Aaron as a 39/3 so exemplifies Elvis' personality, and loving, giving nature, he truly did radiate this soul expression as defined by numerology, as well as his more intense master number eleven.

Elvis' outer personality number was a six indicating one who emanates, "A protective vibration and has a sense of responsibility for others." This also represents a personage who draws others to him for counseling, teaching, and healing; an individual with a keen sense of balance who sees all the pieces as, "Separate and yet parts of the whole." The further delineation of Elvis' outer personality number expressed as 42/6 or 4 + 2 = 6 is, "Complete dedication to peace and understanding" would lend to this individual's role as a minister, and he "would be a fine singer—strong, leaning toward the mystical. They see beauty everywhere and should express it in a tangible way for others to enjoy. Their personal charm and pleasure-loving, generous nature draws others to them. They intuitively realize their needs and work to create a happy atmosphere. They need the sociability of friends and would not be happy living alone. They believe in doing the right thing, sharing equally in all relationships and binding contracts."

Elvis' path of destiny number using 'Aron' to determine it was an eight, indicating someone with magnificent courage, who will attain his goals solely through his own efforts. "Recognition, success and wealth are their proper destiny." The further delineation of the 'path of destiny' number, expressed as 80/8 or 8 + 0 = 8, is not covered in the book 'Numerology and the Divine Triangle.' It does not go beyond 78/6, as it paces the Tarot.[6]

However, one could reason that the eight appearing twice would increase the productive power which eight represents, and as such has been given the title of the 'power number.' The influence of the 'Aaron' name was a force present in Elvis' life through his path of destiny number as well. Using 'Aaron' to determine the number we come up with an 81/9 or 8 + 1 = 9. Nine as a path of destiny number indicates that perfection is the goal, but it is not often attainable. The mission this soul has embarked upon is a charitable one. They meet many tests and setbacks, "but the lesson of forgiveness will bring temperance to those situations."

These persons strive to follow the pattern of an ideal life, inspiring others to do the same. "They desire to better the world through philosophy and philanthropy and become impatient when results come too slowly. They will meet many famous people in their lifetime who will be impressed by the breadth of their thinking. They should not cling to old associations. When they have fulfilled their role with an individual, they must move on. They cannot be limited to a small circle of friends. Their broad philosophy must touch and enlighten the lives of many."

Another great individual with a 'path of destiny' as a nine was the cowboy philosopher, Will Rogers. It is interesting that personally, Elvis was unable to break from his "small circle of friends," other than through his phone friends, but through his music he was able to fully accomplish the complete fulfillment his numerological destiny. In summary, *my inner mystical sources* reveal that Elvis was definitely a combination of 'Aron' and 'Aaron' and that these two names together formulated his special ability to encompass the spiritual and emotional needs of so many millions of people. I now move into the 'Stars' or astrology portion of this chapter with a statement on the true purpose of astrology made by Elvis himself.

'Astrology' by Elvis Presley

"It is designed so as to expose the ultimate in height and depth. To relate the strength and weaknesses of those who are willing to accept and are seeking a closer relationship with the divine. In order to recognize and correct one's faults and be in step. To be capable of understanding the necessity of the changing times. To participate, to create, to express, appreciate, and to more fully understand his individual role in reaching the divine God. For man to more fully understand and to determine his own destiny. The realization that divine God is life itself.

"Upon being able to accept one's faults and weaknesses. To correct them in order to have a better understanding and to be capable of giving love and help to other human beings regardless of color or creed. To appreciate all people. The breaking down of barriers and recognizing individual traits. To be sincere in having the desire to show gratitude and appreciation for that which each individual has given to the world. You create a better understanding for yourself of life and the part you yourself and others play in this world. You are soon recognizing a brighter light within yourself. The sharing of that light with others and feeling the importance of stressing and/or distributing the love and will of God. For Christ, who gave life and hope and faith to the millions of people who have accepted His sacrifice and Ray of Life. He taught the love of God and the importance

> of expressing gratitude and respect for the greatest miracle of all—life itself!"

It was my feeling that some of Elvis' astrology information should be included in this book, especially since all previous charts done on him have been computed with his twin brother Jesse's birth time, and not Elvis,' who was born several minutes after Jesse. While to those somewhat unfamiliar with astrology the few minutes' difference might seem a trivial point, astrologically it often is not.

Therefore, based on the birth time Elvis gave Wanda June Hill as the actual moment of his birth, I sent for a computerized natal astrology chart and mini-analysis from Harriet I. Matysko in Brooklyn, N.Y.. When sending for this reading, I did not give Elvis' name, but identified the natal information as "deceased male, born 1/8/35." When I received the natal astrology material on Elvis from Ms. Matysko, she enclosed a personal note to me which read in part as follows:

> "The departed male had a beautiful chart—a glorious blend of fire, earth and water. What a strong and virile, yet gentle soul he must have been. It's sad that someone so young, so good-looking both from the outside as well as the inside should be taken, when there are those far less worthy roaming this Earth."

When I wrote to Ms. Matysko, informing her that the 'deceased male' was Elvis Presley, she replied in a letter to me:

> "When I gave you the interpretation for the deceased male 1/8/35, I had no idea who it was. What I saw and reported to you was the majestical splendor which emanated from the chart—I was saddened to know that the beautiful chart was of a being who no longer spread his graces on this Earth."

The astrology of Elvis Aaron Presley as done by Ms. Matysko (shortened version):

"Born January 8, 1935 at 4:17 AM, Place of Birth; Tupelo, Mississippi, Rising Sign: 8.33 degrees in Sagittarius, Sun: 17.13 degrees in Capricorn, Moon: 1.50 degrees in Pisces, Mercury: 22.17 degrees in Capricorn, Venus: 29.21 degrees in Capricorn, Mars: 12.48 degrees in Libra, Jupiter: 18.01 degrees in Scorpio, Saturn: 25.39 degrees in Aquarius, Uranus: 27.28 degrees in Aries, Neptune: 14.27 degrees in Virgo retrograde, Pluto: 25.04 degrees in Cancer retrograde, N. Node: 1.07 degrees in Aquarius.

"Capricorn is ruled by the planet Saturn, which is really the executive branch of the Zodiac. You're the boss! The Saturn influence will make you an achiever. You will be aspiring, responsible, controlled, practical, patient and just. With the Moon in Pisces your inner feelings and thoughts are expressed in a manner sympathetic, voluble, kindly and extremely receptive to the influence of others. The Pisces Moon makes you feel emotional, intuitional, artistic and often psychic—you make a very good friend and confidant.

"Your emotions can sometimes fluctuate from the ultimate height of happiness down to the depths of despair. However, the strength and stability of the Capricorn Sun is a saving device for you, and your Sagittarius ascendant blends well with your Pisces Moon to give you a harmonious balance. This gives you the combination of strength, magnetism, with a blending of a sympathetic nature, making you an exceptional individual. Your Pisces Moon is in the 3rd house of communications, giving you a strong flair and feelings for communications. You are an effective communicator with the public in written and verbal form. You no doubt can write poetry and

> tender, sensitive writings. The 3rd house Moon would also give you strong feelings for sisters, brothers and nearby relatives."

In 1972, Wanda June Hill attended a Psychic Fair. She could not resist taking along a photograph of Elvis, sealed in an envelope. Without giving any hint as to the identity of the individual whose picture was enclosed, she handed an envelope which could not be seen through, to a psychic reader at the fair. The following is part of this gentlemen's reading on the unseen photo:

> "This is a male—tall, considered above average in appearance or build—some fashion. He is fun-loving, at present his life is in turmoil. There is a separating factor—someone he cared for is gone from his life—taken away by another—I sense divorce. He is serious, a hard worker and takes things very personally at times when he should not. He possibly is a service worker—dealing with the public. I feel he has many followers—perhaps he teaches in some manner—and he is spiritual, gifted in the way he reaches people. He is well-known among many—a writer or communicator.
>
> "He tries too hard to please. I sense that he needs the approval of women to a great extent, and has often compromised his own needs to attain this approval. It must be that he often feels put upon to return affection he would rather not return in order to have this approval. He is lonely and seeking someone—something—no—some person to fill his heart—his life. I sense this man is in deep personal pain—a broken heart perhaps—or dejection at being betrayed by one he trusted implicitly. This man is also facing a change in his life. He will leave this Earth plane

> early in life and he knows it. The first letter of his name is 'E.'"

Not much more needs to be said to anyone remotely familiar with Elvis' life, and the heartbreak of losing his family life with beloved wife Priscilla and his child Lisa. The following is part of a reading and subsequent intensive interpretation done by Edward L. Nowak M.D B.S. entitled, 'The Soul Purpose and Spiritual Goal of Elvis through Esoteric Astrology.'

> "Many of those who beheld Elvis Presley, saw him as 'through a glass darkly.' Yet in all his raiment, glamour and glory, few realized the power of the soul that animated this unequaled and singularly complex being known as Elvis. In this lifetime, Elvis had the opportunity to 'Prepare the Manger' for the coming of the Christ in his own life.
>
> "Whether this would have manifested as a 'born again' experience, or a greater mental awakening, we will never know. If this had happened, Elvis would have been seen as the revealer/teacher, almost 'guru-like' in his aura of power, of a distraught and wayward humanity. His performances could have been the launching pad to bring a more definite and focused message to the world. However, this was not to be.
>
> "In Esoteric Astrology, the tropical natal chart affects only the uninvolved and average individual. When man begins to emerge out of the Great Illusion, the Sidereal Zodiac affects him at a personality level. The Sidereal chart is the personality chart for the evolved soul. Thus the Sidereal ascendant indicates the Soul's purpose for this and the next several lives. It is from this ascendant that the spiritual struggle is entered into. It is then from the ascendant that we can

describe the soul's purpose, its liberation, and how that purpose will activate.

"The ascendant is the indicator of the limits to which one will go in separating themselves from the glamour and illusions of the world, before one turns within and accepts the linkage and union with the rest of humanity. The sign of the ascendant is the force of the soul, and encapsulates the possibilities for this incarnation and the possibilities for spiritual evolution. The Sidereal Zodiac is approximately 24 degrees (of rotation) behind the Tropical Zodiac. Esoterically, the 12 planets in the 12 houses affects the physical plane expression and the personality life.

"Esoterically, the 12 constellations help to stimulate the soul, bringing about interior changes which transform the way one behaves. In the Sidereal chart of Elvis Presley, the ascendant is in Scorpio.[7] It is here that the intense power of Elvis was concentrated. The Scorpio ascendant is the area of greatest temptation and testing as well as providing the greatest opportunity for spiritual progress. Ruled by Mars esoterically, the soul life also receives the energy of Pluto, but on a higher level. This combination not only gave Elvis the drive and power for accomplishment, but also the ability to survive crisis.

"From time to time Elvis was confronted with the weaknesses that arose from his subconscious, and at the same time, given the opportunity to destroy them. This Scorpio energy gave Elvis the ability to draw upon hidden sources of power to attain his goals, and the magnetic power to attract the masses in a way known only by the soul.

"The Soul Purpose as indicated in this particular

chart is shown by the Scorpio ascendant, and the rest upon the 3 major tests of Scorpio; Reorientation to the life of the soul, the readiness for initiation, and sensitivity to the Plan. These are divided into 9 lesser tests of appetite, desire and will; sex, comfort, money, fear, hatred, ambition, pride, separativeness and cruelty. It would be difficult to determine which of these tests Elvis was subjected to at any given time.

"It may be that he touched upon all of these or any combination. Suffice it to say that here is exemplified the 'Crises of the Battlefield' and desire in its many forms must be consciously brought under control of the soul. Every latent pre-disposition, instinct, every unconquered situation and every controlling fault must be tried, tested and overcome. When these are realized and overcome, the result is the establishment of right relations with the soul and the environment.

"Elvis' purpose was to become the spiritual warrior, not only for the self, but for others; to bring before the masses an image that would become not only an enduring role model, but a teaching that would become a foundation for inspirational living. Elvis showed how anyone could rise from their roots to command power and success. The 9 tests of Scorpio can be spread over 9 lifetimes before victory is attained. Archetypically, through the Scorpio energy, we find the comparison of the symbolic struggle of the 8th Labor of Hercules and the life of Elvis to be similar.

"Hercules was sent to battle the 9-headed hydra, symbolizing the 9 tests of the personality life. But with each assault, the hydra grew stronger and for each head that was severed, 2 grew in its place. Hercules was told by his teacher before going into battle that, 'We rise by kneeling, we conquer by surrendering, and by relinquishing we gain.' Hercules was forced to his knees and from that position of humility, lifted the serpent (accumulated evils) into the air (the realm of the soul where the hydra could not live), cut off the Hydra's immortal head and buried it under a rock. Thus was Hercules delivered. Elvis, like Hercules, also had to realize 3 things; to recognize the existence of the Hydra, search patiently for it, and finally destroy it.

"Elvis needed discrimination to recognize its existence, patience to discover its lair, and humility to bring the fragments of the subconscious to the surface and expose them to the light of wisdom. It is possible that Elvis recognized the existence of the 'Hydra' in his own life, but he did not or could not destroy the many 'heads' that kept arising to take the place of the ones he defeated. Humanity witnessed Elvis from the level of the personality life, but the personality rarely cooperates with the requirements of the soul. Thus was Elvis misunderstood.

"There were times when Elvis, having the willingness and courage to be the 'knower,' released the Eagle aspect of Scorpio. He would then become the rescuer of what or who might otherwise be doomed. This gave him the ability to stimulate others to fight back and transform themselves. The Scorpio ascendant is at 14 deg. 43 min. (for all intents and purposes 15 degrees). 15 degrees of any fixed sign is considered one of the 'Points Of Avatar.' These points suggest power over the elements in one form or another or from one level or another. This highly energized point represents the blending of knowledge from the higher realms.

"It pulls the divergent energy from several areas and gives a more precise unification, one that is more applicable to mankind. The power here must be realized from within and used to become free. Elvis pulled in this divergent energy and gave it form for the masses, but he could not free himself enough to become (complete) master of that power. The fixed star Regulus (the 2nd Archangel Star in a prominent position in the chart, known as the 'Star of human glory among its own kind'), is also conjunct the Leo Mid-Heaven and the point of the Yod (see below).

"This means 'The Little King in the Heart of the Lion.' This position is most propitious. Its placement indicates that this individual will be raised to a high position in life far exceeding the environment he was born into. This cosmic connection brought Elvis into the presence of rulers and famous people. Riches, fame and power came to him quite easily.

"From 'An Astrological Mandala,' the 28th deg. of Leo (Mid-Heaven) states, 'A wide, and perhaps confusing, openness to a multiplicity of inspiring potentials. There is a stage in the spiritual life, which is not different from the everyday life, during which the consciousness, aspiring to greater realizations or more impressive forms of self-expression, feels itself flooded with new ideas and new possibilities. This can be very exciting, yet also quite confusing. It becomes necessary to focus oneself by limiting one's field of vision and activity.'

"Elvis was in conflict with himself, and that others near to him were draining him of the power needed to maintain his focused Soul's purpose. He was striving constantly to balance his warring nature, yet always being shown that which needed to be overcome through those around him. It is rare to have all 4 Archangel Stars in prominent positions in a chart (as did Elvis). This would indicate not only the tremendous energy of evolutionary forces that were available to Elvis, but that his soul life plan was divinely guided and protected in ways we may not know or fully realize until a later time.

"It is interesting to note that in Esoteric Astrology, the Sun, Mercury and Vulcan are considered 'one light.' As man evolves, the influence of Mercury as mediator between the soul and personality is no longer needed and its light 'dims,' leaving its influence behind. Vulcan's influence wanes as man develops a relationship between the soul (Vulcan) and Spirit (Sun).

"Both Mercury and Vulcan become 'invisible' until only the Sun remains. The Sun that remains is not the physical Sun, but the Great Central Spiritual Sun*. Elvis' Physical Sun may have dimmed in his last years on the Earth plane, but the power of his Spiritual Sun remains a mighty and shining Star. His method of approaching the spiritual path should have been one of self-control and discipline, thus gaining balance with the warring factions of his nature.

"He was constantly trying to seek explanations for his mental elations or sufferings through those around him. He may have more than once, sacrificed truth for harmony. He sought the eternal truths that would support him inwardly during times of stress. And he was constantly prepared to break down old values and standards and re-assemble them at a higher level of spirituality.

"At times personal difficulties would deplete Elvis

of the strength he needed to maintain his image, yet maintain it he did, Even if it meant sacrificing his entire life. There was a strong need in Elvis to fulfill a 'father' image either personally, publicly or spiritually. Interpersonal relationships are usually so potent and distracting that the person can become blinded to their own inner knowledge. The person needs encouragement to become more conscious of the potent effect they have on others so they can know that the response from others to them is their teacher. Once they become aware of their effect on others, they release their inner gift. They need to become more conscious about the gift that the culture sees within them.'[8]

"For many of us there are still questions that remain. Did Elvis accomplish what he came in to do? Was he aware of his purpose? His Goal? His spiritual potential? Did he realize it all too late? Perhaps. There is a point to be made here. Perhaps only an idea to ponder. A great dichotomy in the life of Elvis has emerged.

"It is quite possible that Elvis fulfilled the destiny aspect indicated by the Yod pointing to the Leo Mid-Heaven. For it is here that he entered the public 'battlefield' as his life was thrust before the masses in all its glorious reverie. The music, the power, the attraction, the honor, were all placed before him to be conquered by it.

"Yet, he commanded it, took what he could from it and in the end gave it all back. Later in his life, when he began to fall from grace, beset with physical ailments and surrounded by those who would imprison him and drain him of his power, he realized he had no real control over his life or circumstances.

The public battlefield became a star in his crown, but his personal battlefield became the sword that pierced his mighty heart.

"The glory became the burden until the spiritual goal and vision set before him, became only a distant and fading memory. His passing from this plane did not give him time enough to finish his spiritual journey. But the Great Triangle of Destiny found no expression, and he could not truly share what he knew with humanity.

"However, Saturn will not be denied. And he will return anew, unencumbered by success, in a more humble, focused and responsible life to once again point the way as a beacon of light before all mankind. Although surrounded by the crowds and the adulation, Elvis stood alone on a planet he could not call home.

"It should be realized that we cannot know the requirements of the soul in any one life. No one, no matter how evolved, ever fulfills the total opportunity, expresses fully all the energies, or transmutes all the karma★, provided by the parameters indicated in the astrology chart in a single lifetime. For until our experience sings with joy, there will always be more to do. 'The personality is a song sung by the soul, and when there is silence the soul is preparing for a new harmony.'"

"When the magic of the soul acts, the chemistry of transformation is limitless. Who knows what new patterns the soul may weave when the call is heard?" ~ 'The Astrology of the 7 Rays' by Davis and Raifsnider

Chapter 15: SHADOWS

My intention is for this book to be a positive energy and influence on the reader and Elvis. There were however, some dark forces present in Elvis' life. I feel that these dark energies around him were very much part of his soul's mission, that it was given him by the Almighty to love even those who mistreated him and took advantage for their own financial and emotional gain. So I present the following information not to judge, criticize, expose or slander anyone, but to reveal the true tests that Elvis' soul worked through on its path to a greater Light.

In the 'The Minstrel,' Bernard Benson wrote:

> "Power hungry men arranged that their voices could be heard through the world—their pictures could be seen everywhere—greedy men did the same—they would try to attack him with evil words."

> Elvis (1971 or 1972): "People tend to measure life by the things, the material things be it money, houses or business, that they have attained or done when they ought to measure it by the joy, the happiness and love in their life that they've brought to another—by their

deeds, if you will. For that is what makes us different from the animals—we have capacity, the desire to be important, to be more than we are. It is the idea of God, the knowledge that a God does exist who will judge us that gives us the inspiration, the need, to be better, to do good works and attain perfection. And that's good. It is always better for a man to think there is someone or something—God, out there to look upon our life and to make judgments upon it. Otherwise there would be no moral fiber, no reason to try.

"In His wisdom He fashioned this need into man and womankind—gave them His word, and made sure by the many written and spoken words called His word, that we would be aware we'd know and have it down as fact. Man has always had a deep felt desire to attain goals, to Be, and if he'd just take the time to look, to listen, he'd understand that the greatest thing he could achieve is that when he had lived out his life, people would remember that he was a good man, a loving man, and one who cared for his fellow man, his country, and tried to improve it for all. That is immortality; that is greatness—to have even one other person say, I'll miss him, damn, he sure was a friend! God smiles on every handshake, every smile we give someone who needs it, every hand we offer another, every time we bend to help, and he numbers each deed.

"Those are the numbers that count—not dollars and cents! You see, people don't realize, are unable to comprehend the vastness of God's thinking. This intelligence created the Universe—not just ours, not just one in our galaxy, but all of the universes out there too many for mere mortals to understand or imagine. We base all our understanding on our own comprehension and we are so small, so nebulous in any comparison to what God is—you understand me?

"There are no words, no communication devices we know of to explain this vastness, so we stumble along and limit God to our thinking. Yet, in His wisdom He created in each of us a desire to be like Him, to seek His attention, to gain His favor, and that is the essence of the heart and soul. Without that need we become animals and even to say that is wrong because animals love, are devoted, and attempt to please man, therefore they too in their way, know a God.

"But mankind without the need to please the Lord is criminal, insane, if you will, and has no comprehension of good, of doing good, and will in fact, commit harm. I think that those persons without this need are in some way evil, of evil nature and are perhaps sent here by evil forces—Satan—and I believe they number in the thousands and seek to destroy mankind's tie with God. They also attack all of us, especially those trying to be more perfect in His image, trying to bring good to others. The Evil Ones throw down stumbling blocks, often killing the good, the kind. Thus we say, how can one so good die when so many evil ones go on living? God doesn't rule this Earth, not yet, evil does. He tells us that—Jesus intervenes at His will, when it is a step to further that closeness to perfection."

Elvis was Against Racism

Elvis had a special affinity for Afro-Americans and their culture.

He could not have sung Blues and Gospel as he did, had he not carried a strong heart connection to them. Unfortunately, in the early years of his career, a certain government agency considered him a threat. The breaking down of racial barriers through the mass attention being given his music posed a problem for the 'white supremacy' consciousness of the 1950's in America. I have good reason to believe that a governmental agency put forth a slur campaign against Elvis.

One deliberately malicious allegation was that he had criticized minorities, in particular blacks. This was untrue. As told by Mary Jones (Chapter 12), Elvis was to some extent raised by Afro-Americans. One shop owner in Tupelo commented that the Presley's would have starved to death had it not been for black people, who helped them in their time of need. Elvis never forgot this. As a boy, he had so loved to sit outside the local black church, peering through the window and listening to them sing and move to the music. He told friends he just wished he could have, "painted myself black and gone in."

One of his former teenage girlfriends recalled that a young Elvis often took his dates to black gospel sing-ins, where they would be the only white people there. Mary Jenkins was Elvis' personal cook for many years. In 'Elvis, The Way I Knew Him,' which was authored by Mary, she writes what a kind and generous friend he was to her; that there was not a bigoted bone in his body. In fact, all of Elvis' black employees have made similar statements. There were only a few entertainers that Elvis was really close with personally, and among the handful many were black, including Sammy Davis Jr.

> Mary Jenkins, writes about Elvis: "He looked at me with tenderness on his face and said, 'Mary, you have really been putting in some long hours these past few weeks, and in that time I've never seen you with a frown on your face. You're always so pleasant to everyone. I want you to know how much I appreciate you, and I want you to know that I really love you.' He then stuck something in my uniform pocket. It

> was a one hundred dollar bill... Elvis wasn't only generous to me in the form of gifts and material things. He was always heaping compliments on me. I couldn't have loved one of my own (children) any more than I did him."

A black man named Lonnie who served with Elvis in the army, spoke with reporters about him, saying that Elvis had become a good buddy, and he stressed, had no racial prejudice whatsoever. One of those Americans whom Elvis greatly admired was the Reverend Martin Luther King. In 1968, he was given a song to sing which had been written especially for him, expressing his sentiments toward the black leader, and the beliefs they shared. This song was 'If I Can Dream,' which Elvis sang on his 1968 television special. In 1969 Elvis recorded what was to become one of his biggest hits of the latter part of his career. It was a soul-searching song entitled, 'In the Ghetto.' It spoke of the endless cycle of pain born in the poverty and desperation of ghetto life.

In the 1970's after seeing one of Elvis' performances in Fort Worth, Texas, I had the pleasure of sharing a conversation with a young black musician who played for Elvis' back-up singers, 'The Sweet Inspirations,' when they performed one or two songs at the start of Elvis' shows. Around his neck hung a gold 'TCB' (Taking Care of Business) necklace that Elvis had just begun giving his friends.

He gave them only to those who meant a great deal to him. They were expensive jewelry and not trinkets. This young man, his eyes shining with absolute love, told how Elvis had given it to him; the special and genuine way he had done it, which obviously meant more to him than the gift itself. Bear in mind that Elvis was an absolute superstar, while this fellow was just one of three or four guys playing for Elvis' back-up singers.

His group was never even on the stage when Elvis was. And yet as the musician spoke of Elvis, there was no doubt but that this man had touched him very deeply—not in the manner of a celebrity, but one to one, soul to soul. Elvis shared with Wanda June Hill that he had put two of one of his black employee's sons through college—not just regular college, but medical school for one, and law school for the other. He paid for the entire college education for each of them. When Elvis heard that the Ku Klux Klan had burned a cross on the yard of a black family not far from where he lived, although he did not know the family, he had their entire yard re-landscaped and planted so that no sign of the burn was left, and then wrote a strongly worded letter to the Klan.

Here is a quote from Elvis which exemplifies his non-discriminatory nature:

> "Everybody comes from the same source. If you hate another human being you're hating part of yourself."

Elvis also suffered from severe physical ailments in his lifetime, severe enough that they eventually took his life as witnessed by the following information. From a 1979 press release in Memphis, Tennessee, "An autopsy on the death of Elvis Presley showed the singer was dying of bone cancer," his chief security guard says. In a copyrighted book outline, Dick Grob, who supervised security for the singer on his concert tours, said Presley probably would have lived only a few months more if he had not died August 16, 1977, allegedly of cardiac arrhythmia.

"Elvis' death at that moment in time was a very kind deliverance," Grob says in the outline of 'The Elvis Conspiracy,' a book he plans to author (now a published book) with writer Dan Mingori.[1] "His eventual death would have been slow, excruciatingly painful and intolerable to witness. Elvis was dying of bone cancer..." The outline proposes a two-part book on the days following Presley's death. 'A former police officer, Dick Grob, uses his expertise to detail and report facts that have been checked and rechecked and checked again,' the outline said. 'His journal reads like the police report—conspirators of one kind or another and that many questions that have lingered have finally been answered.'"

In 1969 Wanda June Hill came by unexpectedly to visit Elvis at his Palm Springs vacation home. In her book, 'Elvis, Face to Face,' she relates his concern for her safety:

> "After a few minutes of small talk, Elvis bluntly said: 'Please don't come by unless you call first from now on. It would be better for you if you didn't do that. Things are not the same—not as they used to be. There is too much goin' on that you didn't know about—I would rather you not become involved.'
>
> "He was dead serious, his tone one of 'don't question my word'—and though I was full of questions, I accepted his command. Later, I was to learn there were indeed things going on having to do with his career, earning capacity, and unrelated to anything he had control over, and there were death threats. He was worried about his family and friends. When I left, Elvis hugged me, hanging on as if he didn't want to let go of the past—it was a sad feeling, one I never quite understood."

Sean Shaver, in his book 'Elvis, Photographing The King,' writes about Elvis' isolation, imposed upon him by others indicating that he felt in due time we would come to know that most of the people surrounding Elvis were at best incapable and at worst possibly even criminally inclined. When Elvis asked to see someone who was right outside trying to get in to see him, if the 'boys' didn't want Elvis to see this particular person, they would tell Elvis that individual never came and then inform the person waiting Elvis had gone to bed. As Sean stated in his book, "What's Elvis going to do, say, 'Hey, I don't believe you?' Or go downstairs and run through the lobby looking for somebody? I mean, Elvis was at the mercy of whoever was around him."

Marian Cooke, Elvis' nurse in his last few years, recalls in her book, 'I Called Him Babe,' how while upon a flight headed over the Grand Canyon Elvis had quoted something from the song he had sung so many times, 'How Great Thou Art,' by saying, 'When I, in awesome wonder…' Marian goes on to relate how Elvis was so very close to her and how they laughed and cried together. She also related how Elvis had been betrayed by those he believed to be his friends and seriously taken advantage of because of his generosity.

University of Utah's Center for Human Toxicology performed the third and most accurate and decisive toxicological survey of materials taken from Elvis during the family-requested autopsy. Dr. Bryan S. Finkle, director of the University's Toxicology Center, made the following statement on this survey to the press:

> "We have not detected any drug in Elvis that doesn't have a medical rationale to it—only agents prescribed for perfectly normal, rational medical reasons. As a toxicologist, if you ask me why he had drugs in his system, the answer is he needed them medically. All drugs were in a range consistent with therapeutic requirements to known conditions of illness which he had…
>
> "Elvis was not a junkie, as some scandal magazines have tried to say. Dr. Finkle answered some questions, and the two-page report based on his findings—which he wrote at Bio-Science's request—satisfied Shelby (Tennessee) County Medical Examiner, Dr. Jerry T. Francisco, that Elvis' death was not from drug overdose' or even from having a large number of drugs present in his body at one time. Presley family rights prevail, and there are no legal duties to make the information public."
>
> From a newspaper article by Jess Stearn in 1983 quoting Dr. Harry Rosenburg, a friend of Elvis, "After Elvis died, an autopsy revealed what he (Elvis) had

> already suspected. And the almost unbearable pain he felt at times that caused him to use—painkillers. When Elvis died, they said he had drugs in him. He should have had more, the way he suffered in his last few months. With his condition, he was courageous beyond reason if that's all he had in him."

In an NBC network television news report the evening of August 3, 1997, which was a few days prior to the 20th anniversary of Elvis' death, it was stated publicly that Elvis did not die of a drug overdose, but of a massive heart attack.

This report also admitted that he had serious physical conditions for which he was forced to take addictive doses of medication, although the program did not go into detail as to the many serious ailments Elvis had at the time of his death. The news segment did say however, that the steroids he was taking for his enlarged colon caused him to have three compression fractures in his spine and also that, at the time of his death, he had the arteries of an 80 year old man.

One of his doctors stated that before he died Elvis had worked with the doctors in changing his medication to the point where he was no longer addicted to the prescribed drugs. The following list of Elvis' ailments have been spoken and/or written about by Elvis' friends such as Charlie Hodge, Kathy Westmoreland, Larry Geller, Wanda June Hill, and several others, who have either written about some of these ailments in published books on Elvis, or have given me this information personally. I was present at thirty-six of Elvis' concerts and knew several people around him who kept me informed of his severe health problems.

We may never know for sure exactly just what Elvis had or didn't have. I DO know that he was in great pain in the final years of his life and searching for answers to the cause, and remedies for this pain. Despite his debilitating condition, it should be noted that from March of 1976 through June of 1977—two months before his death—Elvis gave a total of 149 stage performances, necessitating that he engage in grueling travel schedules taking him all across the United States.

A Full List of Elvis' Known Ailments

Heart Disease—the autopsy revealed Elvis suffered at least 3 heart attacks before the final one.

Cancer Of The Liver and Bone—Elvis believed he had cancer, and at least one of his doctors (according to Elvis) diagnosed it. It was said to be caused by pernicious anemia, coming from a genetic liver disease.

Erythematous & Systemic Lupus—this is a painful and sometimes deadly disease. There is both an outer epidermal form of it and a type that effects the internal organs. Elvis had both, although for him it was mostly an internal malady.

Hypertension, High Blood Pressure, Diabetes.

Insomnia—a chronic, hereditary clinical disorder.

Glaucoma—This is an extremely painful eye condition which is the third leading cause of blindness in the U.S.

Cluster/Migraine Headaches.

Enlarged And Obstructed Colon—caused severe CONSTIPATION. Elvis' colon was actually deformed. He was born with this abnormality. See also my review of the article by Dr. Daniel Brookoff, MD, PhD below which addresses this condition.

A Partial Colon By-Pass.

Three Compressed Spinal Fractures.

Severe Artery Deterioration and Suppressed Immune System.

Wanda Hill speaking to me: "He (Elvis) was speaking of 'bone marrow' and a form of leukemia at the time and said they were going to transfuse him as he had deformed and many white cells and few red ones. He was very pale at this time and was weak and complained of no strength and severe pain in his bones, especially the legs when he lay down to rest. The headaches he had and the pain he felt in so much of his body, kept him worn out. He also had the severe mid-body pain that doubled him over and he said he'd just as soon 'die' as continue that kind of life of pain. He had a live biopsy which showed the liver damage, what was called a tumor, in fact two types of tumor none of which were operable. And he was told it would eventually kill him.

"Elvis said it was the liquid pain killer that was given by shots and he wasn't using it anymore. I think it was maybe Demerol if that's spelled right? It was to relax his colon and help stop the pain from it. Suzy said that he cried when talking to her because he was so 'tired of hurting' and didn't understand why it was not getting any better when they told him he would get better—that was in '76 and he said then it woke him up even if he had taken sleeping pills and went to sleep. The pain woke him up and that his legs hurt so much he had to get up and walk sometimes. I've had some of that and I sure understand a little of what he felt in that way.

"Suzy said he told her when he was crying that he just wanted to get it over with, if he was 'gonna die—I pray it's soon' he told her. I know he had terrible headaches at times and holed up in his room in the dark (except for that night light) and said he tried to meditate it away but he couldn't do it very well any more. That was in 1976-77 and he said he was having a hard time using self-hypnosis as well. He said, 'I look like hell, but thank God can still sing, it is my salvation so many times.'"

The Autopsy Report

The autopsy report was ONLY to determine what the cause of death was and IF there was a drug overdose or something similar such as poison. The request from the family of Elvis (Vernon Presley) was only for that—and they did not request any further results be made public knowledge. In fact, they requested that NO other facts be made public. The research centers where the details were done, were only to determine if he overdosed and the cause of death—which was the heart and he had ONLY THE PRESCRIBED amounts of the drugs he was taking for his physical conditions in his system. NOTHING else. The autopsy always checks the condition of veins and arteries when looking for heart related or stroke related or hemorrhage related deaths. They also check the heart as it was heart failure in his case—caused by an enlarged heart, a weakened heart muscle due to the enlargement and poor circulation due to artery disease. NOTHING else was required in his case and nothing was to be released other than that.

In April of 2009 an article was posted on the internet (accompanied by a video version) entitled 'Demystifying the Death of Elvis,' by Daniel Brookoff, MD, PhD, Center for Medical Pain Management, Presbyterian St. Luke's Hospital, Denver, Colorado. Dr. Brookoff has since passed away. Dr. Brookoff states that Elvis had a chronic disease he was born with called Hirschsprung's disease. He writes of this condition:

> "...a disease of the colon that really kept him from having normal bowel movements and things that he really didn't want to talk about. There are a lot of people with Hirschsprung's disease that survive into adulthood, and later on in adulthood they start to develop severe bowel problems, and that's exactly what happened to Elvis."

In addition to severe constipation those with this terrible disease also have bouts of "overflow diarrhea." According to Dr. Brookoff, this happened to Elvis on stage once and he was terrified it would happen again. Dr. Brookoff writes that consequentially…

> "He took a medication called Lomotil®, and he insisted that medication be given to him at his own discretion. All his other medications, as it turns out, were very carefully controlled. So it wasn't like he was going out on the street buying drugs or asking for drugs. He was actually taking very little medication, but he did take a lot of Lomotil®."

I interject here that it is important to understand that Elvis had several serious maladies, thus had to take medications for them in order to stay alive—and especially continue to perform as he did. Because the Lomotil® caused even more severe constipation, Elvis finally went as long as two weeks at a time without a bowel movement. This was the case at the time of his death, when two weeks prior he had received a barium enema which had not entirely been evacuated and turned into a cement-like form inside his intestines. It is Dr. Bookoff's opinion that the cause of Elvis' death was due to attempting a very difficult bowel movement:

> "So as he bore down real hard to kind of push things out of his bowel, his heart slowed down and he had an arrhythmia called ventricular tachycardia which killed him. He died on the toilet, which again, I take care of a lot of drug addicts and that's not how they die. They either die with a needle in their arm or they die in bed. He died on the toilet and was taken to hospital, and by the time he got to Baptist Hospital he'd passed on."

To read Dr. Brookoff's complete article and view his video on YouTube, type into the Google search box, 'Demystifying the Death of Elvis.'

> A newspaper article related, "The singer's dad,

> Vernon Presley, and other close friends of Elvis were there when a doctor engaged to perform the private autopsy told the disconsolate father, 'Elvis' cancer was in the advanced stages. He would have deteriorated rapidly and known ever greater pain. When the star's longtime friend Larry Geller spoke to him about it, Vernon was still terribly despondent and could only say, 'Elvis was sicker than anybody knew. For some reason, the cancer was viewed as a stigma by some of those closest to Elvis.
>
> "Elvis' father thought it would be a shock to daughter Lisa Marie and wanted it kept from her, not recognizing that the disclosure of the cancer would explain Elvis' frequent use of painkiller drugs. "While this book ('Elvis, His Spiritual Journey') was being put together, Elvis' foreman Joe Esposito called Larry and asked him not to mention cancer. Larry decided, as I did, that it would be fairer to Elvis' memory to let his public know the truth. (Larry) 'In the last year and a half of his life, he (Elvis) constantly complained to me, sometimes doubled over in agony.'"

Charlie Hodge was Elvis' long-time friend and employee, who also played guitar and sang back-up with him on stage. In Charlie's book, 'Me 'n' Elvis,' he relates that he was present when Elvis' Dr. Nick told Vernon Presley what the autopsy had revealed. He relates how the doctor told then it had to be kept in strict confidence and that Elvis had an advanced stage of bone cancer which had spread throughout his whole body.

In 1979 a French publication, the 'Cine-Revue,' featured an article by a J.V. Cotton. In it, Cotton stated that he was made privy to the secret autopsy report on Elvis signed by Memphis' highest authorities. Cotton's medical knowledge of what he claims to have read on that certificate is quite detailed. He states that the cause of death written on Elvis' autopsy report was 'Erythematous Lupus,' a rare, painful and sometimes deadly disease.

Kathy Westmoreland, one of Elvis' back-up singers for the last seven years of his life, stated in her book, 'Elvis & Kathy,' that he had an enlarged heart which was a hereditary condition, and along with it high blood pressure, diabetes and hypertension. She relates Elvis had also told her he had a type of cancer and that the autopsy had proven it was bone cancer. Kathy also speaks of how Elvis had several other rather debilitating conditions such as glaucoma wherein he had to have fluid removed from his eyes every so often, and that he had suffered several heart attacks prior to the one that finally killed him.

Additional problems Kathy indicated Elvis had to deal with were chronic insomnia, migraines and pernicious anemia… in other words this poor man suffered horribly from a whole host of diseases only one of which would be rather difficult to cope with for the average person. Kathy sadly wrote that:

> "Elvis had mixed feelings about his condition. On the one hand he believed he was going to die. On the other hand, at times, he couldn't figure out why he couldn't heal himself. He believed in healing with laying on of the hands and that God had given him the gift of healing. I never saw him do it, but others did.[2] I was very much aware of the power in his hands."

From Wanda Hill's book 'We Remember, Elvis,' Dr. Harry Rosenberg, a phone friend was quoted as saying:

> "In 1976, Elvis called me once in the middle of the night. His voice very serious, he said 'Harry, I need to ask you some medical questions. Will you be honest with me?' I told him I would try. He wanted to ask about his health, but I told him I couldn't

give him a fair answer because I didn't know all the details of his condition. He said, 'Just tell me this, is it… Harry… is it terminal, or can you tell me? I then had to tell him that I couldn't be sure, but that from what he had told me, it was serious, and he should get expert help.

"He told me he had a good doctor and that when he had been in the hospital they had talked of surgery, but he could not go through that, he just couldn't. I assured him I understood his feelings. The suggested operation was not pleasant and he'd have to live with it for a long time. He said that he thought he would just try the medicine route and pray. 'God will take care of me,' he said. 'His will be done.' When Elvis died, they said he had drugs in him. He should have had more, the way he suffered in his last few months. With his condition, he was courageous beyond reason if that's all he had in him."

In support of Elvis' true outlook on street drugs, while conducting research for their book, 'Elvis In Print,' Maria Colombus, President of the Elvis Special Fan Club, received correspondence from the Department of the Treasury, and Bureau of Alcohol, Tobacco and Firearms. This correspondence indicated that between 1974 and 1976 Elvis had provided cover for a Federal Agent so he could properly develop a number of important investigations. Elvis vouched for this agent saying he was one of their musicians. As a result, Elvis was presented with a Certificate of Appreciation by the Bureau of Alcohol, Tobacco and Firearms by the Regional Director of BATF in 1976. This certificate can be seen on display in the Trophy Room of Graceland.

In 1972, I became casual friends with a young Hilton photo girl who knew Elvis.[3] She told me things I found quite startling at the time. She painted a picture of a lonely, sensitive man, seeking his spiritual role in conversations on mystical topics with the few people he was able to meet in his restricted environment. These were mostly a selection of young women, the only humans available to Elvis for metaphysical discussion, since his men willfully barred most other people from visiting.

Elvis was unaware of the extent of this manipulation, as he was told by his men the individuals whom he wished to see simply did not show up. Elvis essentially rescued these girls from the intentions of his entourage. In his bedroom, he would read to them from the Bible or other metaphysical texts, and lecture them on the spiritual benefits of remaining virgins until the wedding night.

The Hilton photo girl also informed me that certain employees had been overheard discussing how they could "put Elvis out" when he was "being difficult," but that he was "hard to hold down." She said that Elvis once was pleading to the point of desperation with a doctor to stay the night with him in his room, to no avail. It was my friend's opinion that Elvis was terrified of being alone that particular night.

I am quite certain now that Elvis was literally held hostage by the mafia working with and through those around him. I was told this many years ago by a source I trusted, and have heard it repeatedly since. Elvis broke down and wept when speaking to Wanda June Hill as he related the threats made to him on his daughter if he did not comply with their wishes. Even David Stanley, one of his stepbrothers in his book, 'My Life With Elvis,' admitted he knew Elvis was being drugged against his will.

Wanda spoke with Todd Slaughter, a renowned British fan club president[4] who stood and watched helplessly as Elvis was led down the ramp of his plane in 1977 with two men firmly grasping him, one on each side. Elvis was presented to Todd, who reached to shake his hand. The Star was obviously drugged, and on his pale and swollen face was a bright red hand-print, and a split and bloodied lip. He grabbed the proffered hand tightly, and refused to turn loose. Finally

Elvis' manager pried his hand away from Todd's. As Elvis was taken bodily to a waiting car, he turned and rasped to Todd, "They are making me do this."

Another witness[5] described a scenario in a hotel in which Elvis was staying for a performance in that city. This was apparently after the concert. She saw him come down the hall, again with two men holding on to him. Elvis seemed ill, but alert. He looked right at her, and attempted to walk over to her, but the men tightened their grip on him and he was escorted into a room. The door closed.

Later, someone went in and this woman caught a brief flash of Elvis solemnly sitting in a chair with several men around him, none of whom she recognized as being a part of his usual entourage. At one point, she heard what she believes to be Elvis' voice yelling, "No, no, don't do that!" After which another voice said gruffly, "Shut up!" Minutes later, he was brought from the room by the same two men again. He was unconscious, his chin resting on his chest. They threw a cape around him and 'walked' him down the hall.

Before he passed away, Elvis' friend and karate instructor Ed Parker,[6] told of Elvis' face being shoved under a basin of ice and astringent until he struggled for air, and began inhaling and choking on the substance. This was done to get the swelling down from his face caused by the bloating of his failing liver and cortisone medication. They wanted him to 'look good' for the next show. As a result, his lungs and eyes were damaged from the toxic astringent.

I have heard too much from too many different sources through the years not to believe that Elvis was indeed a prisoner from 1969 on. This was something he kept from his family, although his father Vernon became suspicious toward the end. So while it is true that Elvis had very real physical illnesses for which, as Kathy Westmoreland stated, it was necessary for him to take prescribed medication, he was also becoming addicted by larger doses of knock-out drugs administered completely against his will.

Elvis often resisted his 'wardens,' and this was a way to insure his cooperation. I believe that there was an intent to addict him, so that he would be dependent on an artificial reality controlled by them. He was not so easy to subdue in 1972, but by 1977 he could no longer resist them. He at times reached out for help, but those persons he reached out to were afraid to help him. They had their own lives and family to protect.

In a hotel, Elvis' unmade bed was seen full of blood.[7] His men joked that he had been deflowering young maidens. In truth, he often hemorrhaged in his colon, and vomited blood. One can only speculate how the forced drugging done irrespective of his medical needs affected Elvis' sensitive pain-racked body. Recreated scenes which appeared on a tabloid TV show depicting a drugged Elvis unable to stand when he was not on stage are absurd.

He was alert and rational right to the end, most of the time. I have heard a conversation of him talking with some Avon ladies[8]—who sent him some gifts while he was in the hospital—in the last few weeks of his life in which he was discussing the upcoming book written in a fit of betrayal by three of his employees. He was not only completely clear-headed, but so very wise and fair in his assessment of their motives. It was most certainly to his credit that despite terminal illness and great pain, and being periodically rendered nearly comatose by his 'keepers,' he could still exhibit such clarity and wisdom in his final days. The following are excerpts from that taped conversation:

> Elvis: "There's a book that you all will be seeing in the stores, wherever, in paperback, about, uh, an expose of my life, my private life, and I would like to say that all of you who will read it, you can believe what you like, but I would like to say right here that it's been distorted drastically, and, uh, sometimes when people get angry at someone they do things that they regret later, and this is sort of the case. The two

> former employees of mine got very upset and very angry at the fact that we had to let them go, and they know very well why they were discharged and they couldn't accept it, and somebody offered them a lot of money, and you know, uh, you're all aware that nice things don't sell.
>
> "People aren't interested in hearing about how good someone is, or what kindnesses they may do, or if they live a quiet life. They want risqué things and the bizarre. So this is what they've given them—there are a lot of things that are distorted and anybody that followed my career will know that it's impossible for someone to live that type of a life, even behind closed doors, without somebody saying something about it before now. Nobody leads that charmed of a life, especially not myself. As far as the drugs, I did not take drugs—I've never taken any drugs except for medical reasons."

Elvis speaking to Wanda concerning the underlying intrigue that controlled his life in those last years:

> "You see, the guys here, they don't know everything. They think they do, but there's so much more behind Elvis Presley, the name, the image, the-the money, than they know. It's not in their best interest to know, an' that's all I'm sayin' about it. I-I-I wish things were different, but it's too late now. I'm just me—nothin's going to change that, except dyin,' I guess. Godddd, wait 'til the reviews come out 'bout that! Man, it's gonna be tough—on everybody, family and friends. Godddd—'n' Lisa—she's the one who's goin' to-to have to live with it."

Wanda and Elvis discussing the book his bodyguards wrote, which came out the day he died. Elvis had read an advance copy.

Wanda: "Well, I just think they didn't give a damn what they did to you."

> Elvis: "Oh, honey, don't talk that way, don't swear, not from your sweet lips, and honey, don't feel like that, bad toward my friends, please. Just let it be. It doesn't matter what those persons will believe or don't believe. All that matters is we know what's true—you know—my real friends know, my fans know, in your hearts you'll know. That's all that matters. I've loved them for so long and they've stood by me—they'll understand, and they'll also know that it would be impossible for me to live like that for so long and not have it come out before now. I just don't want folks blamin' the boys for that book—it doesn't matter—it's done. Let's forget it.
>
> "Man, my head's killin' me tonight. I just can't think straight, it's so bad. I really miss the old days—talking to them you know—about the old days—I miss that—I have nothin' in common with these guys—most of 'em, they weren't there, you know, at the beginning."

Wanda: "I'm really sorry, Elvis, I really am."

> Elvis: "Too bad I didn't have all that fun they said I had (laughs)."

Wanda: "Well, you were so bombed out on drugs maybe you did and just don't remember it!"

> Elvis: "Yeah! (laughs) Maybe so man, would that be a waste! (laughs more)."

It is the plague of history, that those who have made the greatest contributions to the Spirit of the Earth are often scourged and crucified in one form or another. There are undoubtedly some dark aspects churning in the mire that eventually slew Elvis Presley, another archetypal Sun King[9] sacrificed on an altar of uncertain definition. It has been said, and rightly so, that all history is written by the victors. The history makers who pass from this mortal coil are painted for posterity in the colors and hues of those who outlive them, friend and foe alike.

It is often the enemies and the indifferent who comprise the loudest voice in giving the world their picture of an individual who is no longer able to alter this presentation by his or her living presence. When reflecting upon the defacing books that supposedly reveal the real Elvis, this truth was especially evident to me. The true story of Elvis Presley as told by him to his phone friends from beginning to end, would rock the world.

It can only be revealed in part within the pages of this book, and will probably have to wait for a full telling until those whose special interests wish to keep it buried, are themselves interred in the Earth. But it will one day be told as it has been recorded, by those who know the story. That which has been set down in secret will one day be revealed. It will then be seen as the history of a hidden prophet/priest, and the glory of the truth shall be all that remains.

In the book 'Thomas Jefferson—A Reference Biography,' edited by Merrill D. Peterson, John C. Miller writes of Thomas Jefferson having stated that:

> "…if a historian or biographer, dealing with a person whose character was 'well known and established on satisfactory testimony, imputes to it things incompatible with that character, we reject without hesitation, and assent to that only of what we have better evidence.' In other words, Jefferson warned historians and biographers against embracing improbabilities that violated the principle of consistency of character unless the weight of evidence left no other recourse."

I ask you to review the information presented in this chapter and throughout this book, chronicled from the many who knew Elvis, and whose lives he touched in various ways. Would it not seem that they seriously dispute the opinions and testimony of those few who have painted a negative picture of Elvis Presley which is so contradictory to his actual words and deeds? And would not this portrait be quite the opposite of that which is known through the hearts of so many around the world?

I wish to encourage the readers of this book to emulate the virtues Elvis held so dear to his heart, and to hold those who mistreated or took advantage of him in their hearts with the highest compassion each and every one of you are capable of. It would serve no real positive purpose to harbor feelings of anger, victimization or resentment towards them or Elvis' situation.

In a sense, they represent aspects of each and every one of us, and the only way to eliminate such darkness from the world is to be fully responsible for ourselves, and come to understand how each of us can become a better person who radiates those God given qualities Elvis so exemplified. I am quite sure that this is what Elvis would encourage us to do as well.

Can any of us say that we could have held the love and compassion for our tormentors in the way Elvis did? Perhaps we can never be sure unless it were to happen, but by placing ourselves in the position of even contemplating this question, we shall gain a greater understanding of not only the great light that burned within Elvis, but what the nature of that light truly is within us all.

Chapter 16: STRAIGHT FROM THE HEART

I wrote the following piece in January, 2006, and it is fitting that it opens this amazing tribute to the beauty, love and power of Elvis' amazing soul and person.

A Testament of Light—The Last Years, by Maia

Oh, Lord my God, when I, in awesome wonder,

consider all thy worlds thy hands have made,

I see the stars; I hear the rolling thunder,

They power throughout the universe displayed.

When Christ shall come, with shout of acclamation,

to take me home, what joy shall fill my heart?

Then I shall bow in humble adoration,

and then proclaim my God, how great thou art!

From the song, 'How Great Thou Art.'

They came to Las Vegas to see him still. From Ohio, New York and Texas they came. From Great Britain, Japan and India they came.

From all over the world they came to 'Sin City' in Nevada, U.S.A. with one single purpose in mind: to see, hear and hopefully touch Elvis, and to feel the love and universal kinship he offered them. Terminally ill and in great pain, he lay himself down as a bridge never-too-far for compassion and mutual love to cross over. He was now a hostage of men whose greed blinded them to his beauty. They shoved his face into an ice bucket of astringent until he coughed and sputtered, sucking the solution into his lungs. They cared only that he was now conscious enough to go on stage.

Yet on that stage, surrounded by gambling casinos and prostitution, and all manner of degenerate allurement to the darker side of humanity, he looked up and out—to those seated before him; and he smiled the smile of an angel. He radiated the love of a beloved brother, and all was simple and graceful and RIGHT in that moment. There he stood like a sacred white stone in the Garden of Allah, sweat pouring off him in a libation of holy water from the vials of the gods. He paused in the quiet he had created with a glance. He bowed his head for an instant, and then raised his face to the heavens beyond the plastic Vegas showroom.

His eyes caught sweet celestial fire. He parted his lips and sang 'How Great Thou Art' and the trueness of the sound sent a shaft of light through the heart. His voice rose, trembling, powerful. His hand lifted and curved upward in the single spotlight, reaching above his head, his eyes following it like a beacon above a stormy sea. "Oh my GOD, how GREAT thou art!" Such a cry of the awakened soul! An anthem of spirit returning to Source. He was now in the moment, whole, complete and beyond form and suffering and SO WERE WE.

He took us with him on that golden wave of his hand, lifting us gently, surely into the sunrise above the shore. Every tremulous note from the core of his being contained us and assured us that what he saw we would see with him. What he knew absolutely and without a doubt was THERE, beyond the veil, so we would know with such certainty as well. Surely in that moment, the angels descended into the cauldron of this lost city that never sleeps - a lair of the beast, to reveal that there is no 'evil' anywhere when the being is full of LOVE.

I know this to be true. I was there to witness the miracle of Elvis in the Lion's Den (for the last time, in 1975). I know it remains true even now, thirty-one years later. Evil is only a perception, a shadow cast by the absence of love, of light, of beauty. The only true thing is that God is all and is in all. Elvis knew this. He lived it and he gifted it to us in a master stroke at a time in his life that should have been his darkest hour. It was his lasting Testament of Light.

Presidential Tribute to a Really Great Soul

Elvis had an incredible ability through his limitless personal and spiritual magnetism to bring the hearts of the world together into one large pulsing heart of love. The following are a collection of statements and quotations regarding Elvis that come straight from the hearts of the many individuals that each became a cell in that one very large heart that Elvis started beating many years ago. Some of the following quotes I have collected but have never known exactly where they were originally publicized because they came through my many wonderful Elvis friends.

> President Jimmy Carter, August 17, 1977: "Elvis Presley's death deprives our country of a part of itself. He was unique, and irreplaceable. More than twenty years ago he burst upon the scene with an impact that was unprecedented and will never be equaled. His music and his personality, fusing the styles of white country and black rhythm and blues, permanently changed the face of American popular culture. His following was immense and he was a symbol to a people the world over, of the vitality, rebelliousness, and good humor of his country."

> President Ronald Reagan: "He epitomized America, and for that we shall be eternally grateful. There will never be another like him. Let's rejoice in his music."

President Bill Clinton has publicly professed his admiration and love for Elvis many times.

> Marcus Eliason, an Associated Press newsman in Tel Aviv recalled shortly after Elvis' death in 1977, "When I left Rhodesia and moved to Israel at the age of sixteen, my greatest fear was that I would lose contact with Elvis. If Rhodesia was remote, I reasoned what was the embattled Middle East? My fears were unfounded. The first thing I saw from the Tel Aviv bus station was a slogan in tall Hebrew letters daubed on a tenement wall. Fifteen years later it is still there, 'Long live Elvis.'"

A 1979 article released by the Agency France-Presse stated that in a West German poll, Elvis Presley came in fourth as most admired by young Germans. The youth's mothers and fathers, respectively, came in first and second, with Jesus Christ in third place. Marge Nichols writes in 1982:

> "Earlier this year I received a letter from two young boys ages fourteen and sixteen from the Faroe Islands. I had never heard of such a place. It is a group of eighteen small islands in the middle of the North Atlantic ocean. The only way off the islands is by boat or plane, somewhat like our Hawaiian Islands. These boys just dearly love Elvis, just think about what age they were in 1977. It took more than just being a singer for this amount of love to be focused upon one man, from every corner of Earth from all ages."

Whenever an Elvis record is received by someone in Sri Lanka, the entire country shares it over the radio—it is considered a big occasion. Bill Burk of the Memphis newspaper in 1983 wrote:

> "Barring some unforeseen red tape, the Elvis Presley fan club movement will go behind the Iron Curtain officially for the first time in 1984. Meeting in Antwerp, Belgium recently, the presidents of a number of Presley fan clubs from throughout western Europe voted to stage next year's international fan convention in Budapest, Hungary. Heretofore, Eastern European governments have been on record as considering Presley's music decadent. Privately, however, there are a lot of Presley fans among the Communist bloc governing circles. Fan letters, even donations, have found their way through the Iron Curtain to the Elvis Presley International Memorial Foundation in Memphis during the past three years. Some have been from people in high positions.
>
> "One correspondent from Pravada in Moscow once told me he had long been an Elvis fan despite his government's ban on the playing of Presley music. He said he had listened to Elvis records on Radio Free Europe broadcasts. Mrs. (Janelle) McComb touched the audience (at the Antwerp convention) immensely when she told them, 'The first time I saw Elvis he was two years old. He was looking up at me and crying. The last time I saw Elvis I was looking down at him (in his casket) and crying.' All of our remarks were interpreted in Flemish (for northern Belgians) and French by Ernest Moeyersons, longtime RCA representative in Belgium. It was unusual, to say the least. Those who understood English would applaud interpretation into Flemish, more followed the French."

D.J. Fontana, Elvis' drummer in the 1950s and

'60s, stated in 1992: "In the last few years I have been just about all over the world. I've been all over South America and was in Sweden last year. In 1989, I went to the Sudan, Jordan, Tunisia and all over North Africa. I found that in those Moslem countries that Elvis was very popular with the people; they loved him. We'd walk down the street and they would ask, 'Are you Americans?' And when we said, 'Yes,' they'd say, 'Elvis Presley!'"

Dave Marsh wrote: "Elvis Presley was an explorer of vast new landscapes of dream and illusion. He was a man who refused to be told the best of his dreams would not come true, who refused to be defined by anyone else's conceptions. This is the goal of democracy, the journey on which every prospective American hero sets out. That Elvis made so much of the journey on his own is reason enough to remember him with the honor and love we reserve for the bravest among us. Such men made the only maps we can trust."

A Tibetan Llama, upon seeing Elvis Presley via the 1973 satellite world broadcast, was moved to remark: "There is a very good man."

Frank Sinatra stated, "I'm just a singer, Elvis was the embodiment of the whole American culture. Life just wouldn't have been the same without him."

John Lennon commented, "Nothing really affected me until Elvis—the man was unique—everyone else pales into insignificance."

Richard Eagan, who co-starred with Elvis in the latter's first motion picture said, "Elvis had the ability to stir people's souls."

Stephen King, the author felt that, "Elvis Presley's

talent brightened millions of lives. He widened the horizons of my world certainly. Elvis Presley more than made me feel good, he enriched my life, made it better."

Bob Dylan acknowledged, "I broke down—one of the very few times. I went over my whole life. I went over my whole childhood. I didn't talk to anyone for a week after Elvis died."

Elton John related, "News of his death absolutely stunned me. I stopped drinking."

Sam Phillips, former owner of Sun Records shared, "Elvis wasn't always serious, you know that, but when you took that little quiet facade off, it was unbelievable when that spiritual quality of Elvis came out."

Imelda Marcos expressed her feelings that, "He was ahead of his time because he had such deep feelings. He had the privilege of deep feelings because he was deeply loved by his mother, Gladys. He was able to appreciate profound beauty in sounds. And he started a musical revolution. They say all revolutions start from love."

Jerry Schilling, who was eleven years old when he first met Elvis, and was his friend for 26 years tells us, "Elvis was a rebel, but he was a rebel that had love in his face."

Walter Matthau recalled, "He was quite bright, very intelligent. He was not a punk. He was very elegant, sedate, refined, sophisticated."

Goldie Hawn expressed that, "After Elvis Presley died, I was sitting in a coffee shop and just spurted out this delicate little thing about a sparrow about how we should take care of the people we love."

Gordon Stoker, member of the Jordanaires, who sang backup for Elvis in the 1950's & 60's shared his experience of Elvis in saying, "In all the years I traveled and worked with Elvis I never heard him raise his voice to anyone except one time."

Bill DeNight, President of the 'Elvis Presley Burning Love Fan Club' wrote, "He cared about us very dearly. He gave us everything he had, and we'll never stop caring about him."

Muhammad Ali actually humbled himself in a rare moment when he stated, "I don't admire nobody, but Elvis Presley was the sweetest, most humble and nicest man you'd ever meet."

In a 1979 press article, Bill Farmer states: "Oversights so overwhelmingly obvious sometimes embarrass us—brace yourself. We've forgotten to name the moon. I don't know how we could have overlooked it. We've named everything else in the universe from Kahoutek's Comet to Hot Springs, Arkansas (neither of which we've ever seen!) But not the moon—the difficulty in anointing something as impressive as the moon with a name is finding one that measures up to the occasion.

"Most all of the mythological gods and heroes have been used up in naming everything else in the universe. Names of individuals on Earth who might be candidates for this highest of honors are politically difficult, what with our own planet so checkered with nationalism. No, the moon must be titled after a personage or phenomenon of eternal appeal and

> recognizability—a name that will shine down upon all peoples forever, a name that transcends all boundaries of human experience. I like 'Elvis' myself."

Sylvia Murray, a psychic from Austin, Texas works with the local police in finding missing persons. She is considered very accurate with her insights. A 1992 article on her in a local paper stated that:

> "In light of recent tabloid headlines, Murray was asked to attempt to channel Elvis Presley on his birthday, January 8. Confirming that she believes that the King of Rock'n'Roll is really deceased, she reported that, 'his Spirit is really incredible. His is a powerful Spirit that is very evolved, almost like a Master.'"

In 'Elvis: Images and Fancies,' Patsy Hammontree comments on the youngest of his following:

> "One striking aspect of the Presley phenomenon is the attraction he held for children. Surprisingly, many of these youngsters did not inherit a predisposition to Elvis devotion from their parents. Some were spontaneous in their intense feeling for him—much to the bewilderment of their parents."

An example that illustrates her observation is the seven year old boy who, when asked in 1984 by CNN Cable News who was his hero, replied, "Elvis Pwesly." Asked why, the child said, "Because Elvis is an angel and is going to take care of the world." When asked if his parents were fans, "No, just me."

One little four year old boy, looking at Elvis through binoculars at a concert said to his father, "Daddy, Elvis is singing just for me—he is looking right at me!"

Several years after Elvis died, a man and his wife and four year old daughter came into a novelty shop. The adults browsed throughout the store, while the little girl wandered off on her own. The store owner noticed that she stopped in front of a poster, and stood there staring at it intently all the while her parents were in the store. When the man and woman were ready to leave, they had to call to their daughter to get her attention away from the poster. She seemed reluctant, but dutifully followed her parents from the store.

"Several weeks later, the couple and child returned. Once again, the parents looked at various items in the store, while the child immediately ran over to the poster, and stood mesmerized in front of it until her parents called her to leave again. This time, as she ran after her mother and father, she paused in front of the store owner and pointing to the poster, asked in a small voice, Who is that?" To which he replied, "That's Elvis Presley." The child clasped her hands together, and with an emotion greater than her years, replied, "I'll never forget!" She then dashed out the door after her parents.

Linda Thompson, Elvis' girlfriend of five years (1972-1977), spoke about Elvis in an interview shortly after his death:

> "He had the most riveting presence of any human being I've very encountered. His quest in life was to become a better human being; a more aware human being about spiritual matters. For years and years he read books about God. Once Elvis Presley touched your life, you were never the same again. It is that way with me. It was that way with everyone who knew him. All of us who loved him are so deeply hurt (by his death), but we think of how fortunate we were to have known him, to have shared so much of his life with him. He cared for people, he loved them. No one will ever replace him, not for me, not for anybody who knew him, not for the entire world."

Ginger Alden was Elvis' girlfriend in 1977, for the last several months of his life. She remembers him fondly:

> "He had a smile that gave you the feeling

> everything was all right—I was very lucky and honored that I shared his life, and I'll never forget him. It's impossible—he had a certain kind of love, a deep love, that I have never noticed in anyone else on Earth. Elvis' beliefs have left a strong impression on me. He was into meditation and I meditate every day now. Through it I can really feel his presence. We used to meditate together, holding hands, clearing our minds and giving them to God first. He was a leader among men. He knew where he was going in life and he had a positive purpose: to make others happy. He wanted to entertain, yet he was always ready to meet his God. He gave of himself to the world."

Ann Margaret stated, "He had a tremendous impact on my life. I not only admired and respected Elvis, I loved him."

Elvis had wealth and fame, yet the things that were dearest to him came from the heart. Elvis' cousin Harold Loyd wrote of such a moment with Elvis in his book, 'Graceland Gates,' when he related…

> "My wife and I gave him and Priscilla a Christmas card one Christmas, and I told him I wished we could have given him something he could use. He opened it up and called Priscilla over to look at it. He said, 'Isn't it beautiful!' Then, with tears in his eyes, 'Harold, Marcelle, it's the love and thought that counts. I have everything else I need!'"

Janelle McComb, a native of Elvis' birthplace—Tupelo, Mississippi, knew Elvis since he was two years old until his death in 1977. She told of a time when she was visiting him as they watched Lisa come through the living room on her tricycle. Mrs McComb asked Elvis what his hopes were for his daughter, and he told her, "I would like her to remember, and be remembered for, the lady she will become, not for what she'll acquire." He then suggested to Mrs McComb, who is a regionally popular poet, that she write a poem for him to give to Lisa on her fourth birthday, encompassing the values of life which he wished to impart to his child.

When she finished the poem, 'A Priceless Gift' and handed it to him he exclaimed, "Mrs. Mc Comb, this is just beautiful!" took it in both hands and bounded upstairs. He soon returned, weeping, signed her copy and his tears fell on the poem. He tried to brush them away with his elbow, smearing his signature. He lamented, "Oh, Mrs McComb, I've ruined your copy." The poet replied, "No, Elvis, one day these teardrops will be priceless."

> Also from Mrs McComb emerged this delightful story of man with a 'spiritualized' ego; "Elvis admired the truth in anyone. I remember my niece, who was 13, went with me to visit him once at Graceland. Elvis was teasing her, 'Who's your favorite singer?' And with all the innocence of youth, she named somebody else. He looked at her and said, 'You're in my home and you're naming somebody else? Shame on you.' My niece said to him, 'You wanted me to tell you the truth and you're too old for me.' Elvis just laughed and told her, 'Honey, stay as honest and precious as you are today and the world will be a better place.'"

Joan Buchanan West wrote of her first meeting with an eighteen year old Elvis in 1953, at the home of a mutual friend by sharing:

> "The last one through the door caught my eye and took my breath. He was different in every way. He was quiet, but not sullen; outgoing, but shy; friendly, but bashful. It was truly impossible to take your eyes off him. There was a mystical magnetism about him. Now this same magnetism surrounds Graceland, constantly pulling you to it. It was not anything that he did or said, but simply his presence. He was truly beautiful. At the time, he was blonde and very slender.

> He had navy blue transparent eyes and a smile that could melt the most hardened heart.
>
> "I found myself watching his every movement and not really paying much attention to what he had to say. I found it impossible to listen and look at the same time. (And through all the following years I still had this problem.) He was extremely courteous and kind. He had all the attributes as a teenager that he had when he became a world-famous personality. Elvis never really changed… He never forgot you, no matter how many years might come and go until you would see him again. I can remember very distinctly how empty and void the house and even the air felt after he left (that day in 1953). It was as though everything beautiful had been put away never to be brought out again.
>
> "I remember thinking that I may never see him again and even then it brought a heavy cloak of loneliness over my heart that would only be lifted through the years whenever I saw him. My two oldest sons, who were three and two at the time, stood in absolute awe of the beautiful 'stranger.' He picked them up and played with them and to this day, they still remember their first encounter with 'God's Brightest Star.'"

Alan Wiess, who wrote the screenplays for several of Elvis' motion pictures, remembers his first meeting with Elvis in 1956. It was during the twenty-one year old star's screen test for the producer Hal Wallis:

> "The transformation was incredible. We knew instantly we were in the presence of a phenomenon, electricity bounced off the walls of the sound stage. One felt it as an awesome thing—like an earthquake in progress, only without the implicit threat. Watching this insecure country boy, who apologized when he

> asked for a rehearsal as though he had done something wrong, turn into absolute dynamite when he stepped in the bright lights… he believed in it, and he made you believe it, no matter how 'sophisticated' your musical tastes were. I had not been a fan until that point, but to deny his talent would have been as foolish as it was impossible. He was a force and to fail to recognize it would be the same as sticking a finger into a live socket and denying the existence of electricity."
>
> Jean Dixon, a well-known psychic in the U.S. writes in March, 1979, "Elvis Presley's music will live forever. Not only in the hearts of his fans, but in the great universities that will name libraries and music departments for him. Presley's life and music will also improve tools for psychiatrists in their search for cures for depression. A German psychiatrist will use some of his records in treating patients. Elvis will receive many posthumous honors from governments around the world. The first will probably come from England. Two books are now being written that will try to discredit Elvis. They are by authors who feel they have been misused either by the singer himself or by his family. Elvis fans from all over the country will begin a letter writing campaign against these books that will verge on threats against the author's lives. (*Author: this has happened*) These books will be followed by very inspirational works based on the singer's life and relationships with the many people he helped and inspired."

This also is true, in fact many more books have been written attesting to Elvis' spiritual good than those attempting to taint his memory, however for the most part only the malicious books have been published by large publishing houses and have received extensive media attention.

By the millions, his fans still mourn him. By the thousands they have written about their love for him. I have been privileged to see many of their letters. Written in pencil, pen and crayon on all types of paper, in the awkward printing of the childhood or the trembling hand of old age, they are a moving testimony to the way Elvis touched people not just with his music but with his life. But how? What made him so different from all the other singers, many of whom tried—are still trying—vainly to imitate him.

Anyone who saw Elvis in performance had to be struck by the way he seemed at times to be singing not to the audience but to himself, and to some point in the far-off distance. It was as if his music opened up a window in the sky through which he could catch a glimpse of the peace denied him here on Earth. His music, especially the earlier music that came right from his roots, was his psychic channel to eternity.

I have seen the same expression of intensity, the same look of abstraction, the same awareness of a great beyond on the faces of men and women in all walks of life. It is the sure sign that a person is fulfilling his or her calling. Whatever their profession, they are the lucky ones who have found their God-given talents and brought them to fruition. Like Elvis, they are shaping their future by keeping an eye on their past, never forgetting who they were at birth. That is the true pathway to greatness. Elvis knew that, even though as the years passed the dream seemed to become tarnished and the faith was challenged. That may be why he did not run from death but almost courted it, knowing that the dream to which he had been born had at last run its course.

> In the book 'Meet Elvis Presley' (1971), Favius Freedman relates that, "'Elvis never was a Casanova type, or libertine,' said actress Natalie Wood. Miss Wood was a popular starlet when she and Elvis first met and began dating. She was invited to meet his folks in Memphis. 'He was more like a pleasant high

> school date who had strong religious, almost mystical beliefs, Elvis always talked about a supernatural power that plucked him out of nowhere and made him what he was.'"

In 1973, Mamie Engle, then 84, was given a special encounter with Elvis when he was hospitalized in a room close to hers. Ms. Engle said:

> "I'm sitting on top of the world. I was in my room and I saw this young man being rolled past the door. I waved and he waved back. He had that (oxygen) mask over his face but he seemed to smile. I'm convinced Elvis Presley was sent to me from heaven." That afternoon she received a note that read, "To Miss Engle—I saw you too. Love, Elvis Presley."

The following is a quote from a personal letter to the author dated April 11, 1976, from a friend and Elvis fan reporter. She is discussing her then recent trip to Graceland, and seeing Elvis drive through the gates there. For a split second, their eyes met:

> "I mentioned before about feeling his power and gentleness—but I knew there was something else. I'd never seen him off stage like that (before) and was really floored by it. But I finally found the word for it, it's 'sorrow.' When our eyes met, I felt such deep sadness, as though Elvis was looking out through an ancient tunnel. His eyes echoed an understanding of others (the gentleness) while immersed in a nameless pain of his own. That he goes on and has enjoyable times and gives of himself in performances does not negate this strong impression. That look in his eyes haunts me."

Elvis' record producer Felton Jarvis gave this insight into Elvis' mesmeric quality in 1973:

> "Elvis is kinda shy, reserved, but confident—most people's reactions to him are incredible. You can have twenty people in a room, all of them looking one way and Elvis can walk in behind you and you'll feel him. You'll feel his presence. You'll turn around cause you know something's behind you. Nobody can explain it; there is no explanation. But I've seen it with my own eyes. I've heard musicians (who have never before worked with Elvis) say, 'Man, I don't care about Elvis Presley - it don't shake me up to play on his sessions.' And then they get on the session and they just go to pieces; just completely go to pieces when he walks in the room. And then after he leaves, they'll say, 'Now I see why he's Elvis Presley, man I ain't never been around a guy like that.'"

While Elvis' voice and music is masterful and magnetizing on record, his live performances were nothing short of being spiritually inspired. As one reporter wrote in a review of an Elvis concert, "Reviews of his concerts, by usually credible writers, sometimes resemble Biblical accounts of Heavenly miracles."

The following is a quote from a magazine on Elvis released in November of 1975, whereby the male author is discussing Elvis' appearance in January of that same year:

> "When he came on stage and began to burn, there was still no one who could match him in energy, or in sheer magnetic power. All that counted was the moment when he caught fire, when something suddenly stirred him and he really started working. Then he was superhuman. Twenty years on, he was still, quite simply, the King. His popularity had never stood higher; his followers had never been more devoted. When he went on tour, many hundreds of disciples would journey with him, as if

> on a pilgrimage, tracking him through city after city, never missing a single show. And when he appeared it was no longer just a performance. To those who lived him, it had long since become a litany, a near-religious observance. Nothing less than an act of sacrament."

Sean Shaver, a man who felt it was his historical duty to follow Elvis' concert trail city by city, photographing the master in performance of his magical, musical art, reaches for an accurate description of an Elvis' performance in his book 'Elvis, Photographing The King.'

> He stated, "...no one who was in those audiences could ever forget the feeling, the electric energy which flowed back and forth. There's no way you can explain this, there's no way you can say it. If you were there, you know what I am talking about, if you were not there, you probably think I'm exaggerating..."

> Another reviewer does not attempt description, he merely accepts, "All that is really important is that he came on the stage and something wonderful happened. There was no controlling it, no defining it, but you felt it and the magic was uniquely and unmistakably his alone."

In a 1975 review of an Elvis concert, a mystical accounting was the only language possible in giving an accurate revelation of the event:

> "Something entirely his, driven by two decades of history and myth, all live-in-person, is transformed into an energy that is ecstatic—that is, to use the word in its old sense, illuminating. The over-stated grandeur is suddenly authentic, and Elvis brings a thrill different and far beyond anything else in our culture... It might be the time when he sings 'How Great Thou Art'—it might be at the very end of the night, when he closes his show with 'Can't Help

> Falling In Love With You' and his song takes on a glow that might make you feel his capacity for affection is all but superhuman.
>
> "Whatever it is, it will be music that excludes no one, and still passes on something valuable to everyone who is there… One might think that the great moments Elvis still finds are his refusal of all he can have without struggling. Elvis proves then that the myth of supremacy for which his audience will settle cannot contain him; he is, these moments show, far greater than that."
>
> Carl Wilson of the Beach Boys, "His voice was a total miracle."
>
> One woman's experience was typical of his spiritual impact on ordinary people: "How lucky I have been. To come face to face with Elvis is an experience my words could never describe. The warmth and love I felt from Elvis as he took my hand (from the stage) is something I wish I could share with all of you. Of course I have always known Elvis is beautiful, but the beauty I saw inside the man, behind those eyes, was incredible."

He inspired people through some form of internal revelation, deep within their own spaces.

> Another woman wrote, "The love within that beautiful and wonderful human being has reached through my heart and into my inner soul and touched a chord that makes me know beyond a doubt that I can truly be and do the great things that I have dreamed of being and doing."
>
> In her book, 'Precious Memories,' Sue Wiegert stated: "When some friends went to see Elvis' Las

> Vegas show, they were talking before the show about how beautiful Elvis was. A man at the next table overheard them and leaned over to say that no man is 'beautiful.' He said that 'Elvis may be handsome, but a man is not beautiful.' They didn't argue with him, but when the show began and Elvis came on stage and got into the middle of the first song, this same man leaned over to apologize and admitted, 'You're right, ladies, he truly is beautiful!'"

Elvis' illumination of others did not begin and end with his audiences, as is profoundly emphasized in this 1973 concert review:

> "And not only did the fans hold their hero (Elvis) in awe, so did his musicians and his crew, who gave off vibrations that reflected they were in the presence of greatness. At one point, as Elvis went to the right of the stage, a sound man, who was squatting down below, looked up at him as if he were catching the first glimpse at Shangri-La."

Gordon Stoker, backup singer for Elvis in the 1950's & 1960's, expressed his amazement:

> "There's no way to describe the excitement of being on stage with Elvis Presley. The joy of seeing him, working with him… I've always thought that was one of his secrets of success, that he looked different to anyone I've ever seen in my life. He had a period in his life from the mid-sixties to the mid-seventies when his was the best looking face I've ever looked into. He was beautiful!"
>
> Kathy Westmoreland, backup singer for Elvis in the 1970s: "He taught me the joy of singing. He saw the unity of feeling and singing, like it was all one thing. I remember his smile and the good feelings that

> everyone had just being around him because he was just so full of life. He was more alive than anybody I've ever known—he was more of everything than anyone I've ever known. He lived his faith."
>
> Author, Dave Marsh observed, "Unless you understand that Elvis was more than anything a spiritual leader of our generation—there is really no way to assess his importance, much less the meaning of the music he created… Uniting opposites, of course, is the essence of religion… he obliterated distinctions between musical forms, between races (for a moment at least)."
>
> Elvis' backup singer, J.D. Sumner shares this nugget, "I remember one night, a woman presented Elvis with a gold crown on a small pillow. He asked, 'What's this?' She said, 'It's for you. You're the King.' Elvis said, 'No, honey. Christ is the King. I'm just a singer.'"

Bernard Benson, inventor, scientist and author of 'The Minstrel' a book on Elvis' past incarnation as a Bard, writes in the preface:

> "Elvis Presley had a great gift. He was able to fill with joy the hearts of millions of people, both young and old, throughout the world. This great force cannot be explained by his music alone. He looked upon his life as a miracle, his talent a gift of God, to be used to bring happiness wherever he could."
>
> A press release expounds on the greatness of Elvis: "If Elvis' life had played out its drama a few centuries ago, when there were no electronic media, no communication systems, and writing skills were possessed by only a few, and, all stories and tales of heroic deeds and heroes were passed along by word

of mouth, his greatness might have surpassed that of a worldly King. It almost did in the 20th century."

Caroline Zetland—fan, U.K., 1979: "We cared so much, and caring cannot be turned off, nor can the lifetime habit of reaching out for that voice at times of sadness, happiness, loneliness, in fact there is no time when we do not need that voice. Just as entertaining was life's blood to Elvis, so is Elvis life's blood to us. He brought so much good to the world that with the passing of the years, we must make sure that the world is never allowed to forget this—we never will."

Glenda Boler, a fan: "I would like to set the record straight about the media's impression of an Elvis fan. I love my husband, my children, family and all mankind and am still hopeful that the American Dream can still be achieved. If that makes me odd then I suppose I am. Elvis meant a lot of different things to a lot of different people, but the love for him that millions of us share has helped to bond a lot of people together that may never have known what friends were, were it not for a man named Elvis Presley."

Elvis' aunt, Lorene Pritchett, shared her deeper feelings: "He was a bundle of energy and had a ball of light that rolled inside of him and came out in a thundering laugh and made everyone laugh around him. A man who could look past your eyes and into the depths of your soul, and feel your hurt—to our family he was a gift. He was a giver to the point of exhausting himself—the thing that hurt him the most in his giving was that he pushed himself to the breaking point. He felt so responsible for so many people around the world."

Lisa Marie Presley (a composite taken from two

separate newspaper interviews, speaking about her father): "I remember him very well. It was a very intense feeling to have him around. You would know he was there in the house, you'd know he was there when you drove up the driveway. He was a very powerful person spiritually—he was an incredible and enlightened man. A one of a kind human being."

JoAnna McKenzie's Story of Friendship with Elvis

JoAnna McKenzie

"My name is JoAnna and I am blessed and thankful to be able to call Elvis my friend. I was introduced to him by Starla and Wanda June Hill. I am forever grateful to them. I lost touch with them for a long time, and found them recently through this wonderful website (ElvisLightedCandle.org). I really missed them, they are wonderful, generous, loving people. Elvis is very special to me. My memories are treasured, as are the cards, letters, poems and gifts he gave me. He was a generous, loving man. Always kind and so very funny. I miss him so much, every day, but I know he is always with me.

"Wanda, I so vividly remember those great days in your old home. We had so much fun. Laughing, sharing stories, watching movies and eating vanilla ice cream with some kind a cherry topping (yum yum). The laughter stopped on August 16, 1977. Elvis tried to reach me that morning. He called my home phone and left a message and called my work and left a message. I was on the freeway, driving to work (no cell phones back then). I never got to talk to him again. I got a call at work and was told the news. I left work.

"I remember driving, it was August in California, but it was raining. I was crying so hard, so between the rain and my tears, it was hard to drive. Some girls in another car rolled down their window and asked if I was OK, of course I wasn't. The news hadn't been released to the press yet. I drove to Wanda's house, but I don't remember how I got there. I was so sad for so long.

"After he went to heaven, I received a tape from him and also a card that his secretary found on his plane. He told me to be happy. That's how I've been trying to live my life, with happiness and silliness and laughter. Now, when I think of him, I remember his beautiful smile. His beautiful eyes. His tender, sweet soul. His laughter. I miss him. We shared an incredibly close, tender, intimate friendship…

"I know it's hard to believe or understand, but I felt blessed just to have him in my life. I did not have dreams of marrying him or living with him. He was my friend. I know he loved me, he told me and showed me often, and I loved him dearly and still do. We had very intimate times and conversations. I believe that because he knew he could trust me, he could be intimate with me, and confide in me.

"I first met him—I was sitting around a kitchen table at my friend Pam's house. Across the table was her younger brother and his friend, Julie, they were 5 years younger than us. I was 18 years old. The day was April 1st, the next day was my 19th birthday. Julie kept staring at me until I finally said 'What?' She asked me 'If you could have anyone famous call you for your birthday, who would it be?' I said 'Bob Hope.' She sighed. Then she gave me hints about Memphis and Graceland. I said 'Glen Campbell.' She was in shock. She said something like 'Never mind!' A little later she asked me if I would like Elvis Presley to call me for my birthday. I said something like 'Of course I would!'

"She explained how she and her family knew him and he was her 'Uncle Elvis' and she was his 'Little Julie.' The next morning, my phone rang. The caller said he was Elvis Presley. I started shaking. I knew in my heart it was him (that voice!) but my brain was saying, 'NO WAY!' I asked him who he really was—after all, the day when Julie (Starla) told me all of this was April Fool's Day.

"He said that he thought I was aware that he'd be calling me. Julie had told me things he liked to keep him interested, like football and karate. I was a cheerleader in high school and had 3 brothers, I knew about football. We talked for about an hour. Then when I got to work, he called me again. That was the beginning of our wonderful, beautiful friendship.

> Thank you Julie (Starla). After I had said Bob Hope and Glen Campbell, she could have easily said forget it. But I guess there was something she saw in me that she thought he would like. I am forever grateful to her and to Wanda and Jimmie for being wonderful friends and family to me."

The following photographs are of some of the mementos that JoAnna McKenzie has in her collection as a result of her endearing friendship with Elvis and which she agreed to share with the readers of this book.

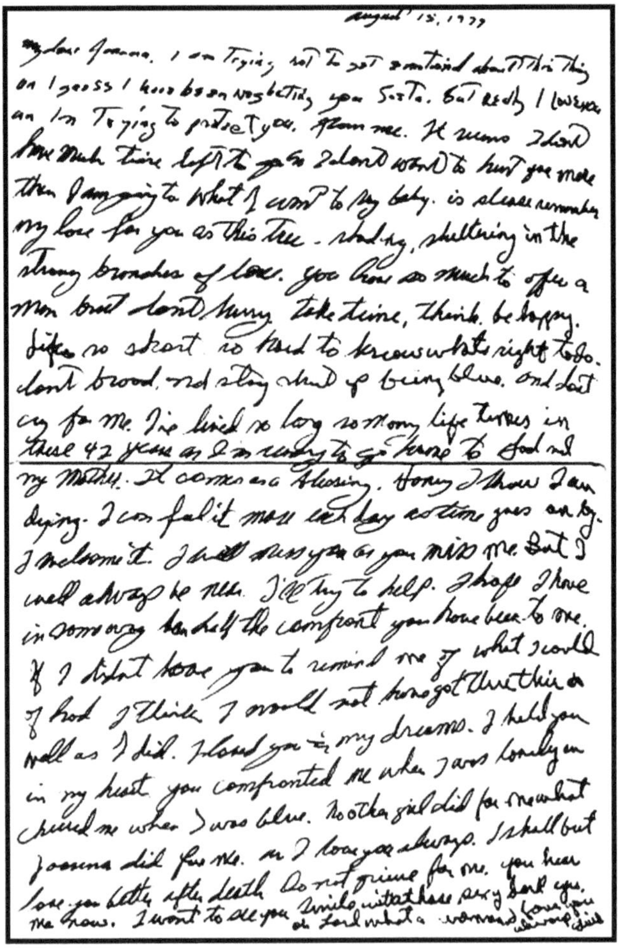

August 15, 1977

My dear Joanna, I am trying not to get emotional about this thing on I guess I have been neglecting you sister. But really I love you an I'm trying to protect you from me. It means I don't [illegible] much time left to go. I don't want to hurt you more than I am going to. What I want to say baby is please remember my love for you as this tree - shading, sheltering in the strong branches of love. You have so much to offer a man but don't hurry take time, think, be happy. Life is so short so hard to know what's right to do. don't brood and stay ahead of being blue. And don't cry for me. I've lived so long so many life times in these 42 years as I'm ready to go home to God and my Mother. It comes as a blessing. Honey I know I am dying. I can feel it more each day as time goes on by. I welcome it. I will miss you as you miss me. But I will always be near. I'll try to help. I hope I have in some way been half the comfort you have been to me. If I didn't have you to remind me of what I could of had I think I would not have got thru this as well as I did. I loved you in my dreams. I held you in my heart you comforted me when I was lonely an cheered me when I was blue. No other girl did for me what Joanna did for me. an I love you always. I shall but love you better after death. Do not grieve for me. you hear me now. I want to see you smile with that sexy [illegible] you. oh Lord what a woman [illegible]

Card from Elvis to JoAnna

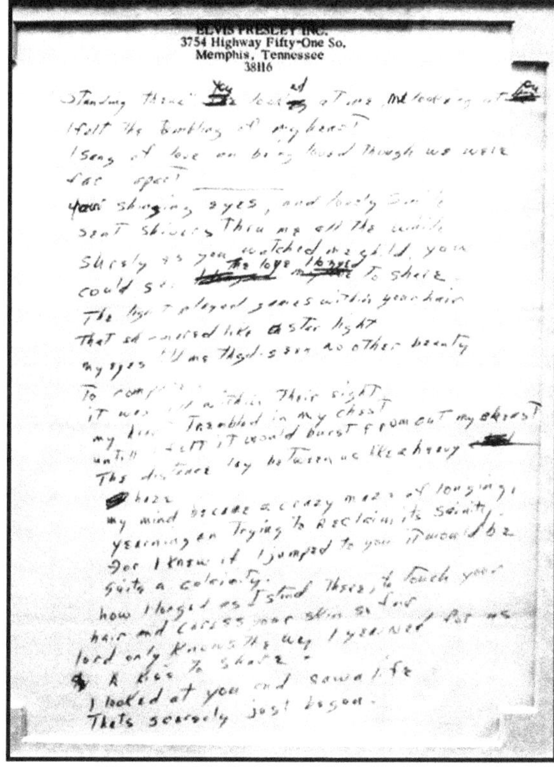

ELVIS PRESLEY INC.
3754 Highway Fifty-One So.
Memphis, Tennessee
38116

Standing there [illegible] looking at me, me looking at [illegible]
I felt the [illegible] of my heart
[illegible] of love [illegible] though we were
far apart
your [illegible] eyes, and lovely [illegible]
sent shivers thru me all the while
surely as you watched me [illegible], you
could see the love I [illegible] to share
The light played games within your hair
That [illegible] like a star light
my eyes [illegible] no other beauty
To [illegible] within their sight
it was [illegible] in my chest
my [illegible] trembled [illegible] it would burst from out my chest
until [illegible]
The distance lay between us like a heavy
haze
my mind became a crazy maze of longing,
yearning and trying to reclaim its sanity,
for I knew if I jumped to you it would be
quite a calamity.
how I longed as I stood there, to touch your
hair and caress your skin so fair
lord only knows the way I yearned for me
a kiss to share
I looked at you and saw a life
That's scarcely just begun.

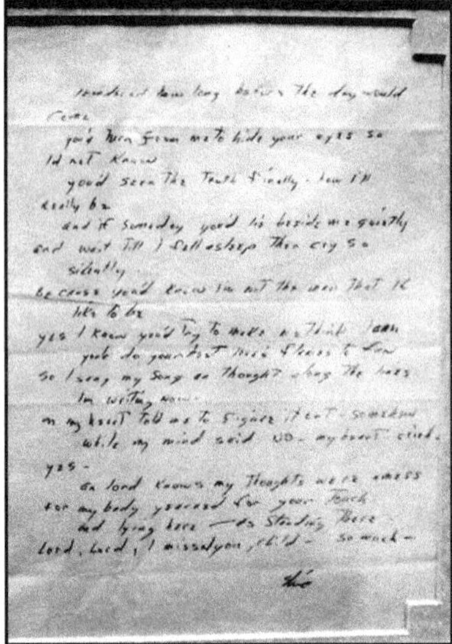

[illegible] how long before the day would
come
you'd turn from me to hide your eyes so
I'd not know
you'd seen the truth finally - how I'll
really be
and if someday you'd lie beside me quietly
and wait till I fall asleep then cry so
silently
because you'd know I'm not the man that I'd
like to be
yes I know you'd try to make me think [illegible]
[illegible] do your best [illegible]
so I sing my song as thought [illegible] the [illegible]
I'm writing now
[illegible] my heart told me to figure it out - somehow
while my mind said NO - my heart cried
yes -
[illegible] lord knows my thoughts were [illegible]
for my body yearned for your touch
and lying here — [illegible] standing there
lord, lord, I missed you, child - so much -

Three poems written by Elvis for JoAnna

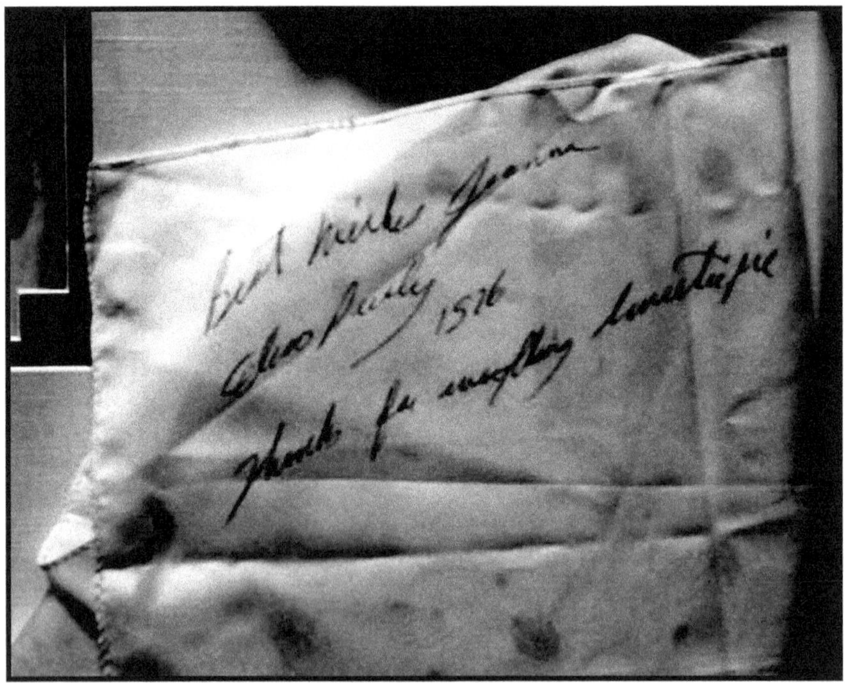

Monogrammed scarf given to JoAnna

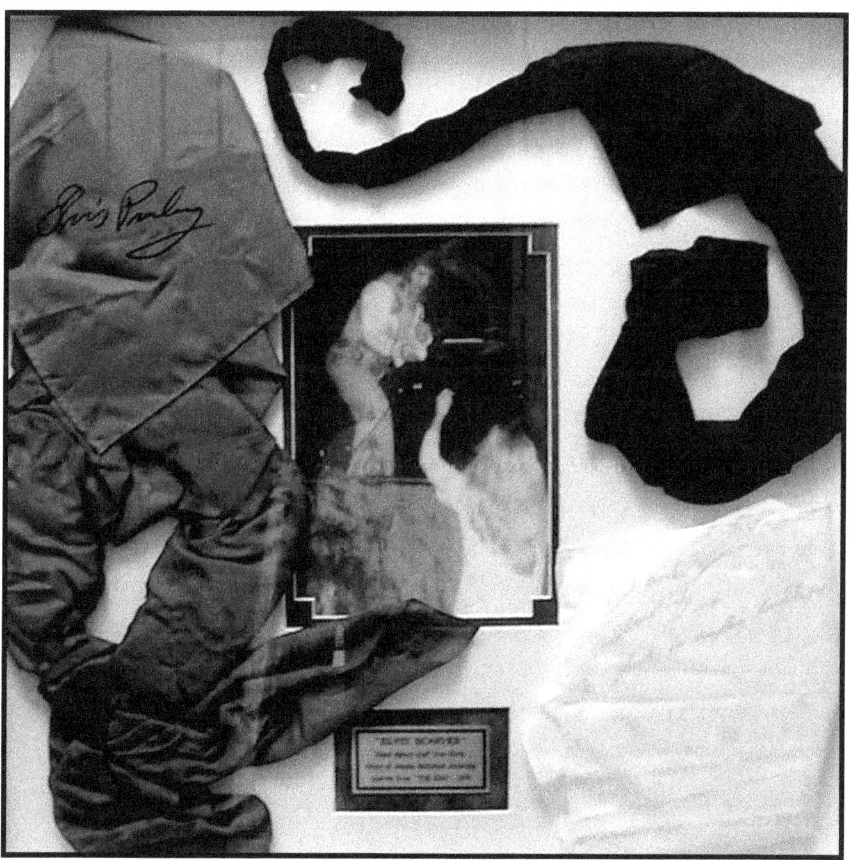

More of JoAnna's scarves

Sean Shaver wrote at the time of Elvis' death in 1977 that, "He was too great for this world. Too perfect of voice and face. Too beautiful on the inside, too. We were drawn to him like magnets. We would look and listen and not believe he was real. Some of us even touched him, still we could not believe. He was the best of us—and now he is gone."

Curt Willis, Shelby County (Tennessee) deputy sheriff shared, "My partner and I had been called to a real tough neighborhood because of a domestic dispute. When we got there, this couple was just about to kill each other. The woman had the man down and was choking him. We pulled them apart… Just then, it came over our walkie-talkie unit that Elvis had died. The woman started crying and the man went limp. This seemed to take their attention from their fight and they went to watching TV and talking about Elvis. It was real strange. We left and didn't hear anything more from them that night."

Michael Hicks, in a letter to 'Elvis International Forum' in 1992 wrote: "…I could not help but remember how the death of the King played an important part of my childhood. I was five years old and remember sitting in the living room of my grandparent's home. I watched as thousands of fans cried at the gates of Graceland. I didn't really know what it was all about at first, but I did notice the tears in the eyes of my mother and father. This was the first time I ever remember seeing both my parents cry. This is when I first knew, what an important part Elvis played in the lives of everybody everywhere."

A seventeen year old Scottish girl reflects on Elvis' imprint upon her life, shortly after his passing in 1977 by saying, "I am confused now in my feeling towards Elvis. Sometimes when in my more depressed moments I think, 'Why do I love Elvis, anyway?' I was nothing to him—one of millions upon millions of people he never knew. I often wonder how we looked through Elvis' eyes.

"I just don't know why I do all this—defend Elvis, love him. I just know it's there and it exists in me. It's too emotional a situation to analyze. I just know Elvis, his music and the life, love and happiness he gave so much will live in us forever and maybe even longer, however much it hurts us now. After I forced myself

> to listen to some selected (Elvis) tracks, I realized Elvis was, is, and always will be a part of my life. The music is the most vital, meaningful thing I know."
>
> Sue Weigert, President of the Blue Hawaiians fan club shared, "None of us will ever be the same again, we cannot be the same because Elvis' death changed forever our feelings and our hopes and our security. But we can be full and rich individuals if we want to be. We need look no further than Elvis for our example. Elvis reached out to be friends with us, he stretched out his hand and shared his kindness with countless millions throughout his career. He had fears, he had insecurities, he had emptiness inside after losing his mother. Yet he shared his extraordinary talent and enriched our otherwise quite ordinary lives, and he left his love with us so we could continue to share it. We must work together, we cannot turn our backs on one another or on the dream Elvis gave us that the world is a lovely place to be. It is up to each of us."

A fan writes from the heart on experiencing Elvis' performance in Las Vegas, August, 1975 when these amazing shows ended abruptly after Elvis collapsed ill backstage. He was forced to cancel the remaining two weeks of his appearance, being flown to the Baptist Hospital in Memphis, Tennessee: He was rubbing his left eye in this show and at last looked into the audience and said, 'Is my Doctor there? Do we have any eye drops, Dr. Nick? I have something in my eye.'

He was again in a beautiful mood, but seemed more tired than for previous shows. Judge how the audience felt about him, however. At the end of a request version of 'Young and Beautiful' as Elvis was pausing and searching mentally for the words a girl yelled, 'You're beautiful!' and Elvis never finished the song because suddenly the whole audience spontaneously applauded and applauded and applauded.

"He just stood there amid it all and looked from JD to Charlie and back again, and shuffled his feet, beaming. Everyone on stage beamed back at him, and it was one of the best moments in an Elvis concert that I've ever experienced. During this and every show his smile broke out constantly. He seemed more relaxed and confident in front of the audience than I've ever seen him.

"When he sat to rest, he had a tranquility and a glow of good-humor which seemed a little different from anything I've observed in him before. The 'tranquility' may have been part of his tiredness in effect, but it didn't seem tired; he seemed calm and quietly happy. I have to say that he still seemed to have a weight problem of some kind, which does not necessarily imply that he's fat. His back view was perfect, and so were his face and limbs, but the front of his body makes him look more heavy.

"Many people I spoke to were sympathetically concerned about this. I never heard anyone criticize him for it. More than ever his audiences seemed to love and cherish him, and give him total appreciation and encouragement with every show. If I say that Elvis looked more beautiful this time than I've ever seen him, those who don't know will probably cringe with horror[1] while those who do will understand. It was something to do with his expression and that peacefulness.

"When he was about to do 'Why Me, Lord?,' he leaned sideways on his chair with his hand over his eyes in an attitude of great tiredness. But he sat up almost immediately and removed his hand as if he realized he shouldn't look like that in front of his audience. Each show was punctuated by Elvis resting on a chair or an amplifier, and he would sit still and pant for a while after a hectic song, but soon the smile would come back and he would be alright again.

"He would always sit by Estelle for the introductions while each of the group's musicians did a solo. He sat quietly in the darkness breathing hard for awhile and blinking as he watched, with an expression of smiling appreciation. Usually he would come up with some seemingly outrageous comment while watching, and would turn back to Estelle who would lean forward to him to communicate it, and then she'd collapse with shocked mirth, and so would JD. Elvis would look sideways at the audience too, with a smile to see if they were enjoying the solos as much as he was.

"Throughout the show, Elvis had received great applause, notably from some very enthusiastic male members of the audience, which is a thing he values. At the end, the people were literally climbing over each other and over the furniture to get to Elvis. The show had in fact been characterized by people's affection for Elvis and their eagerness to hold or shake his hand, even more so than I've seen before. People of all ages would stand and stand until he came to them. The girls climbed over everything, Elvis gave away scarves, accepted more gifts, kissed more people, ducked back under his curtain, and was gone.

"The next thing we knew was the following morning when the place was found stripped of its hundreds of Elvis pictures and posters, the concession stand was gone, and nothing remained to show what had been except three small posters that say, 'The

> remainder of the Elvis Presley engagement has been canceled due to illness.'
>
> "Rumors, panic, and confusion spread, fans fell weeping into each other's arms. You couldn't get on a plane out of Vegas for the numbers leaving, people were on the telephone all day to the Baptist (Memphis hospital) or telling anxious friends as much as they knew, prayers were arranged for Elvis for the following Sundays' services, and we spent some hours in tricky negotiations to change our flight tickets home."

I was present in 1975 for the show before the one described above. My mother and I sat in the darkness, our vision transfixed upon Elvis. His face was grey. I had never seen a living human face that color before or since; and yet his eyes were lit, as if by eternal lamps. His soul poured out of them and into our hearts. When he sang 'How Great Thou Art,' he arched his back, raising his arm upward, as if reaching for a distant star. His voice soared beyond the range of human emotion. Surely the angels were rejoicing in that moment. As he reached the height of crescendo, my 71 year old mother burst into tears. She later told me that she felt his voice lift her into such a sacred space, the emotion of it was momentarily overwhelming.

Bob Green's review of 'This Is Elvis'—consisting mostly of documentary footage on Elvis' life—in the Daily News, May of 1981, stated:

> "I saw 'This Is Elvis' in a theater packed with faces. I expected them to be whooping and hollering during the early parts, when young Elvis dominated the screen. But they were silent, almost reverential, during those scenes… At the end of the movie, when Elvis was so helpless that he had to be guided to and from the stage, the people in the 1981 movie theater began to talk to the screen. As Presley came closer

> and closer to collapse, they began to talk, and then to shout encouragement of him. 'Come on, Elvis' they said.
>
> "These people in the movie theater were still with him—a man in back of me called out, 'Elvis you're still the King,' and the entire theater burst into applause. Here was a man who had been dead almost four years, and hundreds of men and women were cheering him on, trying to let him know they didn't care what he looked like or what had happened to his body; they were still with him, they loved him. That absence of cynicism may seem hard to believe. But if you ever understood anything about Elvis Presley, it makes perfect sense."

Elvis' last concert tour six weeks before his death in 1977 was filmed and later shown on television after his passing. What is seen on this film is a physical body no longer alive in any energetic sense; a corpse of the original being. Yet the soul that animates it is shining, full of the experience of Spirit. While Elvis' breathing is rasping, his vocal tones are deep, rich and astonishing in power. How he could command his lifeless body to perform this task is nothing less than a miracle. His occasional smile is filled with surrender to a greater peace than this mortal realm can provide. He seems already 'beyond the veil,' locked in the embrace of another world.

Prior to the last three years of Elvis' life, his detractors, ignoring his great talent and loving Spirit, attempted to mark his success by his handsome looks and 'sexy' body and movements on stage. In those final years, the truth—what Elvis' fans had been saying all along—was made glaringly obvious. Never had more people flocked to see, hear and touch him than when he was no longer fair of face and form. Their continued and deepening love for him was evident, and he responded by giving of himself unto the end. He told Kathy Westmoreland that he wanted to continue to perform to the very last that he felt this was God's plan for him. On the day he died he was to have begun another concert tour.

Elvis' truest fulfillment came through giving to us. He 'let himself down' and became a river, that we may know him in his time. Surely he was human, yet it was that very humanity in him which we cherished. It revealed the bright sun in each one of us. It was his joy of life, his appreciation of every part of the world's beauty—even the silly little things most people overlook, that awakened this same appreciation in us. We each have a genie within us. Elvis rubbed the lamp of our souls, and freed that part of us from the cocoon of our lesser selves that is ancient, full of joy, and knowledge of life.

The Gift of Burning Love

I originally wrote this lovely piece as a magazine article in 1978 under my previous name of Linda Christine Hayes.

> "Those of us who have lived in an Elvis World for the greater part of our lives find it difficult to separate the living memory of the man from the very foundation of emotion itself. Our moods, our joys and sadness and even our silent fears were moment by moment expanded to encompass Elvis. He was our mirror into which we gazed to dispel fear and sorrow, to encourage our fragile dreams, to face reality refreshed, and to absorb joy from the oasis of his shining eyes.
>
> "It was all there for us to behold, to cherish. When in his presence, his vitality surged through us. He opened the world to us through his eyes and it was beautiful. He was giving us something magnificent, something of Spirit, pure in motivation, deliberately human, that we would not experience again. Like the sand of a crystal hourglass, each grain was a sparkling treasure; each look, whisper, laugh, all the silly things,

all the psalms of life he sang us. He literally fell down on his knees to us and let us bruise his hands and lips.

"We crowded to touch him, to take the sweat from his brow as if it were holy water. He had a tender and personal way with each of us. He mocked himself, but he loved what we saw in him and we became part of his self-honor. Like a flaming phoenix, cape flared and blazing in the light, he bedazzled us. But true to legend, he was devoured by the flame, by the rapture which had sustained his image before us. We could not know the briefness of it all, nor what it took from him to give us our finest hour.

"It can be argued how long he carried it in his heart, but he knew. It seemed he lived his whole life as if another world awaited him. He touched as if it might be the last touch. He studied our faces, penetrating through the darkness as if he wished to remember them into eternity. No doubt there was sorrow for him in this inner knowledge, but a greater emotion rang through him like a clear Christmas bell. The special life God had given him to share with us gave him more joy than any cup could hold. He sang for joy. He transformed our need into his.

"Of the physical gifts, his philanthropy is well known. He gave to fill the needs of the heart as well as the body. To Elvis, poverty was always a shadow of deep exile. He had been forced as a youth to taste the bitter waters of his family's fading dreams. Being a sensitive man, he never forgot the desolate feeling of poverty and wished to vanquish if for at least one triumphant moment in the lives of those he touched. His greatest gift to each one of us was a burning love, an uncommon loving with no thought of reward. His fame and fortune was a sandbox of delight to him in which he built castles reaching into the clouds.

"He rode in chariots of gold and adorned himself with the jewels of kings. Yet he was keenly aware of the ways of the sea of life and the tides that dissolve illusions of grandeur. The only mansion his faith told him could never be crumbled was the one safe in his Father's keeping, in the kingdom he longed to know. The boy whose life began deep in Mississippi sod was borne to his rest in a white cavalcade of sixteen Cadillac's sparkling in the southern sunlight. It could have been no other way. God always laughed with Elvis. They shared a sweet confidence."

Remember Me, by Elvis

"I'd like to be remembered when I'm gone from this Earthly life, for my efforts to bring joy, happiness and a time of freedom from every day cares to other human beings… Just think of me as the redbird, in a winter worn bush on a snowy day—a bit of color in a sometimes dreary world"

Chapter 17: REFLECTIONS

This chapter deals primarily with Elvis' own viewpoint on life, love, giving, God and death as transcribed from Wanda June Hill's telephone conversations with him over time, and shared from Wanda's memories, letters and books in addition to a few other sources. In her letters to me, Wanda wrote of Elvis' impact on her and her family—her personal close encounter:

> "The first time I talked to Elvis by telephone he blanked out my mind completely. I could not remember driving home, going to my sister-in-law's house which was about four miles away, and drew a total blank on which roads I took, if I stopped at signs or lights or what happened for two hours! I woke up at my sister-in-law's house and she was not at home. I say that he did it—not the excitement of talking to Elvis Presley.
>
> "I was not a fan, not that intrigued or anything by him, not familiar with his music, so it was not that. It's just too strange, but from that moment forward Elvis has more or less controlled our life, influenced it, molded it, guided it, and still does to a great extent. His presence or influence comes in when we least expect it. He just is and it's always for good.

I don't understand it, but then I don't care, either. Our lives only got better for knowing him, for having him so involved yet not involved. I can't explain it—why try?"

Elvis confided a great many things to his friend Wanda. Some were funny, much was sad. All his expressed thoughts to her were laced with goodness and wisdom, and prevailing through these many conversations was trust.

Elvis: "I don't have any secrets from you, honey—should I have? Is this too personal for you?"

Wanda: "No—it's just that it surprised me is all. Though I don't know why it should, you've also told me other personal things. But I am taping this you know."

Elvis: "I know—is it so hard to understand that I trust you —with my life, if you will, honey? Is it?"

Wanda: "I guess it is, Elvis. I don't know what to say now."

Elvis: "Well, don't cry! God!"

Wanda: "I'm not—but let's change the subject—away from your trusting me."

Elvis: "Oh. I do. I love you, you're my friend and I do. There's nothin' more to say about that."

Elvis on Delivering Babies

"I think it would have been really wonderful. God's greatest miracle, his greatest! It really is—it would be wonderful to help bring life into the world, to be there at birth and see the soul enter the body—it does you know—with the first breath. God said He breathed the breath of life into mankind. Until we take the first breath we are without a living Spirit—a soul.

"That's my belief. We exist—our minds are there—our past memories are present therein, but without that first breath, that first moment of a living force entering our bodies, we are only partly alive. We cannot live without that breath, without a living spirit controlling our physical bodies and generating the life force within us."

Elvis on Abortion

Elvis: "Abortion is so misunderstood. I believe women should cherish life—their ability to produce the living bodies that house Spirits—but if they cannot handle the reproductive process, then why force them to do so? I don't see the reason behind that."

Wanda: "Well, if it is as you have said, Spirits choose the body they are going to live on Earth in, then if they choose one that is aborted, what happens? Perhaps that is why the moral issue is so strong."

Elvis: "They'll have to try again. The same as if one is born dead—like my brother—he chose to die for me—I believe that. I couldn't have made it through birth had I come first—it would have killed me, as I was weak. He was larger and took the pressure off me. I believe it was his wish, his desire, to let me live this time."

Wanda: "If that's so, then that body that was your brother must have had knowledge—how would he know if he had not taken that first breath—become a living Spirit?"

Elvis: "He didn't, he was born stillbirth—he never breathed—Grandma told me that. He was born blue from lack of oxygen and never changed color, only grew more blue. She said it was as if he was all dried up. He chose not to enter his body. He chose to let it die."

Wanda: "Then you were born shortly after?"

Elvis: "About thirty minutes or so later[1] and I was so small, so I just came right out with a little help and I couldn't breathe well either, so they took us to the hospital and I grew better on the way. I couldn't nurse, so they fixed a rubber glove to feed me at first—squeezed milk into me—and I was sick—couldn't take milk—and then Momma and Grandma and this old black lady who lived nearby, fixed a way for Momma to get out her milk and they fed me with a straw, then got an eyedropper to do it."

Wanda: "It's a wonder you made it."

Elvis: "Yeah—it was meant to be. I had to be here. I had to complete my purpose."

Wanda: "Do you feel you have?"

Elvis: "No, not at all. I-I no one listens to me."

Wanda: "Oh, I do."

Elvis: "I meant others. Sure you do—I appreciate it, but you're just one of very few. It should have been more—much more. Maybe next time…" (end of tape)

Elvis on Friendship and Love

Elvis: "See, it's like a plant really. A tiny seed begins to grow, putting down roots, just as when you meet someone, talk, begin to know them a little and then as the acquaintance turns toward familiarity the stalk pushes up and begins to leaf out and the friendship is off and growing. As long as there is nothing poisoning its roots, it continues to grow and expand and it's nurtured by the sun, the rain—just as people nurture their friends with care and concern and sharing interests.

"But just when a breach of loyalty, a lie, an argument that is not settled amicably, puts a break in the friendship, a chink in the trust of that person, so it is with a plant when branches… or even a severe break, such as (of) the stalk itself, injures the growth; (so it) soils the developing love in people. But if the foundation is there, the initial trust and concern has become love, then as a plant with good roots can re-grow its broken branch or stem, so can people rebuild the friendship.

"And in real love, as a plant grows, reaches maturity, it flowers, puts out new seeds that drop off and start growing, so it is with love. We plant new seeds, we develop new relationships either with other people or we find them in the one person we love above all others. So the world of plants and people is not different. Earth, its animal and plant life is tied together making one whole—all a plan of God—we were made of the same ingredients, the same design in patterns of living. It's just that man is closer to God's image—more like him than the animal or the plant."

Elvis and Wanda on Friendship

Wanda: "I haven't got that many friends—I mean real friends. I know quite a few people, many of them I met because of you, but I don't say they are friends. They're acquaintances."

> Elvis: "I know what you mean—I don't either. I mean, most of my so-called friends are hired employees doin' a job for me, you know? I don't have many people who are actual, true friends, someone I can talk to about things. It's different—they- they look at me as a-a boss, a person they have to please, or lose their position if they don't. It's not easy dealin' with that all the time, I-I get so I don't know for sure how to how to act with them. What they expect of me, you know?"

Wanda: "I think so. I couldn't take it. You have for so long now. I just couldn't take that kind of pressure. It has to be a strain for you at times, always living with them around you and having to be all things to all people. Isn't that how you feel at times?"

> Elvis: "Yeah—how'd you know? You know honey, you-you understand more than-than just about anybody 'n yet you aren't here. You amaze me at times."

Wanda: "I listen well. And I know you pretty well, too. You've been open, and the things you don't say sometimes are more revealing than what you do say. You know that, don't you?"

> Elvis: "I've learned that too. It pays to listen. Yet-yet I feel like you'd understand me 'n if you didn't, you wouldn't harp on me about it. That's nice to know—it's nice to have a friend who listens. You-you don't know how badly I need that at times. Just-jus' someone to listen, to bounce ideas off of an' to-to-to let it out, kind of, you know? It's one thing to remember things, it's another to actually talk about them, understand?"

From a 1950's magazine: "When asked about any marital plans he (Elvis) replied, '...my marriage will depend, not so much on my wife's feelings for me, but on my consideration for her.'"

Elvis Talking About Women

Elvis: "I love women. The way they make over me, the feelings of warmth and concern I experience with them and just the rush a beautiful female can give me with her smile that's for me alone. Life would be dull man, dull, without 'em! I'd like to find a woman who is interested in me, in the things I enjoy doing—certainly. But I realize my life is vastly different than most men's existence and that makes it difficult for anyone, especially a woman who doesn't have any idea what this kind of life is like.

"Sometimes though, I find one who really enjoys the topsy-turvy of it all and we get some laughs out of it. That's when I enjoy their true friendship the most—when we can share the ups as well as the downs and still get along. It happens, it happens. I've learned a hard lesson beginning when I was pretty young—19 or so, and that is nobody is going to wait around for long unless there is some sharing, something between you that bonds emotionally, be it just the fun, sense of humor, or having something in common to share.

"So I try to give back something that they need, want, in my relationships—it makes it so much better for both of us and I enjoy knowing that they understand I'm not just using their time for amusement. It's nicer when I take the time to get to know them, to understand where their head is at and build up a sense of caring, of loving that person. That's what it's all about really, loving each other."

Elvis on Sex

Elvis: "I feel that if you can't control sex—the physical impulse for sex—then you can't control anything in your life. You cannot let your body—it's desires rule you. It cannot master your mind, your heart. If you allow it, then all is lost. Sure I have desires—but by damn, I am the master of my body. I am the deciding factor and I rule. The day comes that I can't, then I'm dead. There is more to life than flexing muscle and I intend to follow a code of honor in my life—that's important. My self-esteem, my feelings of self-worth and living with my heart and conscience. Life is too short to waste in vain regrets."

Elvis' Feelings about Fidelity

From Wanda June Hill's book, 'Elvis Face to Face': "He didn't feel that it was God's intended plan for a man to have more than one wife or mate and therefore he intended to make certain before he married that he had picked a marriage partner for life. 'It is against God and his word to be an adulterer and causes all kinds of suffering both physical and emotional. I'm not gonna be one of those. Priscilla will be able to know that she can count on me. I'll never let her down.' His tone was full of conviction. I had never known him to be quite so serious and I believed him. Elvis never lied. Even when he ought to have done so to protect himself, he would tell the truth."

Priscilla Presley, from a California local TV show, 1987: "Elvis was faithful to me during our marriage. I cheated on him. He passed a lie detector test and until he learned of my indiscretions, Elvis never cheated. Only after I left him. Elvis was a loving, sincere man

> who respected his home and family. His career took him away from us and being so young and naive I thought wrongly that he just didn't care anymore. Had I known then what I do now about this business, I would have been more patient, more able to help him."

In a 1970's magazine concerning the court hearing for Elvis' 1.5 million dollar settlement for his wife, Priscilla—who was the one requesting the divorce:

> "Fain (Elvis' lawyer) then asked if these differences had resulted in an 'irremediable breakdown' of the marriage, the legalistic phrase that is used in California's new divorce law. Elvis said he didn't understand. 'Explain that word to me,' he said. Translated into plainer English, the attorney amended: 'Has the marriage broken down to the point where you can't reconstruct it or reconcile?'
>
> "Again Elvis replied, a little sadly: 'Yes sir.' 'You are satisfied that every effort you could make won't succeed in restoring the marriage?' 'That's true,' Elvis agreed. Priscilla averted her eyes. Elvis had been in a kidding mood up to this critical point. Sensing Priscilla's discomfort, he squeezed her hand, smiled at her and added: 'I don't like her anyway.' Seconds later, he apologized to his attorney and the court for the joking remark, yet he could not resist another when Fain continued…
>
> "'At any rate, Elvis, I take it you and Priscilla are going to remain friends, even though the marriage isn't going to be maintained?' 'Yes, sir. I hope never to see her again as long as I live.' Priscilla giggled, and everyone else laughed, too. 'I'm only kidding, Mr. Fain,' assured Elvis. Lawyer Fain, who has been

> through many a tough divorce contest with wealthy and not so wealthy clients, to the court at the closed hearing said, 'I want to state for the record, rarely have I seen or represented a more genuinely generous and friendly man: warm and an all-sacrificing kind of man.' Elvis said quietly, 'Thank you.' At the conclusion of the hearing, Elvis put his arm around his wife of six years and kissed her on the cheek. Then arm in arm they left the courtroom, all smiles. 'She was just beaming, very happy, as happy as she could be,' said a court observer. 'He seemed happy too, patted her and held her hand...' Lawyer Fain: 'He was most anxious to please his wife and give her what he felt she would be happy with. Now she is...'"

In a television interview after Elvis' death, Priscilla Presley revealed the words Elvis had whispered into her ear when he hugged her in the courtroom that day of the divorce proceedings: 'for always and ever.' According to the newspapers, only days after the proceedings Elvis was once again hospitalized. Excerpts from 'The Promise,' written by Elvis at the time of his divorce, in 1974:

> "I promise to be a father to my baby as long as I shall live; to love the Lord thy God with all my heart and soul and body, as best I can; to wish happiness for Priscilla; to hold no malice against no man as long as I live; to sing with the utmost of my ability, and bring happiness from singing and laughter, with love and joy."

In 1974 Elvis had this following very revealing conversation with Wanda which was initially triggered by a conversation about his ex-wife Priscilla's upcoming visit:

Wanda: "I hope she'll come, that you'll have a wonderful time and if it's what you want and need, I hope she'll stay forever."

Elvis: "That would-would be great. I think I could-could put it all back together then. I'd-I'd have a reason."

Wanda: "Put it back together? What? Your marriage?"

Elvis: "No, my life, my purpose for being, you know? My existence—I'm not gonna be here much longer if-if I don't do it soon. I'm fadin' fast. I know it. I can see the end of the tunnel. I can see the light comin..."

Wanda: "How—why did you say that?"

Elvis: "It's true..."

Wanda: "You think your time is about up?"

Elvis: "I got 'bout maybe three more years or so. I won't make it to fifty, I know that. This is not a-a joke, or to make you down, just a statement of fact. I don't think I'll live to be much older than forty or so, maybe forty-three, forty-four, but not much more (he died at age forty-two). I can't, I'm-I'm burnin' up inside."

Elvis and Wanda 1975-76 Speaking of his Ex-wife, Priscilla

Elvis: "I mean she made me happy—we had fun, some good times. If it wasn't for her—hell, who knows what I'd be turned into? She loved me, Lord she did! And she took care of me—let me tell you this, she tried hard to be a good wife. She did. And she put up with a pack of loud-mouthed, dirty-minded guys layin' around the house day-in and day-out, and she did it for years.

"I should have given her more time, tried harder

to make her happy. I should have listened, noticed what was happening to her. Instead I was selfish, demanding and unreasonable and expected that little thing to understand and put up with it. Lord, no wonder she left me for the first guy who showed her attention—and that's what it was, too—attention. Something she wasn't getting from me, man. It's a shame—a damn shame!"

Wanda: "You're too generous in accepting blame—she did plenty of wrong things—and you know it!"

Elvis: "A lot of it was my fault—I know it and I'm man enough to admit it. I was the major party, you know."

Wanda: "I know—but I also know you've hidden your hurt."

Elvis: "Well, there are things I've done just as hurtful to her that maybe she's hidden."

Wanda: "You'll always defend her, won't you? I guess it is love."

Elvis: "She was the best thing to ever happen to me—her and the baby. It's a hell of a thing that one person can be so-so satisfied and then find out that it was all a lie that the other person was unhappy and dying inside all that time—just putting you on for so long. A hell of a thing. Damn, I was a fool, I guess blind. I really didn't see it comin'—even when she told me, I never listened. You know, nine years[2] I knew her but-but-but I guess we never really did know each other—I mean, really..."

Elvis Reflecting on his Youthful Dreams and Wishes

"I had a need to have a wife, a family, and I wanted kids. God, I had a dream of that—havin' a sweet, little wife loving me and of us with three children. It was always three and then she'd be expectin' the fourth. Silly, huh? But it was there. I day dreamed and I'd always picture a little girl with dark brown hair, big blue eyes and real pretty, saucy lookin' you know. She'd be waiting for me, and the kids were pretty and we'd sing and play. I was just a silly kid dreamin' of a better future for me.

"I wanted a church wedding—her dressed in white, a preacher to marry us and God's blessings. It was the way Momma taught me—she read the Bible to me from the time I was real little and she'd explain it and it's in there plain - a man's supposed to keep his girl a virgin until he marries her—he's supposed to protect her name and keep her pure—it says that. I'm okay on that score. Except for me, I can't remarry because-because I still feel married—I can't get rid of that. I just feel it was my fault and so, I can't be free to really love again. My life is different, I accept it as such. I was born to live this way and I could not adjust to any other way of life. I was different from beginning, from birth and as such, I'm satisfied."

Elvis' Favorite Memory

Wanda (taped 1973): "So what's your favorite memory?"

Elvis: "I guess my favorite one now is when Lisa was born, when I first held her, you know? She was so-so tiny, precious and beautiful. I know all babies look beautiful to their parent, but she was-was special. I guess because I realized she was my child—mine to care for and-and it was a special feeling. It was that I realized it wasn't just me anymore—or Cilla. It was us and they depended on me. I liked it."

Elvis (1970): "Lisa is growing so much, it's hard to believe that she is already a big kid, you know, walking and all, going around saying daddy this and daddy that... she calls me Elvis... she can't say my name right—she says "Alvis" I'll say, "Honey, I'm your daddy, not "Alvis," so she'll say: "Okay daddy, All-viss," (laughs). Kid's smart as a whip. They're re-teachin' her to read and she can print her name and my name. She's somethin.' Man, I love that kid. I understand what they mean when they say they're sweet enough to eat. I could just squeeze her to pieces—eat her whole, you know?"

Wanda (different tape): "Alright—how's the kid?"

Elvis: "Great, just great! She's comin' to stay a couple of weeks soon—I can't wait! God, she's great—so much fun to have around. And she-she makes my life worth livin.' I wish, I wish, but that's silly, it can't be so-so forget it!"

Wanda: "You wish she could stay all the time—I know Elvis, you can admit it—I know."

Elvis: "Well God I do. I do! But I know she's better off with Cilla - I mean, I don't have the time and Lisa'd start feelin' neglected. I know that. I just can't give her the time she'd need so-so besides, I'm not-not a good influence to be around, I'm moody—even Linda (his girlfriend) has to step aside at times. A child wouldn't understand me at all so-so Cilla is the better choice to raise her. I know that but it doesn't make my heart any less empty when she's gone from me. I-I oh hell, I'm gonna cry if-if forgive me, I'm sorry I can't help it. It's just been so long, so long (trying not to cry). I'm such a Gawdamn baby I'm sorry.

"It's just I miss her I miss them both and there is not a hell of a thing I can do about it other than live with it. And it's killin' me, just killin' me inside. Sometimes I think I'd be better off dead then it wouldn't hurt anymore. But that's silly then I sure enough couldn't be with my baby. Sometimes I wish I wish I could let it all out and yell and scream but then that'd make 'em lock me up. God, I love her she's so sweet and you know, the thing that gets me most is when I think of it, which is nearly all the time she is mine, I mean, really mine, you know? Do you understand me? It's almost incomprehensible, isn't it? It makes me have chills—Lordy!"

Elvis on his Philosophy for a Happy Life

Elvis: "Someone to love, something to look forward to, and something to do."

More bits and pieces Elvis spoke or wrote to Wanda June Hill and his other phone friends:

Elvis: "If people look around in their own circle of living they would find more to do, more ways of helping each other than any congressional committee in a year's research. People in love they say, always tend to overlook the loved one's faults, but I think it's more that they see them and love them too much to let it bother them. That to me is what love really is—being willing to accept each other for what you and they are, regardless of flaws or inconsistencies, loving in spite of, instead of because of another's ways.

"You know, if you look into your child's eyes and they look back at you, you can easily see what trust really is and it's scary, because they have such perfect love, without question they have faith and that's what we have to have, that kind of faith, when looking into our Father's eyes. Perfect trust as a little child. It must be why God gives us children, as a teaching tool. A pity is that so many parents don't take the time anymore, to really look into their child's eyes."

Elvis' Love of Children

Elvis' generosity is legendary, but Wanda offered a personal insight in, 'Elvis: Face To Face,' on the compassionate nature that motivated his giving:

"Elvis donated large sums of money to charities, mainly for the benefit of children, although many stories have come out about his generosity to anyone he happened to hear about or come across who was in need. He simply felt that money was to be shared, if it was to be a blessing. He said enjoyment is in the giving. At Easter time he visited a school for the blind and a home for exceptional children. I was one of several people who went along. At the school Elvis knelt, letting children feel him. Tears welled in his eyes as a teenage girl hugged him, felt his face and said that she loved him... He grinned like a possum as she ran her hands over his face saying that he must be 'very handsome.' He replied that he was 'pretty ordinary.'

"A small boy felt his face, his arms up and down his body and Elvis let him. A blind child in a wheel chair came up, Elvis leaned over, put his face up to his and whispered into his ear. The child began to shake uncontrollably. Elvis took him up, held him on his lap and sat in the wheel chair while one of his men pushed them about. The child was crazy with delight, Elvis also. In reality Elvis was more beautiful than his gifts. When the little blind girl wiped his tears he trembled, caught his breath and choked back a sob. As she hugged him, he laid his head on hers, closed his eyes a moment and then opened them. They shone with love.

"His very soul poured out of eyes as blue as the rain-washed sky, in a face soft with tenderness and emotion. The only time I saw eyes look like that were his own again, when he cried for Priscilla. When we arrived at the school there had been no people around the outside, but as we left there were several dozen milling about as word had gotten out that Elvis was there. He was mauled, harassed and pulled at all the way out to the car. He was gracious, smiling, and took it all in stride, but his eyes became glassy…

"Once in the car, he said, 'This is what I live for, did you see those children? This is what it's all about. Weren't they beautiful!' As he spoke one of his men wiped blood from Elvis' hand, which had been clawed in the melee of people trying to touch him. It was all worth it to Elvis. He dearly loved bringing smiles to the faces of children; his inconvenience was nothing to him."

> Elvis: "How can one walk outside and look up into the midnight blue heaven, see the magnitude of stars and not know that God is? I find my breath taken away, chills run down my spine and a soaring in my heart every time I view God's Heaven, a wonder to behold freely."

Written by Elvis in a Bible he gave to a friend: "God's love is a warm glow, to hold your heart in troubles, and a beautiful, often exciting joy to light your world in times of quiet… trust in our Lord's word, and He will fill you with greatness, and your heart will sing always."

A Poem by Elvis

The following was written by Elvis, found in a book belonging to him entitled 'The Light To See,' by J. F. DeVries. It is reprinted here by permission from Wanda June Hill from her private collection.

If I am but I, then who am I?

If I am a man, what man?

I believe I am many men as one man in this existence.

If so, then I am all men I have been and perhaps all

I am ever to be. As one is to all.

I am today all I ever was.

The past is my present as it is my future.

I have been before and will be again—who?

~ Elvis Presley

[Piece written by E.P., found in the book entitled "The Light To See" by J. F. DeVries. The book was given to him by someone named "Bernice" who wrote, "I hope you will enjoy this book Elvis, it reminded me of you."

If I am but I, then who am I?
If I am a man, what man?
I believe I am many men
as 1 man in this existence.
If so, then I am all men
I have been and perhaps all I
am ever to be. As 1 is to all.
I am to day all I ever was.
The past is my present as it
is my future. I have been before
and will be again – who?
EP.

Elvis about God

Also reprinted from Elvis' copy of 'The Light To See,' with the answers written into the book by him. The year was either 1976 or 1977.

The Light To See: If there isn't any God, then what does man become?

> Elvis: Non-existent substance.

The Light To See: Do you think it's hard to be an atheist?

> Elvis: One unable to see God has to be blind. All about us is proof in the birth and death of all living things.

The Light To See: Do you see any danger in reading horoscopes, playing with Ouija boards, and dabbling in the occult?

> Elvis: Yes, if not done in wisdom, and with God's hand in yours. A worthy heart full of love for God's truth is a protector.

The Light To See: What does Deuteronomy 18:10-12 say about these practices?

> Elvis: They are an abomination according to the OLD testament, but the NEW testament states Jesus gave divine wisdom of these certain things. Corinthians 12-31.[3]

The Light To See: Who do you think God is?

> Elvis: My father in Heaven who has spoiled me rotten, because He loves me dearly. I would please him in all ways I may.

From a taped conversation with Wanda:

> Elvis: "Everyone has their place, their importance

to the whole of life, be they dignitaries or working class. One's position in life does not make one's value as a human being go up or down, that I believe. So no matter who it is wanting to see me, if they care that much, to try, to wait or whatever, for me, then the least I can do is be hospitable, obliging. After all, my time is no more valuable than theirs. You have to consider where they're coming from. They want to meet me, shake my hand. Some of 'em want more, you know, in the excitement of the moment, they lose it; but overall, people are great. I'm flattered they care about me, so I try to return the favor, that's all really."

Elvis' Greatest Fear

Wanda: "What is your greatest fear?"

Elvis: "Well-eh-I'd have to say my greatest fear—it wouldn't be to lose everythin' I have because I could begin again—might take me awhile, but I could get it back. My greatest fear—would have to be to somehow lose the affection, the love of the fans. To somehow fall out of favor with them, be alienated from them. I'd have to say that would be my greatest fear—one I don't know if I could handle."

1977—the year of Elvis' death, he discusses with Wanda a dream his father recently had:

Elvis: "He said he was walkin' in the yard at Graceland, 'n' looked up to see Momma comin' up the driveway. She was leadin' a little goat on a string. She come right up to him, smilin,' he said, an' handed him the string holdin' the goat. The next thing I was there with them."

Wanda: "A goat, like maybe a Capricorn symbol?" (Elvis was a Capricorn)

> Elvis: "Maybe that's what I thought too, an' he said she never said anything, just handed him the string, took hold of me, an' we turned 'round and walked off leaving him standin' there with the goat. Now, he was upset with me for goin' and called to me but we just kept walkin' out of sight. What upset him most was that when he looked back at the goat an' the string they'd become a vine that was all tangled up and around itself. He said it was growin' and weavin' itself into everything as he watched it—the thing kept growing and he got scared because it got out of hand, nothin' he could do would stop it-it was takin' over everything, he said. He woke up then, an' was cryin' and callin' for help but I never came."

Elvis' Dreams

Wanda: "Do you have any idea what it means?"

> Elvis: "No, sometimes I dream about 'bout her comin' for me, too. Real clear an' nice dreams. Maybe he just picked up on it, somethin'—dun-no."

Wanda: "Do you dream about being on stage, performing?"

> "At times—mostly it's-it's people, crowds after me, you know (laughs). Hearin' 'em callin' me, my name, you know. Sometimes after a show if I'm there long-long enough to hear 'em after. I hear it in my head, you know, like-like a roar, an' their callin' my name over 'n' over 'til-until I can't shut it out 'n' can't sleep. It's bad, but not all the time, just when I'm real tired or-or been out a while."

Wanda: "What is the one thing you'd really like to do if you could do anything you wanted, without having to ask anyone? Is there anything?"

> Elvis: "Yeah, I'd like—this sounds silly, I know, but I'd like to-to go out an' meet people, just talk an' spend time doin' things that don't mean much to anyone but me, an' others like me, I guess. But you know. I'd like to be able to just, for instance, go to Lisa's school, you know, just go an' be one of the parents. She'd like that. She wanted me to come, then she said, 'Oh, daddy, it'd be too hard on you, so you don't have to. I'll just tell you what the teacher says.' That's a perceptive kid, huh?"

In 1976, Wanda suggested to Elvis that he try and put his feelings about life on paper. He was hesitant at first. With her encouragement, however, he wrote about a day in the life of Elvis Presley and sent it to her. The following is a condensation of this piece. It is important to realize that at the time Elvis was in the last stages of terminal illness and great pain and yet doing a series of 10 day concert tours with little time off between them.

A Day in the Life; When the Night is Ten Days Long

> Elvis (1976): "Sometimes in the night I waken from a cold sweat and the shaking of my limbs. I try to remember where I am, another hotel room, the same as a thousand others yet different in color? Arrangement? No matter. I try to recall where? What city? State? It's too hard so I fumble up the phone and ask the operator to get someone I know. She is so quick to please, so thrilled. 'It's him!' I say the correct words of long habit and in comes Joe, Ed, Jerry, someone familiar. 'Good show boy, good show! Need anything?' he asks, smiling, smoothing my bed,

he flutters through the ritual—please the man, give him what he wants. He tells me: 'Linda, Sue, Mary, Maria (whomever) is waiting in the other room: Do I want her to come in? Yes-no-yes?' She looks at me in wide-eyed fear, yet total excitement. 'God it's him! I'm really here and it's him!' runs past her mind.

"I say all the words, pretend I'm interested in her, ask about her family and their interests. She willingly, eagerly plays the game I hurry through. Lord, all I want to do is sleep but she is so excited and so pretty to see. I lie trying to stop the involuntary trembling of my body. She notices and looks worried, her smile fades off and on. I say it's nothing, she says, 'Oh,' I say, 'Please leave me to sleep until later.' Her eyes dim, she puzzles and then I see the doubt begin. I say she is pretty and I wish I weren't so tired, but later, Baby.

"She leaves after kissing me and purring into my ear. God—I'm glad she left me alone. I try to sleep; I hurt all over, my head throbs and my eyes burn. Sometime later I wake up. She is sitting on the bed kissing me. I try to remember her name; I can't so it's 'Honey.' She quickly falls into the game, so practiced—but aren't they all? Lord, I hurt at the thoughts that come charging into my mind. Why? Why can't my whole world come back to me? My heart pounds in broken memory. She's pretty and bubbly, chattering like a school girl. I flirt a little to see her sparkle. They're so pretty, so cute; what can they believe they are doing here with me?

"She sits beside me; I watch TV; talk a little on the phone to someone somewhere else, trying to pretend I'm like them. I need to forget, I need reassurance; I hope someday I'll pretend long enough to make it come true. The time draws nearer, I think about the show, what songs, which suit, and talk with members of my group: James, Myrna, Charlie. Each one vital to me, important. I couldn't go on if they didn't support me. They know how I feel, they understand, but they don't really know me, not me, just him. But aren't we one? I wonder. I lie down for awhile; I'm so tired but I don't shake except inwardly and my hands tremble.

"It's 45 minutes till show time and I'm ready. My heart pounds as we go down through the hotel. A woman grabs me and I drag her along until Lamar removes her like so much lint. In the car I'm singing, trying to loosen up. Backstage all looks the same. I hear the crowd, I feel my flesh prickle and I'm sweating. My hands burn, knots inside tighten up. Someone tells me: 'Turn left at the stage steps, five feet of prowl space in front of drums. A wild crowd low stage so stay back.' They start the intro, rush me out and I'm on fire as I step on the stage. God, the lights flash like a million fireflies in some giant fruit jar. The noise is a roar, solid. It lifts me out of my fears and I fill with love for them. I feel their love for me, hot, syrupy, flowing over and through me—I love the feeling. Lord, so good, so good. I sing.

"My life, my heart, my dreams, my hopes—everything in me, everything that I am comes pouring out, answering their love. They understand; they love me and share the night in one fantastic love affair. Inside, my soul soars, light fills me, blinding, brilliant, filling me until I can barely hear myself in the din, but I know this feeling. So good, so pure, so right for me, for them. Sweat is pouring off me and I'm so tired I tremble as Charlie tells me, 'Cut it, cut it now.' I say goodbye, the crowd groans disapproval. I don't want to leave them, to end this feeling, but I must. It's too much, I can't take it so long anymore. I walk before them, trying to thank them, then off stage. A wild rush to the car and to the hotel. I can't remember leaving the stage, I'm so full of music I hear little else. I want to sing, so they sing along… They put me to bed; I won't remember tonight tomorrow. Just one more day gone from my life. I sleep and dream I'm someone else."

It seems the greatest souls are tested to the fullest in their initiations of Spirit. Wanda commented on Elvis' physical suffering in those last months of his life:

> "As the end neared in Las Vegas, December, 1976, he stood on stage with his hand hanging down and water dripped off his fingers, making a visible puddle on the floor! I could not believe that I had never seen anyone sweat that way before he couldn't seem to get his breath but there he was working his heart out the best he could. He sat down and was close to us; he was a pale, grey color and his lips were bluish tinted. His eyes were so dull and weak looking, he smiled at us and shook his head as if to say, 'this is all there is, I'm sorry.'
>
> "I knew he was as good as gone. I knew I'd never see him again and it was terrible to just sit there and watch him dying. I fully understand why he didn't tell his people, why he chose to let them think the worst—he couldn't stand letting them know the truth, letting them watch him dying. He said he couldn't bear to see the eyes of the people, to see the way they looked at him. He said, 'I know I look terrible. I wish I could change things, but I just can't seem to do it anymore.'
>
> "Elvis said one time that his life had been blessed. He had been at the height of happiness, had been loved beyond reason by so many and felt he had every blessing known to

God laid at his feet. He was so thankful to have lived and he would have changed only a few things. He felt that under the circumstances he would say he was the luckiest man on Earth. Measured up, the happy times far out-weighed the bad times. If he could be so tolerant, so understanding of his trials and tribulations and have lived through it all, still feeling like that, then how can we sit back and mourn his sorrows? I admire him greatly. His courage—he had it in spades!"

As an example of his remarkable courage and great good humor, in the last months of his life, Elvis joked with Wanda that since he was afraid of the dark, he intended to have a night light put in his coffin!

Elvis in 1977 while in the Hospital

"I saw a cute little baby the other day. A friend of mine came by with his daughter, she's just about eight months old, got this pure, creamy complexion, jet black hair and big blue eyes. Gonna be a doll when she grows up, a real doll and I won't be around. You know, my life's become one big circle, turning in and out and all around, never ending and no real beginning, everyone's changed, everybody's split up, no one's happy. I only wanted to know everyone was happy, contented. I wanted to sit back and know I helped you know, that I had something to do with it—that I was worth something, you know, to someone."

Wanda: "Oh, you are worth something. For heaven's sakes, you just don't know how much you are worth to us. You've made our lives worthwhile. Don't you understand how boring and dull life would be without you?"

Elvis: (he chokes, coughs)

Wanda: "Oh, I choke you to death, huh?"

Elvis: "No-no, it's just that I got this fluttering in my chest and it-it sometimes I when I get up it's bad…"

Wanda: "What are you going to do when they release you?"

Elvis: "I don't know—I suppose go back to work. Then just sit around the house and-and wait."

Wanda: "Stay around the house and wait? What for?"

Elvis: "See what happens. I don't really want to talk about it."

Wanda: "You said you went shopping. What did you buy?"

Elvis: "Oh, a couple of silk shirts. I found one I like. I have it on. It's real pretty—only trouble is it's silk and it spots, so I got all these spots on me—where I drool on myself, you know."

Wanda: "You drool on yourself, huh?"

Elvis: "Yeah (laughs). It's really pretty. See, what happened was Sylvester (cat) jumped on me when I was drinking coffee and spilled it on me, so I got spots. I guess when it's washed it'll come out though. It's really pretty—blue, you know. I'd like to be buried in it."

Wanda: "Oh great. Got it all planned, huh?"

Elvis: "Yeah, daddy bought me one—blue but this one is better. It'd go real good with the white suit daddy bought me."

Wanda: "I don't think I ever knew anyone who went to such great details to prepare for their funeral."

Elvis: "Well, I like to take care of things. You

know, it's been a long time that you and I have been friends."

Wanda: "Yeah—going on fifteen years. It's really strange how things worked out. This last year it's been so strange how events keep leading into other events. Ever since I met you, in fact. Just meeting you—the fact I ever came to California—I never wanted to come here. But the first year—bam! There you were."

Elvis: "Well, it was God, he brought you to me—you brought others and I brought them too—it was fate. It was God—I needed your friendship, I needed you."

Wanda: "Well, I don't know about that, but I needed someone like you—I needed to learn from you, but I don't know what I ever did for you."

Elvis: "Well, I never could tell you, I just-just knew the first time I talked to you we'd be friends, it was like you... it meant a lot to me. I-I can't tell you how much your listening to me, talked to me and I could never do nothing for you; it meant so much. If there's anything I can do for you, give you anything, I wish you could tell me now, so I could do it while I can..."

Wanda: "There isn't anything, just knowing you has been all we wanted, Elvis, really. That's more than enough. Just being your friend. You've provided the other side of my life, taught me so much, and made it entertaining. I can't imagine not knowing you, hearing about your life. We all love you, and gosh, it's been great."

Elvis: "Thank you, honey. It's nice to have friends."

Elvis on Heaven

Wanda (taped 1977): "Tell me something, do you think that by your actions on Earth that you are building up space in heaven?"

> "Yes. I'm gonna have a mansion, not a cottage or house on a hill, I want a mansion. Streets of gold, rainbows for windows, blue sky for ceilings, stars for light. I want a mansion, it says (in the Bible), 'in my Father's house are many mansions,' if it were not true I would have told you. I don't want just a room in a mansion, I want the whole damn thing."

Wanda: "You're not greedy, huh?"

> Elvis: "It's not a matter of greedy, it's just what I want."

Wanda: "Rainbows for windows, huh?"

> Elvis: "Yeah, nothin' prettier than goin' outside after it rains, and seein' the sky open up and there it is, pulsating, God's beauty, nothin' like it. You know in Alaska they have Northern Lights, man, it was pretty, God was so near, and I could have reached up and touched him. I was so excited, my skin prickled, my whole body was excited. I wanted so much to take off into that beautiful sky and be part of it. I really wanted to take off and be part of it."

Elvis on his Death

Elvis discussing his imminent death in the last month of his life:

> Elvis: "We never live long, people like me. I'm only here for a short time on this planet, and then I have to go home, go back and start anew. I told you."

Wanda: "Yeah—but I don't want to think of it."

> Elvis: "You have to one of these days—might as well adjust—I have."

Wanda: "You're different, you've always thought that way, I haven't and it is terrible to think of not having you, not being able to see or talk with you, Elvis. Don't you understand that?"

> "I do. But don't you understand that I want to go home? I want to be with my people again? It's not home here, I've never felt at ease. I need to go back and recharge, I need to have peace. I think I'm going to enjoy the feeling of death. I want to be awake, to feel every sensation. I used to think I'd be better to be asleep, but now I don't, I want to be alive, every second feeling it. I think death will be a beautiful thing. I look forward to it.
>
> "I guess I'm very vain. I don't want to look bad, to lose my voice, and that would be a worse fate. You know, to drag it out, decaying slowly and having to face it every day. I don't want that. I want it quick, easy. God isn't going to be that mean to me, he's going to make it quick, and I'm going to enjoy it. The sensation of my soul leaving this body, pulling away and leaving it all behind, traveling down that white path of light into the love of the Father's brilliance. Man, it gives me chills just thinkin' of it. God's gonna take me quick, you will see, and pleasant, I'll be at home, with my friends, and whatever happens, it'll be taken care of—I know it."

The following is a poem written by Elvis in 1976, which he sent to Wanda June Hill, and was originally published by Ms. Hill in 'We Remember Elvis.'

For All My Friends

> "The times I've shared with you my friends, cannot be bought with money, promises or fame. Though shallowness has become the trend, I'm not the kind to play that game with those I hold so dear. So I'm stating here and now for all of you to hear and before I take my final bow. It's your love that brings the song to me, the melody of my soul is played by your love untold. Without you I am nothing, and could never be so bold. The times we've shared, the laughter and the tears. Priceless memories, treasures all. How could I ever fail? With you I don't fear that at all."
>
> "Wanda, I enclosed a poem I wrote for whatever it's worth. Merry Christmas, for all my friends."

A final bit of wisdom from Elvis depicting his eternal victory over all the difficult circumstances of his life, through the power of Spirit manifest as positive outlook.

> "Life isn't something you are given because it's owed to you. It's given because you need to grow, to learn and to expand your soul and Spirit. Life is often treated as just a time of play and expectation when it ought to be one of service to others; a building often sits empty because people can't picture its potential. And that's how many people's view of life is empty because they don't see what it could be. When I get to the point where I can't be helpful, do something for other people in some way, then I don't want to stay here any longer.
>
> "I'd like to fulfill my purpose in life, but if I can't do everything this time, then I know I'll have another chance. Life is a continuing circle, beginning with

birth, ending with death and then beginning again. I believe that, just as I believe in our Heavenly Father and His Kingdom everlasting. To me that is the most important thing we have to learn, God is, He always will be. Learn that and everything else comes easy. Some people are put on this Earth to help carry the load, the strain; some are here just for show, some are here so that others can come and do what they must do.

"I'm here to bring as much joy, happiness and comfort to the population as I can, and if this causes me some strife, some personal heart aches, it's alright, because I have the privilege of seeing the happiness and joy I bring others. It evens out, I get the greatest highs, the best memories, and I have the knowledge that I can truly do something for other people, especially when they need it. So I'm happy, I don't mind. My petty problems are but tiny thorns on the rose, understand?"

"Elvis is still with us. This man who has moved us so deeply, who saw what was inside of us and released it, even when he may not have known the great change he was creating in our society and in ourselves, has touched us in a way which will never stop." ~ Author unknown

Chapter 18: THE LAST GOODBYE

In person… the last good-bye… This entire chapter is a condensed version of the last chapter of Wanda June Hill's book, 'We Remember, Elvis,' the 2005 revised edition.

"In1976 a friend of ours had a son who was taking classes in Media Production and Film Making at a college in Northern California. He wanted to do something 'that would knock the socks off' his fellow students and the teachers so he asked another friend if he would be willing to 'answer a few questions' in an interview setting. That other friend was Elvis Presley and he said he'd 'think about it.' He did, and said he would be willing to do that if he could pick the person doing the interviewing and that it had to be when he had the time and he would have exclusive rights to anything that might come of it, including what (would not and would be) used in the actual finished piece.

"That said, Elvis asked me to be the interviewer and to choose the questions. He agreed to answer those he felt comfortable with and so we spent several hours during late1976 and into 1977 talking on the phone and in person, taping, cutting and taping again, until it was finished and given Elvis' 'blessing' before being handed over to the young film mogul, who has since gone on to actually working on MTV productions. He gave Elvis the only copy of his college project and I have control of the original interview tapes.

"I've never talked with anyone about the one in-person meeting, he asked me to keep it between us. But it was too painful later and I just wanted to stop the terrible hurt after 8/16/77. I said I'd never cry over him again. I guess I lied to myself, because redoing this book has brought it all back, and it still hurts. I would not trade one minute of the time I spent listening to, talking with, going to see or the time waiting in line and on the pavement for all the fame and fortune in this world. I think I understand what he meant when he said, 'They could put me in a box for 23 hours, let me out on the 24th to do the show, and it'd be worth it.' In my case, he is worth it.

"He said it had been 'awhile' and eight years was a long time. When the door opened and I came into the foyer he stood just inside what must have been his friend's office library though it had a round table, no desk, shelves to the ceiling, full of law books, two comfortable leather chairs and an eight-foot wide fireplace. As huge as that was, the persona of Elvis was far greater, and I was more nervous than he, I think. He grinned, shook his head and held out his arms, saying, 'Come 'ere darlin.' He was dressed completely in black, though the jacket and pants had red overstitching on the seams and he wore a long gold chain with what looked to be a red coral inlaid medallion and another that was the choker type braided cord necklace and medallion he had worn in almost every concert photo I'd seen for the past year 1976-77, the one he said he had received from Lisa.

"He was pale, looked tired and though he was wearing glasses with a smoke tint, his eyes were dancing as he held me by the shoulders and said, 'You still don't mind bein' alone with me?' before pulling me against him in a long hug. He kissed my cheek, nuzzled my hair and softly said, 'Ummmm still smell good baby, been a long time, awhile.' Referring to my having always used White Shoulders perfume that I learned, after 8/16/77 had been one of his favorites. He took my arm and said we'd sit at the table that held a tray with a coffee pot, some cups and a plate of cookies. He asked if I wanted something else, water or soft drink and did I need to plug in a cord for the machine I brought with me, it was full of new batteries, new tape and a good microphone I purchased just to record him.

"He appeared to be calm, though his hand trembled slightly as he picked up the coffee cup, he kept them clasped together on the table when he wasn't fidgeting with his hair, shirt collar, playing with a little cigar that went unlit until he was leaving, or gesturing as he spoke. He kept glancing outside, where two of his boys whom I did not recognize were standing by the car he arrived in, I guess. From what I could see of them, they looked as though they got their clothing from the 'God Father' wardrobe room. He had come incognito he explained, he didn't want the press or anybody else to know he was in town. And said he was going to see a specialist in Los Angeles, but that it wasn't 'nothin' to worry over' and that he had another appointment in a about an hour or so, so he had some time to talk.

'Jus' ask me any thin' you want honey, I'm available ya know,' he said, looking at me from under lowered eyelashes, before letting that strictly Elvis naughty boy grin show. He asked about Jim and 'little Julie' and, that done, I said we'd better get busy or the time would fly out the window. He nodded, pushed his chair back a little and said, 'Let's do it, I don' want to be late, 'n traffic an all.'

"As different subjects, some personal, came up he fidgeted, bit his lip, averted his eyes, then gave straight, honest answers while looking right at me. I watched him closely, trying to keep things light and letting him off the hook if something bothered him and he didn't want to say no, but it was going to be hard for him to continue. Elvis had always, since I had first met him, been very revealing, by his actions, attitude and little subtle body movements, though I don't think he realized at all how much those things gave him away. Had he been aware, he would have altered his behavior and that would have taken away a great deal of what he was all about. He wouldn't have been Elvis. That innocent naturalness also made him a great actor.

"He told some funny things, forgot to use 'proper' English and let the real man/boy show; I don't think he ever changed, he was 41 years old and that little boy was still there. I could have cried over some of that conversation; I struggled not to crack up laughing at others so he could just say whatever he wanted and the time flew right out the window before we knew it. He said as I was about to leave, 'I'm so glad you came, thank you,' his eyes welled up in tears, he hugged me close a second time and I could feel him trembling because he didn't want to cry. He released me, stood close and I couldn't look at him for fear I would cry.

"He leaned down, nuzzled my hair again and whispered, 'It's okay, don' worry 'bout me' in my ear before saying he had to go. The last thing he said was, 'See ya there,' meaning in Vegas. I had never felt such an overwhelming sadness as I drove away; I knew I'd never see him alone again. Months earlier when we had gone to see Elvis On Tour I could barely see the screen for the tears that wouldn't stop and didn't know why, though deep down I felt that he was dying. I guess that he was but didn't want to hurt anyone, so he kept it to himself. After all, he was a male, 'born to take care of business' and he did; his way.

"I think he asked me to meet him so he could say good-bye; he had shared some of his deepest secrets and fears as well as triumphs and joys over those many years, and all because he wanted to talk to someone 'outside' his world. He said I helped keep his feet on the ground and his head out of the sand. All I know is he made our world so much brighter and he didn't have to do any of it. But he did. I promised him I would not sell, make public, nor give any one the recordings we made, he and I, over those few weeks by phone and in person. I intend to keep my promise to him, some of those conversations will never even be in print, but the parts so uniquely him will always 'be available' in print for the next generation of his 'beloved' fans who want to get a glimpse of the 'real' Elvis. I think he would like that."

Appendix A: LETTERS & REMEMBRANCES

In this appendix I share some very special poems and remembrances written about Elvis, some letters and poems from Elvis, some regular letters about Elvis, some notes from Elvis, and finally a beautiful story on how my friend Stephanie James came to know of her unique spiritual connection with Elvis.

Poetic Remembrances

The following poem, written by Terrina Rush, was a result of her inspiration after reading an early version of 'Blue Star Love' which was entitled 'Magii From The Blue Star.'

The Blue Star by Terrina Rush

On the rays of the Blue Star

God sent you to this world

To be the Light of heaven

To be the soul's rebirth

Even as a young boy

The love inside you grew

And soon you were caring
For everyone you knew
Lightning from within you
Touched the Soul of everyone
And little did they know
What the Spirit had begun
Your mother knew the meaning
Of that Blue Star in the sky
The path you were to follow
The heights to which you'd fly
Only you could have touched us
With the love in your blue eyes
Only you could have reached us
With the music in the skies!
When you walked upon the stage
We saw the signs you gave
How you soothed the savage beast
And the captives He did save
You shook the mighty heavens
With the longing of your sighs
The Angels were rejoicing
As they heard your battle cry
The holy Spirit moves now
To do the work He must

And begin the final chapter

For the only one we trust

As God is our witness

We know that you're alive!

You are the Light of heaven

As the Phoenix you will rise!

Some say you're gone now

But we say you live!

We base our love upon it

Now what more could we give?

We follow in your footsteps

We try to sow the seed.

The time is ripe for harvest

To fill our every need.

We watch now for the Blue Star

We stand ready at the Gate

The candles all are lit now

Please don't make us wait!

We watch now for the Blue Star

To shine its Light again

To gather us together

For the new world to begin

This next piece was written by a friend, Stephanie James, upon the occasion of being gifted a tiny pearl from one of Elvis' jumpsuits:

Pearl of Wisdom by Stephanie James

Stars of radiance dance in your glory,

revealing the hidden truth of your surreal existence.

With all your beauty and splendor

Your pearls of wisdom fall on us like that of a warm summer rain,

each pearl individualized to touch the very core of our souls

in only a way you know how.

To look into your blazing blue eyes

Your pure radiance permeates the hazy air

enlightening our souls to the grace of God within.

Your spiritual mastery was perceived by few,

I pray that one day the truth of your

majestic presence may be revealed to the world.

Either way the warm glow of your soul will
remain in our hearts for eternity,

~ In loving memory of Elvis Aaron Presley

Letters from Elvis

The following are letters written by Elvis. They are re-copied here from their original form. These originals are in the possession of Wanda June Hill, with the exception of Elvis' letter to his daughter, Lisa Marie. Letter Three was first published in 1978 in Wanda June Hill's book, 'We Remember, Elvis.'

Letter One

The original of this letter was typewritten by Elvis to Wanda June Hill. It was dated August 3, 1977. She received the letter on the 15th, the day before his death.

"Dear Wanda my friend,

"You remember the first time I talked with you. I can recall thinking how nice it was to talk to someone who sounded like I used to sound and that you were sweet and innocent and nervous. I thought then how much I was going to enjoy knowing you and your family. I felt this ugly thing called jealousy because of your child when I saw her. I wanted her for my own, just because she was so loving and I wanted that loving for myself.

"Listening to you talk about your family life and your husband made me want that kind of relationship too. I never met many married people in California that were happy in marriage until I met you and then some of your friends. I guess it is true about the people you run with influencing your life. Mine has had its bad influences all the way. But I wanted to write to you and tell you that I have enjoyed knowing you and your friends this past year and a half most of all. I have never regretted meeting any of them and I have not one time wished that I did not have you for a friend. I could and feel I will be able to trust and enjoy an open relationship with you and with many of the people that befriend you and your family. I think that is a blessing from heaven and I treasure it.

"Remember when you came to the lot at M.G.M. in the spring of 1963 and I asked you to have lunch with me? I knew then I could trust you and that you would not do anything funny in there with me. I wanted to be able to just relax and with you and I could. I was supposed to have lunch with another girl on the set that day and then you came up and I told her another time but she and I weren't just going to eat lunch, in fact I was skipping lunch but then you were so nice and sweet and cute and I decided to spend it with you instead. You didn't even know that other girl was giving you the evil eye the rest of the day and she damn near tripped you a couple of times and you didn't even know! I'll bet you never even noticed when she chopped at you do you? In fact I'll bet you don't even remember it. That was the kind of girl you used to be, trusting and awful sweet.

"I liked you from the first because you weren't like her. I hope that you don't change as you grow older and more successful. I want to tell you that life is nothing without trust and love and good friends. It is nothing without family and loved ones. And you cannot replace them once they are gone. I know. Believe me. Love them and take care of them and never regret the things required of you by them. For that is what life is about. Loving and caring. Love, Elvis P.

"P.S. If I have done anything to harm or hurt you over the past few years please forgive me for it. I know you have worried about me and spent a lot of time trying to help me, and it did. I would like you to remember me and to help others to do the same. But I don't have the right to ask for a thing. So I'll just hint real loudly, alright?"

Letter Two

This is a portion of a letter written by Elvis to his daughter, Lisa Marie, probably in the 1976-1977 period. During this time Elvis was in the last stages of terminal illness, and his teeth were beginning to give him great difficulty because of the lack of calcium in his bones due to cancer having spread through his bone marrow.

The original is in his handwriting and has been analyzed by a handwriting expert and deemed valid. It was found torn in pieces in the trash of Elvis' Beverly Hills home while it was occupied by Lisa and her mother. Elvis signs his full name to this letter. Lisa was eight or nine years old at the time, and was extremely impressed that her father was 'Elvis Presley.' At first Elvis tried to discourage this, but finally gave up and let her enjoy it in her own way. I feel he was humoring this thrill for her in emphasizing, "your Daddy, Elvis Presley."

> "So honey, I am going to see you real soon. I want you to be a good girl for Mommy, and do the things we talked about so she won't worry about you. I know you will try your best. That's all anybody can do sugar, so just have fun and try real hard in school, too. When I finish working this trip, I'll come by and get you. Honey, we'll go back to Memphis and have lots of fun. I can hardly wait until I can be with you my darling, it seems like a long time since last month to me.
>
> "Guess what happened? I lost a tooth! And the tooth fairy didn't even come say she was sorry, either. You know the one that hurt when you were here last month. It just broke off when I was eating, and I almost ate it. Guess I could chew with my stomach then, huh? I got it fixed, they put a new tooth in for

me and now it's so white it blinds me when I look in the mirror.

"Before I forget, Get-Low (Elvis' Chow-Chow dog) says 'Hello, and hurry up and play ball with me.' He brings me the ball every evening and wags his body to play, but he'd rather play with his baby—you, darling. Me to—I want my baby girl to play with real bad. And sometimes this little daddy cries because his baby isn't here to kissy and cuddly with him.

"I love my baby girl very much. Here's a kissy and a huggy for her and now I'm going to beddy and dream of playing with my sweet Sue-Sue Yessa dolly. XXXX I'll call you when I get to Rhode Island, look at the list I gave you and you'll know what day I am in each city and when you can call me and where I'll be staying.

"Bye, Bye

"Your Daddy,

"Elvis Presley"

Letter Three

The following is the 2nd page of a letter written by Elvis in 1974 to an ex-show girl whom he used to date casually many years before the letter. In 1974 she came to see him when he was performing in Las Vegas.

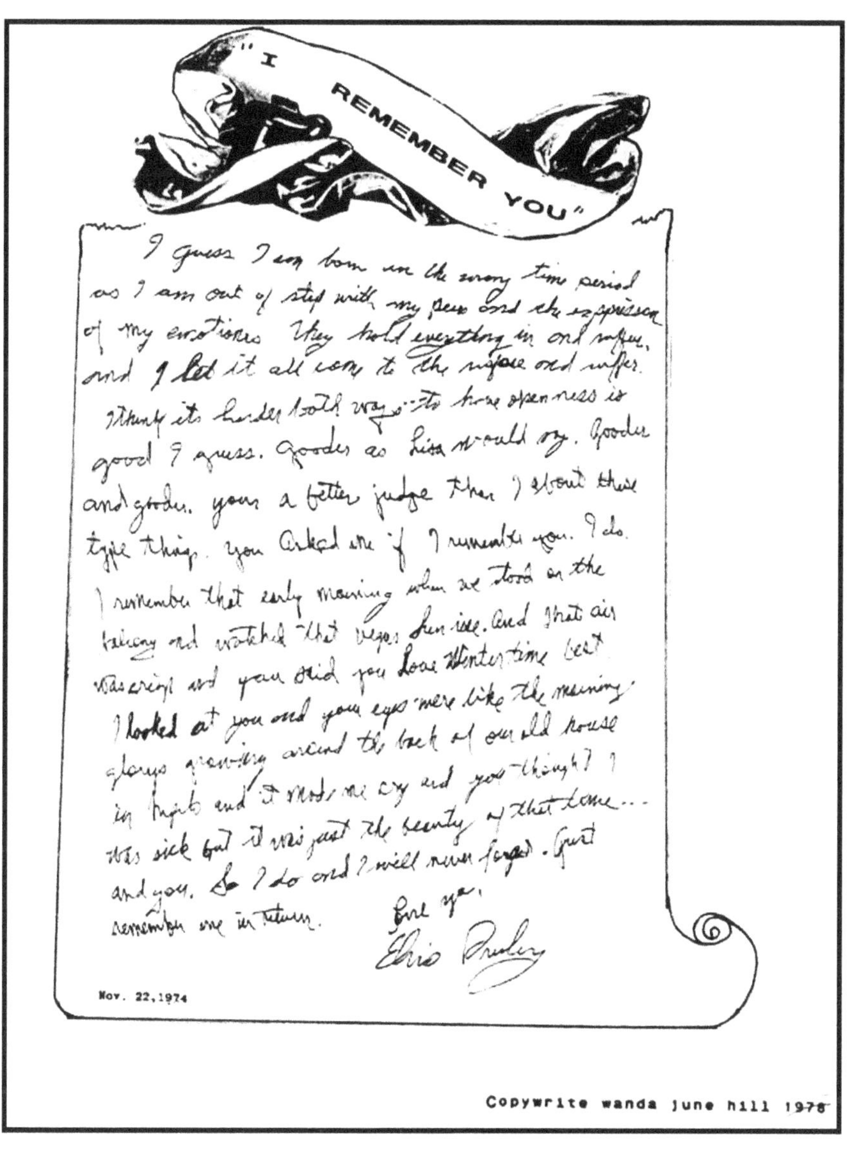

"I REMEMBER YOU"

I guess I am born in the wrong time period
as I am out of step with my peers and the expression
of my emotions. They hold everything in and suffer,
and I let it all come to the surface and suffer.
I think its harder both ways—to have openness is
good I guess. Gooder as Lisa would say. Gooder
and gooder. Your a better judge than I about these
type things. You asked me if I remember you. I do.
I remember that early morning when we stood on the
balcony and watched that Vegas sun rise. And that air
was crisp and you said you love Wintertime best.
I looked at you and your eyes were like the morning
glorys growing around the back of our old house
in Tupelo and it made me cry and you thought I
was sick but it was just the beauty of that time...
and you. So I do and I will never forget. Just
remember me in return.

Love ya,
Elvis Presley

Nov. 22, 1974

After the show, she went backstage to visit with him. In her letter to Wanda June Hill she recalled:

> "Elvis was very ill when I saw him and from what I was told at the time—he was due for surgery but was refusing to go until he had finished his tour of concerts. So like him to think only of others. He

> was too tired out to stand up and said that he had to rest though he really would have liked to stay and talk to all the people there to see him in the dressing rooms.
>
> "I felt great sorrow as I looked upon him—it was as if I knew he was dying. I've never experienced that kind of feeling at any other time. I cried most of the way home and my husband who was with me at the time said, 'Babs, he's really sick, really sick. I don't think he'll live much longer. I'm so glad you got to see him again'—(Elvis) was so dear and had a beautiful heart and soul and this letter shows that well."

The ex-girlfriend wrote to Elvis shortly after seeing him that night. This is a portion of his written response back to her:

> "I guess I am born in the wrong time period as I am out of step with my peers and the expression of my emotions. They hold everything in and suffer and I let it all come to the surface and suffer. I think it's hard both ways—to have openness is good I guess, Gooder, as Lisa would say, gooder and gooder. You're a better judge than I about these type things.
>
> "You asked me if I remember you. I do. I remember that early morning when we stood on the balcony and watched that Vegas Sunrise and that air was crisp and you said you loved Wintertime best. I looked at you and your eyes were like the morning glories growing around the back of our old house in Tupelo and it made me cry, and you thought I was sick, but it was just the beauty of that time—and you. So I do, and I will never forget. Just remember me in return. Love ya, Elvis Presley"

Letter Four

The following are scanned copies of a six page letter typewritten by Elvis which he obviously sent to more than one person. Wanda Hill received a copy from him, but others would have as well—probably all or most of them his "phone friends" with whom he felt comfortable sharing his feelings and thoughts about spiritual-mystical topics. Wanda believes that he wrote it about 1974, possibly on Linda Thompson's portable typewriter. There is a handwritten addition on the last page of the letter (from the private collection of Wanda June Hill). Below are photos of the letter with some excerpts appearing below the pages they are taken from.

Hello,

I am trying to sleep and can't so Im going to write a letter to ever
body and say how it is. Tonight will make just four more shows and
you can bet Im eager to finish it off. Its been good for several and
they been getting their money's worth I can saftly say. I been really
"gittin it on" ever show and the sqeals and shirkes are proff positive
that its getting through to them. I been goofing off for so many
shows I figured Id better get on the ball and get some work done or I
may not have a job next time. Hell I got alot of things to catch up
on being sick for so long and all. I feel better. Just plugged up
in the lungs. It hurts like hell when I cough but I haven't had too
much of that. Its good to be able to stop shaking and chilling like
I was. Going on that stage was something else when I was so cold I
couldn't stop shaking through the whole stint. But everyone was so
nice about it and considerate of my feelings. They sent me get well
cards and notes thanking me for doing it even when I felt so rotten.
Its worth a hundred bouts with the flu because the folks think so much
of me. You see it isn't how much I want to do my thing as much as how
well I can entertain them and make them happy and glad they came to see
the show. Thats all I care about...making the people enjoy themselves
for awhile. I love seeing and hearing them laugh and yell and show
their happiness because of what I am doing up there. Even the girls
wanting to kiss me means alot because they wouldn't want to if I had
not given them something they couldn't get anywhere else. I guess its
kind of like a love affair. I am in love with the people's happiness.
And in return they are in love with the idea of me. In reality I am
nothing..I know that is true. Im pretty much like the next guy..no
better and no worse but because of all the publicity and the talk I
have been made into something greater than reality. It feeds my ego
sure. I need feeding that way or else I wouldNSt have chosen this
type of work. And yet I am shy and inhibited untill I get out stage.
Strange man that I am it is pretty hard to explain much less understand
I talked about the weird things that happen to me and around me to all
of you people at some time or another. As I said I grew up with it
and so wasn't aware untill a few years ago that I was kind of strange.
But with all the other weird people Ive met these past few years I am
pretty sure Im low on the pole of strangeness. I just see and hear
things. And do them and kind of have them happen to me and around me.
But I don't make it a life study or lifes work so that lets me down.
I guess that its something one is born with or develops later in life
when the time becomes right for them to do so. Now me..I have been
like this all my life but lately it has gotten stronger because the
times are changing and because I am in touch with so many many people.
I have found that when things get too much for me prayer is a main
stay in my life. I put ever thing into [illegible] hands and into His [illegible]
judgement. Sometimes I thought that I could not go on living with all
the things going on around me. The times that I could not find the
faith and strength within myself to fight the desperate thoughts in
my heart and mind I turned to God for He is the only one who understand
exactly what is on the inside of the human heart. No matter how we
try to explain and tell another person how we feel it just won't come
out the way we want it to. There is no way to explain to another just
what is going on inside our minds and hearts. But God knows. He can
know before we try to tell it and just the knowledge that He knows can
be such a blessing to a troubled heart. If not for Him I could not
cope with the buffeting and blowing of evil winds that strike me down.

Page One

"I am in love with the people's happiness. And in return they are in love with the idea of me. In reality I am nothing, I know that is true. I'm pretty much like the next guy... not better and no worse, but because of all the publicity and the talk I have been made into something greater than reality. It feeds my ego, sure. I need feeding that way or else I would not have chosen this type of work. And yet I am shy and inhibited until I get out on stage. Sometimes I thought that I could not go on living with all the things going on around me.

"The times that I could not find the faith and strength within myself to fight the desperate thought in my heart and mind, I turned to God for He is the only one who understands exactly what it is on the inside of the human heart. No matter how we try to explain and tell another person how we feel it just won't come out the way we want it to. There is no way to explain to another just what is going on inside our minds and hearts. But God knows. He can know before we try to tell it and just the knowledge that he knows can be such a blessing to a troubled heart.

There is around all of us a kind of curtain made up of our own persona vibrations. Each of us is entirely different in this respect..we have no vibrations exactly like anyone else on earth. And the color of it is different..like no other. Its called and arua and other names too. This vibration can tell us many things. Like when someone walks up quietly behind us we can sense it. It can tell us when someone is talking or thinking about us too. It can be very sensitive and again if we haven't become aware of it-it can be very un-sensitive. Most people will admit to knowing that they for some reason, are aware at times of things they don't know how to explain. Like knowing or thinking that a thing is going to happen or has happened but not ever knowing for certain how they knew. To some people this is scary. They don't like it and since they can't explain the things or someone who has this ability they start thinking that they are wrong or some how evil or nuts or should be put away. But it is their own crazy ideas and not the strange persons at all which should be analzed. A person with a narrow unseeing understanding is to be pitied for they go through life missing most of lifes greatest joys and blessings God provide each of us with a brain and the ability to use it. If we go through life using only a part of our reasoning then we are wasting His gift to us. As a child we are born inquistive and eager to learn but to some a time comes that we shut down our minds and refuse to listen or even to try to hear or understand anothers mind. This I beleive is the reason for so many wars and misunderstanding between the races. We each tend to feel ourselves superiour to the other and only because we don't listen to each other. We just go through life thinking that we are right because we only listen to ourselves and so how could we known that perhaps someone else has a different opinion than ours and perhaps it is the correct one after all. I think that it is the fear we all have that perhaps we are wrong and somoen else is going to find it out that keeps us from opening our minds and hearts to another. What I am trying to say that is important to me and to everyone with the ability to reason is this...God intended that we explore our world and our ablities given to us or He would not have bothered to give us reasoning ability in the first place. He meant that we use our brain and our sensitivity and our hearts to open the doors to understanding and knowledge. God works in many ways His wonders to perform. It sometimes seems that everything is wrong but with faith,hope and trust in God the end works out for the best. We argue and fight it and try to change it and end up in a worse mess than ever but when we turn to Him in honesty and love the end is always right even when it is not what we would have for ourselves. Time all ways will ~~even our wants and needs~~ out if we just have faith. Its so hard to wait sometimes and so hard to keep faith and so difficult to understand when all around us is black and we can't see the light but sometimes darkness is in its self a blessing. Well anyway we have to learn to understand the things that come to us and to"read"what our senses tell us. The seventh sense is the one that is given to us according to our grace with God. Some never develop it and others it begins to develope almost before they are aware of it. And when it does it is a direct line to God. So many fear what they do not under-stand and in doing so they lose touch with God. They become so wraped up in fear and doubts and scoffing that they miss the treasure that could be theirs. Certainly it is hard to take when you become aware of anothers heartache and pain and the knowledge that one you love is going to suffer in the near future. It can drive you crazy to know you must stand by and can do nothing..but there is also a blessing to this for in knowing the future you can prepare and make ready a way to give help and comfront to those loved ones that you could not have done had you not known in advance. God's ways are never happhazard.

Page Two

"God works in many ways His wonders to perform. It sometimes seems that everything is wrong, but with faith, hope and trust in God the end works out for the best. We argue and fight it and try to change it and end up in a worse mess than ever, but when we turn to Him in honesty and love the end is always right even when it is not what we would have for ourselves.

"Certainly it is hard to take when you become aware of another's heartache and pain and the knowledge that one you love is going to suffer in the near future. It can drive you crazy to know you must stand by and can do nothing... but there is also a blessing to this, for in knowing the future you can prepare and make ready a way to give help and comfort to those loved ones that you could not have done, had you not known in advance.

3

There have been so much written about the seventh sense and most of it treats it as hocus-pocus malarky. There are science fiction stories made up about it,witches,super-natural mysterious and so forth. But this is just the same old thing....someone not understanding and making light of and money from other peoples fears,ideas,knowledge and misunderstanding But through the years, dispite ridicule and all the rest, the super-natural and seventh sense has survived and will continue to do so. Becaus there are people like myself and others all over the world. Some more psyic than I and many with greater powers. I can"read"the future at times and I can predict things at times and I hear voices continualy telling me things. Some of them not so good but most of them very good. I hear poems and songs and music which I put into my own material and into words for others. They are usually big on the charts every time I use them. I hear stories that are heartbreaking and some of them give me the will and strength to go on with my life. I admit to being many times on the verge of leaving by my own hand. And there were times that I felt I could not ever be a whole person again but through the knowledge and widom of those departed who come to me with these words of strength and wisdom I have conqured my weakness. This I beleive to be a direct line to God. I beleive he sends his angels to us here on earth if we would but listen. And I think that ~~when there is a need he will [illegible] to us in~~ order than we be forced to listen..to oepn our minds and slow down enough to hear from Him. There again some people become so drug down in self-pity they still hear nothing...but they are the losers in this world. No one can find happiness when wallowering in self-pity. It is so easy to give up..I know..I gave up..but God wouldn't let me go. He had other plans..someday I hope to be able to live up to them. Someday I know I wil know what I am to do for God. Untill then I intend to do the best I can with the gifts that I have. I can sing, I can make people happy, I can help with the money I earn from doing that, and I can reach people who are unreachable. All because I happen to be sensitive to the seventh sense. The drawbacks to being so sensitive are many true..but the blessings far exceed them. I am grateful and indebeted to my Lord every day I live. I had to be brought to my knees in spirit as well as body before I knew how great was this force given me. Before I would listen to His voice. Of course being this way I pick up the pain and suffering of all I meet. I pick up other things also. I can tell what goes through their minds at times and I don't want to know every thing like that so I have learned to shut it off...by thinking of something else at the time it begins to come in. The active body and mind has no time for dwelling on such things. That is the secret of living with psyicism..you have to keep your mind busy on creative thinking. Brooding and worrying about things only make them worse. Bad thinking strengthens evil and trouble. You attract just what you think. So think good. If you can't find a good thing to say or think of someone...keep silent...think of something good regardless. It will shut off the bad influence comeing into you and bring a good one. You have to have good pleasant thoughts going from you inorder to bring them to you. Get good books and read...increase your understanding of the world around you. Shut your mind to nothing but neagitive thought. Keep an open heart. Never go to bed mad or with bad thinking...it will only foul up your vibrations and send you on a bad spiritual trip while you sleep. This can make you sick..physicaly so. I have found that to be so. If you keep good thoughts,good deeds always before you then your body will heal itsself much faster and you'll in turn feel better. It has kept me alive when I should be dead. I am living through God and by His will I know that. I will never leave Him. Always pray before sleeping.Always. Never ask for yourself anything that you can do without. Ask nothing but Gods will be done. He knows what you need...so just thank Him for knowing and for giving it to you. For instance don't ask for strength..thank Him for it. You already have been given the strength...and in acknowledging that you have it you will make it real unto yourself and thus find ...

Page Three

“I hear stories that are heartbreaking and some of them give me the will and strength to go on with my life. I admit to being many times on the verge of leaving by my own hand. And there were times that I felt I could not ever be a whole person again, but through the knowledge and wisdom of those departed who come to me with these words of strength and wisdom I have conquered my weakness. I can sing, I can make people happy, I can help with the money I earn from doing that, and I can reach people who are unreachable.

“All because I happen to be sensitive to the seventh sense. I am grateful and indebted to my Lord every day that I live. If you keep good thoughts, good deeds always before you then your body will heal itself much faster and you’ll in turn feel better. It has kept me alive when I should have been dead. I am living through God and by His will, I know that. I will never leave him. He knows what you need so just thank him for knowing and for giving it to you.

4

Find a time just for yourself and keep it that way. Every day be alone with yourself and try to find the faults you have and get rid of them. The way to do that is to lay them out before you and then forget them one by one. Say that you know you have them and then say that you will over come them. Then don't worry about it again. Put it aside and when you find yourself relenting into whatever they are...you will be aware of it and can stop it. The same goes for smoking...tell yourself each night and each day that you will overcome the need for tobacco and that each time you start to feel the urge for one that you will find it tastes bad. So bad you won't want it. This works..I have just stoped smoking cigars and beleive me my need for them was more than physical...it was in my mind and tied up with my nerveousness. Just a crutch. I no longer find myself reaching for one or wanting one when I see another with one. I notice but I don't hurt for it now. I have conqured it. I find that you must never for one minute doubt that you can do it. That is where the fault lies...thinking that you might not be able to quit or that you lack will power...you do not...unless you al low yourself to think you do. Each neggtave thought weakens the will power. Think positive and add the strength to the will. The same applies to a bad temper, doubting people, finding fault with another, lying, cheating, stealing or any of the vices people are prone to. Usually whatever one cannot stand in another is the very fault in themselves. This I've found to be so true. So I try not to find fault with anyone and if I can I try to find the good in them and dwell on it. I look for the same trait in myself that offends me in another..I usually can find it in myself. The thing that bugs me most in another is narrowmindness...so I try to be open about my own. I sometimes fail but I am nothing like I once was. I have opened a door so wide and so wonderfull that I could never shut it. I opened the door to love and it has warmed my whole life with a glow that is striaght from God's heart. I couldn't stand to be shut off from it again. By this love I mean the love of the whole wide wonderful world of people and the things connected with living. I love everybody and even those who hate me and hurt me I try to understand and many times I find that by trying I make them do the same and like as not they end up liking me and loving goes into their hearts just like it does to mine. There is noone on this earth that God does not love....he intended us to feel the same. He made one world. He made one race..the human race..He just made varity in their color and thinking to enhance the one world and the one race. If we were not different how dull and how boring it would be. And we would not learn the ways of God or of living. Someday everyone will know and understand these ways and then we can say we are again one with God. Untill then it is the duty and the privledge of each of us to try to do all we can to bring this about. Those who do not try are not going to ever have peace of mind or the joy of God in their hearts. I beleive it. I don't know why I am writing all this down but it seems to be coming from my Heart and I just keep writing it. I guess there must be a reason other than one that I might have had in the begining for I had not intended to come on about this. It just came out. I hope that it is useful. My hands just seem to be going of their own accord or else someone is using me for a go between. Sometimes that happens too. This is when you are sensitive to the departed spirits who want to communicate with another or with you and so they use your body and mind and voice to do so. Or that of another...this is what mediumship is about. This is what sceance and other such things are about...but again they are used materialy and have lost their true meaning through underhanded people. But it is a good force and should be treasured if one has it. I do. There are forces of evil in the world and they are always trying to take over the good ones. They try to put doubts and bad thoughts into the mind to build their own force. And they can do this. They can take over the body the same as a good one can. There are so many evil forces around today because so many are willing to think the worst and dwell on evil doings. Just as one can build a good force one can build a bad one. Thoughts give strength and they must be good thoughts or one will suffer through evil.

Page Four

"Usually whatever one cannot stand in another is the very fault in themselves. This I've found to be true. So I try not to find fault with anyone and if I can, I try to find the good in them and dwell on it. I look for the same trait in myself that offends me in another. I usually can find it in my myself. The thing that bugs me most in another is narrow mindedness so I try to be open about my own. I sometimes fail, but

I am nothing like I once was. I have opened a door so wide and so wonderful that I could never shut it.

"I opened the door to love and it has warmed my whole life with a glow that is straight from God's heart. I couldn't stand to be shut off from it again. By this love, I mean the love of the whole wide wonderful world of people and the things connected with living."

5

We tend to feel through others more sensitive to things that we are at times also. We can feel the hurt and pain of whomever those more in tune are feeling. It can be so strong as to make us think we are ill or dying when we are in fact heabthy. I have many times gone to a doctor for a thing only to find it was not me at all. People are forever doing this. And millions of dollars has been spent for treatment they didn't need. I have passed my own sypptoms around to my friends alot xx And I have had to learn to control this on my own for they didn't know what was on. I can hyptnoize myself or anyone else without much effort on my part and so I do this often to keep my friends from feeling what I feel. I can take it-they cant. It is hard to control it at times and if I am feeling real bad I sometimes can't do it. I hate that but I can't always help it. The fact that I can hyptnoize my self helped me through the shows this past few weeks. I kept the pain from bothering me through the show. I don't like to do this because I don't know if something bad really is on me untill I come out of it. Then it may be too late you know. So I have to watch that. So far I have been fine. Just nose bleeding and the like. And to when I use hyptnoisess I cannot control my own psyecsim and so I can't be sure what I do in spirit. Thats funny sounding but true. I do travel around in spirit and I do things ... very well. So do the people who see me...like as not. Also my illness seems to travel to others when Im under also. This is what bothered me about Bob. I wonder if he picked up what I had. It sure sounded like it. For I hyptnozed myself just a few minutes before I came on stage so I wouldn't feel the chill or pain in my chest and so I wouldn't be nervous. I also had a stomache ache bad and was short of breath and sweating cold and felt pretty dizzy and like I might faint from the junk given me. I felt good after I did it though. Its possible I gave him my sypmtoms because you all were on my mind at the time because I expected to see you out front and I had just went to the edge of the curtain and tried to see you and then Ifelt so bad I knew Id have to fix it to give a good show. So I may have done it right then. For shame! If so it will pass after a little while. And like as not the doctors won't find a thing to explain it. You see I also was doing the hyp bit the other time you were there too. I had to in order to do the show. I guess maybe the tie must be broken if this keeps on. I don't want to do it but it will have to be. Or you all will have to learn how to put it aside and control it. It can be done. It should be done for not only will you pick up from me but from everyother person with the similiar vibrations that respond to yours. Like it or not..its true. We all,that are sensitive to any degree, have ties and when we come in contact with them in any true way..mental,spiritual or physicialy we tie in with them and pass our ailments back and forth. Thats how it is and how it will always be unless we learn to hold it off. I know that it can be helpful..for I can take the pain of another and help ease their hurts...and others can do that for me..but we have to learn how to let it go too..or suffer ourselves needlessly.

Well I am about wore out and Ive got to sleep or Ill blow it tonight. Of all nights I can't blow this one. So bye and God's love to all. Elvis

Page Five

Yes, Wonderful this life would be...
If everyone could go..through every day with confidence...

To conquer every woe...if we could go along unnerved
By detractors of this life...Im sure we'd be more equeal...
To the great torments of strife..

If only people would possess..more faith in God above
They could, I know, find happiness and give heartaches a shove.

The key to having confidence..is first to know yourself..
Have high ideals, and store them on your priceless mental shelf..

Hope for the best however rough..the road of life may be
Through hope you'll gain the confidence to forge a golden key.

Above all this pray as you go..and prayer will show the way..more people would have confidence..if more people would only pray.

The golden key to happiness is confidence in doing what you know is right, what you believe in, stand by and uphold in life. you have the key to life use it and it unlocks the world of God's love and blessings. Knowledge is that golden key. whether it be knowing someone, or something, knowledge is the key. use it wisely. strive for it and turn not away. use the key - and follow the path of rightiousness and God's blessings will come

Page Six

Letter Five

Wanda received the following letter from Elvis in June of 1974, a copy of the original follows the transcribed version—from the private collection of Wanda June Hill.

"Dear Wanda and family,

"I am writing this on the plane so if its messier than usual you will know why-as we are over the way to Boston where they would never let me play before. thanks a kick believe me. As I said on the phone when last we spoke, I'm no longer married, it's soon final. Funny tho' it still feels the same to me guess it takes a while to get the feeling back of being free again. Wonder why 'tis called 'free.' I felt freer married. Don't tell anyone but it just feels like fear to me. Maybe I'm just out of practice? Know any nice girls who'd like to practice with me? I'm kidding. I got my 'hands full as it is' (Figure of speech)

"Elvis Presley

"We're in a storm / Turblance (he messed up his name)

"rockin 'n rollin' up here"—Over

Wanda: This part below was on the back and I xeroxed it… (appears below)

"I'll call when we get to Providence-if you can please look up the information I wanted. If you have time. I'm using it now and it's got some side effects I know now. Not too bad though. Man-this is a STORM. God's temper is up to the top. I Love it!"

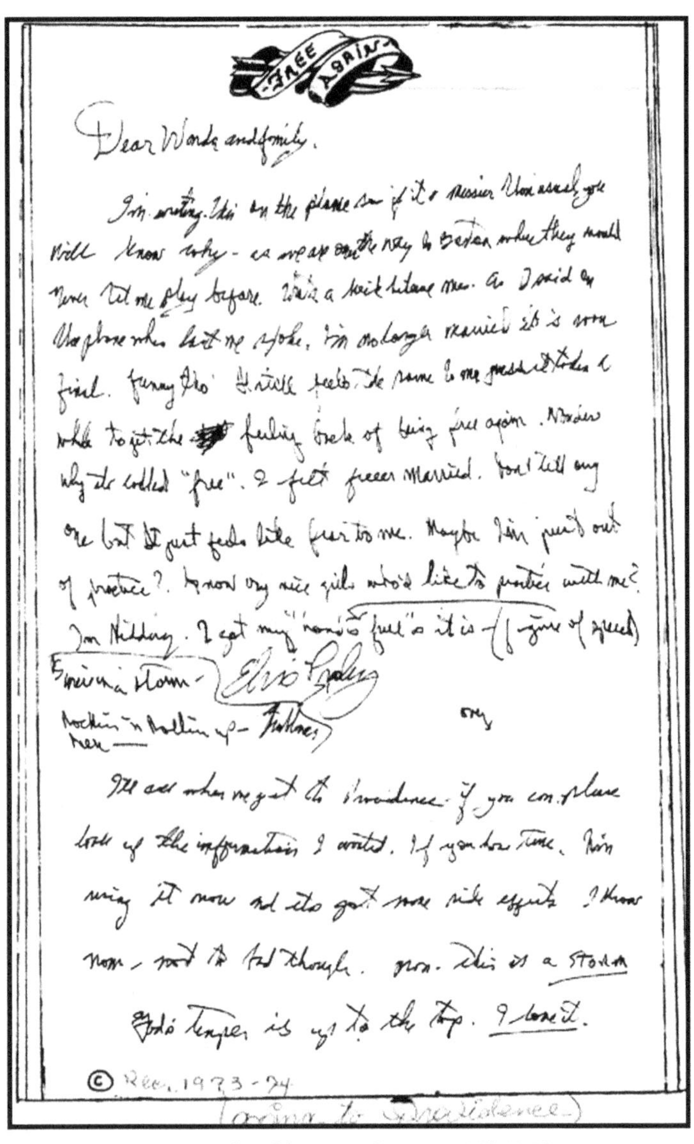

Copyrighted by Wanda June Hill 1978

Letter Six

Wanda June Hill to Maia Nartoomid the author:

“This was written on the cardboard inside a manila envelope with black and white still photos from Easy Come Easy Go… Elvis was just beside himself over that film and hated most of it… he felt it was a 'put down' to some of his 'new age' friends and also his thoughts on such things… but he did it and he did the best he could with what he had to do with. He did enjoy going to the ship and 'being a sailor' for a little while out there… and he liked his co-star but he sure didn't think much of the script. I couldn't believe he put it in writing—that was certainly one of the worst I guess, for him to do that.

"We went to see it twice—he couldn't believe we would sit through it twice! I told him we went because we could see him I remember saying that's why most people go Elvis, to SEE you. I recall that because he wrote that and also because he was dead quiet for several long moments and then said, 'I'll try to remember that…' in a very somber, quiet voice and then he abruptly changed the subject and I thought I had hurt his feelings or something—I wasn't sure exactly what he thought. I had the feeling though it put more of a pressure on him and I hadn't intended to do that. It was just the truth—but I should have joked about it instead or something."

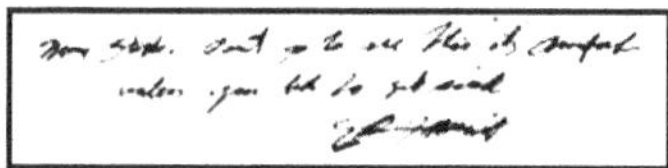

"More Stills. Don't go to see this, it's awful, unless you like to be sick—Elvis"

Letter Seven - Elvis' Birthday Letter to Wanda

Wanda June Hill: "The following are excerpts from letter inside birthday card I received from Elvis on June 29th, 1977. He had told me in May that I would get my birthday present on the 4th of July—my birthday is May 30th and I asked why did I have to wait until then?

"In that on stage sultry tone of voice he said, 'I want to… light your fire, honey!' Then said it was being made and there had been problems. I got the card and letter in June and since it was one of the 3 actual 'letters' in nearly 15 years, that would have been more than enough! I wouldn't take gifts from him very often—he had to sneak them in and after I as he said 'got all over' him for 'spoiling my little girl' and returned several things that were way too expensive I thought; he was very careful what he 'sneaked in.' But this time, for some reason, I didn't give him any static about getting me something-and I didn't ask for anything usually other than him playing guitar, organ or just being funny.

"He always tried to do that—to please us any way he could though he'd grumble that 'wasn't a gift—it's just more of the same—me bein' a durn fool.' Jimmie and I laughed over that 'fool' a lot. I teased Elvis about his having made 'two fatal mistakes' in our relationship—he made me angry a couple of times—but we got passed it. I told him he just had one more mistake—that was as far as I'd go and—he'd better not let me find it or that would be the bitter end! He took that seriously, though I would have forgiven him. He wasn't sure, and had to ask like a little boy thinking he might somehow fail to live up to expectations."

Here is Elvis' birthday letter to Wanda:

> "I hope honey, you will know that I appreciated all the times you have ran around for me, and listened to me and tried to help me out of an emotional maze. I could never repay you for the time and attention you've given to me and the worry I know that I have been. But in giving you this ring... let me also say that it is encircled with love and crowned with praise for you are a wonderful friend... whom I love dearly and from whom I will hurt to part from.
>
> "Please don't find that third mistake when checking my records. I don't want to be cut off and the door

shut between us as friends. I need your friendship and I need to know that you won't leave me. The time is fast approaching when I am going to be in dire need of all the friends I can get. Please don't leave me.

"I know that I have never sat down and written a letter to you like this and I know that it may seem a little weird for me to do so now. I was going to send a taped message but I just wasn't in the mood for it. I will run off some music and soon, but not this minute. I'll have the time a little later on I'm sure. It's just a matter of time before I'll have to stay at home and will need something to keep me busy that can sort of be entertaining for others. In closing, thank you very much for everything and please be happy, and live for me. I'll need you. Sincerely, Elvis Presley

"P.S. My girlfriend's writing this for me, it takes me too long to find the right letters and I can't do spelling. Her name's Cindy and she's going on tour with me a couple days. Her hair's as red as yours, you know me—got a thing for those red haired girls and this little one's got freckles too. Hot damn, connect the dots. XOXO (hugs 'n kisses)"

Letters About Elvis

The following quotations are from letters written to Wanda June Hill by several different women after having read Wanda's books: 'We Remember, Elvis' and 'Elvis—Face to Face.' These women knew Elvis at different periods in the 1960's and 1970's:

Letter One

"I am married, I stayed a virgin until I found Eddie (her husband) because Elvis told me I should. I am so glad too, because I love Eddie as much as I love

Elvis. He (Elvis) told his guys to keep their hands off me and that he would personally kill them if he found out they'd messed around with me. They never did it in front of him, but they tried behind his back. Elvis treated me like a lady, like his little sister whom he protected and cared for. I'll never forget him or his sweet, gentle ways."

Letter Two

Comparing another girl's experience with Elvis to hers, "…he wasn't dirty-mouthed or said cuss words or used four-letter words at all and said poems and sweet things… and he was like a cat, she said, he about purred and he was so beautiful, all his skin and everything, just like I thought, too, and that he gave her an electrical charge too. He was so different, and not real, like men are, you know. Elvis was special and like a real good man, like women everywhere want men to be and they aren't."

Letter Three

"And he (Elvis) went on to explain that the man was his friend and that sometimes friends had to go one step further to help each other. He said something I have remembered. When I commented that maybe he had to draw the line somewhere he said, 'Does your friendship have limitations?' I said 'yes, sometimes.' He looked at me a moment, smiled and said, 'My friendship doesn't - I can't live that way. Maybe if I could things would be easier at times, but I'd feel that I was a failure somehow. I guess,' he said, 'I feel the need to care for others even when it sometimes hurts.'

"And he patted my shoulder and told me not

everyone could or was meant to carry the world on their backs—some of us are like the ducks—it runs off—others are more like the Earth soaking it up, then flowering as spring blossoms, and then there were his type—sponges who soak it up, hold it in and carry the weight for those who can't.

"I never forgot that little speech, it was so sincerely spoken, love shone from his eyes and each word was placed before me as if on a tray. How did he know I carried a load of guilt because I 'ran out' on a friend who had burdened me with so many troubles until I couldn't take it? He didn't know—yet he did, and that talk eased my guilt because I know now, I'm a duck!"

Letter Four

"I know there are many persons who could write such things (as Wanda has written on Elvis) if they would or if they knew how. So many people had personal experiences with this man said to be a 'recluse' and 'have no friends' yet he met so many, cared about them and related with them.

"I was fortunate enough to be among those people—I had my Elvis experience in 1971, shortly after Elvis' wife left, apparently for the first time. Elvis was in Las Vegas and he was devastated. I never had a more interesting evening with a real man. Elvis was divine, kind, intelligent and he listened! He asked questions and he paid attention to me when I answered.

"He never took liberties, he told me that his wife and daughter were 'at home' and that he missed them so much. He said that it was his fault that they weren't getting along, he just couldn't handle the constant pressure of career and home life and that it wasn't really anyone's fault—just the way things were. I was terrible, I do admit to that. I wanted him to lose control, wanted to take him to bed and wipe his pain away, make him happy.

"It was awful, he sat there, tears filling his blue-blue eyes, one trickled down his cheek, running all the way to his jaw bone and I wiped it off. His lip trembled but he said, 'I don't know what I'm going to do. I-I need love, warmth and I'm not the kind of human being who can do without those things. You are so beautiful, warm and loving it makes me know how much I miss those things.

"Please understand, I'm not turning you down for any reason other than I just feel I can't do this to my family. Maybe we can make it right soon, I pray for that. I need help with this, I can't go on alone.' Those were his exact words, I wrote them down as soon as I was out of his sight. I am an ordinary woman, Elvis could have done anything he wanted, I welcomed his attentions, but he sat there, holding in his heartache and watched television, while I sat there wishing for a way to reach him, to help him.

"I married four years after his (Elvis') death. My husband died two years later of cancer of the colon. He looked exactly like Elvis did before he died, bloated, thin of limb and puffy of face with eyes deadened by pain, hopelessness and dejection. When I saw pictures of Ray (her husband) taken four months before he died, I saw all the same things in those (pictures) of Elvis taken weeks before his death. I knew beyond a doubt what killed him."

Letter Five

"I stayed for 5 weeks, day and night, every minute of each day and never left him alone. All of his medication was at the direction of two doctors. It was carefully monitored at the time and Elvis did have a bad stomach, he suffered from constipation all of the time due to a blocked colon. Sometimes he bent double in pain, his face would go white, then grey and he would lie on the bed or floor biting his lips until it passed. He took pain-killers for those bouts, and somctimes they, with the sleeping pills, would just make him pass out wherever he was.

"I was always scared for him at those times, for his life, but no one else worried. They merely picked him up and put him to bed to 'sleep it off.' I was told it was not my business and to butt out. I heard he had cancer, I don't doubt that he did—he complained that his bones hurt, ached, and at night he would sometimes moan in his sleep and rub his legs as if they hurt him.

"I've so many fond memories, I learned so much from him. I loved teasing him, to get him to really laugh—to break up and giggle. He was so charming, sweet, and always had something adorable and nice to say—never spiteful and mean, not to me anyway. He was grateful for my help, for my concern, and he often said thank you when he didn't have to. Even when he felt so tough, couldn't keep food down and was in pain, he would be sweet and kind to me.

"The thing I remember most of Elvis is his sense of humor and understanding of when to laugh and when to be serious. He had it well in hand, and could laugh at himself. That knowledge was a saving grace for him, he could laugh at his trials and tribulations and it kept him strong enough to face life. He was so kind, so patient with everyone, great and small, it didn't matter to him. Each was deserving of his time and attention; that made him a great man, a loving man."

Letter Six

"Elvis was a wonderful, kind man, a tender man, good-hearted and innocent of evil thought or deed. To say he was misunderstood is trite, but there are no words to explain just how confused people appear to be about him, even those who ought to know him, who lived in his presence. I found him delightful, funny, sweet and passionate about many things. To say he was a great man is also trite—he was better than great, he was a lover and a loving man."

Letter Seven

"I knew Elvis for 22 years. Watched him grow into a man, become a super entertainer, husband and father. He developed from a boy into a thoughtful and loving young man during those years, and I watched him mature into a respectful, dedicated husband and daddy. The last time I saw him he had become a divorced, heartbroken man who was resentful of the time his newly won back fame took from his private life.

"He talked for some while about this sad turn of events and asked if I thought other people went through the same type thing in other kinds of demanding jobs. I told him in many ways they did, he wasn't an unusual case. That appeared to relieve his mind somewhat and he began to smile a little and to speak of happier things. It was heartrending to see the anguish in his eyes, the strain had sharpened his features and he was no longer the sad-eyed dreamer I had come to love and cherish."

Letter Eight

"I'll always remember Elvis' smile, the gentle way he treated me and his wonderful laugh. He was such a special friend and I sure did love him. I wished so many times that my mother had been able to meet him but she died just before he stopped by the first time (to her father's store). Sometimes I think that he was sent to my dad and me, sort of to help us over the loss of momma.

"Elvis told me how it hurt when his mother died and he talked to my dad some about that too—the very first time he came by. He just started to talk about his mother—and he had no way of knowing we had just lost momma a week earlier. It helped my dad talk about it and it sure helped me to meet Elvis and to look forward to seeing him now and then. It gave me a reason to live I guess.

"I told him that the last time I saw him—in Vegas. He leaned down and kissed me and whispered, 'Love never dies—be it mine or yours or a loved one's devotion to another. I love you little Mollydolly,' which is what he called me from the first time he saw me and was introduced. 'My Mollydolly' he would say, 'come here and let me look at you. Man, you're a real doll!' It was pretty confidence building let me tell you! And he'd laugh and wink, then tell my dad he'd better keep an eye on me!"

Many of the letters Wanda June Hill has received in response to her two books on Elvis have been from those who knew him, most of them briefly, and yet he seemed to enter their lives when he was most needed. Several of the women who wrote to Wanda stated that Elvis had 'saved their lives.' He touched them in a way that reversed their destructive life-pattern. Such is the power of true spiritual, cosmic love.

Notes from Elvis

In December of 1976, a terminally ill Elvis poured out his heart to God in a series of personal statements written in his hand on the stationary of the Hilton Hotel in Las Vegas. These 'notes' he tossed in the wastebasket, only to be retrieved by a friend and not released to the public until after Elvis' death. They read as follows:

♫

> "I don't know who I can talk to anymore. Nor to turn to. I only have myself and the Lord. Help me Lord to know the right thing."

♫

> "I will be glad when this engagement is over. I need some rest from all of this. But I can't stop. Won't stop. Maybe I will take everyone to Hawaii for awhile."

♫

> "I wish there was someone who I could trust and talk to. Prayer is my only salvation now. I feel lost sometimes. Be still and know I am God. Feel me within before you can know I am there."

The following note is in the possession of Wayne Newton, who wrote a song called 'The Letter' based on Elvis' plea:

♫

> "I am glad everyone is gone now. I will probably not rest tonight. I have no need for all of this. Help Me Lord."

The first three of the above quotes appeared in the article, 'Crying for Help' from the tribute magazine, 'Elvis—An American Legend.' The author of 'Crying for Help' ends with this heartfelt statement:

> "That someone of Elvis' incredible talent and saintly generosity could not find sanctuary for himself is a modern-day tragedy. Elvis lived to bring his fans pleasure and perform on stage. His golden voice, innocence and incredible God-given talent attracted so many to him. Those who took joy from all that Elvis was, know that there will never be anyone who can compare and wish that somebody could have helped."

Stephanie's Story With Elvis

Stephanie James was a twenty-seven year old woman who came into my life in 1996. I was moved by her feelings for and experiences with Elvis since his death, and therefore wished to share this story she sent me about her connection to Elvis. It demonstrates how there is so much more to life that we often believe there is. I hope it inspires you to explore the possibilities more deeply too!

> "I have been a disciple of the mystical realm for many years. I am here to tell you a story, a true story involving my personal experience with the soul we know as Elvis Presley. Before I begin I must state a fact that I feel is relevant to the story. I did not know Elvis during his most recent incarnation as Mr. Presley for I was only six years old when he died, but that does not denounce the experiences I have bore witness to since Elvis' death. I have been an Elvis fan ever since I can remember. I found it very easy to love and admire the

man and his music at a very early age. This admiration has continued into adulthood and I will always admire the man for sharing his love and his life with us.

"Now to begin the story of my spiritual journey. To help you understand the path I have been traveling, I will start by saying that prior to my spiritual experiences with Elvis' soul I was confused, in a grey area of my life, and did not know the correct path to take. The path I chose begins with a psychic reading given to me by an expert in the area.

"During this reading she tells me of my own psychic abilities and asked why I had not used these powers to answer my own questions. She told me of a master, an angel on High that was watching over me quite attentively. She proceeded to tell me that this master had been assigned to me as a guardian spirit for my soul, and its purpose here was to help guide my way on the enlightened path. She told me this angel (master soul) had gained physical immortality as well as spiritual immortality and that I knew of him, and his presence was ever present in my life.

"I did not understand what she meant, but I was intrigued by what she was telling me. She did not drop any names and the session was over before I could ask. At the end of the session she suggested I use my intuitive abilities and try to contact the master that guides me. So I went home and took her advice. I meditated and tried to contact this soul but could not. It was late so I went to bed.

"I had a dream that I was in a darkened room sitting on a red crushed velvet couch with a similar couch adjacent to the one I was on. Encompassing the room were thick red velvet stage curtains. There were two people sitting on the couch facing me and they were conversing with me telepathically. They told me I was going to be visited by my guardian spirit and he would be here shortly. I sat with them and waited until I felt a tap on my shoulder through the curtain and I responded by jumping out of my seat.

"I turned to see a hand through the curtain that was adorned with many rings. I was no longer frightened and took the hand willingly. I felt this overwhelming presence of light and love and felt an illumination from within. Then the dream dissolved in the mist and I was in my own room still holding onto the hand but I was rubbing against the ceiling, floating in the air. The hand I was holding onto seemed to come from outside of the house and was reaching inward.

"At this time I looked at my body lying there sleeping and then looked at the hand again, this time getting a better look at the rings. One had the initials 'EP' in a diamond cluster and the other one was encrusted with jewels with the insignia 'TCB.' The hand seemed to be encouraging me to follow it out into the sky. This caused me to become scared and I made a leap for my body below.

"I remember feeling a tingling sensation that I had never experienced before and my eyes were streaming with tears. I am normally a heavy sleeper, but I was wide awake. I looked at the ceiling and there was no hand so I then looked at my bed and could not believe what I saw. I have a textured, stucco ceiling and there were little white pellets of ceiling all over my bed. I knew then I had had my first out-of-body experience.

"After this dream I wanted more proof of the existence of life after death, so I began an extensive search into the supernatural phenomena. I realized that I could induce out-of-body experiences, channel spirits, and read tarot cards very easily. I had an innate ability that I had not used or tapped into before. This was all well and good but the dream still sat heavily in my mind. I asked for Elvis' help and guidance and that is exactly what I got.

"I went to work the following day and a friend said she had something for me. It was a magazine that she had come across at the doctor's office and felt an urge to take it with her. It was an 'Angel Times' magazine with Elvis gracing the cover. The headline read 'Elvis and his Angelic Connection.' I found this to be quite a coincidence and ran home to read it. It was all about the spiritual happenings in Elvis' childhood and his commitment to God in his lifetime. The article in Angel Times was written by Maia (the author of this book), and used a picture painted by Isabelle Tanner. The addresses for these ladies was at the end of the article and I felt compelled to write to them. I was excited to know that I could learn more about the subject so personal to my life.

"I ordered Isabelle Tanner's book. While I was waiting for the book, I once again asked Elvis' soul to give me yet more proof of his after-life existence and that he in fact was communicating with me. This time I was a little more demanding, knowing from the article that Miss Tanner was an artist and has painted many portraits of Elvis, I asked him to show me the truth about our connection via one of the portraits. I waited for the response from Miss Tanner for what seemed like a very long time.

"Then several weeks before Christmas the package finally arrived. I tore the package open so quickly some of its contents spilled on the floor. The book was oversized and beautifully handcrafted. It was titled 'Elvis, A Guide to My Soul,' which I found quite appropriate. On the inside cover she had autographed the book with the words 'Through the loving care of Elvis—Love, Isabelle.' I flipped through the pages and did not find the picture that Elvis had promised me. I was disappointed and thought maybe, just maybe, my mind had been playing tricks on me all along.

"I put the book down and went to pick up all the papers on the floor I had dropped while opening the package. I was looking through it when I came across a Christmas card she sent along with the book. I sat there in awe for several minutes. The picture on the card was of an angel giving Elvis his wings, and Elvis was lying beneath the angel ready to receive them. That was not the reason I was astonished, however. The angel looked exactly like me. To say the least, I was overwhelmed by feelings of love and admiration. Elvis had truly been communicating with me all along and here was my proof. I can't begin to explain to you how excited I was that I was privileged with the true knowledge of my gift to communicate with Elvis' soul.

"Very shortly after this, I wrote to Maia and sent for the book she had written and excerpted to form the article for 'Angel Times' at the advice of Elvis. Her book arrived quickly and I was able to delve into Elvis' spiritual side, the book went way beyond my expectations with the vast array of information contained within it. Its name was 'Magii From The

Blue Star—The Spiritual Drama and Mystic Heritage of Elvis Aaron Presley'(*Author: the earlier version of this book*).

"After reading the book I felt closer to Elvis than ever before. The voice became clearer and clearer in my mind as well as his visitations in my dreams. I wrote to Maia and told her my story. While I was waiting for her reply, a remarkable thing happened to me. I was sitting on the couch one night watching TV, when I got an overwhelming feeling that there was a presence in the room.

"I felt a warm tingly feeling and smelt something like that of electricity. My cats were staring into the corner of the hallway and that's when I heard this voice say 'over here, here, see me for I am here.' I looked to where the voice was coming from which was the corner of the hallway and that's when I saw him. It was Elvis, yes Elvis. Not the Elvis that we loved on this Earth, but a different Elvis. He was filled with light from within.

"The only way I can describe it to you is take a negative from a picture and shine a flashlight through the back of it. He was just the outline of Elvis, he was an illuminated being. The image of Elvis spoke to me telepathically and told me not of our connection to one another but of a world to come. He told me not to fear death because death is life in another dimension, and that our earthly minds cannot conceive the beauty and the peace that awaits us when we die.

"He further explained that our souls never die. We live on and on into infinity. We are only here, he explained, to seek and find our soul's purpose in each incarnation that we encompass. We are also to try to live in unity, peace and harmony while on this earthly plane; but because of personal will this fact of unity is becoming more difficult and complex as the years pass on. That is why in order to accomplish this task given to us at the beginning of time we must give up our personal will to spirit, that spirit being God the Almighty.

"He then went on to explain that this is the true key to Heaven on Earth. He then told me he was my guardian angel and he said he had to go now but he would always be there when I needed his assistance. I either passed out or fell asleep and woke up the next morning wondering if this experience had really happened or it was just a dream. I went upstairs, took a shower and returned downstairs.

"I happened to look up at my hutch when passing it and saw a sign that the dream had in fact had been real. On the hutch wedged in between the rail of the hutch and a book was a card from a deck of cards. It was the King of Hearts. I then heard the voice of Elvis say to me that it was real and to spread the message of light to all who love the King. I started crying and knew, right then and there, that I would be able to do as he asked. I am doing this by telling you this personal story right here and now.

"I wrote to Maia again telling her of my story and she gave me a spiritual reading to find out how Elvis and I were connected. I will give you a short summary of my reading to better explain my connection to Elvis. She started out by telling me that I had known the soul of Elvis in several past lives and that I had once saved his life from people who were going to kill him by hiding him in my house.

“She also told me of an order called ‘Aberu’ in ancient Atlantis* that Elvis’ soul and mine were a part of. The order had made a pact to remember past incarnations when incarnating in a new body and the rest of the order would guardian over the incarnating soul through his or her lifetime. Maia explained it as being kind of like musical chairs, and that it did not happen in every incarnation but only key ones.

“This to me explains my connection with his soul in this lifetime, as well as the Angel picture on the Christmas card, the one which I so treasure and truly looks like me, the one with the Angel giving Elvis his wings I mentioned previously. I had not mentioned this before, but Elvis had told me before I ever received the card or the spiritual reading from Maia, that I had been Elvis’ guardian in his incarnation as Elvis. Now it was all beginning to be validated.

“Maia then told me that I almost incarnated as Elvis’ daughter in this lifetime, but instead decided against it because of the limitations I would endure being Elvis’ daughter, as is exemplified in his daughter Lisa Marie’s challenges. I could give you countless examples of my communion with Elvis’ soul, but that is truly not the purpose for my writing this. I have given you some background into my life so you would believe what I am about to convey to you about the true essence of life via my conversations with Elvis’ soul. There is a God, and He goes by many names and is worshiped by many different religions, but he is the one and only Creator.

“So many of us turn our backs on Him and are disbelievers because we feel if he were real he would not let us suffer with trials and tribulations the way we all do. But in reality our incarnations on this Earth serve a divine purpose. We are all here to serve God and are all Sons and Daughters of Light. We are all part of the Master’s plan to create Heaven on Earth instead of it being two different realms of existence. This will come to pass in the near future and the time is now at hand to regain our spiritual heritage that is inside us all, waiting to emerge. Elvis and I both realize that this can be a long journey for some and a walk in the park for others. But no matter what spiritual level you are now on, there is always room for improvement. So please open your heart and soul to the beauty of God, so that we may attain Heaven here on Earth. You may ask, ‘how can I do this?’

“The answer is simple; with an open mind and just one ounce of faith all things are possible. Elvis and I also realize that some of you may need assistance in this incredible endeavor. I am here to say that we are both here to help all true seekers. As far as Elvis is concerned, he extends his hand to help all those in need of his assistance in their search for God and their Divine Purpose. All you have to do is call on him for help with love in your heart and he will help show you the way.

“Now that this story has been told so that you too may find the path to God and Spirit, I have fulfilled one of the many tasks in God’s Master Plan. I wish you the best of luck in your spiritual seeking and also extend my hand to help all those wishing to find God, and even wishing to feel the Spirit of Elvis.

I invite you to write to me with your God and/or Elvis experiences either just to share them with me, or for maybe a more divine purpose. Either way, I look forward to hearing from you and always remember that our loved ones are just a heartbeat away, waiting for us to look into ourselves and find that they have been waiting there for us all along.

"Elvis Presley in my opinion was a hidden Master. He was not able to reveal this to the world for fear of losing his image and he couldn't risk losing the love of his fans due to them misinterpreting him wrong. So he went out on a quest to show them the truth, love and Light of God through his music; especially his gospel music. Throughout his life-time he loved, shared and gave us his all for no other reason than love. He is best described in this piece from the Instruction of Amenemope from an Egyptian papyrus writing:

"The truly silent man holds himself Apart.

"He is like a tree growing in a garden

"It flourishes; it doubles its fruit

"It stands before its Lord.

"It's fruit is sweet, its shade is pleasant

"Since Elvis Presley no longer resides on the earthly plane living out his karma like the rest of us, most people believe he is but a precious memory even though his legend lives on in our hearts.

"Blessings, Peace and Harmony to all, Stephanie James"

Appendix B: ELVIS' SPIRITUAL BOOKS

During Elvis' lifetime he read over 1,000 books on a variety of topics from medicine, politics and history to spiritual philosophy and metaphysics. Three hundred of these books he took with him wherever he went. Unfortunately, after his death, most of them were either lost or destroyed. This appendix presents a listing of some of Elvis' favorite spiritual-metaphysical texts, which he read often and shared with friends. We have chosen to section them under the following headings:

- **List A:** Larry Geller's list from his book on Elvis, 'If I Can Dream.'
- **List B:** The book list Elvis gave Wanda June Hill (minus the repetitions from Larry Geller's list).
- **List C:** Our own additions, books Elvis personally gave to Wanda June Hill.

List A—Larry Geller's List

- The Scientific Search for the Face of Jesus by Frank Adams.
- The Initiation of the World by Vera Stanley Alder.

- The Finding of the Third Eye by Vera Stanley Alder.
- The Fifth Dimension by Vera Stanley Alder.
- The Secret of the Atomic Age by Vera Stanley Alder.
- The City of God by Saint Augustine.
- The Light of the Soul by Alice A. Bailey.
- Initiation of Human and Solar by Alice A. Bailey.
- Glamour: A World Problem by Alice A. Bailey.
- The Reappearance of Christ by Alice A. Bailey.
- Esoteric Healing by Alice A. Bailey.
- From Intellect to Intuition by Alice A. Bailey.
- The Externalization of the Hierarchy by by Alice A. Bailey.
- Beyond the Himalayas by Murdo MacDonald Bayne.
- The Impersonal Life by Joseph Benner.
- Brotherhood by Joseph Benner.
- The Way to the Kingdom by Joseph Benner.
- Isis Unveiled by Helena Petrovna (Madame) Blavatsky.
- The Secret Doctrine by Helena Petrovna (Madame) Blavatsky.
- Wisdom of the Overself by Paul Brunton.
- Hidden Teachings Beyond Yoga by Paul Brunton.
- In Search of Secret India by Paul Brunton.
- The Secret Path by Paul Brunton.
- Discover Yourself by Paul Brunton.
- A Hermit in the Himalayas by Paul Brunton.

- The Quest for the Overself by Paul Brunton.
- Ten Unveiled: The Brydlovan Theory of the Origin of Numbers by Dozema Brydlova.
- Cosmic Consciousness by Richard Maurice Bucke M.D.
- The Lost Books of the Bible and the Forgotten Books of Eden.
- Cheiro's Book of Numbers by Cheiro (Count Louis Harmon).
- When Were You Born? by Cheiro (Count Louis Harmon).
- Cheiro's World Predictions by Cheiro (Count Louis Harmon).
- Fate in the Making by Cheiro (Count Louis Harmon).
- Science and Health with the Key to the Scriptures by Mary Baker Eddy.
- Gracian's Manual by Martin Fisher (trans.).
- The New Age Voice (magazine) by Larry Geller.
- The Prophet by Kahlil Gibran.
- The Spiritual Sayings of Kahlil Gibran.
- Thoughts and Meditations by Kahlil Gibran.
- The Infinite Way by Joel Goldsmith.
- The Gospel According to Thomas, from the Nag Hamadi Library.
- Meetings with Remarkable Men by G.I. Gurdjieff.
- Man, Grand Symbol of the Mysteries by Manly P. Hall.
- The Mystical Christ by Manly P. Hall.
- The Phoenix by Manly P. Hall.

- Twelve World Teachers by Manly P. Hall.
- The Secret Teachings of All Ages by Manly P. Hall.
- The Lost Keys of Freemasonry by Manly P. Hall.
- Old Testament Wisdom by Manly P. Hall.
- The Rosicrucian Cosmo-Conception by Max Heindal.
- America's Invisible Guidance by Corinne Heline.
- Color and Music in the New Age by Corinne Heline.
- Music: The Keynote of Human Evolution by Corinne Heline.
- The Sacred Science of Numbers by Corinne Heline.
- New Age Bible Interpretation, Volume I by Corinne Heline.
- The Hidden Wisdom of the Holy Bible, Volumes I and II by Geoffrey Hodson.
- You are the World by Krishnamurti.
- The First and the Last Freedom by Krishnamurti.
- The Masters and the Path by C.W. Leadbeater.
- The Inner Life by C.W. Leadbeater.
- The Chakras by C.W. Leadbeater.
- Levi by C.W. Leadbeater.
- The Aquarian Gospel of Jesus the Christ by C.W. Leadbeater.
- The Huna Code in Religions by Max Freedom Long.
- Only Love by Sri Daya Mata.
- Light on the Path by Mabel Collins.

- Metaphysical Bible Dictionary by Charles Fillmore.
- Morya by Helena Roerich.
- Leaves of Morya's Garden, Volumes I and II by Helena Roerich.
- Agni Yogi by Helena Roerich.
- Aum by Helena Roerich.
- Brotherhood by Helena Roerich.
- Hierarchy by Helena Roerich.
- Heart by Helena Roerich.
- Fiery World, Volumes I and II by Helena Roerich.
- Infinity, Volumes I and II by Helena Roerich.
- Letters of Helena Roerich, Volumes I and II.
- The New Man by Maurice Nicoll.
- In Search of the Miraculous by P.D. Ouspensky.
- The Fourth Way by P.D. Ouspensky.
- Thinking and Destiny by Harold Percival.
- Masonry and Its Symbols by Harold Percival.
- Morals and Dogma by Albert Pike.
- Ramacharaka by Albert Pike.
- Fourteen Lessons in Yogi Philosophy by Albert Pike.
- New Mansions for New Men by Dane Rudhyar.
- Fire Out of the Stone by Dane Rudhyar.
- The Secret of Light by Walter Russell.

- Pyramidology: The Science of the Divine Message of the Great Pyramid by Adam Rutherford.
- Pyramidology: The Glory of Christ as Revealed by the Great Pyramid by Adam Rutherford.
- The Adventure of Consciousness by Satprem.
- Life and Teachings of the Masters of the Far East, Volumes I-V by Baird Spaulding.
- The Urantia Book.
- Holy Bible; Old and New Testaments, King James version.
- The Holy Kabalah by A.E. Waite.
- Autobiography of a Yogi by Paramahansa Yogananda.
- How You Can Talk with God by Paramahansa Yogananda.
- Science of Religion by Paramahansa Yogananda.
- Man's Eternal Quest by Paramahansa Yogananda.
- The Holy Science by Sri Yukteswar.

List B—The List Elvis Gave Wanda

less repetitions from Larry Geller's list above

- The Agony of Christianity by Miguel De Unamuno.
- Red Tree by Christine Hayes (this author by her former name).
- The World Around Us by Sandra Hillstrom-Svercek.
- The Inner Reality.
- Just One Voice.
- The Life of Christ.
- The Mystical Christ by Murdo MacDonald Bayne.

- Joyful Wisdom by Friedrich Wilhelm Nietzsche.

List C—Books Elvis Gave Wanda

- The Teachings of Buddha from B.D.K.
- The Light to See by J.F. DeVries.
- Strange World by Frank Edwards.
- The Search for a Soul by Jess Stearn.

Below is shown a page from one of Elvis' many books. You can see his writing showing through from the other side, which is shown directly in the second image (from the private collection of Maia Nartoomid - given to her by Wanda June Hill).

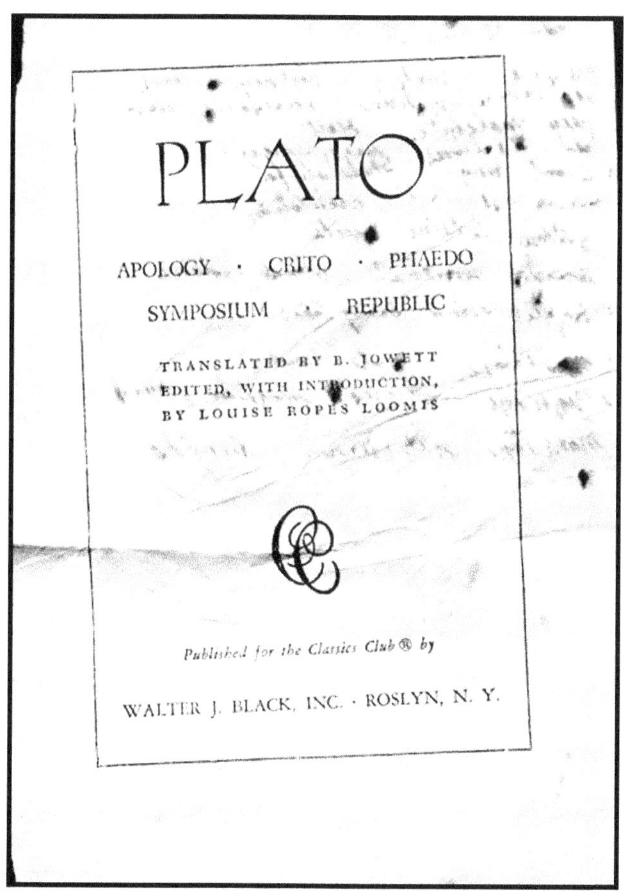

PLATO

APOLOGY · CRITO · PHAEDO
SYMPOSIUM · REPUBLIC

TRANSLATED BY B. JOWETT
EDITED, WITH INTRODUCTION,
BY LOUISE ROPES LOOMIS

Published for the Classics Club® by

WALTER J. BLACK, INC. · ROSLYN, N. Y.

Colors & Sacred Stones

rose pink quartz kidneys blood
aquamarine ovulating nervousness, ulcers
green malachite heart
red carnelian lungs, energy
Black onyx stress reliefer
silver hematite circulation
yellow citrine guts
lavender amethyst glands system
Agate mind, body toner
obsidian guts stress
tiger eye pancreas magnetic ground
moonstone colitis varicosed, lymphs

COPYRIGHT, 1942
BY WALTER J. BLACK, INC.

PRINTED IN THE UNITED STATES OF AMERICA

Appendix C: ELVIS' KNOWN CHARITIES

List of charities which either Elvis donated to himself or serve to honor him specifically. The first was built after his death in honor of him. The last three he gave to generously during his lifetime.

The Elvis Presley Memorial Trauma Center

The Med Foundation

877 Jefferson Avenue

Memphis, TN 38103

www.the-med.org/services/trauma-center

Le Bonheur Children's Hospital

One Children's Plaza

Memphis, TN 38103

www.lebonheur.org

Porter Leath Children's Center

868 N. Manassas

Memphis, TN 38107

www.porterleath.org

St Jude Children's Research Hospital

ALSAC

501 St. Jude Place

Memphis, TN 38105

www.stjude.org

Appendix D: GLOSSARY

These are the terms which were marked in the text of this book with and asterisk*. In this glossary we have also maintained the format of placing an asterisk* after any terms contained in this glossary so that if in reading one definition you are not familiar with a term used therein, you can cross reference it wherever possible.

Acu-points

'Energy points' identified by the ancient Chinese through the science and practice of acupuncture performed generally on the human body. When these points are stimulated in a particular manner a specific result can be witnessed, many times as simple as pain relief or the alleviation of disease. Moreover, these points were considered to be connected by energy lines called meridians, which acted much like wires.

Modern research done by Dr. Robert Becker and others has shown that these points and meridians do indeed exist, and that the points are 'transmission booster' stations for very minute electrical signals traveling along the meridians. The meridians have been shown to exist within the skin and subcutaneous tissue of human flesh, there being an actual measurable difference in the electrical conductivity of the skin and tissue along these 'meridian lines*.'

So the actual mechanism for pain relief via acupuncture is that the needle when inserted into the acu-point disturbs the flow of electrical energy moving through that circuit. As the pain signal has been found through research to travel actually through these circuits to the brain, rather than using the more commonly thought nervous system, the pain signal is effectively blocked from ever reaching the brain.

This principle of acu-points on the human body is also repeated on the 'body' of the Earth. There are acu-points and meridians present on the Earth, and they are responsible for the electromagnetic anomalies mapped out by the military and other governmental agencies primarily for the purpose of pinpointing 'hot spots' that are dangerous to air travel due to their effect on electrical instrumentation aboard aircraft. There also acu-points on other 'energy structures' such as pyramids and ancient temples, which can be worked with by those knowledgeable in such matters, and this is what Elvis refers to in Chapter 6.

Alchemist

One who practices alchemy. Alchemy in its more ordinary understanding is the doctrine, study and practice of chemistry as performed in the Middle Ages, which was primarily focused upon transmuting ordinary metals into gold, and finding a universal remedy for all diseases.

Esoterically and spiritually, alchemy encompasses a much more expansive realm of endeavor, and in its highest forms of expression is the actual transformation of consciousness from its lesser base states to the more highly refined spiritual states. When working to 'better' ourselves, to attain to ever higher moralistic and humanitarian goals, we are affecting a form of alchemy within ourselves.

All-Seeing Eye

The inner vision of one's Higher Self Wisdom. In ancient Egypt, this inner vision was represented in the Eye of Ra, the Eye of Horus, and also the Eye of Isis. Each of the 'eyes' was identified with a particular type of inner sight or wisdom. My inner spiritual sources tell me that the Eye of Ra is the pure 'solar' consciousness; that is the Wisdom and Knowledge of the Central Sun (see also Great Central Spiritual Sun this glossary) of All Creation, from which all things arose. The Eye of Horus is the vision of discernment, of spiritual law in the world of matter, and teaching universal principle to humanity. The Eye of Isis is the unfolding of Love-Wisdom in the heart; listening to one's inner compassion through acceptance of all-being as coming from the One Source.

Apollo

A Greek god of mythology who was the son of Zeus and Leto, a demi-goddess. According to legend, Leto gave birth to twins named Apollo and Artemis on the Greek island of Delos. Apollo was a Sun god, strongly associated with the oracle site of Delphi.

Aquarian Age

The period when Earth in the scheme of the 'Great Year' passes through the influence of the astrological* sign of Aquarius. It takes Earth approximately 26,000 years to pass through all of the Zodiacal signs, about 2,150 years for each sign. This occurs due to a great stellar cycle called the 'Precession of the Equinoxes.' Earth is considered by some to have entered the 'Age of Aquarius' early in the 19th century. Others believe this will not occur for another few hundred years. While the Age of Pisces has represented a time of suffering and separation from God Source, the Age of Aquarius is to be a time of reconciliation and return to the God Source.

Aquarius

The astrological* sign which lies between Capricorn and Pisces. It is considered the 11th sign of the Zodiac. Aquarius, despite its name, is an 'air sign,' and represents an enlightened or illumined persona and expression in its higher manifestations.

Archetypal

Pertaining to an archetype—see 'Archetype' below.

Archetype(s)

An archetype is any pattern that can be duplicated in thought or form. This could be as simple as the image of an object or product to be manufactured such as Coca-Cola, or as complex as human consciousness patterns. There are many different variations on archetypes. The noted psychologist Carl Jung's archetypes are those born partly of God essence, and partly of humanities own lesser variations of that essence. These types of archetypes are an underlying pattern of consciousness generally existing within the subconscious or unconscious mind.

Many of the ancient 'gods' and deities are symbolic of certain archetypes. In our world, we have a mixture of different categories of archetypes. The archetypes Carl Jung identified represent ways of thinking and behaving that humans would adopt, many times without being fully conscious of the pattern they were emulating. These patterns greatly influence an individual's perception. These archetypes come to us in our dreams and visions to bring us a message in pictures.

Through a basic understanding of archetypes we can begin to see the message more clearly, whether that message was given in the dream / vision state, or through a representative figure in society. Myths and legends are rich with the presentation of archetypes to deliver their message. The stories presented within these myths and legends are designed to lead one into deeper aspects of the sub/unconscious mind and to a greater understanding of themselves and their world.

Astral Projection

This can take many forms, one of which is commonly referred to as 'Out of Body' experiences. There are different levels of astral projection possibly depending upon the amount of consciousness that is actually 'transferred' to the other states of mind. A more complete transfer would allow an individual to be fully conscious within the experience and to feel the texture of the material in walls and other solid objects as they pass through them. A less complete transfer might be a flying dream or vision. The types of experiences possible are almost infinite due to the many variables affecting states of consciousness. This is called astral projection because it is the subtle astral* levels of reality that one projects into when this phenomenon occurs.

Astral

The astral plane is a dimension of reality where dreams, disembodied spirits, ghosts, poltergeists, out of body experiences and other psychic phenomenon occur. It is also where Angels and other spiritual beings may appear or interface with us as humans. The astral dimension has many different levels of reality, from the very lowest to the very highest, just as here on Earth. In the Biblical correlative, the very lowest astral regions could be equated to Hell, the middle astral regions to purgatory, and the higher astral regions to Heaven.

Astrology/Astrological

Astrology is the science and study of astronomical influences pertaining to an individual's personality and life events. However, it can also influence an entire country, organization or world. In the astrological 'forecast,' the position of various planets in our Solar system, the Sun and Moon, relative to each other, and the position of the individual at birth, are used to determine influences present in their life. Each planet and celestial orb has an associated symbolic energy and these combinations are defined in the astrological chart.

Atlantis

An ancient civilization for which there is little or no remaining evidence. Plato spoke of the people of this continent in his writings, but somewhat cryptically. According to *my inner mystical sources*, the Atlanteans were highly advanced, in many ways; attuned to Spirit more than our current civilization. Their downfall was working with spiritual powers beyond their total comprehension. They made some key errors in judgment eventually leading to the destruction of not only their civilization, but the entire continent of Atlantis.

While this may boggle the mind of current day humans, the Atlanteans were working with energy forces contained within nature, incomprehensible to our way of thinking. The closest powerful thing in our experience is the atom bomb. However, it is important to understand that they did not develop weapons of destruction or dominance with this power, they were simply using it to attempt to create a greater spiritual reality that would shortcut the spiritual development process for mankind, an experiment which ended in catastrophe.

Auras

This is the energy field which surrounds all matter, especially living things. Humans have an aura, or subtle energy field around their bodies, which can be perceived by those with their psychic abilities opened. The aura changes colors with the moods, health, age and spiritual advancement of the individual. Those people who have a greater spiritual presence will have auras which extend out beyond their physical body for a great distance usually, and they will have very beautiful and spiritual colors in their aura. Less advanced humans will have smaller auras, and if they have patterns of anger, hatred, jealousy etc. many times the aura will have 'muddy' looking colors, or even dark spots and holes in it. The aura is the mechanism by which we 'feel' things intangible, it is the sensor for our sixth sense.

Avalon

The realm of the Fairies, an in-between realm that is a higher spiritual reality not completely removed from the Earth reality. It is from this realm that many myths and legends have originated, thought to be 'Fairy Tales,' and truly they are! (see also 'Crystal Isle' this glossary).

Camelot

The place where King Arthur and the Knights of the Round Table are presented in the Grail mysteries. The Somerset hill-fort of Cadbury Castle, England has long been thought to have been the ancient 'Camelot,' however, more recent archeological evidence suggests the Isle of Man is the more likely location for the historical version of this mystical kingdom.

Central Earth Incan Clan

One of the clans of the Inner Earth populace. Many of the remnants of the Incan culture retreated into the regions of the naturally hollow sphere near the center of the Earth. For centuries, persons have claimed to have had experiences with Inner Earth races, either within caverns, or further, being taken within the natural hollow and allowed to return again.

Chakra(s)

These are the main energy centers on the physical human body, and are identified and mentioned in Eastern scriptures a great deal. The endocrine glands each correlate with a specific chakra. There are generally seven main chakras or energy centers recognized in the human body, with a myriad of lesser ones. The main ones are generally located about the mid-line of the body in the following locations:

- 1st or Base chakra—on the perineum.
- 2nd or Navel chakra—usually just below the navel.
- 3rd or Solar Plexus chakra—just below the sternum.
- 4th or Heart chakra—next to the physical heart.
- 5th or Throat chakra—at the recess at the base of the throat.
- 6th or Brow chakra—also called the third eye, on the center of the forehead just above or even with the eyebrows.
- 7th or Crown chakra—on the top center of the head.
- Each chakra has a specific 'consciousness' focus:
- 1st—survival issues.
- 2nd—creativity and sexuality.
- 3rd—power and will.
- 4th—love, compassion.
- 5th—communication and expression.
- 6th—psychic ability, clairvoyance some mental powers.
- 7th—higher spiritual knowledge and mental powers.

Other chakras are located in the center of the palms (used in 'hands on' healing) and soles of the feet. The chakras are where subtler energies enter our experience, allowing us to have spiritual experience while in a physical body. The aura* is intimately involved and each chakra has an color, but is not limited in that color for its emanation. The colors of the specific chakras can be visualized to help 'tune' a chakra to its optimum operating condition.

Channa (see 'Ki' this glossary)

Channeled

This is a form of Spirit communication. There are many forms of 'channeling.' We could consider in the truest meaning of the term, that anytime we receive a message from Spirit that we have 'channeled' the information. We must use caution here though many forms of medium-ship communicate with negative beings and entities that truly lead to no good purpose for anyone. Conversely, there are souls who have the ability to access higher spiritual beings and who have as their sole purpose helping humanity reach higher levels of spiritual attainment and understanding—both are vastly different in their results. As an example of the possible extremes that this term could encompass, participating in a séance or communing with poltergeists might lie at the bottom end of the scale, while the highly evolved spiritual knowledge that Jesus Christ imparted to his disciples would lie at the other end of it.

It is important to on the one hand not openly accept anything that someone who is channeling brings through simply because it is given by a being without a body, and on the other to not totally dismiss the possibility that we can be helped by a higher being not embodied on Earth at this time. We must come to 'feel' in our hearts what is correct for us and what is not, and use that inner discernment as our primary criteria as to what is truth and what is not.

Christic Merovingian

The Merovingian dynasty ruled over large parts of France and Germany between the 5th and 6th centuries. It has been suggested they descended from the family of Jesus Christ. *My inner mystical sources* concur. The Merovingians were called 'sorcerer kings' as they were said to possess much arcane wisdom and knowledge of the mystical. They were also called the long-haired monarchs, as they prided themselves on the wearing of long hair believing that, like Samson, it gave them strength. 'Christic' Merovingian then implies the genetic connection of this dynasty to Jesus Christ.

Confucius

From 551-479 B.C., Confucius was one of China's most famous teachers, philosophers and political theorists. He greatly influenced the civilizations of Eastern Asia. While he isn't normally considered a religious leader—his primary focus and teachings were on social ethics and reform—he embodied higher spiritual principle in his writings and teachings. Many of his books became the basic Chinese educational curriculum for nearly 2,000 years.

Corpus

Latin for 'body.' 'Corpus Christi,' meaning the body of Christ, is often used in the context of the Christian religion.

Cosmic Emissary

Anyone with a greater purpose or message, a soul who incarnates with a greater purpose, such as Elvis; or an illumined Light being, who appears to us in a vision; or an Angel, etc.

Crystal Isle

This was the legendary title given to Glastonbury in England and to the otherworld of Avalon. Glastonbury and Avalon are the same place, in essence. *My inner mystical sources* state however, that Glastonbury was a consciousness 'doorway' to the realm of the Fairy, otherwise known as Avalon. The Crystal Isle then, is both the earthen realm of Glastonbury, and the spiritual realm of Avalon working in close harmony with one another. It is akin to an 'Island' that exists neither here-nor-there exactly, an in-between place for souls to experience spiritual states of existence, without fully leaving the earthen realm.

Glastonbury is a sacred place. It is the site of the first Christian Church in Great Britain founded by Joseph of Arimathea*, according to *my inner mystical sources.* In ancient times, it was a stronghold for the Druids*. Factions of the Druids honored 'One God' and others were notorious for human sacrifice and other negative and harmful practices. I therefore speak here of the Druids who remained true to God principle. Joseph of Arimathea is said to have brought his young nephew Jesus to this region when the latter was a child, and in later years Joseph returned with the 'Three Marys' (Mother Mary, Mary Magdalene and Mary Martha).

Dharma

The state of existence when the soul comes into a full expression of its purpose for incarnation in that particular embodiment. While dharma does not mean the soul is operating free of karma*, it does mean it has moved far enough beyond the karmic circumstance to be able to receive knowledge of its greater purpose for the current incarnation.

Druids

A name given to priests and priestesses of the ancient British Isles and Europe. They were highly scholastic, religious and founded universities of learning. Their religion centered on the glory and divinity of nature as a living being, much like the 'Gaia* Hypothesis' of today. When the Romans invaded the British Isles, France and Germany, they found the Druids threatening their power. The Druids gave the native peoples identity and respect for their culture.

The Romans, however, wanted to keep the conquered nations in fear and ignorance and began a campaign to justify their slaughter of the Druids, by proclaiming they were perverse, blood thirsty and evil, deserving of elimination. The eradication of the Druids by the Romans did not take place over night. These religious scholars were a powerful authority in their time and the Romans needed their cooperation to maintain law and order. Eventually, however, the Romans dispensed with them altogether.

Elephantine

Elephantine Island near Aswan, Egypt, on the Nile, is the site of some ancient temples. The Temple of Khnum is here and considered the home of the god Hapi.

Enoch

Enoch was a main figure in the Old Testament of the Bible, and is to be a Master of the Light. There is an inter-testamental scroll called the 'Book of Enoch' which contains a great deal of wisdom. Enoch also represents a specific consciousness, which the being Enoch exemplified, this is another example of archetypes*.

Ether

Also spelled 'aether,' this is a subtle energy or 'substance' from which matter forms. Although it is not limited to that function, being the medium through which we can astral project (see astral projection) and accomplish other psychic feats. Quantum physics now recognizes aether.

Etymology

The study of the origins and meanings of words many deriving their meaning from ancient mythology.

Gaia

The spiritual being or consciousness inhabiting Earth. We are all Gaia's children. She is our Earth Mother.

Galahad

The knight who sought and found the Holy Grail* in the Grail Mysteries; in mythos, the son of Lancelot du Lac and Elaine, daughter of Pelles. My inner spiritual sources state that Galahad was the son of Elaine by Ban, who was the son of Merlin and when Ban died his soul entered the body of the fetus as yet unborn, who was to become Galahad.

Gnostics

Gnostic—'truth' and Gnosticism—esoteric practice and study of attaining higher levels of spiritual truth. Students—Gnostics.

Golden Age

When mankind receives higher spiritual influence inherent in the Age of Aquarius*. This age will bring the end of war, famine and hardship and has been predicted by the Bible, the Baghavad Gita, and many other scriptures, prophets and seers. We are about to enter the Golden Age now and the more we focus the quicker we enter.

Golden Age of Horus

When the wisdom of the Horus* and those he represented return to Earth.

Golden Spiral

A golden spiral or 'golden mean spiral'—a sacred geometric progression which holds the key to eternal life. It can be expressed as a mathematical equation, when plotted results in a never-ending spiral. When viewed from the air, the Sphinx, and the three main pyramids at Giza, Egypt can be plotted exactly upon a golden mean spiral when starting at the Sphinx.

This suggests very high levels of knowledge in the planning of these structures, which were not even built at the same time. A lesser version of the golden mean is called the Fibonacci sequence or spiral. The Fibonacci spiral or mathematical equation is intricately interwoven into all of life on the planet; it determines the correct number of flowers on a plant, the size of our fingers in relation to our hands, lower arm bone length to upper arm bone length etc.

Grail Legends

The Grail Legends of King Arthur, Guenevere, Camelot, Parcifal, Fisher King, Merlin, Galahad and Sir Lancelot—while these legends have some basis in actual historic personages and events, few realize the symbolic importance of these stories to the spiritual evolutionary unfolding of humanity. The essence within the legends is that the spiritual seeker must find divine expression within their own experience.

When enough individuals on the planet have found this inner source, the Grail is returned to the planet as a whole. According to *my inner mystical sources*, there is also a physical Holy Grail* cup which remains hidden to this day. This Grail Cup is the one used by Jesus and the Apostles at the Last Supper. This object is significant, in that it is infused with the holy essence of the consciousness of the Christ and the rite he performed at the Last Supper with his closest disciples.

Grail Mystery

This is the sacred knowledge that, if attained, would free one to become the Grail or Christed being. The Grail Mystery is elusive, not because anyone wishes for us to remain in the spiritual darkness, but because humanity has blocked understanding. Only those with a higher level of consciousness fully understand consciousness and all of Jesus' parables although he ensured many were decipherable by the masses.

Great Central Spiritual Sun

The esoteric Source of All Being, which could also be referred to as the Heart and Mind of God, is also called the 'Kolob' in some scriptures and is the true focus of 'Sun Worship' in its undefiled state. In later ages, once the ancient wisdom had departed from humanities grasp, worship of the Sun took the true 'Sun Worship's' place. While our Solar Sun is also a higher spiritual entity, later forms of Sun Worship employed a large measure of superstition to 'appease' the gods so crops would be successful. This practice is based on fear not wisdom.

Great Pyramid

The largest of the pyramids in the complex at Giza, Egypt. While whole books have been written on the mysteries subject, quite simply the Great Pyramid at Giza is generally considered by those knowledgeable in esotericism, to be an ancient edifice built for the purpose of spiritual initiation, and not for the entombment of a Pharaoh. In support of this, is that fact that there have been no artifacts or mummies found in the Great Pyramid as there have been in other tombs, nor are there any hieroglyphs depicting the deceased, no hieroglyphs at all for that matter.

Harmonic Convergence

The Mayans predicted the Harmonic Convergence, a major alignment of the planets in our Solar System, with the Sun. The date was August 16-17, 1987. This momentous occasion issued in a new era for Earth's humanity, where we were to remember our connection to God and move into harmony with each other again. It must be understood that this 'convergence' will take some time to mature.

Hermes Trismesgistus

The Greek Hermes Trismesgistus, also known as Thoth or

Tehuti, also spent time in that area, although he was not known at Greece in that time. Hermes is the name for Greek God Mercury, or spiritualized mind; Trismesgistus means 'thrice great' and represented his mastery of the three great alchemical principles of Love, Power and Wisdom. Hermes Trismesgistus wrote many sacred texts as a legacy for humanity. He was a great being whose soul comes from another world more highly evolved than our own, to help humanity surmount its own plight.

Hermetic

Of or pertaining to Hermes' (see 'Hermes Trismesgistus' above) teachings and philosophy.

Hidden Name

Names believed sacred by the ancients as they signified the essence of the individual, for the purpose of good or ill. A 'hidden name' was one not revealed to the masses, but kept secret from all but initiates who understood its true meaning.

Hierophant

A sage or seer at a high level of spiritual achievement, an interpreter of sacred inner mysteries and higher esoteric principles, the Hierophant must be able to 'see' clearly into the soul of others and safely facilitate their higher initiation. The Hierophant holds the key to great love, wisdom and power and transfers this to the spiritually prepared.

High Llamas

Tibetan religious leaders are called Llamas and the High Llamas are the upper echelon of the Tibetan religious hierarchy.

Hiram Abiff

The Master architect of King Hiram, sent to King Solomon to

build his temple. Hiram Abiff was ritually slain by three unknown persons of an oppositional force before the completion of Solomon's temple.

Holy Grail

Said to be the cup from which Christ drank at the Last Supper and the central theme of the Arthurian legend; the prize King Arthur's knights sought to obtain in a holy quest. This Cup is more significant if understood symbolically as a sacred Mystery representing the blood and body of Christ, the Corpus Christi.

It is a crucible for consciousness, handed down through the alchemical properties of blood from one generation to another, representing the ability of all human races to awaken to the Spirit within, through the commonality of the blood which all share from one original God. Corinne Heline states in her book, 'Mysteries of the Holy Grail': "The power of the Grail belongs to the Christ Mystery, in which the heart becomes an organ of divine illumination under the control of will."

In other words, the Christ consciousness awaits those who can learn to think with their hearts, and love with their minds. The Holy Grail, as a container for 'sacred blood,' signifies the human form for within us are the remnants of great and illumined races. Yet the Grail is also the cauldron or creation pattern of the Goddess within the Earth. In this form, it comes not from the patriarchal lineages, but from the maternal lineages of the Earth. It is nevertheless the same in essence, human beings are an interwoven product of many sacred genetic vines, those of the Earth mixed with those from the stars.

Holy Tone

The sound used to initiate creation of our world by the God Force. This term can also be used to denote the use of sacred sound to initiate spiritual principle or reveal sacred inner mystery. Sound as a creational principle may seem a novel idea, but the Bible says, "In the beginning was the Word" referring to this principle.

Our science is now finding out that everything, even seemingly solid objects, is energy, and has a specific vibration or 'sound frequency' to it. Sound is vibration and the extrapolation can be made to demonstrate this principle, by saying that it is conceivable there could be a Divine sound which may have initially put life into motion by combining particles into atoms into molecules etc., all induced through the added vibration imparted by the 'Divine Word' or sound.

Homer

Greek author of several mythological stories including the 'Odyssey' and 'Iliad,' it is presumed Homer might have lived sometime in the 8th or 9th century but virtually nothing is known about his life.

Horus

In Egyptian mythos, Horus is the son of Isis and Osiris. He is a sun god, often depicted with a falcon head. Esoterically, Horus was a star being who established temples of wisdom throughout ancient Egypt.

Incarnation

The physical cycle a soul goes through here on Earth until they have realized their highest potential. Then the soul returns to the greater Light of the Godhead. The process of incarnating is that of a soul taking life in a physical body to learn within Earth's great school curriculum.

Initiates of Aryana

This comes from a quote of Corinne Heline which states: "Orpheus was the first of the 'human gods' (Initiates of Aryana)."

Ms. Heline does not give any further information on these Initiates. *My inner mystical source*, Thoth Hermes, tells us that Aryana was a state of joy attained within the heart of devotees to God, as such the 'Initiates of Aryana' would have been those who devoted themselves to this end.

Joseph of Arimathea

Joseph was a wealthy friend and follower of Jesus Christ—he arranged for the tomb, oils and shroud for the body of Jesus. Esoterically, Joseph was Jesus' uncle, his wealth having been attained in the tin business which took him to the British Isles. It is believed Joseph brought his young nephew, Yeshua (Jesus), to Glastonbury, England on one such journey. After Jesus' crucifixion Joseph then returned to Glastonbury to build the first Christian church in the British Isles.

Kaballistic Tree of Life

The sacred formula for spiritual attainment, the template which all humanity is based upon according to the teachings of the Kabbalah.

Kabbala/Kabbalah

According to this teaching there are ten main points of Light or consciousness on a 'Tree of Life' that humanity must attain in order to realize their full God potential. There are interconnecting pathways between these points of realization one must travel in order to achieve the potential of the 'point of Light.' It is an esoteric spiritual teaching still commonly used today, and while it originated in the Jewish tradition, is accepted by many esotericists outside that practice as being highly viable.

Kachina

A Kachina is a powerful Spirit from the stars in the religion and

Shamanism of the North American Hopi Indians. From *my inner mystical sources*, 'Kachinas' can be various types of star beings as well as Earth spirits. The Hopi were able to commune with these beings, who shared insight about the plight of humanity and the true path of returning to our Divine heritage.

Karma

Balance of energy within the law of cause and effect—involving action, words or deeds. The purest essence of karma is not that God is wrathful, but there are spiritual laws we must abide by. If the total of a soul's good actions outweigh the bad, that soul will generate good karma.

Ki

Also spelled 'Chi' or 'Qi,' it is the spiritual energy which keeps our bodies alive and well. Ki has also been called channa, prana, life force, etheric energy and many others. It is Ki energy martial arts' masters learn to harness, concentrate and then release in a focused manner to achieve some of their almost miraculous feats. When we are ill, our Ki is low and must be rejuvenated to become well again. The Eastern and alternative healing arts utilize knowledge of the way Ki flows in our bodies to help heal and keep us healthy.

King Arthur

The legend of King Arthur, Queen Guenevere and the knights of his court are allegedly fiction based on some vague historical fact. However, the city of Troy was alleged to be fiction prior to discovery of its physical ruins in northwestern Anatolia. To quote Gareth Knight, in his book 'The Secret Tradition in Arthurian Legend,' this legend, "Enshrine(s) a secret Mystery Tradition that stems from beyond the Western Ocean, and which was also the guiding force behind the old stone circles and ancient trackways of Western Europe. This ancient tradition, preserved in Celtic myth and legend was recast by initiated Troubadours and Trouv`eres of the twelfth century, and spread all over the Christian world." *My inner mystical sources* reveal such a King did exist and many of the legendary characters are genuine historical figures, however some are composites of true personages.

In her book 'Mysteries of the Holy Grail,' Corinne Heline writes of the beginnings of such legends: "Ageless wisdom, the first religion given to the early patriarchs by the angelic messengers of the gods, was transmitted whole from the spiritual world to early leaders of mankind. These Wise Ones, masters of other days, were men above creed and class. They served not idols but ideals. Theologies and philosophies grew up around them, yet each divine leader was greater than the Order he founded. Melchizedek, of biblical fame, was one of these. King Arthur was another. From the same place they all came forth."

King Solomon

Son and successor of David, King Solomon (mid-10th century B.C.) was considered the greatest King who ever ruled Israel. He built his famous temple in Jerusalem, was also a sage and a poet, and considered author of the 'Song of Solomon.' The true Temple of Solomon has yet to be uncovered. King Solomon's temple was destroyed in 587 B.C. by the armies of Nebuchadnezzar who burned Jerusalem. A second was built in 538 B.C. over the ruins of this first temple.

Kundalini

The sacred spirit fire or energy stored in the sacrum at the base of the human spine. When the individual reaches a high level of evolution, this spiritual energy will release into the spinal column. This process unfolds over time and, if the individual is balanced in all other ways, will generally proceed incrementally until the kundalini energy reaches the brain and effects an illumined or enlightened state of consciousness. There are dangers involved if released before the individual is ready. Sometimes there can be pre-mature release of this sacred energy.

Unless the soul is under the tutelage and surveillance of a spiritual master who knows what they are doing, this can be dangerous. Release is best naturally, a result of the individual's efforts to live higher spiritual principles. Kundalini is represented by the rising serpent and is the origin of two serpents upon the caduceus now used by physicians. This symbol dates back to ancient Egypt, and the two serpents are the rising kundalini wrapped around the shaft which represents the spinal column, as they rise up to meet the winged sphere, which is the illumined mind of the individual who has had the kundalini reach all the way up the spine to the brain. The winged sphere represents the illumined mind or spiritual sun.

Labyrinth

Also known as a 'maze,' it is an elaborate and usually circular pattern composed of many passages. Only one of these passages leads into the center and out again. The significance of the labyrinth is mystical, based on occult knowledge. When the human body passes through a spiraling movement of twists and turns, the brain receives re-orientation to enable greater spiritual knowledge and wisdom.

Lemuria

A continent (also known as 'Mu') believed to have existed many thousands of years ago in the Pacific Ocean. It met its end in a cataclysmic event long before recorded history. James Churchward, a scholar of the early 20th century, researched fragments of ancient texts he found in Tibet, South America, and other locations, concerning the possible existence of Lemuria.

Lemurian(s)

People or beings that dwelt on the now-sunken continent of Lemuria*.

Light Races

Millions of years ago these beings from other star systems mixed with Earth races to populate this planet with more intelligent and loving beings.

Magi

An esoteric term—'Wise Men' or learned scholars.

Masonry

An esoteric order of architects in ancient times who employed 'sacred geometry' in the design of temples, cathedrals, churches and other buildings used for sacred purpose. Sacred geometry is the use of geometric configurations and numbers that correspond to universal patterns of creation. Many molecules and atoms, when viewed under high-powered microscopes, reveal geometric designs inherent to their structure. These geometric designs are also indicative of the universal patterns of creation and found in all matter. Therefore, creating temples, cathedrals and churches with such design, helps to align the structure, and all souls within it, to divine patterns.

Master Tomer

One who led musical renderings of perpetual choirs*.

Melchizedek Priest(hood)

Priests within the Order of Melchizedek*. While there are current day orders that prepare and ordain one to the priesthood of Melchizedek, it must be understood that these are lesser variations of the true spiritual Order of Melchizedek. Once a soul has been spiritually ordained a Melchizedekean Priest that soul always remains a Melchizedekean Priest throughout all of its lifetimes. It is also true there will be incarnations where that soul is more or less aligned to this part of its greater beingness.

Mental Projection

The act of projecting one's inner mental vision to another location or spiritual / dimensional realm (see 'astral projection' this glossary), also called 'remote viewing' and psychic vision.

Meridian Lines

Magnetic Earth lines criss-crossing the planet, like acu-lines in the body, the Earth's meridians channel powerful energies, connecting various vortices of energy on the planet (see 'acu-points' this glossary).

Merovingian Dynasty

See 'Christic Merovingian' this glossary.

Metaphysics

The science of cause and effect and the knowledge of invisible subtle energies and consciousness which make the universe work the way it does.

Mount Olympus

The holy mountain upon which the gods of Greece dwelt according to their legends.

Multidimensional Beings

Refers to the simultaneous state we all experience in many realities. When we dream, we are experiencing aspects of ourselves that are in these other 'dimensions.' This term can also be used to denote beings able to consciously move between different dimensions of reality and different worlds. This last technique is the ultimate potential for space travel between stars and worlds, through pure consciousness manipulations, not mechanical technology.

Music of the Spheres

The Greek mystic and mathematician Pythagoras stated that all planets in the universe vibrate in harmonic tones. These tones are the 'sound' that particular celestial orb makes. Pythagoras called these tones the 'Music of the Spheres.' It is possible for an attuned individual to hear these sounds in deep meditation. They have been recorded by space probes and sophisticated electronic equipment. The diatonic musical scale, with which we are most familiar is based upon the relational distance between the planets of our solar system. It is as though they were tuning forks affecting each other based upon how close they are to one another.

Mystic Crosses

In this book, 'mystic crosses' are lines in the palms of the hand that cross in a certain way, a sign of some special, mystical destiny for the individual according to the science of Palmistry.

Nature Magic

The science of occult practices using the elements of nature. These practices have been used for both dark and light purposes. Many indigenous peoples have used nature magic in their healing rituals, ceremonies to invoke rain etc.

Numerological

The use of numerology* in application; of or pertaining to numerology.

Numerology

Science of numbers as an insight into the nature and character of Spirit. A number such as 12 can be 'reduced' to a base digit, in this case 3 (1 + 2 = 3). Each letter of the alphabet is assigned a number from 1-9. A person's name can be assigned a numerological value by adding up the numbers for each letter of the name then reducing them to a base digit, which is given a meaning. Numbers of birth dates, names and combinations thereof are used to make the personal 'forecast' or determine the personality profile.

Oracles

An oracle prophecies or sees into the Wisdom of the Ages through inner spiritual sight. In ancient times, oracles were kept distant from the masses, coming forth only in great ceremony to announce their visions. The most famous oracles were those of Delphi in Greece.

Order of Melchizedek

An esoteric order aligned to the ancient wisdom and knowledge of Lemuria★ and Atlantis★. Originally, this order contained a balance between the male and female powers in the temple but, after a revolt of priests in Lemuria and later in Atlantis, the Order of Melchizedek on Earth became solely patriarchal in nature and lost its spiritual focus. However, there are many souls who have participated in this Order in an attempt to bring it back into balance through their greater vision.

Osiris

Osiris was one of the foremost gods of ancient Egypt—his more primeval name being 'Ausar.' He was a god of regenerative power and therefore presided over the Dead. He was the brother / husband of Isis and the father of Horus. In legend, Horus was killed by his evil brother, Set (also called Seth or Typhon), who cut his body into fourteen parts and scattered them to the winds.

Osiris' wife Isis, searched for the parts of his body, finally bringing them all back together (with the exception of the phallus—Isis substituted a wooden facsimile of it and attached it to his body) so that he could pass into the Underworld. Before his passing, Osiris magically came to life long enough for Isis to conceive a child by him. This child was Horus. This story represents the evil forces (Set) having 'scrambled' the divine or Christic consciousness (Osiris) of this world, and the love of the Spirit (Isis) attempting to bring it all back together again.

This story oddly enough, is not a great deal different SYMBOLICALLY than Humpty Dumpty. The underlying essence of both was that something sacred, innocent and joyful had been scattered or lost and, through an effort of love, an attempt to resurrect this essence. The story of Isis and Osiris is much deeper and contains a greater mystery. As the phallus represents the regenerative organ, it indicates that Isis could not 'physically' correct all the damage. On a spiritual level, she solved the problem in giving birth to Horus—something akin to the concept of the 'Immaculate Conception,' but in presented Egyptian symbology.

Perpetual Choirs

Choirs developed in medieval Europe and the British Isles which continually sang. This was accomplished through a constant rotation of its members. The superficial intent was to praise God eternally, but the tradition contained a greater purpose; that of creating a harmonious sound vibration which would send a spiritual consciousness into the ethers* of the planet. Similar perpetual chanting was practiced in the temples of Egypt, Atlantis* and Lemuria*.

Pinnacle of Olympus

Utmost point on the sacred mountain of the gods (see 'Mount Olympus' this glossary), also denotes utmost attainment in consciousness available, where one would be able to commune with the Gods.

Planetary Transformation

The Spiritual journey of Earth in its return to the Light of the Father / Mother God, including all forms of change humans must undergo, to move beyond conflict into the greater love of God, and be able to express that to all of our human brethren.

Ptah

Considered by many to be the greatest of all the old gods of Memphis (Egypt). In Egyptian mythology, Ptah made new bodies for the dead who were to reincarnate. He is identified as a smelter, caster, and sculptor and is also supposed to have fashioned the iron slab that symbolically formed the floor of heaven. While the female counterpart of Ptah is Sekhmet, the lion goddess, he is also connected with Maat, the goddess of cosmic law. Ptah was also the master of the 'Holy Tone*.' As is true with many of the Egyptian and other ancient deities, Ptah was/is both a soul and an archetype* that still exists for those who are knowledgeable in how to access it.

Pythagorean

That which contains the science and philosophy of the Greek mystic and mathematician, Pythagoras, who was born sometime between 600 and 590 B.C. He was a world traveler who studied the sacred mysteries of many cultures and was initiated into their sacred temples. Pythagoras was said to be the first man to call himself a 'philosopher.' Much of the current day geometry taught in our schools is derived from the theories of Pythagoras.

Quetzalcoatl

Aztec name for a mysterious 'White God' or luminous being

who appeared before ancient South American people as a spiritual leader.

Ra

'Ra' means 'creative power.' As an Egyptian Sun God, he was seen as the generator of all life by the sacred rays of his presence (the spiritual Sun). Pharaohs were given the divine right to rule when they were named 'the son of Ra,' as Ra was perceived the supreme ruler.

Reincarnation

The concept that the soul returns many times in order to complete its spiritual evolution on Earth. In the Bible it says that we are created in God's image and that God is life eternal, without beginning or end. If we are created in God's image we too must be eternal. The soul is what we truly are and that is the aspect of us that is eternal and as such continues to be 'born again' upon the Earth until it has enough wisdom to adhere to God's greater plan, whereupon it is then free to move onto God's other 'Kingdom's beyond the Earth in the higher heavens.

Rennes-le-Chateau

A small village in southern France which, along with its surrounding region, was the site of several mysteries of the past. It is said to be the area where both the Order of the Knights Templar and the Cathars hid their sacred books and wealth. Moreover, it is considered holy ground by those who believe that Mary Magdalene journeyed into this region. There is an edifice built at Renne-le-Chateau in her memory called the Magdalene Tower.

Royal Divinator

One who performs divination and who prophecies for royal ruler.

Saqquara

Ancient city of Egypt said to be the location of Ptah's* most sacred temple. There is an impressive step pyramid still at Saqquara.

Self-Realization Fellowship

An organization founded by Paramahansa Yogananda, a spiritual leader and yogi from India with headquarters in California. The organization maintains an ashram there, and perpetuates the ancient yogic wisdom teachings of Yogananda's lineage. A portion of the focus of this organization is to bring the Eastern religious philosophy and teachings to the Western world and into harmony with Christian beliefs.

Sethian Era

In the context of the quotation in Chapter 9, the 'Sethian era' (named after the evil Egyptian god, Seth or Set) refers to our current age, when evil has yet to be vanquished. 'Set' was the evil brother of Osiris in the Egyptian hierarchy of Gods.

Shaman

One who has knowledge of the worlds of Spirit and Nature, and works with those realms, usually for the benefit of healing the body, mind and soul. Like all things, there are and have been 'dark' shamans as well as 'Light' ones. Shamans also work with nature magic*.

Solar Initiate

One who has been initiated into the 'Solar Mysteries'—the knowledge of ancient wisdom that is connected to the Sun. The Sun in these teachings, is a spiritual consciousness that one may attain by understanding the deeper meaning of self and life (see also 'Great Central Spiritual Sun' this glossary).

Source Translation/Translator/Translated

One who receives and translates information from the Akashic records—vibrational fields of Earth, containing all thought, past, present and future events. This is the source of information for many psychics, although there are different levels of ability information available. Source translated is information received/translated by source translator★.

Spiritual Science

Science based upon the spiritual principles of the universe—from the dynamics of interpersonal relationships, to the science of physics beyond the speed of light.

Spiritual Hierarchy

Highly evolved beings who form the greater agency for overseeing Earth's spiritual evolution—Masters, Archangels etc.

Star Person

A human on Earth who contains a significant percentage of genetics from other races in the universe. Many times these 'genetics' are of the soul which then incarnates into earthen genetic form in our world, creating a combination of the two making them nearly indistinguishable from other humans. It is their more highly evolved nature, generally expressed as unconditional love that sets them apart.

Star-Energy

Energy transferred from the universal stellar worlds into the Earth (in our context). Star energy is consciousness itself. Different stars represent differing types of consciousness.

Sun Bow Clan

According to *my inner mystical sources*, these people are from the Orion constellation and established the first 'Temples' on Earth many millions of years ago, before the race of Adam.

Tantric Forces

The creative energy power we possess as a humanity. This energy is most frequently associated with sexuality, but that is only one expression of it, as it takes form as artistic expression and through any other creative avenue offered it by the individual. In its more highly evolved expressions, Tantric energy can be used for healing others and self, and to perform paranormal feats which are generally called miracles by our standard. As with all things, the energy can be used in perverted or destructive ways by individuals with poor or evil intent. It is then not the energy itself which is bad, but rather the individual's misuse of it.

Telepathic

Of telepathy*.

Telepathy

The ability to send and receive thought from one mind to another. This ability is not limited by distance, and is nearly instantaneous, responding to laws of physics which are beyond the known bounds of science currently.

Template

A pattern or form from which other similar patterns may be developed. However, in these chapters, this word is applied as a title for one who was a master of knowledge in the Order of the Sacred Three within the Druids* of the White Grail*.

Ten Holy Sephiroth

Ten spheres of Light of the Kabbalistic Tree of Life*.

Thoth Hermes Trismesgistus

See 'Hermes Trismesgistus' this glossary.

Unicorn

A creature of mythology and some say fact, which has the body of a horse and a spiraled horn upon its forehead. Mystically it represents 'Christ in Nature' with its mantle of purity being the white coat and its sword of heavenly power symbolized in the mighty horn upon its brow. There are also black unicorns, which represent the veiled or hidden 'Christ in Nature.'

Valhalla

Final heavenly resting place for Viking soldiers.

Vulgate

Latin Bible used by the Roman Catholic Church. The translation was begun by Jerome in 383 and completed in 405 A.D. In 1546 the Council of Trent decreed that the Vulgate was the exclusive Latin authority for the Bible.

White Grail

Same as the 'Grail of the White Rose.' *My inner mystical sources* tell me that there are two paths for the Grail Mystery: the 'White Rose' and the 'Black Rose.' Both are of God, but one is more of feminine role (white) and the other masculine (black).

World Karma

The karma* of the human race as a whole. In a more personalized sense, karma or spiritual debt taken upon the soul, not for its own errors, but for those of the world; as in the case of the Christ Jesus 'dying for our sins.' There are other souls who operate in this capacity, albeit to a lesser degree.

Zoroaster

An Iranian religious reformer and mystical initiate born in 628 B.C. who founded Zoroastrianism, or Parsiism, as it is known in India.

Appendix E: AUTHENTICITY DOCUMENTATION

Below I present handwriting analysis and voice spectrum analysis done by experts verifying the authenticity of both the tapes Wanda June Hill transcribed from her conversations with Elvis, and the letters in his hand sent to her.

Spectrographologist Voice Identification Report

Wanda June Hill took all of her taped conversations with Elvis, eight hours of dialogue, to voice analysis expert Arland Johnson, who had formerly worked for the Los Angeles Police Department. In Ms. Hill's presence, he listened to and analyzed these tapes. Mr. Johnson was moved by what he heard and there were moments during the playing of the tapes when he openly wept. The first document is the actual analysis report. The date on this document is January 12, 1979.

PROFESSIONAL SOUND MASTERS INC.
10377 La Saria St.
Los, Angeles, California
90069-237

January 12th, 1979

To Whom It May Concern:

The second week of January, Wanda June Hill brought to my office several cassettes containing conversations with a male, said to be the late Elvis Presley. I took those tapes, ran through extensive electroalysis and compared the voice prints to those taken from a spoken portion of Elvis Presley's Las Vegas recording. I determined that her recorded tapes were in fact Elvis Presley. It is my opinion, determined by 6 voice print check points, that 5 out of 6 checked to be positively Elvis Presley's voice. The 6th test was natural and could be read as positive.

At that time I "cleaned" the recordings, boosted the clarity of the quality and copied them for her on new tape. She took all copies with her and I have no print or copy in my possession.

Dated: 1-12-1979

Signed: Arland Johnson engineer

Witnessed: Marcella Cummings asst

PERSONALLY APPEARED
1. Wanda June Hill
SUBSCRIBED, SWORN AND ACKNOWLEDGED BEFORE ME TO BE WITHIN INSTRUMENT ON THIS DATE January 12 1979
NOTARY PUBLIC
2. Arland Johnson
3. Marcella Cummings

The Municipal Court
WHITTIER JUDICIAL DISTRICT
CLERK
ADMINISTRATIVE OFFICER

This is accompanied by a second document, which is a further verification of the findings signed by Mr. Johnson on January 12, 1979.

SPECTROGRAPHOLOGIST
Voice Identification Report

__Submitted:__

Fifteen [15] audio cassette containing the voices of (1.) a woman, Wanda June Hill, (2) a male said to be Elvis A. Presley.

One (1.) phonograph record containing the voice of Elvis Presley, live, in concert 1969, Las Vegas upon which is a 4.31 minute monolog by Presley.

__Analysis Performed:__

Extensive spectrographic search using standards set forth by Voice Identification/Crime Lab Detection for magnetic tapes via telephone and microphone recording. Comparision of 62 words and phrases, speech patterns, and syllabic resonance over all concluded sufficient match up of the two male voices.

__Determination:__

Tape quality and variables of recording proceedures of more than four (4) variations, over electromagnetic cable [telephone], lower resonance microphones [at least two], and high frequency microphones, at least one, prevented full use of all aural and spectrographic examination possible in the range of magnetic testing. Without the original recordings which were no longer available, further testing is/would not be conclusive.

__Findings:__

It is my conclusion based on the extensive comparison examinations performed on each separate conversation [3? in all] found on the cassettes in question that the male voice contained on all 15 cassettes is Elvis A. Presley. The female voice found on each of the cassettes is Wanda June Hill, except for one female voice on one cassette and in one conversation is of unknown origin. The third voice found in the background noise of one conversation on one cassette is that of an unknown male speaking to Elvis Presley which was recorded in the phone conversation. On all of the cassettes the background noise is varied, consisting of various radio programing, television programing, phonograph recordings, traffic sounds, household noises, office equipment noise, a baby crying, animal noises [dogs, cats and birds] and other human voices of unobtrusive nature.

Arland Johnson
Spectroanalyst
Voice Identification
LAPD

Then there is a third document which is a another letter from Arland Johnson written on January 9, 1986, responding to a letter written to him by Wanda June Hill, requesting that he re-confirm his findings on the voice analysis of the 'Elvis tapes' which he originally made in 1979.

LONDON HILTON ON PARK LANE

LONDON W1A 2HH · TELEPHONE 01 493 8000 · TELEX 24873 · CABLES HILTELS

Arland Johnson
London, England
January 9, 1986

Dear Mrs. Hill

I received word you were trying to contact me concerning your tape recordings with Elvis Presley. In regard to the voice print tests I made in 1979, I can only say again the test was postive. It was without a doubt Elvis on the telephone oposite you. There is nothing further I can do for you in this regard as I no longer am involved in electronic science.

I hope that this will be the information you would have from me. It is the best I can do for you at this time. I would hope Mrs. Hill, that you would not release the intimate and personal confidances you have on tape with Mr. Presley. I admired the man, found him to be of deep personal integrity and find it difficult to condone breaching his confidance, when he was being candid, revealing and quite trusting in his relationship with you. I hope your steadfast declarations of his faith remain.

I have been located in Europe for some years and will continue to reside therein. At this time, due to a case I am working, I am not staying at my home here in London. Please feel free to write me at the address you have now.

Faithfully yours,

Arland M. Johnson
Detective

By 1985 Mr. Johnson was employed by INTERPOL in Europe. In this letter, Arland Johnson is expressing his concern that Ms. Hill not release, "the intimate and personal confidences you have on tape with Mr. Presley." He is not referring to the type of transcribed material we have included in this book, but conversations of a far greater personal nature concerning his broken marriage and other deep sorrows which were the burden of Elvis Presley. These more personal comments from him have been kept personal and confidential. Ms. Hill has not, nor will she ever violate the trust Elvis placed in her.

Handwriting Analysis

A letter from handwriting analyst Karla C. Huntz written to Wanda June Hill on September 25, 1979 concerning her analysis of the handwriting submitted to her by Ms. Hill purported to be that of Elvis Presley's. In this letter she is referring strictly to what she has gleaned in the personality of the individual's (Elvis') handwriting. At a later time she compared known handwriting of Elvis Presley's with those specimens presented to her by Wanda and found them to have been written by the same individual. Unfortunately, this latter verification has not survived in any written form. A copy of Karla Huntz's letter to Wanda June Hill, dated September 25, 1979 appears below:

KARLA C. HUNTZ
251 Des Peupliers Quest, No.5B
Quebec 3, P. Q. G1l 1H5

Sept. 25th, 1979

Mrs. Wanda June Hill
10941 Trask Avenue
Garden Grove, Calif. 92650

My dear Mrs. Hill,

I was quite pleased to learn that the handwriting specimens you sent for analysis were the writing of Elvis Presley. I was delighted to be able to study his handwriting and to inform you that all 3 were written by Elvis and none other. They represent different phases of his life, emotional state and personality changes brought on by those times in his life, but show him quite stable and controled. He was a very special man, gifted and his writing reveals the sensitivity, the generousness and graciousness of his nature. As I mentioned in my analysis, this man was quite unique in many ways and very much the loving, tender man he revealed to the world at large as well as the secretive, often nervous and introspective man that he kept hidden from all but those most near to him. I wish I could have known him on a personal level but now that I have had this oppertunity to study his script, I feel I do know him and I thank you for that.

Good luck with your project!

Yours,

Karla Huntz

Karla C. Huntz
Graphologist

This next piece of documentation is a letter written by Mary L. Jones dated July 16, 1978 to Wanda June Hill. Mary is the elderly lady mentioned in Chapter 12: The Elysian Song, who knew Elvis when he was a boy. Mrs. Jones is no longer living. Because Mrs. Jones' letter to Wanda is so difficult to read, it has been transcribed below.

> "Dear Wanda June Hill,
>
> "I am very pleased that someone finally got around to writing a book telling the truth about our friend Elvis Presley, as there have been so many lies wrote. As I told you on the phone, my family and I knew the Presleys when they moved to Memphis and lived next door to us until Elvis was thirteen. (Mary Jones later told Wanda that they had also lived near to him in Tupelo as well, and moved to Memphis first, the Presleys following sometime later.) I would appreciate it if you would be sure and get one of the personally autographed books. (Mary is asking Wanda to send her a personally autographed copy of 'We Remember, Elvis.') Thank you and the other people (who contributed to the book).
>
> "Mary L. Jones
>
> "P.S. My house is full of Elvis pictures and posters tee shirts and records. Elvis used to eat at our house. He was a good kid. Please call me.
>
> "I'm not well."

Wanda June Hill sent Elvis' father, Vernon Presley, a copy of her first book, 'We Remember, Elvis.' This letter from Vernon Presley below is his reply to her upon receiving and reading the book.

Vernon Presley

3764 Elvis Presley Blvd.

Memphis, Tennessee

Mrs. Wanda June Hill
10741 Trask Avenue
Garden Grove, California

Dear Mrs. Hill,

We received the beautiful book We Remember, Elvis yesterday. I wanted to extend my personal thank you for it. After viewing the contents and reflecting on the work that went in to this lovely tribute to my son, I have to say that you are a friend.

Thank you again, he would enjoy knowing how much his fans and friends care about him today as well as yesterday.

Yours sincerely,

Vernon Presley

Vernon Presley
-Secretary

VP/g

Appendix F: ENDNOTES

Chapter 1

1. Manly P. Hall, now deceased, was an esotericist* of long-standing whose works included such masterpieces of enlightenment as 'The Secret Teachings of All Ages,' which was one of Elvis' favorite books.

2. The key Egyptian initiations took place at various temple sites along the Nile River. The Nile was considered the equivalent to the human spine, with the various initiation temples representing the seven main chakras of the human body spread out from south to north along the length of the river. As each chakra represents a specific level or aspect of consciousness, the individual temples allotted to the initiation of that chakra would be specifically oriented in its teachings to further the development and opening of that level of consciousness.

Chapter 2

1. Elvis had spoken of this in private conversations with Wanda June Hill.

2. By royal lineage I intend to indicate that there are certain bloodlines which have genetics more conducive to supporting a being of much higher consciousness in its soul mission of planetary service than others. This does not mean that all souls incarnated within those genetics will be enlightened, or be beings of higher awareness. Conversely, there are many enlightened beings who have incarnated into 'ordinary' bloodlines, and many 'ordinary' beings that have incarnated into royal bloodlines.

3. See Chapter 5 for more information on this topic.

4. Archetypes are mentioned frequently throughout this book. An archetype is an underlying pattern of consciousness generally existing within the subconscious or unconscious mind. Many of the ancient 'gods' are symbolic of certain archetypes. In our world we have a mixture of different categories of archetypes. There are those which are still pure and close to the Divine mind, and others that are a product of Divine mind and the human mind in varying degrees of mixture.

Carl Jung identified many of the latter type of archetypes. These archetypes come to us in our dreams and visions to bring us a message in pictures. Through a basic understanding of archetypes we can begin to see the message more clearly, whether that message was given in the dream/vision state, or through a representative figure in society. Myths and legends are rich with the presentation of archetypes to deliver their message.

The stories presented within these myths and legends are designed so as to lead the recipient of the story into deeper aspects of their own un/subconscious mind and to a greater understanding of themselves and their world. In addition, something such as Coca Cola could also be considered an archetype, albeit a lesser version of the concept. For further study in archetypes see 'Appendix D: RECOMMENDED READING' at the back of this book.

5. Another way of seeing this is that the downward pointing

triangle represents Heaven coming to Earth, and the upward pointing triangle represents the Earth moving towards Heaven. When you put these two triangles on top of one another, you have a six pointed star, which has been called the 'Star of David' in mystical circles, and this combined movement is what it represents essentially.

6. What I mean to say here is that Elvis had 'created' a 'Temple' from the seemingly normal estate Graceland had been through his devotion to higher spiritual principles in all that he did. As this was his home, it would have become his Temple by default. This is just a different, perhaps more spiritual way of alluding to the old statement that "a man's home is his Palace."

Chapter 3

No endnotes in this chapter.

Chapter 4

1. See Chapter 1 for more information on 'The Time of the Light.'

2. I handed this book to Elvis from the edge of the stage, as related in 'About the Author—My Personal Story With Elvis': "In 1972 I began to give Elvis my mystical works from the edge of the stage. I first gave him my then recently published book, 'Red Tree' (the book published by Naylor Company in Texas mentioned previously). In it I had written a chapter on an ancient Lemurian* (Lemuria is considered by metaphysicians and mystics to be one of the lost civilizations/continents of the pre-history epochs) healer by the name of Kartum.

Although I did not declare it in the book, I knew Kartum to be a past life of Elvis.' Thus, inside the copy I gave him I wrote "To Kartum, in Remembrance." I had brought the book with me to Las Vegas, intent on handing it to him, but not knowing at the time if he was at all open to anything of this nature. Then I met a young woman working in the showroom as a photo girl who knew Elvis personally. Upon seeing my book and hearing a little about my work, she informed me that Elvis was a student of metaphysics and spiritual matters, and would be quite receptive to 'Red Tree.'

That night I was able to hand the book to him from the edge of the stage, although considering my competition for his attention, it was most certainly ordained from the ranks of Spirit that I reach him. When he took the book in his hand and looked at the ancient symbols on the cover, it was as if a shock wave passed through him. It seemed to affect him profoundly. Sometime later when the same young woman photographer asked him if he had read 'Red Tree,' he exclaimed excitedly, "Oh, let me explain it to you."

3. The Holy Tone is the sacred sound of Creation, referred to in the Bible as the 'Word,' and in Eastern scriptures as 'OM.'

4. Very ancient Egypt before the floods that Noah set sail upon with his Ark.

5. It is said that Elvis had the ability to control weather in his most recent lifetime in which we knew him as Elvis also. From Chapter 3: Graceland: "Elvis was known by those around him to on occasion, control the weather in mystical fashion. On the last day of Elvis' life, his cousin Billy Smith complained to him about the drizzle that had been coming down for hours. Elvis went outside, lifted up his hand to the sky, closed his eyes for a moment… and the rain had stopped! As the sun shone down upon him, Elvis turned to his stunned cousin and said with a crooked grin, "You never know, Billy, you never know."

6. The One Star is synonymous with the One God.

7. See Chapter 13 for more information on this technique.

8. See Chapter 13 for more on the wheel he installed.

9. See Chapter 6 for Elvis relating his inner experience of reliving a moment in this lifetime.

10. Pre-deluge is before the Great Flood of Noah's time.

11. See Chapter 13 for a correlative accounting of this lifetime from Wanda June Hill.

12. Black in the mystical and esoterical context denotes that which is veiled or hidden, awaiting the time when the world is ready for the unveiling of the purity, the time when that purity will not be in danger of violation.

13. A true understanding of 'Sun Worship' is that the Great Central Sun of the universe esoterically represents the pure essence of God, and as the visible Solar Sun also brought life to all things, it was natural for that to become a focal point for worship of God to the ancients.

14. These chakras★ are explained Appendix D.

Chapter 5

1. Actually one of Elvis' previous lives as an orator and statesman of Greece, see Chapter 4.

2. 355 B.C. from which 'mausoleum' was derived.

3. Final heavenly resting place for valiant Viking soldiers.

4. The essence of the Grail legends is that the seeker must find the divine feminine expression within their own experience, which is what the Grail represents. When enough individuals on the planet have truly found this inner source, the Grail is returned to the planet as a whole. As the planet has been out of balance in respect to male/female energy for some time, the seeking of the divine feminine (Grail) is designed to restore balance, not to turn a patriarchy into the opposite imbalance of matriarchy. According to *my inner mystical sources*, there is also a physical Holy Grail★ cup which remains hidden to this day. This object is significant in that it is a focusing point for the spiritual Grail, or divine feminine consciousness.

5. Cellular consciousness can be equated to the innate intelligence inherent in our whole being, similar to intuition, and is not dependent on health necessarily as an indication of its state of evolution, particularly in souls such as Elvis' who have embodied for a particular purpose to sacrifice their very form for humanity.

6. From Chapter 6: "Upon opening the casket, all present were astonished to find Elvis' body in an uncorrupted state. Despite embalming, the corpse should not have appeared in such condition. It was not just the preservation that startled them. There was an other-worldly look about it of almost transparent beauty. Elvis was fascinated by the Yogis and Saints ability to achieve transition of this physical realm at will, and studied the teachings of Parahamsaji Yogananda, whose body remained in a perfect non-deteriorated state for quite some time after his death transition also."

7. Reference: 'The Haindl Tarot' by Rachel Pollack.

Chapter 6

1. Pillars of Fire in the biblical and mystical context refers to Divine Light, as in the 'Flame of the Holy Spirit.' Many times in mystical vision or divine revelation the seer perceives columns of Divine Light, or Pillars of Fire. The Pyramids were erected as monuments of the Divine, and served the function as a Pillar of Fire or Divine Light for the planet. Also, truly great souls such as Jesus or the Buddha could be considered Pillars of Fire as well.

2. From Chapter 3 "According to *my inner mystical sources*, Nostradamus predicted the Elvis mystery and its secret: 'The Divine voice shall be struck by heaven so that he cannot proceed any further. The secret of the close-mouthed one shall be closed, that people shall tread upon and before it.'"

3. This refers to the pyramids effect in higher energy zones, where those knowledgeable in such matters could then use the effect to escape the hold of gravity.

4. It is commonly believed in metaphysical/spiritual circles that as human beings evolve to a high enough degree, they will be able to move into higher levels of experience, some able to take their physical bodies with them as did Jesus. Jesus said, "these acts ye shall do and many more." This would be considered the ultimate act of transformation, and esoterically/metaphysically it is commonly understood that temples and pyramids were used to help accomplish this transformation as they were built in accordance with certain sacred geometry principles that helped to raise the energy level of those who entered within them to attempt this type of thing.

You can see this principle demonstrated in the example of ice turning to water, then water turning to steam. As energy is added to the ice in the form of heat, it then changes its state and becomes water. With the addition of even more heat energy the water transforms to steam and is then in a 'different dimension' of reality no longer so easily bound by the laws of gravity etc.. In a similar way, when a spiritual seeker raises their level of consciousness to a high enough degree, they are adding energy to the ice/water of their humanness. At some point when enough energy has been attained, the act of taking the consciousness and physical body into another dimension of reality like Jesus, and some less well known Masters have done, becomes possible.

In the example, the ice/water would seem to have disappeared but it has not disappeared but rather exists in a very much less dense energy state. This is the entire basis for other beings and life forms (i.e. Angels, beings from other planets etc.) being able to exist in our same life space without our being able to see them normally with the physical eyes.

5. This would be an invisible energy grid that is composed of gravitational and magnetic lines of spiritual Earth force which have intersecting points that form the 'grid' or energy net.

6. Metaphysical or spiritual principle has it that an individual must be able to recognize where they have gone wrong so they may

become all the wiser and continue to evolve into a God based higher consciousness, without having feelings of guilt about the wrong doing. Contrary to what is popularly thought, the guilt only serves to take us even further from God. Guilt needs to be replaced with atonement.

7. Many original Biblical texts were written in ancient Hebraic language. This has been one of the inherent problems in their translation, as the Hebraic language has concepts conveyed with a single word, which can take an entire paragraph to explain in English and some other languages.

Chapter 7

1. Chapter 1: "Elvis had spoken to Wanda in 1966 about the Blue Star, and that the ninth moon of Jupiter was somehow an energetic entrance or portal to his planet. *My inner mystical sources* reveal Jupiter's ninth moon is an energy doorway to Orion and Rigel."

2. See Chapter 4 for a list of some of Elvis' incarnations including this one.

3. See Chapter 4 for this and other of Elvis' past incarnations.

4. The Sacred Three—offshoot of Atlantean Melchizedek Order.

5. In Chapter 12, Elvis talks about his childhood visitations at another time.

Chapter 8

1. Black is also used esoterically to denote that which is hidden but sacred, waiting to be revealed—i.e. the 'Black Madonna.'

2. This correlates with the various comments elsewhere in this book about Elvis' 'presence' being felt when he walked into a room. This effect is due to the very large aura he had, which always is present around highly evolved spiritual souls.

3. From 'We Remember, Elvis,' by Wanda June Hill.

Chapter 9

1. Each teacher has been taught by a teacher, who has been taught by a teacher, etc.—this is the 'lineage.' Bob's teacher was taught by a teacher who was taught by Ed Parker.

2. A revealing analogous, symbolic reference to the pig face mask and hippopotamus suit: In ancient Egypt, the hippopotamus and also the wild boar were representations of the archetype Set, who was the equivalent of the Prince of Darkness or Satan. Set's color was red and thus he was often portrayed with red hair and red eyes. His hieroglyph was the khat or physical body which is liable to decadence and decay. Could it have been that the subconscious of those who maliciously required Sarah to wear these atrocities, chose these symbols as representations of their own lower desires?

Chapter 10

1. See Chapter 8 for an accounting of what really went on his room with these women. Generally he read the Bible, or spoke of spiritual things to them.

2. From Sean Shaver's book, 'Elvis Through My Lens.'

3. The name of this reporter was eliminated here as we felt it served no purpose to use it, the story stands by itself to demonstrate Elvis' playful 'Trickster' nature. Anyone who wants to know the name of this reporter can find it in Wanda June Hill's book 'We Remember, Elvis.'

4. Interestingly enough I had received through *my inner mystical sources* that Elvis had actually been incarnated as the person named Galahad. See Chapter 4 for more on this lifetime.

5. See Chapter 15 for more information to support the statement that he was held captive against his will.

6. See Chapter 9 for the story.

7. Einstein's theory of relativity establishes a relative relationship between matter, energy and the speed of light. In a meta-scientific understanding thoughts and feelings are energy, and according to the theory of relativity energy cannot be destroyed, so therefore the energy (in this case of Elvis' laughter) continues on through the universe for eternity.

Chapter 11

1. A partial tone or sound that is in harmony with the full tone or sound of the atom. This would be similar to each member of a symphony playing their individual part, which alone would be not as harmonious and powerful, nor as effective when combined with the sounds of the other instruments.

2. By pre-historic I mean to convey that these cultures existed before the time of our commonly understood recorded history, and not that they were primitive in nature. Quite conversely these cultures were much more advanced than our own in many ways, particularly spiritually, but also in technologies that were in harmony with the Earth rather than those that would destroy the environment their cultures lived within.

3. The Holy Tone carries the same significance as the 'Word of God.' Both denote sound as a creation principle. If you were to watch particles of sand upon a piece of glass being vibrated by sound from a loudspeaker, you would witness a similar effect to how sound creates at higher energy levels of reality. You would see the sand move into specific patterns that were determined by the sounds emitted by the speaker.

The Holy Tone then, is a non-audible (to the normal hearing of humans) sound produced by God which is further defined by His other beings of Light (i.e. Angels) whose job it is to assist such matters. It is this sound that caused the building blocks of matter to coalesce into specific elements, and specific elements to join into molecules and so on. Then we have complex combinations known to us as elements and compounds which then form human, animal and vegetal life forms, minerals etc. All of this occurs in a similar manner to the way the sand (matter) responded to sound (the Holy Tone) on the glass (this reality).

4. Scientifically light is simply a higher frequency of vibrational energy than sound, but both are harmonic with each other. In other words, if the frequency of light is slowed down at some point it theoretically could become sound. This is similar in principle to a dog whistle. The only reason humans do not hear the dog whistle is their ears cannot detect the higher frequency of sound, but the dog's ears can. If the sound of the whistle is slowed down, then humans could hear it. While this analogy uses only sound, the principle is nevertheless demonstrated. Another way to look at it is to see that visible purple light, is a slowed down version of invisible ultra-violet light.

5. Think of the planets as atomic particles in a larger system. Radio astronomers have been listening to very narrow ranges of sound emitted from distant stars for years. These sounds they hear are incomplete renditions of the Music of the Spheres. This is like listening to a stereo recording of your favorite music with the balance turned all the way to the left or right, and the treble and bass controls turned all the way down.

6. In other words, the sounds emitted by the planets act as a balancing mechanism for the sounds of the stars. This could be compared to the way one instrument synchronizes with and balances another when harmonious music is played together by more than one individual at a time. In this case the stars would be playing the 'lead' and the planets the rhythm and bass.

7. This pure primal force has been known to many of the ancients as the power of the 'Goddess,' who has been known by many names such as Isis, Mother Mary and Athena to name a few. It is this sacred

force, which is the key to all manifestation and presents itself in all matter.

8. This was indicated to me by *my inner mystical sources.*

9. The prophesied new era of humanity where God's Law and love shall prevail.

10. The 'Solar Force' is akin to the creative energy of our finer energy system. This energy can be expressed through any creative endeavor engendered through love.

11. Representing Christian and Jewish/Hebraic traditions.

12. Corinne Heline was a modern day Christian Mystic and the author of work which is referred to throughout this book.

Chapter 12

1. The Elysian song is known as the song of the Angels, the celestial choir and sounds of the divine that may be heard when one is attuned to them, usually in deep meditation or prayer.

2. The White Brotherhood is not a racist connotation, as it may sound; it refers to orders of higher beings such as Angels and Masters that are brilliantly radiating the white Light of God.

3. Quoted from Chapter 6: "When he came offstage, he sometimes fainted from sensitivity to the energy blasting he received from an enthusiastic audience. Unconscious, he would begin to speak in an unknown language. Regaining consciousness, he had no memory of the occurrence, and so on one occasion a friend tape recorded his trance-like jargon. Elvis did not recognize the language, but took the recording to a language expert, who identified it as 'ancient Hebrew.'

Chapter 13

1. Edgar Cayce was widely known for his 'sleeping trances' which

allowed him to access information on healing and many other topics including past lives and ancient civilizations. He was commonly called 'The Sleeping Prophet.'

2. In a past life reading I am able through my psychic, spiritual and mystical gifts to travel back in time and 'read' the events, thoughts and feelings for the individual from the 'recording' of them made in what is known metaphysically as the Akashic records. The Akashic records are like a magnetic recording tape, but they are in a subtler dimension of reality and so have no 'physical' mechanism, rather working as does the human memory system we are more familiar with.

3. August is astrologically in the sign of Leo, a fire sign and also considered to be the sign of the Sun traditionally.

4. White Magician meaning one who worked with true spiritual magic for the good of others, rather than selfishly for themselves as would a Dark or Black Magician.

5. In spiritual and metaphysical realms of thought (and even in the leading edge of quantum physics now), it is held that everything is energy and vibration, so that an individual with the proper knowledge could use his mind energy to set up 'invisible shields' that would keep those who were not of good intention away from sacred records. This is the same principle that many accept in regards to say, a Church being protected by the power of God. In this case, individuals acting in behalf of the God force can use the God Light to do much the same.

6. There are many beings of great stature in the Angelic kingdoms that are doing most of the work, but they need a human counterpart(s) to make the link to this world complete.

7. What he is saying here is that the Tree of Life, and the Path of the Flaming Sword represent a descent of Spirit into matter in stages. In other words, the flow of God into our world and our own

beingness as they were created was not all in one step, but happened in successive stages.

8. From Chapter 3, as quoted from Nostradamus: "The Divine voice shall be struck by Heaven so that he cannot proceed any further. The secret of the close-mouthed one shall be closed, that people shall tread upon and before it."

9. Bibliographical reference 'The Symphony of the Zodiac,' by Torkom Saraydarian on information regarding the three sacred fires, and all information relating to the Goat/Crocodile/Unicorn.

10. While this may smack of typical 'tabloid' weirdness, I ask you to consider the following:

i) It was a regular press release,

ii) Elvis often wore a turban as part of his disguise when he attempted to go out 'incognito.'

iii) A phrase which he would speak sincerely to people when he had pre-cognitive insight about a troubling situation in their lives was, "Everything is going to be alright." It was always my feeling that he said this not as a gesture of consolation, but as a kind of psychic-spiritual infusion into the troubled soul of that individual.

Chapter 14

1. Etymology is the study of the origins and meanings of words, many of which derive their meanings from ancient mythology and times long past.

2. An actual past life of Elvis,' see Chapter 4 for more information on Elvis' past lives.

3. In numerology a number 0-9 is assigned to each letter of the alphabet, and the letters of that individual's name are then converted to their assigned numbers, whereby they are then added up and

reduced to a base (single) digit. Therefore, any change in the name will affect the numerology.

4. In numerology each letter of the alphabet is assigned a number, which are then added up. A key difference in the adding of these numbers from the usual mathematical methods of addition are that for example, 27 is equal to a nine via 2 + 7 = 9. So if the person's first name was 27 and their last name were 41, then through this method we would reduce the 27 to 9, and the 41 to 5 and have 9 + 5 = 14, which then would be reduced further to 5 via 1 + 4 = 5. The greater number from which the final result was reduced, also has significance in numerology, i.e. the '14' that we just derived the 5 from.

5. The base digit for 11 would be 2 (1 + 1 = 2).

6. In the Tarot there are 78 cards or archetypes.

7. Remember the 'Eagle' of Scorpio he had on the suit he wore at the concert in Hawaii when I was in Teotihuacan. This story can be found in Chapter 13.

8. This paragraph is from 'Chiron: Rainbow Bridge Between the Inner and Outer Planets' by Barbara Hand Clow.

Chapter 15

1. This book is now available.

2. See Chapter 9.

3. Elvis' record producer, Felton Jarvis, relayed these events to the Hilton photo girl, Janey Steele. In a card Janey sent to me dated 11/05/74 she wrote: "I went to Elvis' closing night party—very bad—he's just not himself. I left after an hour. His record producer (Felton Jarvis) stopped by here. He left Elvis in Tahoe. He says Elvis won't live another 3 years unless they put him into a hospital and get him well. His kidneys aren't functioning right for one thing. My friend is really worried—so am I."

4. Todd Slaughter wrote about his experience in a fan club newsletter, but later told Wanda in a long-distance telephone conversation the undiluted version given in this text.

5. The witness's name is Fran Dale, a friend of Wanda June Hill's. She told Wanda about this personally witnessed episode, as well as other revelations on Elvis' mistreatment which she gleaned from her conversations with Ed Parker.

6. This incident was told by Ed to Fran Dale. It was also written by Larry Geller a spiritual confidant of Elvis,' in his book, 'If I Can Dream.' Larry's version states that the bowl contained ice and water, but Ed told Fran that he too, had thought it was water until he later went over to the bowl and inspected it more closely, at which time he realized that the fluid it contained was astringent.

7. Ed Parker was the witness to the bloody bed and told this to Fran Dale. Also from a second source Casey Korenek: Casey's friend Kay Reynolds-Hunter was a hairdresser for Elvis and his entourage for a time in the last years of his life. Kay was with Ed Parker when she saw Elvis' blood soaked bed.

8. One of the Avon ladies knew Wanda June Hill and gave her a copy of the taped conversation which this author has heard.

9. See Chapter 5 for a description of this archetype.

Chapter 16

1. Elvis was very swollen from a combination of his genetic liver disease and the cortisone medication he was taking.

Chapter 17

1. In Larry Geller's second book on Elvis, 'If I Can Dream,' he states that Vernon Presley said Elvis was the first to be born of two brothers. When his father made this statement, he believed it to be true. However, by the time Elvis had the conversation with Wanda

given in this chapter in which he discussed his birth, he had found from others who had been present then that Vernon's remembrance was not correct. Instead, Jesse had been the first to see the light.

This made perfect sense to Elvis, since he had never felt that the astrology chart done previously had really suited him. When his chart was re-done using his new found time of birth, he felt it to be a true reflection of his persona and soul in this lifetime—see Chapter 14 for information on Elvis' astrology chart. Vernon's interview in Good Housekeeping in the January 1978 issue substantiates this new information on Elvis' birth time. In the 1978 interview, Vernon is quoted as saying:

> "My parents were at our house with us, along with two women, one a midwife, who told us it was time to call the doctor. After what seemed to me an eternity, a baby boy was born dead. I was desolate at the loss of our child. But then my father put his hand on my wife's stomach and announced, 'Vernon, there's another baby in here.'"

While it may seem odd that Vernon could forget such a traumatic experience, much water had passed under the bridge since that day of struggle and joy in Tupelo. Perhaps Elvis' father had chosen to let go of certain memories that remained in such a different world than the one in which he presently dwelt.

2. I believe Elvis is referring to the period of time he knew Priscilla before they got married in this statement.

3. This was in Elvis' writing, we believe he refers to Corinthians I 12:12-31 which starting with verse 12 says; "Now concerning spiritual gifts, I would not have you ignorant."

Chapter 18

No endnotes in this chapter.

CPSIA information can be obtained
at www.ICGtesting.com
Printed in the USA
FSHW012124150219
55723FS

9 781452 562865